More Praise for *Legal Gladiator*

"Solomon Schmidt's biography explores the highs and lows of Alan's life in a gripping narrative. Read this book!"

—Greta Van Susteren, eminent news anchor;
current host of Newsmax's *The Record*

"Alan Dershowitz's portfolio is unique in the annals of legal history, and Solomon Schmidt has told his life story brilliantly in *Legal Gladiator*."

—Robert Shapiro, acclaimed criminal defense attorney;
co-founder of LegalZoom

"Solomon Schmidt has written a captivating story. This is a significant new biography about a significant figure. Do read it."

—Lord Daniel Finkelstein, OBE, former executive editor of
The Times; bestselling author

"Alan Dershowitz is one of the sharpest, bravest, and most principled legal minds in America. Interviewing him is always a challenge, because you have to be on your A-game, but an enjoyable one."

—Piers Morgan, internationally renowned media personality

"A fascinating account about one of the greatest lawyers of our generation. This is a must read."

—Jay Sekulow, famed religious liberties litigator; host of the
radio and TV show *Sekulow*

"Solomon Schmidt has skillfully recounted Alan's life in *Legal Gladiator*, and the result is a fascinating, inspiring story."

—Arthur Aidala, noted defense lawyer; host of the radio show
The Arthur Aidala Power Hour

"Here is the case for Alan Dershowitz . . . This frank but friendly biography is not written by or for lawyers, and it is all the more enjoyable for that reason."

—Geoffrey Robertson, prominent human rights lawyer; author
of bestseller *Rather His Own Man*

"A lively portrait of America's most famous lawyer, revealing the funny and endearing man behind the legal theories, the celebrity clients, and the colorful controversies."

—Steven Pinker, Johnstone Family Professor of Psychology, Harvard University; bestselling author

LEGAL
GLADIATOR

LEGAL
GLADIATOR

THE LIFE OF ALAN DERSHOWITZ

SOLOMON SCHMIDT

Skyhorse Publishing

Skyhorse Publishing books may be purchased in bulk at special discounts for sales promotion, corporate gifts, fund-raising, or educational purposes. Special editions can also be created to specifications. For details, contact the Special Sales Department, Skyhorse Publishing, 307 West 36th Street, 11th Floor, New York, NY 10018 or info@skyhorsepublishing.com.

Skyhorse® and Skyhorse Publishing® are registered trademarks of Skyhorse Publishing, Inc.®, a Delaware corporation.

Visit our website at www.skyhorsepublishing.com.

10 9 8 7 6 5 4 3 2 1

Library of Congress Cataloging-in-Publication Data is available on file.

Print ISBN: 978-1-5107-8064-4
eBook ISBN: 978-1-5107-8065-1

Cover design by David Ter-Avanesyan
Cover photograph by Getty Images

Printed in the United States of America

This book is dedicated to Harvey Silverglate—a kind man, a hard worker, and a brilliant lawyer. Harvey has been a dear friend and supporter to me in my work, and without him, this project on Professor Dershowitz would not have been possible.

To my mom, Lisa, who taught me how to read, who loved and watched out for me when I was most vulnerable, and who helped ground me in the principles I hold today.

And to my dad, Mike, a lion of a father and a friend, who gave me the idea of writing my first book and who has unendingly supported, helped, and encouraged me in every single aspect of my work.

In nomine Jesu.

First they came for the socialists, and I did not speak out—because I was not a socialist. Then they came for the trade unionists, and I did not speak out—because I was not a trade unionist. Then they came for the Jews, and I did not speak out—because I was not a Jew. Then they came for me— and there was no one left to speak for me.

—Martin Niemöller, philosopher

In whatever arena of life one may meet the challenge of courage, whatever may be the sacrifices he faces if he follows his conscience—the loss of his friends, his fortune, his contentment, even the esteem of his fellow men— each man must decide for himself the course he will follow.

—John F. Kennedy, *Profiles in Courage*

CONTENTS

PROLOGUE

"It's disgusting! Your whole enclave—it's disgusting. You're disgusting!"

It was a summer day in 2021, and Alan Dershowitz found himself in the Chilmark General Store on Martha's Vineyard being shouted at by someone he had once regarded as a friend.

Over the previous twenty-five years, Dershowitz and comedian Larry David had formed a special relationship. On the Vineyard, they played poker and volleyball often and shared lively conversations on the porch of the General Store. David used Dershowitz's home gym, and the two periodically had dinner together with their wives. On top of this, David had once spoken at an event honoring Dershowitz's work on behalf of human rights, and Dershowitz had made a phone call to help one of David's children get into college.

Then came the era of Trump. Dershowitz frequently advocated for Trump's civil liberties, advised his Middle East team, and represented him on the floor of the Senate during Trump's first impeachment trial. In the process, he formed close ties within conservative circles.

It was all too much for many in the liberal community, including Larry David, who slowly cooled in his interactions with Dershowitz. When he saw Dershowitz in the Chilmark General Store in August 2021, he turned around to leave the store.

"We can still talk, Larry," Dershowitz called after him.

"No. No. We really can't," said David, turning around in a rage. "I saw you. I saw you with your arm around Pompeo!" He was referring to a publicized visit Dershowitz had made to the White House in 2020, during which Trump had unveiled a plan for peace in the Middle East and Dershowitz had been spotted patting Secretary of State Mike Pompeo on the back.

"He's my former student," Dershowitz said to David. "I greet all of my former students that way. I can't greet my former students?"

"It's disgusting," retorted David, voice raised, veins bulging, and face reddening. "Your whole enclave—it's disgusting. You're disgusting!"

* * *

Alan Dershowitz is to the law what Churchill is to politics, what Ali is to sports, what Shakespeare is to literature, and what Einstein is to science. He is arguably the most iconic lawyer in American history.

Over a fifty-year career at Harvard, Dershowitz taught around ten thousand students, and in addition to his signature course "Introduction to Criminal Law," he offered nearly twenty different courses over the years. As a scholar and author, he has written almost sixty books, which have sold over one million copies in dozens of foreign languages. As a speaker and debater, he has been heard in person by nearly two million people in venues such as Carnegie Hall, the Sydney Opera House, the Kremlin, Madison Square Garden, the French Assembly, the House of Lords, the Knesset, and the US Senate. As a ubiquitous commentator in the media for sixty years, he has appeared thousands of times on media outlets like *Firing Line with William Buckley, Larry King Live, Geraldo Rivera, The Record with Greta Van Susteren, Oprah, Sean Hannity, The View,* and many others. As a Zionist, he has known (and in various cases advised) Israeli prime ministers Golda Meir, Yitzhak Rabin, Menachem Begin, Shimon Peres, Ehud Barak, Ariel Sharon, Ehud Olmert, and Benjamin Netanyahu. And finally, as a lawyer, he has litigated upward of three hundred cases, including high-profile murder and rape cases, *pro bono* efforts on behalf of foreign dissidents, and the impeachment proceedings of two US presidents.

Since his childhood, Dershowitz has always been a lightning rod for controversy. But who could have predicted that his eighth decade would bring the most vehement controversies of his life on account of a mysterious financier named Jeffrey Epstein and a businessman and TV host named Donald Trump? Who could have foreseen that Dershowitz would be panned by members of a liberal community that once widely admired him?

"What I appreciated from Alan was the risk he took by choosing a side that most of the people my wife and I know opposed," says Dershowitz's friend Geraldo Rivera. "As became apparent with the Russia collusion hoax, sometimes the right wing is right. Trump did not deserve to be convicted in that impeachment trial. Alan did the right thing. He was true to his profession."

"I was not surprised by Alan's decision to represent President Trump," says Justice Stephen Breyer, who has known Dershowitz since the 1960s. "He determined things on principle and followed through with his decisions. He wanted everybody to be represented, including people who may themselves be terrible. I think that's a good thing for the bar and the bench—for everybody—because those people are entitled to it."

"People would impugn Alan and say he did it for notoriety or some other non-noble purpose, but I truly believe he's a crusader through and through for the rights of people who are hated," notes Nadine Strossen, former president of the ACLU and a student of Dershowitz's in the 1970s. "I don't think he courted the adverse publicity and shunning he was subjected to."

"I feel like people who are disappointed don't understand what a criminal defense lawyer does," comments Megyn Kelly, who has often invited Dershowitz onto her shows. "It's not an endorsement of the client or their misdeeds for someone to represent them. When you're in criminal defense, you're going to be representing some very bad people. That's the nature of the job. People need to grow up.

"I was probably a little bit more to the right than Alan was, and occasionally, I'd disagree with him on something political," Kelly continues. "But I can say that Alan was incredibly principled. In the day and age in which he defended Trump, when everybody was selling out for their partisan leanings, few people stood in the small circle that is their own objective values. Alan did, and that is incredibly rare, sadly."

"I believe him when he said that he wasn't defending Donald Trump's ideology," says Pulitzer Prize–winning journalist Glenn Greenwald, who sparred with Dershowitz in the prestigious Munk Debates in Toronto after breaking the Edward Snowden story in 2013. "I believe he was defending principles and not Trump's ideology. I think that's always a difficult thing to do, and it's a part of Alan I find admirable."

"Having talked with Alan about it, I don't think he did it for any ulterior motive, for attention or anything like that," says Robert F. Kennedy Jr., a friend of Dershowitz's from Martha's Vineyard. "Even though I think he felt that Trump was not good for our country, he honestly believed that the law was being used against Trump in ways that were not good for our country. It was kind of like letting the Nazis march through Skokie— stand up for the principle even though the people that you're protecting are reprehensible people."

"It certainly didn't surprise me that Alan took a legal position that was dramatically opposed to his personal political beliefs," comments Robert Shapiro, who worked with Dershowitz on the O. J. Simpson case. "Alan was a true believer in the Constitution. It wouldn't have surprised me any more than seeing the ACLU take a position that was against my social and moral compass. I will say this, though: I didn't expect that Alan Dershowitz would get involved in a political controversy. After thinking about it and discussing it with him, however, there was no reason why a constitutional scholar could not take positions that were different from what his supporters would believe he'd subscribe to."

"Of all the people I've known for decades, Alan remained absolutely consistent," says civil liberties attorney Harvey Silverglate, who was a student in Dershowitz's first-ever class at Harvard in 1964. "He would represent the most despicable human beings, which is what criminal defense lawyers do. He was not afraid to take controversial cases and risks, whatever that entailed."

Dershowitz's momentous life story begins in a Depression-hit Jewish community in Brooklyn, while far away in Europe the clouds of an impending Holocaust were looming.

PART ONE

RISE

A WORLD OF STRUGGLES

September 1938 found Harry and Claire Dershowitz, two Orthodox Jews living in Brooklyn, with a baby boy. Per Jewish custom, they gave him a Hebrew name, Avraham Mordecai, from which they derived an American name: Allen Morton. In time, Avraham Mordecai Dershowitz became known as "Avi" to family and close friends.

Dershowitz's father, Harry, worked six days a week to provide for his family, selling men's clothing in a dry goods store in Manhattan—resting only on the Sabbath. After closing his shop each night, Harry took multiple trains from the wealthier hub of Manhattan across the Williamsburg Bridge to his home in Brooklyn, where an ever-growing number of Jewish refugees were settling from Europe.

Over the last several years in Germany, Adolf Hitler's government had enacted a series of laws which steadily took away the rights of Jewish citizens, forbidding them from serving in the military, teaching at or attending public schools, marrying or having sex with non-Jews, or practicing law. During this time, Aaron Dershowitz gathered his wife and two children in their spacious apartment in Czechoslovakia. Aaron, a successful businessman and a cousin of Harry Dershowitz, had listened to radio reports in March that announced Hitler's takeover of Austria, and in his home city of Brno, antiaircraft guns were installed on the roofs of buildings. Aaron was warned by his aging father: "This guy Hitler is different from all the others. Get out."

His friends, however, sought to calm him down. "Come on! Hitler's just another anti-Semite," one said. "We've gone through the tsars, we've gone through everything else. We'll manage." Aaron decided to listen to

his father and told his family, "Europe is no longer a place for the Jews."
He made plans to follow his cousins to America.

Under the cover of night, on December 31, 1938, the Dershowitzes
left Czechoslovakia and crossed the border into Poland, where they eventually boarded a tourist ship and reached America on February 7 the following year. Thirty-six days later, Hitler's army invaded Czechoslovakia.
For Aaron's friends and family members who had decided to stay and trust
that this leader was just another anti-Semite, it was too late to get out.
"And of course," Aaron's son Zvi recalled eight decades later, "they didn't
make it."

* * *

When Aaron Dershowitz and his family arrived in the *goldene medina*, a
Yiddish term for the United States meaning "the golden country," they
were welcomed by a bespectacled and cigar-smoking man named Louis,
Avi Dershowitz's paternal grandfather. Professionally, Louis was a printer
and a paper salesman, who made a meager income to provide for his wife,
Ida, and their children. Privately, though, he had taken upon himself the
role of protector of the family. News had drifted to his community of the
violence and discrimination against European Jews of all different classes
and nationalities. Louis wanted to help as many Dershowitzes as possible
to emigrate; however, this was a difficult time to find refuge in America.
Quotas had been put in place by the government, limiting the number of
Jewish immigrants, and on top of this, less than 5 percent of the American
public wanted to allow Jewish refugees to enter the country.

This did not stop Louis. For almost ten years leading up to World War
II, he contacted relatives in Poland and Czechoslovakia who needed aid,
including Aaron Dershowitz's family. He arranged meetings with wealthy
relatives in the United States, including one who owned a theater chain
in New York, to secure financial backing for affidavits which certified that
an immigrant would not become a nuisance to the country. Louis also
capitalized on the US government's favoritism toward immigrants of a
religious or academic background. He sent for a particular male relative
in Europe to relocate with his family to America and serve as a rabbi for
his father Zecharia's *shtieble*, a sort of family synagogue located in the

basement of his home in Williamsburg. After a couple of weeks, the new rabbi was fired, and another relative was brought over from Europe to fill the role. This legal masquerade was repeated several times, and through all his efforts, Louis saved twenty-nine family members from the coming Holocaust.

Devotion to family was a trait Louis passed on to his second son, Harry, a warm-hearted, quiet, yet tough man who engaged in physical fights with bullies who shouted anti-Jewish obscenities to his brothers. "Harry was extremely devoted to my parents," recalled his youngest brother, Zecharia. "He was the brother who, after my father died, made it his business to visit my mother most often." Born in 1909, Harry spent the first year of his life in the Lower East Side neighborhood of Manhattan and lived in high-rise, slum-like conditions before the family packed up and crossed the East River to the burgeoning Williamsburg neighborhood in Brooklyn. After several years of struggling through both secular and religious schooling, Harry dropped out of high school and went into business, partnering with two of his uncles to open a dry goods store and managing to earn a yearly income of $7,500.

* * *

At the beginning of the twentieth century, Naftuli Ringel—Avi Dershowitz's maternal grandfather—was a Jewish peasant living in the city of Przemyśl in Galicia, a region which extended from present-day Krakow, Poland, to Lviv, Ukraine. Unwilling to kill a person even in battle, Naftuli hoped to avoid conscription into the army of the Austro-Hungarian Empire and decided to join a wave of Polish immigrants making the journey to America. In 1907, he temporarily left his wife, Blima, and three children in the hopes of starting a new life in the *goldene medina*. After his arrival, he worked as a peddler in Manhattan, scraping together the funds necessary to bring his family over. A few years later, Blima sailed with the young ones across the Atlantic Ocean.

Soon thereafter, in July 1913, she gave birth to a baby girl named Claire. Like her future husband, she for a time grew up in crowded housing developments on the Lower East Side, but moved to Williamsburg around 1923.

Unlike her future husband, Claire Ringel excelled academically. She graduated from high school at the top of her class at fifteen years old, and in 1929, she enrolled at City College in New York, called the "Jewish Harvard." Brilliant, inquisitive, and articulate, she was the first of the Ringels ever to attend college, but her hopes of eventually becoming a schoolteacher were cut short after only a month by the stock market crash. Her father, Naftuli, needed additional income to support their family, and Claire dropped out of college to take a job as a bookkeeper, which became a lifelong career.

Harry and Claire's families knew each other from the Williamsburg community, and during the slump of the Great Depression, they met and fell in love. They were married on January 9, 1937, and less than two years later, Claire gave birth to Avraham Mordecai Dershowitz in a Williamsburg hospital. As was customary among Galician Jews, his Hebrew name was the first name of Naftuli's father, the patriarch of the Ringel family. On the eighth day of his life, he was circumcised, physically signifying his place in the four-thousand-year-old Jewish community.

Dershowitz's first years were spent in the ground floor of a house at 193 Hewes St. in Williamsburg, and as a child, he played with his cousin Zvi, who had recently escaped Hitler's invasion of Czechoslovakia.

Harry and Claire were intent on raising their son in the traditions of Orthodox Judaism, which their families had followed for generations. One of the core observances was the regular wearing of a *yarmulke*, which denotes the lowliness of man before the holiness of Jehovah. Once, when Avi was three, his parents took him shopping for a pair of tall leather shoes, and as they were waiting to cross a street in Brooklyn, the maverick toddler decided to go ahead on his own. In the process, an eighteen-wheeler ran over his foot and only missed crushing him entirely when Harry pulled him to safety. Avi's leather boots had saved his foot from being flattened, but the truck's wheel had broken some of his bones. Harry and Claire took him to a nearby Catholic hospital, where he was to spend the night after being examined. Later that evening, Claire received a call from the hospital, and the nurse informed her, "Your son wants to go to Florida."

"He's never even heard of Florida," responded Claire, who went to the hospital to investigate. There was her three-year-old son in front of his meal shouting, "Miami!!" Claire proceeded to explain to the nurse that Avi was saying, "My yami!"—meaning his *yarmulke*, without which he could not begin his meal.

Around this time, Dershowitz's grandfather Naftuli Ringel died and was buried with a small bag of sand he had gathered in Palestine. He left his wife Blima a widow, and she was unable to afford the rent for her apartment in the neighborhood of Borough Park. Harry Dershowitz decided to move his family into Blima's apartment and take care of the rent for his mother-in-law. While he and Claire plodded on with their jobs as salesman and bookkeeper, on May 5, 1942, they welcomed a second son to their family. Naftuli Zeaf (Americanized to "Nathan Zeff") was to be Avi's only sibling and received the nickname "Tully" from his Hebrew first name. Soon after Nathan's birth, the Dershowitzes moved into an apartment complex on the corner of 14th Avenue and 53rd Street. They spent the war years living in this two-bedroom apartment for thirty-five dollars a month.

The core neighborhood of Borough Park was less than one square mile and contained a population of 100,000 Jews, along with communities of Italians and Irish. Although it was filled with houses and shops, it was a well-kept and clean area of Brooklyn. In fact, the Dershowitzes were able to buy fresh corn and chickens on farmland just a few blocks from home. Borough Park's residents tended to be modern (liberal) in their religious views.

Modern Orthodox Jews like Harry and Claire allowed their children to dress in American clothes, rather than black coats and prayer shawls of the ultra-Orthodox Hasidim sect. Harry and Claire also made sure Avi spoke clear English in addition to Yiddish, the language spoken by Ashkenazi Jews. "My family wanted us to be as American as possible," recalls Dershowitz. Louis Dershowitz told his grandson to "be a good American" because America was "a wonderful country for the Jews."

* * *

When he departed for a new life in America, Dershowitz's great-grandfather Zecharia had left behind seven siblings in his hometown of Pilzno in present-day Poland. Although his son Louis rescued a number of these relatives before World War II broke out, he could not save them all. After the fall of western Poland, Pilzno came into German hands, and the members of the Dershowitzes' extended family in the area were ordered to wear a yellow-and-black cloth in the shape of the Star of David, a symbol that derived from the shields used by King David's army in biblical times. Between 1939 and the summer of 1942, sporadic attacks were carried out in Pilzno, but in July 1942, most of the Jews were rounded up and disappeared to concentration camps. Those who did not suffer this fate, such as the family of Benjamin Dershowitz, were killed in late 1944 when an order arrived to shoot the remaining Jews in the town.

Dershowitz's maternal family met the same end. Despite an armed stand against the Nazis' arrival, two of Naftuli Ringel's three siblings, in addition to many nieces, nephews, and cousins, were shot in 1942 along with their fellow 17,000 Jews in Przemyśl. Out of the many Ringels who had lived in the city, a handful survived—and only because they had fled while there was still time.

By the spring of 1945, approximately six million Jews had been killed across Europe, and the Allied armies were preparing for the final assault on Hitler's Berlin. Dershowitz and his father listened to news updates about the war on their small white radio. Although they would not learn the full extent of the genocide until after World War II, the Borough Park community knew that relatives were disappearing in Europe. Letters would suddenly stop arriving from family members they had corresponded with frequently. Harry told his son that the rate at which the Allies conquered Nazi land would determine how many of their family members would stay alive. Dershowitz helped his father move thumbtacks on a map of Europe to indicate the positions of both Dwight Eisenhower's and Georgy Zhukov's forces advancing on Berlin.

Once the conflict at last came to a close in August that same year, evidence of the atrocities of the Holocaust began to seep into Dershowitz's young life. As more immigrants arrived, he occasionally noticed classmates and fellow synagogue attendees with numbers tattooed onto their wrists. One day, Dershowitz's friend Barry Zimmerman overheard his mother and grandfather sitting in their kitchen crying over reports of killed relatives. "It was very common," he says.

But an aura of silence surrounded the Holocaust among the community until many years later. "Everyone knew about the Holocaust. It wasn't discussed in our community, though," said Dershowitz as an adult. "It just was not talked about." And life went on.

* * *

Along with most of Borough Park, Dershowitz and his family revered the Democratic leaders who had led them through World War II. Mayor LaGuardia spoke fluent Yiddish, and his solidarity with Jewish constituents and anti-Nazi stances endeared him to the community. President Roosevelt's surname was affectionately Judaized to "Rosenfelt" by Dershowitz's Grandma Ringel in part because of his appointing Ashkenazi justice Felix Frankfurter to the Supreme Court.

Dershowitz and his family were thoroughly liberal in their political views. "We supported desegregation, opposed capital punishment, and contributed to the ACLU and NAACP," stated Dershowitz later in life. When Dershowitz stopped by to visit his close friend Carl Meshenberg, Carl's father, a left-leaning immigrant, was always talking politics. "I didn't know there was another team," joked Dershowitz's close friend from Manhattan, Norman Sohn.

Above all, though, after the end of World War II, devotion to Zionism was the highest ideal. The establishment of a nation-state for the Jewish people took on a renewed priority after the Holocaust. The Dershowitzes contributed their part to the Zionist dream by keeping a *pushka* can in their home next to the telephone. Each time Avi Dershowitz wanted to make a call to a friend, he had to place a nickel through the slit on top of the can. Through an organization called the Jewish National Fund, the money that American Jews deposited into their *pushkas* went toward buying plots of land in Palestine and aiding poor Jews in the region.

When David Ben-Gurion declared the establishment of Israel on May 14, 1948, Dershowitz and the rest of his neighborhood were jubilant. There was dancing in the streets of Borough Park, and at Dershowitz's elementary school, prayers were raised during school hours for the new Jewish nation. "To us," explained Dershowitz, "Israel was always in the right, and its Arab enemies were always in the wrong."

Joy turned to apprehension, though, when immediately after Israel's formation, several Arab countries, including Iraq, Lebanon, Syria, Transjordan, and Egypt, launched attacks into the new country. As the war raged, in the summer of 1948, Dershowitz attended a Hebrew-speaking camp in the Poconos called Camp Massad (Hebrew for "foundation"). Due to Israel's ongoing war, individual bunks were named after kibbutzim in Israel. The Israeli anthem "Hatikvah" was regularly sung, and during mealtime, news updates on the war were played over the radio.

Dershowitz would later learn that a nineteen-year-old named Noam Chomsky was also at the camp, working as a counselor in a nearby bunk. The elder son of Sephardic Jews in Philadelphia, Chomsky became dedicated to socialism in his teen years. "There would have been no way for Dershowitz to know it, but in the '40s I was a Zionist youth leader," recounted Chomsky, who would not make Dershowitz's acquaintance until the 1960s. "I was closely associated with Zionist groups that opposed a Jewish state (a Zionist position at the time) and sought an Arab-Jewish cooperative commonwealth based on working class cooperation."

* * *

The fall of 1948 brought a new school year for Dershowitz, and with it, a set of struggles for the restless boy. After two years at a Yiddish-speaking elementary school called Torahs Emes, Harry and Claire transferred him to a Zionist, Hebrew-speaking school named Etz Chaim (Hebrew for "Tree of Life"). In the morning, he and his classmates were immersed in Old Testament studies, Jewish Ethics and Literature, and Rituals, which was followed by math, science, American history, English, art, music, gym, Jewish history, Hebrew, and Zionism studies in the afternoon.

From the time he was little, Dershowitz possessed an innate tendency to question and argue. "Avi was outspoken and opinionated," said Carl Meshenberg. "I used to be a goody-two-shoes," said Dershowitz's classmate Hal Jacobs. "But Avi was always a wise guy."

During the morning religious subjects, the rabbis emphasized to the boys that the Torah was the unquestionable word of God. This did not sit well with Dershowitz, inherently a skeptic when it came to religion. When he was around twelve, he created a *bracha* (Hebrew: "blessing") for skeptics, which was a play off a traditional blessing which stated, "*Baruch atah Adonoy*"—"Blessed are Thou, Adonai." "*Baruch atah* I deny," read Dershowitz's blessing. "*Baruch atah* I'm not sure, *Baruch atah* show me why."

"I would occasionally ask impertinent questions that got me tossed out of class," mentioned Dershowitz as an adult. "I remember upsetting a teacher by asking where Cain's wife came from, since Adam and Eve had no daughters."

It was not only impertinence that got him into trouble, but at times plain old mischief. This ranged from shooting an occasional spitball to one episode when he and Carl terrorized their sixth-grade teacher Rabbi Oretsky, who had survived air raids and the Holocaust, by mimicking the sounds of a falling bomb and jumping out suddenly to frighten him. Barry Zimmerman recalled that when Dershowitz could not fill his time with pranks, he would hide comic books inside his thick religious text-books and detach while the teacher droned on. "We were real jerks," said Dershowitz.

At times, Dershowitz reaped the rewards of his misbehavior. During first and second grade, Rabbi Schwartz routinely made him pull down his pants around his knees, lie face-down on the teacher's desk, and embrace the *boom, boom, boom* of the pedagogue's paddle.

A sixth grade report card showed that Dershowitz achieved Ds in "Effort," "Conduct," and "Respects the Rights of Others," and his principal, Rabbi Shulman, reported to Harry and Claire: "Avi's mind is dirty; he refuses to show respect to his rabbis." While Dershowitz's mind may have been corrupted, it was obviously functioning properly. That same year, Dershowitz and his classmates were administered IQ tests to determine whether they would be in Class A, B, or C the following year. Dershowitz secured one of the highest grades possible, but his then-principal suspected he had cheated.

In the spring of 1951, Dershowitz graduated Etz Chaim, and as the fall approached, he prepared to not only turn thirteen—the age at which a Jewish male is considered a "man"—but also to begin the formative years of high school (in those days there was no middle school). Handwritten notes from Dershowitz's final Etz Chaim yearbook included: "Dear Avi,

If you want to be successful, put your shoulder to the wheel. Do not procrastinate. Do not depend upon others" from his father and the following ditty from his classmate Josh Weisberger: "All the guys who love you, all love you swell, but the guys who hate you, can go to hell!"

Dershowitz had desperately wanted to follow his friends Bernie Beck and Hal Jacobs to the nearby "elite" Flatbush Yeshiva High School, but horrific grades barred his admittance, along with an apprehensive principal who had learned of Dershowitz's less-than-stellar performance in elementary school. He was forced to go to the less-prestigious Yeshiva University High School.

That September, Dershowitz had his bar mitzvah ceremony. During the traditional ceremony, a young Jewish man is required to read a portion of the Torah in its original language, made difficult because the written text contains no vowels or dots over letters. One week after his thirteenth birthday, Dershowitz stood on the raised platform of the Young Israel Synagogue, while his rabbi, Samuel Mirsky, and many of his family and friends looked on. The portion of Scripture he was assigned happened to be a classic verse from Deuteronomy about justice and the rule of law. "*Tzedek, tzedek, tirdoff*—Justice, justice shall you pursue," rang out the words as Dershowitz chanted with proper intonation and pronunciation. He delivered a perfect performance.

The following month, Dershowitz and his community gathered for another coming-of-age ceremony for his classmate Jerry Blau, a shy but respectful student. He delivered a terrible performance, stumbling and stuttering through his Torah portion and speech. When he had finished, Rabbi Mirsky looked at the congregation and declared, "Sometimes there are boys who read perfectly from the Torah, but we do not judge them as well as boys who live a deeply religious life and who are well behaved." Dershowitz had just been indirectly called out in front of his entire Borough Park community. He and his father later agreed that the rabbi's actions were unfair at the least, and Dershowitz would comment over sixty years later: "Even when I did something perfectly, they would find some way to turn my success against me."

* * *

The 1950s was the age of the nuclear family, and Dershowitz's was no exception. Several years back, Harry and Claire had purchased a three-story brick house on 48th Street in Borough Park for seven thousand dollars. Knowing their relatives needed a place to live, they let Harry's cousin Buddy and his bride, Selma, move into the basement, while Claire's brother Hedgy moved into the top floor with his wife, Muriel, and their son, Norman. Harry and Claire lived on the first floor, which contained one bathroom, sitting room, and foyer, along with a bedroom for the parents and a room to be shared by Avi and his brother. The house was nearly bereft of artwork and books, excluding a few basic publications located in a case in the sitting room: Hebrew and English Old Testaments, some *Reader's Digest* condensed titles, and a two-volume, yellow-covered dictionary Avi frequently perused.

On Friday nights, the Dershowitzes gathered in the foyer of 1558 48th Street for the weekly Sabbath dinner. Grandma Ringel always attended, and other family members and friends occasionally joined in. A hearty meal of chicken soup, *gefilte* fish, flank steak, and dessert was followed by religious songs. "There was a lot of singing," remembers Norman Sohn. "Avi's home was beautiful on the Sabbath."

Conversation flowed around the table. "My father . . . always encouraged dialogue and debate," recalls Dershowitz. "He rarely injected himself into the conversation, except to ask 'Is it fair?' or 'How would that help the underdog?'"

"He was the second oldest of many siblings," Dershowitz continues. "His older brother, Jack, was sickly and unable to defend himself. My father was strong, and so he became the guy who defended his family and Jews in Williamsburg when they were attacked. He even bought me boxing gloves when I was very young. He always lectured me about defending the underdog, including not just Jews, but also African Americans, who were some of his best customers. My father was always telling me: don't be a bully, fight against people who are stronger than you."

"If my mother had the opportunity, she would have been Ruth Bader Ginsburg," says Dershowitz.

Claire was intelligent and outspoken. "She was very, very intellectually superior and expressed her opinions forcefully and often," recalls Hal

Jacobs. "Mrs. Dershowitz forced us—and I'm sure she forced Alan all the time—to think things through," reports Bernie Beck. "'Why do you say that—what's your motive?' she'd say. 'What about other things that might affect it? Are you letting your emotions affect it?' She was just wonderful that way. She was a very inquisitive person—always challenging you. If you said it was a hot day out, she'd say, 'Compared to what?'"

Frequently, Claire had to travel to Yeshiva University High School to serve as Avi's defense attorney before the school principal. "They wanted to throw him out many, many times," explains Avi's cousin Norman Ringel, who ranked Avi third on an unofficial list of most-pigheaded family members, behind only Claire Dershowitz and Norman's father Hedgy.

"My sister Claire must have been called to the principal's office every other day," says Shirley Ringel. "'Oh my God, I have to go to the office again,' she'd say."

Claire was fiercely loyal to both Avi and his younger brother, Nathan, who described Avi as a "pain in the ass."

"Avi was a wise guy for as long as I can remember," recalls Nathan Dershowitz. "He was sufficiently manipulative to get out of punishments that were to be imposed." The brothers shared a messy room and played basketball together using a board that had been nailed into the side of their small white garage. Before Nathan became a teenager, Avi utilized his size advantage to pick on his kid brother and beat him handily in basketball games.

At one point, the brothers had to share their bedroom with a boarder, and a white sheet had to be placed across the middle of the bedroom to divide it. Their parents always needed extra money. Dershowitz remembers "desperately wanting" Mounds bars, but his family could not afford them since they were ten cents each, whereas regular candies cost a nickel. "It was only a real treat when we could get a Mounds bar."

* * *

At the beginning of high school, Dershowitz had been placed in the so-called "garbage class" for misbehaving students with lousy academics. He constantly flunked classes and butted heads with his teachers. "[One] time the kid sitting next to me in class lifted an athletic supporter from my gym bag and tossed it at the rabbi," recalls Dershowitz. "Finding my incriminating name tape on the offending item—my mother sewed name tapes onto every item we owned, from handkerchiefs to baseball mitts—the rabbi kicked me out of class. My friend Jake [Greenfield], never one to pass up an opportunity, cautioned the rabbi that I had a 'gang.' When I reached the street I told two drunks who were coming down Bedford Avenue that they could get free drinks if they went to the classroom and said, 'Dersh sent us.' As soon as they walked in and spoke their lines, Jake piped up, 'That's Dersh's gang, I recognize them.' The rabbi made a beeline for the door. I was suspended for several weeks and made to sit in the library reading old copies of *Life* magazine, to the apparent mutual satisfaction of everyone involved, except my mortified parents."

Along with some classmates, Dershowitz formed a so-called "gang": the Shields, which was in reference to the iconic Star of David symbol that had adorned the shields of King David's ancient army. Dershowitz and his friends took pride in rebelling against their rabbis. After school hours, they made a point of wearing chartreuse-and-black uniforms, which had been banned by the rabbis because of their "provocative" colors.

A group of seven core friends in Brooklyn were Dershowitz's lifeline through these tumultuous high school years. All told, they were the "Big 8": Avi Dershowitz, Barry Zimmerman, Bernie Beck, Carl Meshenberg, Zollie Eisenstadt, Murray Altman, Josh Weisberger, and Hal Jacobs. As a group, the boys were staunch Zionists and liberal in their politics.

Whether it was on a train ride racing over the city as they traveled to their individual schools, over a game of pool at Bernie's house on Saturday afternoons, or outside the synagogue after sneaking out of a boring sermon from the rabbi, the boys thrived on conversation. "We were a very, very verbal, interactive society," recounted Dershowitz. A variety of subjects were discussed: the creation versus evolution debate, American politics, and current events in Israel.

"I remember very much that if there was an argument, Avi would say 'So which side do you want me to argue?'" says Hal Jacobs. "And he could argue either side extremely effectively. He had a way of crafting things to always support his viewpoint. One never won an argument against him."

"Avi's brilliance was intimidating," says Bernie. "He just knew everything about anything."

Oftentimes, though, the boys simply chatted about the goings-on of life, particularly how their beloved Brooklyn Dodgers were faring. Along with the Dodgers star Jewish pitcher Sandy Koufax—"who was like God to us," says Bernie Beck—Dershowitz enthusiastically rooted for Jackie Robinson, who was the only Black player in the MLB when he started his career in 1947. "I grew up in a home entirely free of any racial prejudice," Dershowitz says. "My parents admired black leaders, and my father had black customers in his store whom he treated as equals."

The subject of girls was also increasingly fascinating to the boys. In those days there was no premarital sex, but Dershowitz liked to be salacious. One time, he brought a copy of the racy novel *The Amboy Dukes* to Barry's house and began to read the dirty portions until Mr. Zimmerman peeked his furious face into the room and put a stop to it. Through his high school years, Dershowitz bounced from one girlfriend to another. Physical interactions extended to holding hands while on a "cheap date" in Greenwood Cemetery, seeing movies at Loew's Theatre on 46th Street—the border between the Italian and Jewish neighborhoods—and going to the zoo.

Even in the girl department, Dershowitz faced failure. In his freshman year, a school prom was hosted by a panel of girls who graded all the boys on their looks. Category A was the best, and D was the worst. A boy could only pick a girl who had the same ranking. Dershowitz was sweet on Karen, a beautiful blonde, but when he came to the judges' table, the girls laughed at red-haired, freckled Dershowitz and told him, "Don't you know that Karen is on the A list and you're on the C list?" To add insult to injury, several mothers in Borough Park told their daughters that he was "a boy with no future."

* * *

By 1953, Dershowitz was approaching his third year of high school, and his relations with his teachers were unendingly difficult. Tough questions and new ideas were suppressed. "If your idea is so good," a teacher would say, "then the ancient rabbis, who were so much smarter than you, would have come up with it first."

"The issue that was very much on my mind at the time," says Dershowitz, "was how a person could believe in God after the Holocaust."

At the end of 1953, Dershowitz took a statewide Regents exam in History, the only subject that interested him. He scored an 88—astonishingly high in the minds of his teachers. Mr. Lilker, the history instructor, summoned the teenager to his office. "Avi, don't let it go to your head," he said, trying to prevent Dershowitz from getting his hopes up. "You're a 75 student. You've always been a 75 student, and you'll always be a 75 student."

"I believed it and stopped studying," says Dershowitz. "I could get 70s without much work, and if that's who I was anyway, why take time away from activities I enjoyed, such as sports, jokes, girls, and messing around?"

As his senior year loomed, Dershowitz's parents had no commitment of scrimping to send him to college, even if that was something he desired. His potential career options were bleak: according to an employment agency his mother took him to, he could succeed as a salesman, ad executive, or funeral director.

It was in this disheartening time that Dershowitz had an encounter which changed the course of his life.

Yitzchak Greenberg was a respected young member of the Borough Park neighborhood. He had been a well-behaved student and debater through high school and was on his way to Harvard. Everyone knew "Yitz," as he was eventually nicknamed. He was smiley, soft-spoken, and extremely intelligent.

The summer of 1954 found both Greenberg and Dershowitz attending a camp in the rolling, green hills near Rhinebeck, New York. Greenberg was reprising his role as the camp dramatics counselor, and fifteen-year-old Dershowitz was working as a waiter during mealtime. Each year, Greenberg selected Broadway-style plays and scoured the ranks of campers for potential actors and actresses. 1954's production was the intricate, tragic French masterpiece *Cyrano de Bergerac*, which tells the story of an eloquent, kind-hearted intellectual named Cyrano, who is trying to win the heart of the lady he loves.

Greenberg was acquainted with Harry and Claire Dershowitz, but was not yet close with their older son. He got to know Dershowitz during the audition process and decided to cast him in the lead role of Cyrano. "He had emotion, and he had style," remembers Greenberg. "The part required a major amount of memorization. Avi was terrific. He jumped right into it." With speed that shocked his director, Dershowitz memorized the lengthy soliloquies his part called for, and during the production process, he helped Greenberg with any practical tasks that had to be taken care of. "He thought of the other people, not just himself, and he was smart as hell," says Greenberg. After weeks of rehearsal, Dershowitz shined during the final performance.

As his time at Camp Eton came to an end, his senior year was hanging over his head. Greenberg struck up a conversation with Dershowitz about his plans for the future and asked if he would be attending college. Dershowitz related his school woes, telling Greenberg that his teachers wanted to expel him and had refused to give him a recommendation for college. "I'm a terrible student," said Dershowitz.

Greenberg was taken aback. "Avi was brilliant," he recalls. "He was smart. He was sharp. He was lively. He was dramatic. He was charismatic."

"Don't believe what people say," Greenberg said to Dershowitz. "Your mind just works in a different way. You're very smart." As if his teachers' rejection was not imposing enough, Dershowitz told Greenberg that his parents, too, had no plans to send him to college. "Of course you have to go to college!" Greenberg exclaimed. "There's no doubt in my mind that you're capable of being a top student in not just any school, but the best schools in the world."

Soon after this conversation, Greenberg got on the phone with Dershowitz's parents. "You can't do this," he told them. "Someday, Avi will get interested in school and he'll click. He'll be top in his class—he'll be top at whatever it is." At first, Harry and Claire were resistant to Greenberg's pleadings. "I'm telling you, you have a brilliant son," he pressed. "I'm sorry he's not a good student now—he will be someday." After a bit of back-and-forth, they came around to Greenberg's viewpoint and told him they would support sending Dershowitz to college.

At the advice of Greenberg, Dershowitz began broadening his interests in music and reading. He listened to classical music—particularly Tchaikovsky's Fifth—on his heavy, reel-to-reel Webcor tape recorder and read many entries out of the twenty-volume *Encyclopedia Americana* that he purchased at a bookstore on Fourth Avenue.

During this time, he was elected captain of the varsity debate team, a coveted position at Yeshiva University High School, where debaters and athletes were equally revered. A national organization would determine the subjects and assign the students what position to argue. Dershowitz's friend Artie Edelman, who was standby on the team, commented that in this style of debating, "There was no one truth," which was freeing to Dershowitz. To win, one had to be effective at presenting either side of an issue, along with cross-examining your opponent. Dershowitz shined. "I never lost a debate in high school," Dershowitz recounts. "I just was a natural debater." After leading his team to championships in back-to-back years, Dershowitz was designated the organization's "Outstanding Debater," and he was nicknamed "Henry Clay" in his high school's 1955 yearbook.

"I loved conflict, doubt, questions, debates, and uncertainty," admits Dershowitz. This trait caused him to soak in the Talmud, a collection of debates and analysis by ancient scholars over minute aspects of Jewish law. "In the Talmud, you read the majority opinion [and] the dissenting opinion," states Dershowitz. "I recall vividly a class in Talmud [at school] in which I learned that a Jewish Sanhedrin (religious court) that had imposed the death penalty by a unanimous vote could not carry out the sentence, since unanimity meant that the accused did not have a zealous advocate presenting his arguments within the tribunal." Some of his friends noted that during his senior year, Dershowitz slipped away on Saturday afternoons to study Talmud with his learned Uncle Joe. According to his friends, it was around this time that Dershowitz's attitude toward academics began to change.

Unfortunately, Dershowitz's grades at high school were still abysmal. By taking the Regents exam for certain subjects, Dershowitz managed to raise his grades in subjects he had flunked, but he still graduated in the spring of 1955 with an average of 78.6—"not good," as his brother states.

One day near the end of the school year, Rabbi Zuroff, Dershowitz's principal, called the seventeen-year-old into his office. "Dershowitz, you have a big mouth, but not many brains," he proclaimed and then proceeded to offer Dershowitz a piece of unasked-for career advice. "You should be a Conservative rabbi," he began with a jab at his non-Orthodox Jewish brothers, "or—you should become a lawyer."

COMING INTO HIS OWN

Dershowitz had known for some time that the legal profession was a possibility due to his aptitude for Talmud and debate, but his college options were limited due to his family's lack of financial resources and his appalling academic record.

Increasing his dilemma was a sordid tactic his high school employed. "They wanted the school to be regarded as a first-class school, so they would actually encourage the best students to cheat on competitive exams like the Regents," says Dershowitz. A certain teacher, Dr. Leibowitz, left the classroom periodically to permit better students to gather and aid each other on tests, thereby raising their individual scores—all without the teacher's express approval, of course.

This same Dr. Leibowitz was the school's college advisor and in charge of recommending students for Arista, the Senior Honor Society. One day in Dershowitz's senior year, Leibowitz stood at the front of the class for the traditional announcement of student nominations. "It's with great honor that I recommend the following people for Arista," he began. After reading the list of names, he rotely announced that there was no opposition to the names selected. "No, there is opposition," called out Dershowitz, standing up from his desk.

"Among the eleven people who have been proposed for Arista, four are chronic cheaters," he declared. "I'm not going to name them because they're my fellow students, but I am going to name the facilitator of the four cheaters." Pointing his finger at the graying, bespectacled Leibowitz, he declared, "Dr. Leibowitz, the head of Arista is the problem."

Dershowitz was immediately suspended for this classroom protest. He faced little to no discipline at home. While he never condoned misbehavior, Dershowitz's father always encouraged him to speak up in the face of what he perceived to be an injustice.

Dershowitz's most obvious choice for an undergraduate school was Yeshiva University, for which his high school regularly served as a feeder-institution. After a personal intercession from principal Rabbi Zuroff, though, the university turned Dershowitz down cold. This was no disappointment to Dershowitz. Another parochial, religious education was the last thing he wanted. His hope was to follow Norman Sohn to City College in Manhattan, but his GPA was too low and the school was too "out-of-town" for his parents' preference.

Brooklyn College, however, was less than a fifteen-minute drive from home in the Flatbush neighborhood and free to City residents. Claire filled out an application, but unfortunately for Dershowitz, his 78.6 percent was below Brooklyn's required 82 percent high school average for boys seeking admittance. To get into Brooklyn, he had to take a stringent test for non-qualifying students. He passed by the skin of his teeth. On the day his mother received the acceptance letter, she cried tears of joy.

Even though Brooklyn required no tuition, Dershowitz wanted to attempt the statewide Regents Scholarship exam, which awarded a tremendously high sum of $1,400. He entreated Rabbi Zuroff, but the principal denied him permission to take the exam. Undeterred, Dershowitz filed the first petition of his life to the Regents board, who took his side and ordered Zuroff to grant Dershowitz's request. Dershowitz sat for the test and passed. Zuroff was incensed and accused him of cheating. Fortunately, Dershowitz could prove he sat behind a student named Aaron Bachman, whose academic performance was so poor that no one would ever think of cheating from his answers.

"Avi winning the Regents scholarship shocked everybody," says Barry Zimmerman. Dershowitz immediately deposited his $1,400 earnings in an interest-generating account, and in the fall of 1955, he began his first college semester at Brooklyn.

Amid the bustle and unsightliness of City thoroughfares, traffic, and tenements, Brooklyn College was bedecked with a grassy quad, red-brick study buildings, and a colonial-style library with a clock tower rising above the campus. When Dershowitz enrolled, a majority of the students were

Jewish, and the remaining were a mix of Irish, Puerto Rican, Italian, and African American. Despite the fact that the faculty was almost completely composed of white, Anglo-Saxon Protestants (WASPs), the college was a haven for immigrant children due to quota systems in place at Ivy League schools.

"I decided that the lack of a positive goal had been a significant drawback in high school and so I was determined not to repeat the same mistake," says Dershowitz. "I selected law as my goal and set out to achieve it."

Dershowitz's professors were a critical component of his transformation. These were not the religious instructors of his youth. "When I got to Brooklyn College," begins Dershowitz, "I found a place where creativity was rewarded, rote memorization frowned upon, and respect was something to be earned, not merely accorded by the title of rabbi."

John Hospers was the professor of philosophy and ethics, and according to Dershowitz, he was "the single best teacher I ever had in any subject anywhere." Though a conservative, Hospers refrained from bringing his political views into the classroom. "Our minds worked the same way," Dershowitz declared.

Dershowitz bounded into Hospers's classes. There were no hand-raising protocols or pontifications. Hospers masterfully employed the Socratic method, throwing out hypotheticals and seeking the students' engagement and presentation of differing views. He and Dershowitz went back and forth. "Every time he came up with a question you couldn't answer, he'd come up with a harder question," recounts Dershowitz. "I just loved that. I couldn't wait to get to class."

Hospers was part of an influx of brilliant young teachers that had joined the Brooklyn staff in the 1950s. Another member of this wunderkind wave was John Hope Franklin. Son of a victim of the 1921 rampage against Black families and businessmen in Tulsa, Franklin rose above the hatred of his day and became an internationally recognized author through his bestselling account of Black history titled *From Slavery to Freedom*. When Brooklyn College voted in favor of Franklin leading their Department of History, *The New York Times* carried the story on its front page.

Dershowitz took Franklin's American Studies course, an amalgam of US history, philosophy, and culture. Despite coming from a persecuted

Black family, Franklin did not preach to his students. One scholar notes that he supported "the right of an intellectual to express ideas that were not popular."

"It was very hard for me to disagree with him about anything because he was analytic," comments Dershowitz. "He just gave us the facts of history and had us come up with our own conclusions. I remember clearly a discussion about the Civil War in which Professor Franklin told us the series of events that led up to the war and then asked us to explain what we personally believed was the cause of the war. We had a long debate about that."

Although Dershowitz did not grow up in a prejudiced home, Franklin was the first African American friend he ever had, simply because of the homogeneity of Borough Park. In addition to classes, Dershowitz spent time socially with Franklin and wrote papers under his supervision. "He had an enormous impact on me," says Dershowitz.

Dershowitz flourished at Brooklyn. "Debate filled the classrooms, the lunchrooms, and the quad," he recalls. For the first time in his life, Dershowitz enjoyed the subjects he was learning, from political science to Middle East politics to police work and beyond. He did not take a single note in class during his four years at the college. Instead, he digested the teachers' point and decided whether he agreed or if it required a follow-up question. Dershowitz was actively involved to the point that students occasionally thought he had been assigned to co-teach the class. "I loved arguing with my professors," he admits.

After eighteen years of struggling, Dershowitz was coming into his own. He decided to change the name on his birth certificate to "Alan," the spelling of which he preferred to "Allen." Close friends and family still called him "Avi," but from this time on, everyone else knew him as "Alan."

* * *

Back at 1558 48th Street, Alan's family life was not stellar. For the most part, classes ended around three o'clock, and he headed home to find Grandma Ringel keeping house while Harry and Claire were out working. Alan took his college work seriously. "When he went to Brooklyn, he suddenly needed to study, which he had never done in high school," says his brother. "Boy, my brother was a pain in the ass. He screamed like a banshee if my cousin, Norman, and I made any noise playing basketball while he was studying." One day, Alan took a knife and cut up Norman's basketball, and Norman got revenge by flicking pebbles at Alan's bedroom window while he was studying.

Despite a rocky relationship with his brother, Dershowitz's friendships tightened at Brooklyn. He had earned his driver's license and persuaded his Uncle Morris to sell a ramshackle 1948 Dodge that had a large hole at the foot of the passenger seat. Josh Weisberger, Hal Jacobs, and Barry Zimmerman (who all went to Brooklyn) piled in the back seat, and Dershowitz drove everyone to college and then back home after classes were finished for the day. All through college, the Big 8 continued to get together on Saturday afternoons after the Sabbath morning service. Carl Meshenberg came over to 1558 48th Street to visit Dershowitz and discuss politics or books they were reading. "He was quite analytical," comments Meshenberg.

The summers were brightened by a two-month-long camp located next to the peaceful Maple Lake in the Catskill Mountains. "As a counselor, Alan took good care of his campers," says Norman Sohn, who attended Maple Lake with Dershowitz. "They loved him very much." Sohn remembers Dershowitz as a loyal friend. Once, they were doing kitchen work together, and while carrying a large stack of soup plates, Sohn lost his footing and crashed to the floor with the plates. The camp owner was furious. Dershowitz immediately came to his friend's defense. "I saw him—he slipped on the floor!" he told the owner, who doubted Sohn's explanation. "There was soup on the floor!" Dershowitz pointed out. "He was defending me right off the bat," relays Sohn. "He was playing the part of my lawyer!"

Camp Maple Lake was known as a place ripe for *shidachs*, a Yiddish word meaning "meetings that result in marriages." In the summer of 1955, Dershowitz met a sixteen-year-old Orthodox girl named Sue Barlach, who had black hair and a pretty face. Sue was a compassionate, intelligent person who loved books. Her father, Bernie, was a recent immigrant from the Ukraine, where he had inadvertently avoided the Holocaust by coming to America to take up a job his relatives had secured for him. At the time she attended Camp Maple Lake, Sue and her family lived in Bayonne, New Jersey.

Sue and Alan developed a close relationship at Maple Lake, and in addition to summer camp each year, Alan regularly made the trip over the Hudson River to visit Sue in Bayonne. "In those early days, Alan and Sue had a happy relationship," says Bernie Beck. While Alan was at Brooklyn, Sue was beginning to pursue a major in education at Rutgers. The two enjoyed each other's conversation and bonded over car rides, movie nights, double dates, and occasional tennis games. Premarital sex was unthinkable among members of the Borough Park community, but even in the absence of a conjugal relationship, Alan and Sue's romance blossomed.

* * *

While at Brooklyn, human rights was becoming an increasingly important part of Dershowitz's life. In his first year, he took a trip to Washington, DC, with Alan Zwiebel, a classmate at Brooklyn, to "see the government in action," as Zwiebel remembers. King Saud of Saudi Arabia was on a state visit, and the green flag of his country was hanging on small poles around the Lincoln Memorial. Knowing that the King owned slaves and was an enemy of Israel, Dershowitz walked up to one of the poles and impulsively ripped down the Saudi flag. Unfortunately, Capitol Police witnessed the act and took Dershowitz in for questioning.

"Alan was charged with a misdemeanor, and we were all taken into a federal courthouse, where Alan stood before a judge for sentencing," recalls Alan Zweibel. "Alan immediately started into his very first oral argument, defending himself and telling the judge that he wanted to go to law school and someday become an attorney. He asked the judge for mercy, arguing this would be a bad mark on his record and may even endanger the possibility of his being admitted to the bar. And he succeeded! The judge bought his argument, told him to behave, and let him go."

Dershowitz placed high value on being an American citizen, but the welfare of Israel was always top of mind. Around the time of the 1956 Suez Crisis between Israel, Britain, France, and Egypt, Dershowitz delivered a speech to the Young Israel Synagogue in Borough Park on the role American Jews should play in advocating for Israel. "We must convince the

American policy makers of the benefits [that] they will receive from a more favorable Israel policy," he told congregants. "We must show these policy authors that . . . we are fighting a war of principles and morals and not one of strength or might, that this war will be won or lost not on the battlefield, but on the basis of the extension of American democracy abroad."

In addition to following international politics, Dershowitz became actively engaged in school government. Inspired by Professor John Hope Franklin, he became a leading member of the Brooklyn chapter of NAACP, considered a radical organization at the time. In the fall of 1958, he was elected president of the student government in a landslide, after running on a platform of free parking at the college and creating a varsity football team for Brooklyn. Dershowitz used his new position for the benefit of his fellow Jews. During his presidency, five Orthodox Jews were elected to the executive council, and many others were accepted into drama societies, singing clubs, opera guilds, and newspaper jobs.

Dershowitz also used his platform to stand up to the anti-communist policies of college president Harry Gideonse. Gideonse was a conservative who believed colleges were responsible for training young people to be moral and ethical people. As president, he censored newspapers and societies that did not meet his approval and assumed power over the selection of deans and department personnel. He placed leaflets written by students on the college bulletin board with corrections of their views placed overtop in red pen. "Around that time, I was the cartoonist for the school paper *The Kingsman*," says Alan Zwiebel. "I had several cartoons killed because Gideonse thought they were too liberal."

The era of McCarthyism was on the decline by the time Dershowitz enrolled at Brooklyn, but Gideonse took it upon himself to make sure Brooklyn College did not become a "little Red schoolhouse." Around the time Dershowitz became student president, Gideonse fired Professor Harry Slochower, who had pleaded the Fifth before a congressional committee over the question of whether he had once been a member of the Communist Party. Slochower's firing received support from some on the faculty, including Professor Eugene Scalia, father of the future Justice Antonin Scalia. Dershowitz, on the other hand, publicly criticized Gideonse's decision.

Dershowitz had no time for communism as a philosophy. Handwritten notecards he prepared for a speech in 1955 contain the following statements: (1). children of communists are forced to love "socialism" and the "Party"; (2). these children play with "red army soldiers" and "march to Commy songs"; (3). these children are "slaves"; and (4). "We teach how to think. . . . [Communists] teach what to think."

Despite this, Dershowitz advocated for the right of alleged communists like Slochower to publicly present their views. Through meetings, speeches, and articles in the school paper, Dershowitz opposed Gideonse's censorship attempts.

"Alan was an issue-raiser even then," says Alan Zwiebel. "From day one, he was a left-leaning, principled person who spoke out for issues he believed in and would not quietly slip away into the shadows. He was a firebrand, and he was nearly always at odds with President Gideonse."

In addition to bucking Gideonse's anti-communist policies, Dershowitz also angered the president by taking members of the "radical" NAACP down to Washington, DC, for a protest calling for racial integration. They traveled on a bus draped with Brooklyn College banners, to boot.

Dershowitz shined at Brooklyn. In addition to being student president, he was president of the House Plan Association, Forensic Society, and Delta Sigma Rho—a nationwide honor society devoted to public speaking. By his second-to-last semester, he had achieved straight A's in all his subjects (excluding a B in phys ed), and in his senior year, he was elected to Phi Beta Kappa.

"Alan became a well-grounded person at Brooklyn," says Bernie Beck. "He became an activist instead of a smart aleck."

"I didn't do anything very different from what I had done in high school," says Dershowitz, taking a slightly different view than Bernie. "I was still a 'smart aleck' and a 'wise guy,' but these qualities were appreciated and rewarded at Brooklyn College. They let me be me in college, and they wanted me to be someone else in high school."

In an unprecedented move, all five City Colleges of New York put their heads together and nominated Dershowitz for a Rhodes scholarship. If Dershowitz was selected by the trustees, the grant would pay all his expenses for a university education in England at a school of his choosing.

Excitedly, Dershowitz drafted an application that articulated his success in academics and student government, including his efforts to create a level playing field for Orthodox Jews at Brooklyn. "If admitted to Oxford," Dershowitz wrote, "I would read for the Oxford B.A. in the Honor School of Jurisprudence and then enter Law School in the United States."

He never got an interview. The Rhodes trustees rejected this Jewish application, following in the footsteps of the scholarship's namesake: Cecil Rhodes, nineteenth-century diamond magnate and governor of the British Empire's Cape Colony, who believed in the superiority of the Anglo-Saxon race and once wrote: "There is nothing so certain than the natural inequality of men."

Dershowitz thought otherwise, but he could do nothing to change the outcome of this act of blacklisting.

Notwithstanding this snub from the Rhodes trustees, Dershowitz was accepted into Harvard, Yale, NYU, Columbia, and Stanford, with NYU and Columbia offering him full rides. Claire Dershowitz wanted her son to select Harvard, which she saw as the cream of the crop, but he opted for Yale. "Yale looked at law as part of a broader discipline of politics and philosophy," he says, "not strictly just reading statutes and decisions. There was law and psychiatry, there was law and economics, and law and diplomacy. That's what I liked about it."

After two decades, Alan was leaving Borough Park, but before he took off to New Haven, Connecticut, Claire made sure that he had a significant layer of protection from the outside world. Both his parents were worried that their boy would find an "unacceptable" Jewish girl—non-Orthodox—if he left home as a bachelor. And so, on June 21, Alan married Sue Barlach in a traditional Orthodox ceremony at the Broadway Central Hotel in New York. Not yet twenty-one years old, Alan required a guardian's signature on his marriage license. His bride was nineteen, and over the summer of 1959, they packed their belongings and moved to an apartment on Norton Street in New Haven, which his parents picked due its proximity to New Haven's Young Israel synagogue.

Dershowitz's Brooklyn identity emerged in the classrooms at Yale. Although Yale did not explicitly discriminate against Jews, Dershowitz's student body was made up in large part of white Protestants who were wealthy and well connected. His classmates included descendants of William Brennan, John Marshall, Earl Warren, and William Howard Taft. Dershowitz stuck out. With its prolonged vowels and mismatched consonants, his accent caused snickering among students the first time he was called upon to do a reading in front of the class.

On Dershowitz's first day, he walked into torts class with Professor Guido Calabresi, who had just begun teaching at Yale that fall. Calabresi's parents had fled Mussolini's fascist government in 1939, and Calabresi eventually earned a Rhodes scholarship and gained high honors from Oxford before being hired by Yale.

Donned in gray flannel trousers and a sports jacket, Calabresi looked as young as he was. Dershowitz thoroughly enjoyed the class, and early on in the semester, he was assigned to write a short legal memo. Calabresi's assistant reviewed the paper and unhesitatingly assigned it a D. Devastated, Dershowitz called his teacher to ask why he had merited such a low grade. "You write like you're having a conversation with your friends in Brooklyn," came Calabresi's answer.

Despite this criticism, Calabresi believed it was the best paper that had been submitted. "To me, it was the most interesting because it had the most ideas," he recalls. "Alan knew how to form his ideas in a way that presented the argument he wanted to make, putting them on like salt and pepper.

"I told the teaching assistant that we had to work with Alan very, very hard. If he wrote exams that way in other classes, a lot of teachers would have graded him badly, and he would have disappeared in the middle of the class, which would have been a shame because he had more ideas than any other student."

With Dershowitz's enthusiasm and perseverance, Calabresi mentored him throughout the class. In November, Dershowitz wrote an essay that examined whether a TV station is liable for repeating the potentially unlawful speech of a political candidate. On the last page, a note from Calabresi was scrawled in green pen: "A very good piece of work, indeed! . . . a good analysis & a logical presentation. Your style remains ponderous—but is at least clear and clean & that is all one can ask, I guess." By the end of the semester, "Alan had gotten his writing sufficiently under control," reports Calabresi.

* * *

1960 began with a climactic development in Israel. Prime Minister Ben-Gurion announced that agents of the Mossad had apprehended Adolf Eichmann, an architect of the Holocaust, who had managed to slip away to Argentina after the war. Many of Eichmann's associates had not been as lucky. During the Nuremberg Trials, Chief Prosecutor Telford Taylor secured over one hundred convictions of former Nazis. Following Nuremberg, Taylor took up a private law practice and vehemently opposed the ravings of Joseph McCarthy's anti-communist hearings in the 1950s. He eventually landed the role of visiting professor at Yale Law School and taught constitutional litigation.

Dershowitz was enamored with his new teacher. Articulate, polite, and endlessly fascinating, Taylor was a jack-of-all-trades in the legal profession. He wrote popular books and argued before the Supreme Court as a constitutional lawyer in addition to teaching. "He taught me that you don't have to choose between being a professor or a lawyer or a writer. You can do all of that," recalls Dershowitz. Over the course of law school, he and Taylor developed a close working relationship.

One professor that Dershowitz said "defied conventional labels such as liberal or conservative" was Alexander Mordechai Bickel. Born in Romania in 1924, "Alex" spent his adolescence in New York City and was a machine gunner in Italy and France during World War II. He clerked for Felix Frankfurter before becoming a professor of constitutional law at Yale. With a cigarette in hand, he paced the aisles and "would walk right up to students, stare them down, and begin a relentless cross-examination," Dershowitz remembers.

A *New York Times* piece described Bickel: "In politics a liberal Democrat, in legal philosophy a constitutional conservative." However, as with John Hospers at Brooklyn College, he did not bring political views into the classroom. He once said to a colleague: "I would lose my way intellectually if I started thinking about the political impact of position."

"Alex was tough as nails," recalls Dershowitz. "He let students get away with nothing. I learned a lot about teaching from him because there was never a right answer. In Alex's class, he would always double down, press you, and question you." Since he was constantly writing, Bickel did not allow himself to begin teaching for the day until he had written three thousand words. "I learned that kind of discipline of writing from Alex," Dershowitz reflects.

Joseph Goldstein, Dershowitz's professor of criminal law, had failed his bar exam and never practiced law. Quiet and methodical, he "influenced my legal thinking more than any other teacher," Dershowitz states. "Joe made us rethink and question every aspect of the law. 'Why is there a privilege against self-incrimination?' he'd ask. 'Why is there a presumption of innocence when people charged with crimes are virtually all guilty? How can you justify that?' I . . . was deeply influenced by his approach to law, which was the opposite of my rabbinical teachers who had demanded acceptance of what previous rabbis had decreed."

In a culminating moment of the school year, Dershowitz put his legal training to the test in Yale's "moot court" competition, a requirement for all first-years. Two students squared off as mock lawyers to argue a real-life appeal in front of a judges panel usually composed of faculty members. Dershowitz's opponent was set to be Robert Taft III, great-grandson of the twenty-seventh president of the United States. Harry and Claire worried that their son could not successfully compete with this "big-name opponent" and traveled to New Haven to support him.

Dershowitz's classmate and friend Stephen Joel Trachtenberg also came to watch Dershowitz square off with Taft. He recalls that Dershowitz "cleaned Taft's clock."

"Alan had a particularly exuberant role in the class," says Trachtenberg, who took Joseph Goldstein's courses with Dershowitz. "Alan had a lot to say, and he was very up on the material. He kept the class moving."

Recalling Dershowitz's rise at Yale, Trachtenberg comments that Dershowitz "very quickly became a member of the royalty at the law school." Students' grades were posted for everyone to see, and due to his outstanding performance in classes, Dershowitz began to receive invitations to sit at certain lunch tables and hobnob with the faculty. In his second year, Dershowitz was selected by his fellow students to be editor in chief of the *Yale Law Journal*, which was published every month and had an average length of 150 footnoted pages. To be editor in chief required diligence and a sound intellect. Dershowitz had both, and he worked zeal-ously in his new role.

"I loved Yale Law School," Dershowitz says. "The only hierarchy I ever saw was based on grades."

"Alan was much more sophisticated and settled at Yale," his friend Artie Edelman notes. "His accomplishments changed his whole demeanor. He didn't have to prove himself anymore, and he was a completely different person as a result."

During this time, Sue became pregnant. At the end of Alan's second year, in June 1961, she gave birth to a boy, whom they named Eliezer Manakin, after Sue's grandfather who died in the Holocaust. His American name was Elon. Sue devoted herself to raising Elon. Sometimes Alan's brother Nathan traveled to New Haven to babysit Elon, and he brought along his new girlfriend, Marilyn Barlach, younger sister of Sue.

Alan recalls that he "virtually lived" at Yale. Between classes, tasks for the *Journal*, and his social life at the school, he was not home often, though he slept at their apartment. It was during this time that he and Sue began growing apart. A close relative recalls that he put pressure on Sue to keep pace with his prodigious and hectic life at the Law School. "She was not as bright as he was," reflects Norman Sohn, who was a close friend of both Alan and Sue. "He was really a sharp guy, and she was much slower. I don't think she was intellectually up to him." Though they continued to attend synagogue services and social functions together and share an occasional lighthearted moment, their relationship was strained.

* * *

Customary for those aspiring to a job in the legal world, in his second summer at Yale, Dershowitz applied for an assistant position at the law firms of Wall Street. His impressive résumé in hand, Dershowitz showed up for interviews with thirty-two firms. One by one, all thirty-two turned him down. The non-Jewish corporations did not give him a second glance. Sullivan & Cromwell, a mixed (half-Jewish, half-non) firm, conjured an amusing excuse. Their Jewish representative informed Dershowitz they did not accept C students, referring to a lone C Dershowitz had earned in contracts, even though he had achieved an A in advanced contracts.

Taken aback, Dershowitz met with Dean Eugene Rostow, who was Jewish and previously worked on Wall Street, and asked if there was an anti-Jewish policy permeating these firms. "Of course there is," answered Rostow. "If you were a German Jew with wealthy parents in banking, you'd be able to get a job. It's not just that you're Jewish; it's that you're an Eastern European Jew, and you're not a fit for these firms."

After exhausting the non-Jewish firms on Wall Street, Dershowitz received an offer from the Jewish firm Kaye, Scholer. He accepted and spent several weeks working as an assistant to Milton Handler, the company's rainmaker. This new job brought Dershowitz much-needed paychecks. With $100 a week rolling in, for the first time in his life he could afford luxuries like a hardcover book, a tie, and his favorite childhood candy: a Mounds bar.

The fall of 1961 brought Dershowitz's third and final year at Yale, during which he achieved twenty-one A's (the highest unit) and three B minuses. Initially, Dershowitz considered becoming an attorney upon earning his law degree. He had become fascinated with the careers of Louis Brandeis, Thurgood Marshall, and Clarence Darrow—the legendary "Attorney for the Damned." Darrow had defended murderers, communists, railway strikers, and segregated Black people, with his most famous being the 1925 Scopes Monkey Trial on the question of evolutionary education in public schools. The story of the trial, including Darrow's dramatic showdown with prosecutor William Jennings Bryan, became the basis for a Broadway show called *Inherit the Wind*. Dershowitz had seen it at the National Theatre in Manhattan when it debuted in 1955, and it partially inspired him to become a lawyer.

Dynamic courtroom confrontations and intriguing cases were not on Claire Dershowitz's mind. She saw her son as an attorney serving the needs of Borough Park and had her eyes on a vacant pharmacy for rent on 50th Street and 16th Avenue. But Dershowitz had no interest in becoming a notary public. While at Brooklyn, Dershowitz's professor of political science, Martin Landau, had taken him aside one day and told him, "Alan, you're the smartest student I've ever had—too smart to be an ordinary lawyer. You have to be a professor." Since then, Dershowitz had harbored an interest in working as a law professor as well as a lawyer, and after

witnessing Telford Taylor in action, he realized this was a serious possibility. One major phase of education remained in front of him before he
could pursue this ambition.

BIG FEET

On June 11, 1962, all the graduating students of Yale Law School gathered on the grounds of the school to hear an address from President Kennedy, himself a Yale alumnus. During the ceremony, Kennedy shook hands with Dershowitz, who had received the honor of "class marshal" after finishing first out of 175 students in his entering class.

Per standard protocol for elite students, Dershowitz shopped around for a clerkship with an elite judge. "Alan, I'm going to recommend you for clerkships, but you have to promise me you're going to turn off at least one of your barrels when you clerk," Professor Alex Bickel told him. "Judges aren't used to being confronted, and you have to be respectful and polite."

Dershowitz's first choice was Supreme Court Justice Hugo Black, for whom Guido Calabresi had clerked. Unfortunately, another teacher at Yale, Professor Fred Rodell, not only had Black's ear but also had a bone to pick with Dershowitz. Dershowitz had refused to attend Rodell's constitutional law class because it was being held at a private club called Mory's which excluded women from membership. On top of this snub, Dershowitz also replaced Rodell's seminar with one by Alex Bickel, an intellectual rival of Rodell.

After learning of Dershowitz's interest in working for Hugo Black, Professor Rodell took a train to Washington, DC, to dissuade Black from accepting him. The justice replied and told Dershowitz that he would be considered for the following year. This left Dershowitz free to pursue a clerkship with one of the most dynamic and influential figures in the US judicial system: David Lionel Bazelon.

Born to a poverty-ridden family in Wisconsin in 1909, Bazelon rose above his humble beginnings and earned a law degree from Northwestern

University. Upon receiving his law degree, he climbed the ladder of the Democratic Party, eventually securing a position at the Department of Justice before being nominated to the DC Court of Appeals by Harry Truman.

Bazelon used his new position to help those Americans nearest to his heart—the indigent and defenseless. Bazelon had recently served on the President's Panel on Mental Retardation and was known as one of the most liberal judges in America. His most famous decision came in 1954 in an appeal for Monte Durham, a DC burglar with mental disorders. During the case proceedings, Judge Bazelon ruled that a defendant cannot be found guilty if the person is shown to have a mental defect, which became known as the "Durham Rule."

Bazelon happened to be both Jewish and an unwavering Zionist who was friends with distinguished Jewish politicians. Bazelon accepted Dershowitz as a clerk, and in the summer of 1962, Dershowitz's family packed their belongings and moved to a tiny one-bedroom apartment in Hyattsville, Maryland, just northeast of the capital.

Soon after the start of Dershowitz's clerkship, Bazelon was named Chief Judge of the DC Court, which was the second-most-powerful judicial body in America after the Supreme Court. When a DC-area defendant submitted an appeal to the court, Dershowitz was responsible for carefully reading the defense attorney's brief and oftentimes the trial transcript, a written record of every word spoken in the district court proceedings. Bazelon wanted to know whether the lower court had committed a legal error while trying the case and also whether the case touched on social issues important to him. Once Dershowitz completed his study of the documents, he met with Bazelon, and together they discussed whether or not to affirm or reverse the conviction. Occasionally, Bazelon permitted Dershowitz to leave his desk and watch parts of the court proceedings, particularly when the lawyers delivered oral arguments.

Bazelon was a taskmaster, who required his clerks to be in the office before he arrived and work after hours. "It's only a one-year job and that means 365 days," he explained to Dershowitz. "Bazelon was my best and worst boss at once," says Dershowitz. "He worked me to the bone; he didn't hesitate to call at 2 a.m." He pushed Dershowitz to continually refine his work.

Bazelon was also capable of tremendous kindness. "One day he wanted to bring together some of Washington's wealthiest contributors to build a pool in an African American community which had no access to decent recreational facilities, especially during the hot summer," says Dershowitz. "He invited me to the meeting where then–Attorney General Robert Kennedy said a few words and then Bazelon went to work. He got everyone in the room . . . to make a significant contribution.

"The decisions of which he was most proud involved obscure bag ladies, homeless mentally ill men and voiceless immigrants," continues Dershowitz. Once, when he and Judge Bazelon were discussing Dershowitz's bar mitzvah Torah portion—"Justice, justice you shall pursue"—Dershowitz shared his view that the first "Justice" referred to legal justice and the second to compassionate justice. The judge replied to his young clerk, "Alan, compassion must come before law."

* * *

In the winter of 1962, Dershowitz received a once-in-a-lifetime job offer. During his time at Yale, Dershowitz had written several academic articles on constitutional and criminal law which caught the eyes of some of the faculty at Harvard Law School. After being told of Dershowitz's brilliance, Dean Erwin Griswold of the Law School arranged an interview with him, following which he invited the twenty-four-year-old to take up a position as assistant professor of law. Dershowitz immediately accepted, thrilled at the opportunity to join one of the greatest universities in the world.

As if this offer from Harvard was not overwhelming enough, in January 1963, Sue gave birth to a second son, Jamin. Ever the taskmaster, Bazelon had frowned on his clerk taking a day off work for Jamin's birth. Unfazed, Dershowitz extracted Bazelon's schedule from his secretary to find out which days he would be out of the office, and luckily, one of the dates was Sue's delivery. Without informing his boss, Dershowitz slipped out to the hospital to meet his son for the first time.

Under Bazelon's watchful eye, Dershowitz's knowledge of the legal world grew every day. Dershowitz was shocked to learn that in some cases, police officers use any methods possible—even illegal ones—to ensure the conviction of an offending citizen. "Somehow, the suspect always 'dropped' the drugs before the police officer arrested him. Bazelon called this 'dropsie testimony,'" says Dershowitz, "Or the suspect would 'blurt out' a confession before being interrogated. Bazelon called this a 'blurtsie confession.'" Once, in 1957, Bazelon had reversed the conviction of an accused rapist because the man had been forced to confess his crime before appearing in front of a magistrate.

As spring arrived and Dershowitz's year with Bazelon came to a close, the judge urged him not to follow anyone's footsteps in a cookie-cutter fashion. He encouraged Dershowitz instead to forge his own unique career and practice, telling Dershowitz: "Your feet are too big to fit anyone else's print."

Around this time, Dershowitz also sat for the DC bar exam. Once the tests had been graded, Dershowitz's result was mailed to Bazelon, who stormed to Dershowitz's desk and slammed down the evaluation paper. "You didn't need time off," he declared angrily, referring to the days Dershowitz had spent studying for the exam. "You got the g*d-damned highest grade in the city!"

* * *

It was important to both Harvard and Dershowitz for him to gain the prestige of a Supreme Court clerkship before moving to Cambridge, Massachusetts. After reviewing the current justices, Dershowitz arranged a meeting with Arthur Goldberg, who had joined the court a few months previously, and he eagerly accepted when Goldberg offered him a job.

The youngest in a long line of siblings, Arthur Goldberg was born in 1908 in a ghetto of Chicago. Through the sacrifice of his siblings, he was eventually able to attend college at Northwestern University, where he graduated first in his class. As a young man, he was also active in midwestern Zionist organizations and became friends with a young Golda Meir, whom he knew as "Goldie."

Moved by the suffering of Americans in the Great Depression, Goldberg committed his legal practice to aiding causes of the labor movement. His brokering between the AFL and CIO led to the merging of these mammoth labor unions in 1955, and just a few years later, Goldberg became part of JFK's cabinet as secretary of labor. Kennedy once told an associate that Goldberg was "the smartest man I ever met," and he selected him to fill a Supreme Court vacancy in 1962.

"Goldberg was a man of action," Dershowitz remarks. "He came to the high court with an agenda—a list of changes he wanted to engender." The most pressing of these was to have the death penalty declared unconstitutional. Believing the government had no right to take human life, Goldberg was passionately opposed to capital punishment, which had been widely implemented in America since its founding. Goldberg firmly believed it was in violation of the Eighth Amendment's ban on the infliction of "cruel and unusual punishments."

In July 1963, Dershowitz had his first work meeting with Goldberg. Sitting across from Dershowitz, Goldberg chucked a ten-page legal paper onto the desk and asked him to read it. After Dershowitz did so, the white-haired justice inquired, "What do you see in it?" "It's a pro se cert petition in a capital case," said Dershowitz, referring to certiorari petitions that are filed to the Supreme Court by defendants seeking to overturn their sentences. "No," Goldberg corrected him. "What you're holding in your hands is the vehicle by which we can end capital punishment in the United States."

Goldberg explained to Dershowitz the number one item on his judicial "to-do" list. Because it was still a widely implemented policy throughout the country, abolishing the death penalty would have to start with gathering support from certain liberal justices to coauthor a document which would powerfully argue this punishment to be in violation of the Constitution. This, in turn, would provide the lower courts with an impetus to begin opposing it throughout different regions of the nation. As Dershowitz describes, Goldberg wanted Dershowitz to "make [its abolition] seem like a natural progression from existing law and authority." He was to search the nooks and crannies of the statute books for evidence of Goldberg's viewpoint on the Eighth Amendment's "cruel and unusual punishments" clause and then write a thorough memorandum that summarized his findings.

Drawing on the growing public sympathy for civil rights, Goldberg selected a case titled *Rudolph v. Alabama*, which was an appeal from a black man sentenced to death for raping a white woman. The Supreme Court had refused to hear his case, and Goldberg wanted to dissent from this denial. He planned to use Dershowitz's memorandum to help convince fellow justices to join him. After receiving his assignment, Dershowitz spent many weeks over the summer of 1963 researching capital cases throughout American history and prepared a rough draft of his memorandum. His concluding argument was that the "institutionalized taking of human life by the state" was "barbaric and inhuman."

Goldberg's entire plan would not even get off the ground, though, unless another justice would join his dissent. William Brennan was their best shot. Brennan avidly supported liberal policies, including affirmative action and opposition to the death penalty. "Unless Justice Brennan agreed to join, the entire project would be scuttled, since Justice Goldberg, the Court's rookie, did not want to 'be out there alone' against the chief justice and the rest of the Court," Dershowitz explains. Goldberg gave his twenty-four-year-old clerk the responsibility to persuade Brennan to join the dissent.

Dershowitz arranged a private meeting with Brennan, who had an office next door to Goldberg's. At the appointed time, he walked over with the memo in hand and found Brennan in a short-sleeve shirt with his tie loose. "Justice Brennan was just about the nicest, sweetest, most modest important person I had ever met," Dershowitz says. Brennan asked Dershowitz to summarize his findings in the memo. "I . . . told Justice Brennan that our research had disclosed a widespread pattern of unequal application of the death penalty on racial grounds," says Dershowitz. "I cited national prison statistics showing that between 1937 and 1951, 233 blacks were executed for rape in the United States, while only 26 whites were executed for that crime." After twenty minutes of Dershowitz making his case, Brennan said his arguments were "very, very impressive and very persuasive." He took Dershowitz's memo home and read the entire piece.

Soon after, Brennan informed Goldberg he would join Goldberg's dissent of the Court's refusal to hear *Rudolph v. Alabama*. Unfortunately for the defendant, they were ultimately unsuccessful in sparing his life, but nevertheless, in part through Dershowitz's efforts, the campaign for the abolition of the death penalty in America was underway.

* * *

The 1963–1964 term was one of the most critical in the history of the
Supreme Court, and Dershowitz had a front-row seat for it all. Arthur
Goldberg authored eight dissents and fourteen opinions as the major-
ity's representative. Significantly, he helped to lay the groundwork for the
Miranda rights in a case titled *Escobedo v. Illinois*. Danny Escobedo was a
Mexican American who murdered a relative and was hounded by police
until admitting to the crime—without a defense attorney at his side.
Escobedo brought a suit which eventually reached the Supreme Court.
Because of Dershowitz's expertise in criminal law from his time at Yale,
Goldberg asked him to write an opinion in defense of Escobedo. In a
persuasive conclusion, Dershowitz wrote, "If the exercise of constitutional
rights will thwart the effectiveness of a system of law enforcement, then
there is something very wrong with that system." Five justices agreed.
Escobedo was saved, and the powers of the police were checked.

During the time Dershowitz was working on the *Escobedo* case, a young
Oxford graduate named Stephen Breyer showed up at Goldberg's chambers to interview as a prospective clerk for the next Supreme Court term.
Upon entering the office, he saw Dershowitz working away, and the two
struck up a conversation. "Goldberg liked him, and he liked Goldberg.
They were clearly getting on," recalls Breyer. "Alan was very bright and
good at debating."

"Alan's directness and his debate experience were at first disturbing to
some of the other justices' law clerks," continues McTurnan. "In some
of the clerks' lunch-gatherings, disagreements were expressed with legal
theories and positions that Alan had described. Sometimes Alan went into
a debate mode—not hostile but directly dissecting what he analyzed as
weaknesses or mistakes. That ruffled feathers on some clerks to whom it
felt like a personal attack on them or perhaps their justices who may have
expressed the views being criticized. In any event, those irritations seemed
to fade away or be significantly softened during the year. Alan had been
focused on content, without assaults on individuals or character."

Goldberg hoped Dershowitz would model his boss's career path and
become a justice on the Supreme Court, asking Dershowitz whether

he would like Goldberg to arrange him a job as an assistant to Robert Kennedy so he could get his foot in the door of Washington politics. But Dershowitz's mind was set on Harvard. "I had a lot of ideas jammed in my head that I wanted to start writing about, particularly concerning the role of prevention in the legal system," says Dershowitz. "I had spent two years in DC and thought it was time to settle down." In the summer of 1964, Dershowitz's family packed up their belongings for the third time in five years and drove to their new apartment in Brookline, Massachusetts, just across the Charles River from the legendary law school.

BOY PROFESSOR

Founded by Puritan minister John Harvard in the early 1600s, over the centuries, Harvard became the Goliath of American universities, producing students like John Adams and his son John Quincy, Ralph Waldo Emerson, Rutherford B. Hayes, Theodore Roosevelt and his cousin Franklin D. Roosevelt, Oliver Wendell Holmes, W. E. B. Du Bois, and John F. Kennedy.

Harvard's graduate law school bore the distinction of being the oldest continuously running law school in the United States with a birthdate of 1817. Dershowitz arrived at HLS in the summer of 1964 to take up his position as assistant professor of law. At twenty-five, he was the youngest member of the faculty, and he planned to work toward gaining tenure, a full-time pursuit that would require him to focus on teaching and writing academic papers. At the same time, he would glean batches of wisdom from the elder statesmen on the faculty, so he thought.

Alex Bickel had warned Dershowitz about accepting a position at HLS. "Don't go to Harvard," he told Dershowitz. "You'll never fit in there."

When Dershowitz arrived, the HLS faculty was composed of nearly forty professors—all men. Led by Erwin Griswold, an Ohioan who had been dean since 1946, Dershowitz's new colleagues were a coterie of old-fashioned academics. Paul Freund had been a professor since 1940 and turned down an offer from JFK to be solicitor general because Freund wanted to finish editing a textbook on the Supreme Court instead. JFK's response to this decline was, "I'm sorry [Freund]. I hoped you would prefer making history to writing it." As a young man, Professor Henry Hart had done postgraduate work with Justice Felix Frankfurter and had been teaching at Harvard for over thirty years. Paul Bator was a fresh addition to the faculty, but had clerked for the stuffy, aristocratic Justice John M. Harlan II. As at Brooklyn College, Dershowitz's radical personality and ideology had the potential to make waves among this conventional faculty.

"When I first came [to Harvard]," Dershowitz notes, "I found a stifling uniformity of views about law on the Harvard faculty. . . . You'd sit down at the dinner table with your colleagues, and [Erwin] Griswold or one other professor would pronounce the prevailing view of law, and everyone else would shake their heads in unison." Dershowitz intended to shake things up at the school.

The fall semester of 1964 dawned, and on September 1, Dershowitz arrived at the law school at 7:00 a.m. for the first day of his criminal law class, which he had prepared for all through the summer. He pulled his Peugeot into the first parking spot and got in his classroom in Austin Hall early enough to write out questions for his incoming students and fiddle with the script he had prepared for the day. His curly reddish hair neatly cropped, Dershowitz stood dressed in a sport jacket and tie as his similarly clad students began filing in at nine o'clock and took their seats in semicircular rows in front of the professor and his blackboard. By the time he was ready to begin, Dershowitz was looking out at over one hundred students, many of whom were older than him. "I was very nervous and very arrogant all at once," he says. "Here I could unload both barrels and not worry that I was offending a teacher or judge. I was the teacher. My students were worried about offending me!"

"Alan's lectures were intensely interesting," says Harvey Silverglate, who arrived at Harvard as a student at the same time Dershowitz joined the faculty. Summoning all his powers of Socratic dialogue, Dershowitz would walk briskly up and down the aisles of the classroom, engaging multiple students at a time in his thick Brooklyn accent. "I loved it," Silverglate said. "It was mind games. It was logic and hypotheticals, and a ton of philosophy and psychology."

"Alan was totally brilliant. He was a professor coming straight from a Supreme Court clerkship, which is very unusual," says Stuart Eizenstat, who enrolled in Dershowitz's first class in 1964 and eventually became Jimmy Carter's domestic policy adviser. "Alan was very energetic and very into his topic. He was very engaged and would use forceful arm gestures to make a point. He was highly analytic, and yet open to dialogue. If a student made a good comment, he would acknowledge it. He wasn't arrogant, as some of the professors were." For all Dershowitz's charisma, Eizenstat says Dershowitz was not one to make off-color remarks, and he kept his political opinions "out of the classroom." "He was a very strong defender of criminal defendants' rights even at that point," says Eizenstat. "I think his attitude was very much shaped by his passion for supporting the underdog."

Dershowitz was labeled the "Boy Professor" in an October 1964 edition of the *Harvard Law Record*, and students around campus referred to him as "the Dersh."

As the end of the year approached, a group of Dershowitz's students asked him for a favor. The dynamic and controversial Black rights leader Malcolm X had been invited to speak at Harvard, but none of the law school faculty would agree to give opening remarks before his speech. "They deemed him too radical," says Dershowitz, who was himself put off by Malcolm's recent inflammatory comments regarding Israel. In September, he had told the *Egyptian Gazette*: "These Israeli Zionists religiously believe their Jewish God has chosen them to replace the outdated European colonialism with a new form of colonialism."

Despite this smear, Dershowitz agreed to the students' request, and on the evening of December 16, Malcolm X entered a large, packed Harvard auditorium to make his speech with a camera case over his shoulder. At the time, Dershowitz was not aware that the case contained a gun, and he took the podium to deliver the introduction.

"Our speaker this evening was born Malcolm Little about forty years ago in Omaha, Nebraska," he said to the audience. "Although still a Muslim, he has recently broken with the Black Muslim Movement, where he served as chief minister. He is now chairman of an organization known as the Organization of Afro-American Unity [OAAU]—the description of which I shall leave to him . . . Mr. Malcolm X."

Following Malcolm's speech about the importance of using any means necessary to oppose the hatred of the KKK and others, Dershowitz and Malcolm X sat next to each other at dinner and debated the Middle East. Dershowitz asked if Malcolm X would consider visiting Israel, and though

Malcolm X said he would not, he made an interesting aside, saying that "I would be much safer in Israel than in the Arab countries I visited, and safer than I am here in the United States."

Two months after their dinner conversation, Malcolm X was assassinated by a member of a rival Islamic organization while giving a speech in New York.

At the time of Malcolm X's assassination, Dershowitz was in the midst of teaching a family law elective course to around sixty students, many of whom were women. There were few women in his criminal law class, as compared to the family law elective, since "women lawyers were thought suitable to practice in such 'soft' areas of law as divorce and child custody," as Dershowitz explains. Certain members of the faculty held this view, and Dershowitz noticed that one professor, Richard Baxter, purposefully gave a female student lower grades than she deserved. To fight against this misogyny, Dershowitz decided to blindly grade his students' papers. Among the students taking his "soft" course in family law were future congresswoman Elizabeth Holtzman and Elizabeth Dole, who would eventually work in four presidential administrations, run for president, and serve as a Republican senator from North Carolina.

When student evaluations were distributed, Dershowitz received the highest rating of all the teachers at the law school. He would later say the faculty was "pissed off" at the fact that a punk with a Brooklyn accent was now the most popular professor.

Capping off a remarkable first year, Dershowitz helped organize a "Special Summer Program for Negroes," whose stated purpose was to "encourage Negro college students to consider a career in law." He spent weeks recruiting students in historically Black schools throughout the South and working on administrative details. During the program in August, he taught a class on constitutional and criminal law to a group of twenty students, and in pictures taken of the program participants, Dershowitz is one of only a few white faculty standing with the Black students.

"I think Alan came to Harvard Law School thinking of himself as David going up against Goliath," his colleague Dr. Alan Stone reflected. "[He] was the boy gladiator."

During the 1965–1966 academic year, Dershowitz co-taught a course on the relationship between psychoanalysis, psychiatry, and the law with Alan Stone. As Dershowitz studied the impact of psychiatry on the American legal system, he discovered disturbing facts about state governments' use of mental hospitals to detain a person who they believed was potentially dangerous and might commit a crime in the future. The U.S. Census Bureau had recorded in 1960 that of the nearly two million Americans incarcerated in institutions, only 346,000 were in correctional facilities and receiving help to change the direction of their lives. Around 700,000 were kept in mental hospitals. These "predictive prisoners" included psychiatric patients, pretrial detainees, people with communicable diseases, and "others deemed too dangerous to be left at liberty," explains Dershowitz.

Dershowitz's tenure piece—a paper all assistant professors had to write in order to be considered for tenure—would make the case that psychiatry's role in the legal world was a double-edged sword. In Dershowitz's opinion, the decision to commit someone to a mental institution should be made by a jury, rather than a psychiatrist or judge, and his piece would advocate for this change.

By the summer of 1967, the Harvard Board of Overseers were coming to a decision about his tenure appointment. The feisty young teacher did not help his chances. While driving home one evening, he was parked at a red light on Massachusetts Avenue, and the driver behind him was honking the horn and ticking him off. Dershowitz turned and gave the finger, only to realize that the driver was Professor Louis Loss from the tenure committee. He quickly apologized.

Fortunately, Dershowitz's tenure piece, titled "Psychiatry and the Legal Process: A Knife that Cuts Both Ways," was approved by his colleagues, and the committee unanimously voted to grant him tenure, effective July 1, 1967. Two months before his twenty-ninth birthday, Dershowitz was the youngest tenured professor in the history of Harvard Law School.

* * *

Around the time he became a full professor at Harvard, Dershowitz attracted the attention of eminent liberal politicians for his expertise on

the law's relation to the sciences, particularly psychiatry. He exchanged letters with Robert Kennedy, then serving as a senator, who told Dershowitz
he was working on "legislation providing for the care and treatment of
those acquitted in federal courts on the ground of insanity." Dershowitz
reviewed drafts of the bill, and Kennedy wrote to him afterward to
acknowledge that Dershowitz's suggestions "were extremely constructive." Kennedy's younger brother Edward ("Ted") also made Dershowitz's
acquaintance. One of Massachusetts' two senators, Ted Kennedy was a
member of the Committee on Labor and Public Welfare, and in February
1967, he arranged a meeting with Dershowitz to discuss crime. Afterward,
he sent Dershowitz a letter thanking him for his "helpful advice," adding
that he hoped the two could keep in touch.

Over the coming months, Dershowitz received a license to practice
law from the Bar of Massachusetts and was also elected to a three-year
term on the National Board of the American Civil Liberties Union after
being urged to join by his colleague Professor Mark DeWolfe Howe, who
wanted to increase the number of liberals on the board. During this time,
Dershowitz was also working with Kennedy's staff on a new gun control
law which would limit the amount of ammunition a citizen could purchase, rather than the number of guns one could purchase.

It was a violent time. In April, Martin Luther King Jr. became a martyr
for his cause after being shot dead in Memphis by James Earl Ray. At that
same time, Robert Kennedy was in the thick of a race to replace Lyndon
Johnson in the upcoming 1968 presidential election. He became the
front-runner of the Democratic candidates, winning four out of the first
five primaries. According to Dershowitz, Kennedy's staff had earmarked
Dershowitz for a job in the administration if Kennedy was elected president. On June 4, Kennedy won the California primary, and Dershowitz
went to bed thrilled by the victory.

The next morning, he woke up to news that Kennedy was on death's
door. In the early hours of June 5, Kennedy had given a speech to his
impassioned supporters at the Ambassador Hotel in Los Angeles. As he
was leaving through a kitchen hallway, a young Palestinian named Sirhan
Sirhan fired several shots into his body, and Kennedy fell sprawled onto
the ground. With bullets in his armpit and head, the doctors could not

save him. Surrounded by family—including his fourteen-year-old son Robert Jr., he died the following day. Dershowitz was devastated.

Kennedy had been a shoo-in for the Democratic nomination, partly because President Johnson's war in Vietnam was so unpopular. Hundreds of thousands of Americans were fighting in this never-ending conflict between communist-led North Vietnam and American lackey-state South Vietnam in Southeast Asia—far away from the cares and concerns of many young Americans. When the government called for fresh troops in the aftermath of North Vietnam's massive Tet Offensive in March 1968, protests erupted throughout America. The Selective Service Act had made it illegal to resist the draft, but that did not stop many citizens from trying.

Dershowitz did not believe there was any constitutional right to resist the draft, but he was vehemently opposed to the government's treatment of protesters and the war itself. That year he signed his name to a petition calling for peace in Vietnam, which was published in *The Boston Globe*. The document bore the signatures of many Bostonian academics, including Dershowitz's colleague Laurence "Larry" Tribe and Stephen Breyer, who had joined the faculty at Harvard after clerking for Arthur Goldberg. "We believe that it is wrong and dangerous in these circumstances [of terrible violence against the Vietnamese people] to continue to subordinate desperately needed domestic programs to the increasing demands this war is imposing on our nation's resources and moral energies," read their petition.

A local informant of the FBI forwarded a copy of the petition to J. Edgar Hoover. "Enclosed for the Bureau are eleven copies of a letterhead memorandum concerning an advertisement contained in . . . 'The Boston Globe,'" read the informant's letter. "The Bureau's attention is specifically invited to the name of [*blanked*] who is listed as one of the Harvard Law School faculty signers in the advertisement set forth in the attached letterhead memorandum." The FBI was keeping its watchful eye on the "Boy Professor."

* * *

One of Dershowitz's intellectual allies during the Vietnam era was Dr. Noam Chomsky, who in 1948 had attended the Jewish summer camp

Massad at the same time as Dershowitz. Chomsky was now a professor at MIT, just down the road from Harvard Law School. Following a stint as a junior fellow at Harvard, Chomsky received his PhD in linguistics from the University of Pennsylvania. He was hired by MIT in 1956 and became involved in politics early on in his tenure. "[Chomsky] argued that the Vietnam War was only one in a series of cases in which the United States used its military power to gain or consolidate economic control over increasingly larger areas of the developing world," says scholar James McGilvray.

In keeping with these beliefs, Chomsky drummed up support for the anti-war movement through lectures across the country and also by linking arms with like-minded individuals. Chomsky remembers that he first met Dershowitz in the mid-1960s "when I was becoming involved in direct resistance to the Vietnam War and was interested in learning more about legal ramifications. . . . He had a reputation then as being critical of the war. I met him at his office at the Law School . . . [and] we had a cordial and for me useful conversation."

The passion of the anti-war community boiled over in August 1968 at the Democratic National Convention in Chicago. Protesters disrupted the proceedings, and violence took place as police tried to enforce an 11:00 p.m. curfew in the city. Eight men were identified as leaders of the riots and arrested: Abbie Hoffman, Tom Hayden, Jerry Rubin, David Dellinger, Rennie Davis, Lee Weiner, John Froines, and Bobby Seale. Seale received a separate trial, and the remaining seven were brought before the completely unsympathetic Judge Julius Hoffman. As the trial unfolded, the "Chicago Seven"—and their eccentric lawyer William Kunstler— tried to mock the proceedings. They blew kisses, ate candy, wore colorful clothes, and made provocative comments. Consequently, Judge Hoffman charged both Kunstler and his clients with contempt of the court.

When the contempt charges were slapped on Kunstler and the Chicago Seven, Dershowitz circulated a letter among the Harvard faculty declaring it "an outrage." Kunstler knew Dershowitz through the ACLU and asked him to join his legal team. Dershowitz eagerly agreed, helping Kunstler's New Jersey lawyers draft a brief related to the contempt charges. During this time, Dershowitz also participated in a forum at Harvard with

William Kunstler, in which he declared to the audience that "the first step in the process of tyranny is the harassment of lawyers." In the end, the contempt charges against all eight defendants were overturned on appeal.

On campus, Dershowitz went before Harvard's Disciplinary Board on multiple occasions to argue on behalf of student protesters who flashed the "finger" at supporters of the war, heckled speeches delivered by South Vietnamese supporters, and even disrupted moments of silence for fallen soldiers.

Amid the swelling Vietnam protests around the country, Dershowitz and his family sought a reprieve from the busyness of Cambridge life. He and his brother, who was working at a law firm after graduating NYU, rented a house on Fire Island in the summer of 1969, along with their wives and children. On the evening of July 19, Dershowitz and his family were watching the moon landing on their black-and-white television when the telephone rang. James Frug, a former law clerk of David Bazelon who had become Ted Kennedy's administrator, told Dershowitz to travel to Martha's Vineyard as soon as possible.

An island off the coast of Cape Cod, the Vineyard had been a hub of the whaling and fishing industries in the 1800s, and by the late twentieth century, it was an exclusive getaway and home to resort towns like Chilmark and Edgartown. When Dershowitz arrived on the Vineyard, he could not get anywhere near Ted Kennedy, as the senator was encased in throngs of lawyers and reporters. Dershowitz consulted with Kennedy's staff while the nation learned of the sordid incident that had thrust the Senator into this mess.

On the night of July 18, Kennedy and five other men had attended a reunion of Robert Kennedy's "Boiler Room girls" on the tiny island of Chappaquiddick, just off the east coast of the Vineyard. These "Boiler Room girls" had worked tirelessly as assistants to Robert Kennedy during his presidential campaign and received their unceremonious nickname due to working in a hot office space that had once been a boiler room. The reunion of the "Boiler Room girls" on Chappaquiddick found six men—five of them married, including Ted Kennedy—partying with six single women.

Around midnight, Ted Kennedy took one of the ladies, twenty-eight-year-old Mary Jo Kopechne, for a ride in his Oldsmobile Delmont. As they were crossing a narrow bridge with no guardrails, Kennedy drove off into the tidal creek below, and the car landed upside down on its roof and sank underwater. Kennedy managed to get out, but Mary Jo was trapped. She drowned, and it was not until ten hours had passed that the senator notified the authorities of what happened.

Kennedy, an early Democratic front-runner for president in 1972, found himself ensconced in legal troubles. Dershowitz aided his lawyers by writing a ten-page brief that petitioned the courts to handle Kennedy's case with due process. "The petitioners are not seeking in any way to obstruct the inquest into the death of Mary [Jo Kopechne], nor to impede the fullest inquiry into any information they might have relevant to that matter," Dershowitz's document stated. "The specific relief that the petitioners ask is that if the proceedings are to be open and the results made public, the district court be instructed to limit the scope of the inquiry to matters clearly relevant to the death of Mary Jo [Kopechne], that the petitioners be assured the assistance of counsel, the right to cross-examine witnesses, and the opportunity to produce and examine witnesses." Kennedy managed to avoid extremely serious legal consequences and never lost his Senate seat, but his name was tarnished throughout America.

Meanwhile, Dershowitz's relaxing getaway on Fire Island was interrupted once again when he and his brother took part in a public demonstration against a notorious local community called Point O'Woods. As *The Local Voice* newspaper put it, Point O'Woods was an "anachronistic fenced-in retreat for vacationing WASPs with nary a Jew or a black to disturb the storied ecology of familied gentiles." When Dershowitz tried to book a room at the POW Inn, he was refused accommodation. In response, he, his brother, and a group of fellow radical lawyers led a rally down the beaches in front of the community and stood outside the POW Inn holding signs that read: "Guess Who's Coming to Dinner" and "Bring Law & Order to Point O'Woods." Dershowitz was interviewed by *The Local Voice*: "This is a racist, discriminating club," he declared.

It was also during this trip to Fire Island that family members noticed a significant rift developing between Sue and Alan. They had "horrendous" shouting matches, as one relative recalls, which was particularly hard on Nathan because his wife, Marilyn, was Sue's younger sister. Alan and Sue's relationship had become characterized by tension and was only getting worse.

* * *

By the early 1970s, nearly 400,000 American troops were halfway around the world bogged down in the never-ending, increasingly intensifying conflict in Vietnam. Over 50,000 American soldiers had died since the start of the war. In 1970, Dershowitz and several other scholars supported a Massachusetts bill that gave citizens the right to petition the attorney general for a revocation of their draft order. It was eventually signed into law by the governor.

Around this time, Dershowitz argued in a publication of *The New York Times* that Richard Nixon's government was threatening civil liberties. "The evidences are all around us," he said, "witness the recent spate of conspiracy prosecutions in Boston, Chicago and Seattle; or the newly enacted legislation authorizing 'no knock' entry into homes, wiretapping of phones, and pretrial detention of suspects." A lawyer and friend of Nixon's named Lewis Powell Jr.—who was soon to be appointed to the Supreme Court by Nixon—wrote an article in the *F.B.I. Law Enforcement Bulletin* replying to Dershowitz and reprimanding him for his criticism of the government. It was noticed by someone with prominent connections in the FBI, who wrote the following letter to Powell:

> I just wanted to voice a word of gratitude for your article appearing in . . . the F.B.I Law Enforcement Bulletin, which I trust will continue to receive wide circulation.
>
> As a Harvard Law School alumnus, who has done more than his share for that institution, I think your reference to Professor Allan [*sic*] Dershowitz was altogether appropriate. His continued presence on the faculty has caused me to cease all support of the school, and I daresay I am not alone in my attitude.

The name on the letter is blacked out, but the author cc'd J. Edgar Hoover and was evidently an associate of the Bureau director.

In addition to FBI surveillance, Dershowitz also began receiving audits by the Nixon-controlled IRS. His reputation as a radical professor and attorney was growing. Earlier, in 1970, he had flashed the finger at the Nixon administration when he came to the defense of a scandalous new film titled *I Am Curious (Yellow)*, which told the story of a young woman of the Vietnam era who comes to maturity both politically and sexually. It was the first commercially distributed film in the United States to show sexual intercourse. "I found it boring, mediocre, and preachy," says Dershowitz. "I didn't care for it."

The depiction of intercourse shocked many Americans, and the film was ultimately banned throughout the country. Under Nixon, the government labeled obscenity one of the top five most important causes for prosecution. The government came after Grove Press, who owned the rights to *I Am Curious (Yellow)*. Aware of Dershowitz's reputation as a liberal member of the ACLU, the owner of Grove Press asked him to aid their legal representation. "At that time, there was a great debate going on about the First Amendment implications of erotic films," says Dershowitz. "The First Amendment applies mostly to fringe groups— like the Chicago Seven—and so it was inevitable I'd get involved with the fringe."

After agreeing to help Grove Press, Dershowitz was assigned to represent one of the theaters in Boston which was being prosecuted for showing *I Am Curious (Yellow)*. Instead of engaging in a back-and-forth with the prosecution over whether the film was truly obscene, Dershowitz devised a different strategy. While representing the case in a district court in Massachusetts, he argued that even if the film was pornographic, it was none of the government's business what full-grown adults chose to watch in a private setting like a theater, so long as adequate warning was given to theatergoers as to what they were about to view.

"The only valid basis for punishing obscenity," declared Dershowitz, "is to protect people from being offended, from having something thrust on them in an unwilling manner and also to protect youngsters." He cited a recent Supreme Court decision, *Stanley v. Georgia*, in which the justices ruled that the government could not prevent citizens from possessing pornographic films in their homes. The district court was persuaded and ruled in favor of Dershowitz's arguments. But the prosecution appealed, and the case made it to the Supreme Court. At thirty-one years old, Dershowitz traveled to Washington, DC, to appear before America's highest judicial body.

"I was somewhat nervous as I entered the hushed marble and mahogany courtroom," says Dershowitz. "I had prepared extensively for my fifteen-minute presentation—but I could not anticipate what awaited me."

Draped in a black robe, with white hair adorning his temples and his booming voice coming down from the dais where he sat at the center of the nine justices, Chief Justice Warren Burger was an imposing figure. Back during his days on the DC Court of Appeals, the conservative Burger had regularly butted heads with David Bazelon, and following Earl Warren's resignation in 1969, he had been appointed chief justice by Nixon. When Dershowitz reached the lectern to make his argument, Burger pounced on Bazelon's former clerk.

Burger asked Dershowitz if he thought the government had the power to prohibit a bear-baiting contest. Utterly confused as to what a bear-baiting contest was, Dershowitz took a shot in the dark and stated that torturing bears was unconstitutional because the government is required to prevent the suffering of animals. "I think the example would be better if it were a film of bear-baiting," Dershowitz suggested to Burger and then tried to begin his prepared argument.

But Burger persisted. While the other justices sat looking embarrassed, their colleague read off a list of prepared questions to Dershowitz about bear-baiting, without even discussing the issues of the *I Am Curious (Yellow)* case. After nearly fifteen minutes of seemingly nonsensical hypotheticals—to which Dershowitz was obliged to respond—Burger ended his filibuster. "It was the dumbest series of questions I have ever been asked during an oral argument," says Dershowitz, "and it was probably the stupidest conversation I've ever had with anyone about the First Amendment." Dershowitz found himself with just a few remaining moments to sum up his argument: "[A] theater with its curtains drawn deserves [at least as much constitutional protection as] a home with its shades drawn up," he told the justices.

Dershowitz was ultimately able to settle the case in favor of Grove Press and the Boston theater, but the high court refrained from issuing a decision based upon the broad-scope argument Dershowitz had made to the district court.

"During this time, I visited Alan in his office when I was lecturing at Harvard, and I was shocked to learn he was defending the filmmakers of *I Am Curious (Yellow)*—a porn film," says Phyllis Chesler, a prominent feminist author who had been acquainted with Dershowitz and his family while growing up in Borough Park. "Alan and I had a rational discussion about how everyone deserves a lawyer and how every issue is complicated. That's when I first understood Alan has a commitment to defending 'bad boys,' shall we say. I don't think he is a 'bad boy' himself because I know his character, but he defends them. I think this is how he may express his rebellion against the restrictive Orthodox Judaism of his youth."

In the classrooms at Harvard, Dershowitz remained as charismatic and fiery as he had been in the yeshivas of Borough Park during his childhood. In the early 1970s, it was reported in the *New York Post* that Dershowitz offended some female students during a discussion about crime. "He said that rape should not be punishable by death because it didn't endanger life," wrote the *Post*, which also noted that Dershowitz's female students had labeled him an "anti-feminist." Dershowitz responded, "A lot of girls got upset, but I would have thought that liberated women in particular would understand that places where rape is punishable by death are places where women are put on a pedestal."

Not all his female students found Dershowitz reprehensible. Nadine Strossen was a budding lawyer who would eventually become the first female president of the ACLU. During her time at Harvard, Dershowitz offered to meet, free of charge, with any students potentially interested in the criminal defense field. "It was a fairly small group of us," says Strossen. "And I will never, ever forget what he said. Right at the get-go, he said: 'You must accept the fact that all of your clients will be guilty.'"

Shocked and somewhat disturbed, Strossen ultimately decided not to pursue that career, instead signing up for a seminar Dershowitz offered about civil liberties and the Constitution. Seated around a table, Dershowitz participated in riveting dialogues with the students. "In addition to being a very engaging teacher," recounts Strossen, "Alan also did something that was unheard of—and that was to have all his students over to his home for a meal and for socializing."

"Alan had no airs about him," says Strossen's husband Eli Noam, an Israeli who was also enrolled in Dershowitz's classes and also taught his sons some Hebrew at Dershowitz's request. "Outside of class and in his home, he would just be a kind of friendly interlocutor—a conversationalist, probing and always curious."

Years later, in the early 1980s, Dershowitz also befriended a new addition to the Harvard faculty named Susan Estrich, an enterprising feminist who had been raped as a young woman. When she was hired by Harvard Law School, Estrich decided to teach a new course about legal issues surrounding rape. At the time, the subject had been virtually untouched at HLS, where most of the students were men. When she announced to her largely male class that she was a rape victim and that rape would no longer be a hush-hush subject, some people were furious.

Dershowitz stood by Estrich's side. "Alan was a famous figure around the law school who was supportive of our efforts to push for more women on the faculty of the law school," says Estrich. "Rape wasn't taught when I started teaching criminal law because people didn't think it was interesting enough. Of all the criminal law professors, Alan was the one who most readily agreed with me that rape was a subject worth including in the criminal law curriculum. I think he welcomed my interests and wanted to take on a challenging topic. And he knew damn well that the students were going to have a different reaction to him than they did to me."

* * *

Even with his busy schedule, Dershowitz prioritized spending time with his sons. He came home late in the afternoon to play with them and made a point of attending all their soccer games. When he was not at school or doing homework, Elon's private hobby was magic. Although he had frequent headaches and seizures which could make life miserable, he loved performing individual tricks and putting on magic shows. At times he would go into his father's office at home and interrupt his work, and Alan never shooed him off.

Sometimes Alan sat by Elon's bed and asked him legal hypotheticals before he went to sleep. "Okay, now, someone is walking across the street," he would say. "They're drunk and have had one heart attack. They're staggering across the street, somebody hits them, and they have a second heart attack and die. Who is responsible?"

In the summer of 1971, Alan and his family drove across the country to sunny Palo Alto, California, where he was to spend a year's sabbatical at Stanford University, working on an academic book titled *Predictive Justice: Toward a Jurisprudence of Crime Prevention*. He was relieved to have a year away from the rigmarole of Harvard. An up-and-coming lawyer named Joel Klein came along as his research assistant for the year. "Alan worked in an incredibly intense, focused way," says Klein. "He pushed, he challenged. He's got the kind of mind that, when other people's minds may get lost, his starts to shine. It's a deeply penetrating, analytic mind."

When the Jewish New Year Rosh Hashanah rolled around in the fall, Dershowitz received an unexpected invitation. Michael Cernea, an economics professor visiting Stanford from Romania, asked Dershowitz to go on a walk with him in the woods around the university. As soon as they were out of view from any bystanders, Michael revealed his true identity to Dershowitz. His birth name was Moishe Catz, and he was Jewish. He desperately wanted to get himself, his wife, and children out of communist Romania and emigrate to America or Israel.

"It was obvious from my physical appearance that I was Jewish, and Moishe had also evidently known I'd been involved in Jewish causes by that point," says Dershowitz. "He swore me to secrecy and asked if I would become his pro bono lawyer in what would surely be a long-term activity, since his family was being held hostage in Romania." Dershowitz instantly agreed, and the two went back to Dershowitz's house where they discussed his situation further and listened to some traditional Jewish melodies, which Moishe had not heard since before the coming of the Nazis and Communists. While the music played, both men teared up.

At the same time Dershowitz agreed to help Moishe reunite his family, his own family unity was hanging by a thread. The tense relationship between him and Sue had reached its breaking point. For years, Alan had been taking on an increasing workload and trying to advance his career, while Sue simply wanted their life to stay the way it had been during the early days at Harvard when the two regularly attended social events together. A family member recalled one situation during this time when

Sue became angry that Alan was too busy to change a lightbulb. After one heated argument in Palo Alto, Sue got in the family car and took off—where she was heading was anyone's guess. She eventually returned, but their relationship was on the brink of divorce, which would be the first in Dershowitz family history.

"Claire always said Sue couldn't handle Alan being out in the world and his increasing publicity," says Alan's aunt Shirley Ringel. "She became overwhelmed when they had children, and Alan wasn't available much," says another close relative. "He put undue pressure on her when she had no support. For example, he insisted she make dinner parties without any real help."

"We always had help around the house from students," says Dershowitz, disagreeing with that characterization. "I don't think Sue ever hosted a dinner party in which she didn't have the assistance of one or two students.

"I think Sue and I were incompatible," Dershowitz continues. "We had as close to an arranged marriage as possible. On paper, it was a match made in heaven, but Sue had a difficult time adjusting to my lifestyle. I was energetic, ambitious, and constantly on-the-go. She was content to basically stay home and do her job. She didn't share the excitement of life with me. We really couldn't exchange ideas. We were both cognizant that it was an incompatible relationship. It had nothing to do with other people—I didn't have anyone else I was in love with. It just became a very difficult relationship, and I did not look forward to coming home each day."

Any plans for divorce were put on hold when they learned in December that ten-year-old Elon had an enormous, malignant brain tumor and was at death's door. He had been experiencing headaches and seizures, but his parents did not think it could be a tumor until a doctor friend warned them of the possibility. Once this horrible reality was confirmed, Alan dropped all his work and devoted his energies to saving his son. Hour after hour, he scoured books and articles in the medical library of Stanford to determine the best possible hospitals and treatment strategy. "It was an extraordinary tour de force effort," says Joel Klein. "When Alan becomes single minded, he brings an intensity to bear that you rarely see from people."

"Doctors told me Elon was going to die a painful death," says Dershowitz. "It was the most devastating moment of my life, and I had to fight for Elon as hard as I could."

At the recommendation of his friend Norman Sohn, who had become a surgeon, Alan flew with Elon back to Massachusetts, where Elon underwent surgery by the renowned Dr. John Shilito at Boston's Children's Hospital. Alan could not afford this first-rate medical treatment, and so David Bazelon, Elon's godfather, covered the expense.

"My father knew many local Boston sports figures, and as a surprise before I went in for my operation, he arranged for me to go to the Bruins locker room and meet Bobby Orr and get a signed stick," says Elon, who kept the stick near his bed in the hospital room as a comfort during that difficult time.

Claire Dershowitz came up from New York to wait with her son during Elon's seven-hour operation. The Beatles' song "Yesterday" had recently been released, and as Alan sat in the waiting room during Elon's surgery, the song played over and over in his head, as he thought about how happy he had been "yesterday" before Elon had become sick.

When the surgery ended, the doctor emerged and reported that Elon's tumor had been successfully removed. Alan's son was alive for now, but the road ahead would be marked with uncertainty as the family wondered if Elon's cancer would return and as Elon began a difficult regimen of radiation therapy. Unfortunately, as much as she loved Elon, Sue could not bring herself to take him to radiation therapy because every time she did, another one of the children who had been undergoing therapy alongside Elon had succumbed to their cancer.

As for Alan, Elon's brush with death completely changed the direction of his academic life. "I couldn't look at a blank paper," he says. "Every time I looked at a blank paper, I just teared up and couldn't continue to work." Long-term projects—scholarly articles and hefty academic books—became nearly impossible to complete. "I decided [that] instead of just allowing myself to drift on this way, which would be endless, I [would take] on short-term projects with deadlines that I had to meet," he comments.

After struggling through a tumultuous "sabbatical" year at Stanford, Alan and his family started driving back east, leaving the blue waters of Palo Alto behind.

NEXT YEAR IN JERUSALEM!

It had been a turbulent year at Stanford, and during the long drive back to Massachusetts, Dershowitz and his family stopped for a respite in Wyoming's breathtaking Grand Teton National Park. While out camping, Dershowitz was located by a park ranger who told him someone was trying to reach him with an urgent message. When Dershowitz got to a phone and dialed the caller, it turned out to be Marty Elefant, a lawyer who had grown up in Borough Park a few doors down the road from Dershowitz on 48th Street.

Marty told Dershowitz that three young Jewish men had just been arrested for complicity in a deadly bombing in New York City. They were facing the possibility of the electric chair, which would be the first time such an execution had been administered since the Rosenberg case in the 1950s. Like most people in Borough Park, where Dershowitz had become a mini-celebrity, Marty was aware of Dershowitz's budding reputation as a lawyer and asked Dershowitz if he would represent one of the three young men named Sheldon Seigel.

Like Dershowitz, Seigel spent his childhood in Borough Park. He was acquainted with the Dershowitz family and even went to summer camp with Dershowitz's brother. But unlike the Dershowitz brothers, Seigel's homelife had been anything but warm and loving. His mother died when he was a teenager, and his father remarried soon after. Seigel's stepmother was cruel. She constantly insulted the young man and berated him for not earning his own living. Tall and gawky, Seigel was not good at sports and had few friends. He found an escape from the sorrows of life through studying science and creating inventions.

After leaving home and drifting around several colleges, Seigel threw his lot in with the Jewish Defense League, or JDL. Founded by a fiery and controversial Orthodox rabbi named Meir Kahane, the JDL began as a benign group that protected elderly Jews in New York City from ethnic attacks. Following the Six-Day War and increasing Jewish persecution in the Soviet Union, the JDL devolved into an organization that orchestrated violent acts against Soviets and Soviet supporters.

In April 1971, the JDL planted a bomb—created by Seigel—in the Armtorg, the Soviet trade mission to the United States. They got away with the crime, but the government began to keep a close watch on the JDL. Nixon told George H. W. Bush, the ambassador to the UN, that the organization had to be stopped at any cost, in order to preserve the administration's détente relations with the Soviets.

When the JDL carried out another bombing in 1972, the government reacted swiftly. This time a smoke bomb—again designed by Seigel—had been placed in the offices of Sol Hurok, a wealthy impresario who supported cultural exchanges with the Soviet Union. The JDL's smoke bomb was meant to frighten, not kill, but when it exploded in Hurok's office, bluish-pink flames filled the room and a young staff member named Iris Kones became trapped in the smoke and increasing heat. Coughing and choking, Kones died of asphyxiation. What was supposed to be a mere scare tactic resulted in the death of a twenty-seven-year-old Jewish girl.

Somehow, the government had been able to trace the crime to Seigel and two compatriots and was threatening them with the death penalty. Even the rabbis of Borough Park publicly condemned the young men.

These were the facts that confronted Dershowitz after he arrived home from Wyoming and learned more about the disturbing case. "How could I presume to take on a murder case of this complexity as my first real trial?" Dershowitz wondered aloud in later years. "But then, how could I turn down a case involving someone I had known as a kid? Why should I represent a bunch of JDL hoodlums . . . ? But aren't Jewish hoodlums entitled to representation?" Against the opposition of his relatives in Borough Park—including his mother—Dershowitz decided to accept the case.

"[Despite] my need for money, I quickly agreed to put together a team to try to save Shelley's life," said Dershowitz, who took the case pro bono.

The case was to be tried in the federal courthouse in New York City, which would require Dershowitz to commute between Cambridge and New York weekly.

Since he had no experience as a trial lawyer, Dershowitz turned to his former student Harvey Silverglate for help. Since attending Dershowitz's first course in 1964, Silverglate had established himself as a premier defense attorney in Boston, gaining notoriety in the late 1960s after successfully defending anti-war protesters at Harvard who stormed one of the campus buildings called University Hall. Silverglate and his beloved wife, Elsa, socialized with Alan and Sue, and Elsa—who was a talented Polaroid photographer—gave photography classes to Elon and his classmates. Silverglate and Dershowitz became fast friends, partly due to their shared heritage as Jewish kids from Brooklyn.

"[Harvey] gently [reminded] me that I barely knew how to find the federal courthouse and had no experience in preparing the necessary pretrial motions and complying with other such technical requirements," says Dershowitz. "He offered a role reversal: he would become my teacher for this case." Silverglate also enlisted the help of his research assistant, a young Jewish woman with long black hair and a brilliant legal mind named Jeanne Baker. Together, the three lawyers set about trying to get Seigel off the hook.

The judge assigned to their case, Arnold Bauman, was determined to make their efforts unsuccessful. A former prosecutor, Bauman had been appointed to the district court by Richard Nixon and seemed to be in the government's camp when it came to the JDL case. As Silverglate bluntly put it, Bauman was also "a nasty piece of work."

At this point, the death penalty was no longer hanging over Seigel's head. Due to a 1972 Supreme Court ruling in *Furman v. Georgia*, most death penalty statutes had been declared unconstitutional. Even still, Seigel faced the possibility of over twenty years in prison.

Dershowitz's initial goal was to prove that incendiary devices like the bomb that went off in Hurok's office were not technically "explosives" as defined by the statute books. His strategy radically changed, though, when he developed a hunch that the government was being fed dirt on the JDL by an informant—and that the informant was a member of the JDL. "It made sense that the government would try to plant a 'mole' within the organization; that is standard practice in dealing with a subversive organization," says Dershowitz. "Despite its acknowledgment that it had neither eyewitnesses nor fingerprints, [the government] seemed suspiciously overconfident."

Dershowitz discussed the possibility of an informant with his brother Nathan, who was working full-time as a criminal defense attorney at a New York law firm. "How do you know it isn't your client?" Nathan asked unhesitatingly. Dershowitz rejected the notion out of hand, but his brother, who had been a counselor of Seigel's at summer camp, pressed his point. "That kid's a bag full of trouble," Nathan warned. "He's sneaky, he's a loner, and he develops loyalty to the last person who's nice to him."

As the weeks went by and he continued to put in long hours of work at no charge, Dershowitz decided to act on his brother's suspicion. In the fall of 1972, Dershowitz made a call to Seigel. "I've come to the conclusion that you are the informant," Dershowitz told him. He heard crying from the other end of the line. "Thank God you know," sobbed Seigel. "I've wanted to tell you a hundred times, but I was sure you'd hate me and abandon me. Please help me get out of this mess."

Dershowitz was livid. Weeks of strategizing and preparation had been wasted. Worse than that, he had been double-crossed by his own client! After hanging up with Seigel, Dershowitz dialed Silverglate, who was also furious. "We have to get out of the case," Silverglate said to Dershowitz. "Let the government get him a lawyer. He's their boy." Dershowitz explained to Silverglate that Seigel was claiming to have been illegally forced into this position and that he did not want to be an informant for the government. "Every fink has his excuse," Silverglate retorted, "but it's not my job to make the government's case easy."

Despite Silverglate's frustration, Dershowitz persuaded him to give their client a chance to present his side of the story. They met up with Seigel in Brooklyn at a small kosher restaurant and demanded the whole truth.

According to Seigel, soon after the Armtorg incident in 1971—when the JDL placed a bomb in the Soviet trade mission—the government had somehow discovered that Shelley was the bomb-maker for the JDL. The government sensed an opportunity to wreak havoc on the JDL's operations by using Seigel as an informant. A police officer named Santo Parola, who had grown up in Borough Park and was an expert in demolitions, tracked Seigel down and told him that the government knew of his complicity in the Armtorg bombing. He threatened the young man with decades in prison unless he agreed to provide information to the government on the inside operations of the JDL. Agonized by the thought of betraying his friends, Seigel reluctantly agreed, but without Parola's knowledge, he began to secretly tape their conversations on a cassette recorder.

When the bomb went off in Sol Hurok's offices in mid-1972, the government was caught by surprise. They had not been forewarned by Seigel, who unbeknownst to them had planned the Hurok operation with his friends and created the bomb that ultimately killed Iris Kones. The government suspected the JDL's involvement, and Parola was tasked with squeezing information out of Seigel. It was only after Parola promised Seigel he would not be called as a witness in court against his friends that Seigel confessed to the crime. Despite Parola's promise, once the trial proceedings had begun, the government double-crossed Seigel. They denied ever promising something in return for information on the JDL and were preparing to publicly call Seigel as a witness against his friends.

After Seigel explained this sordid situation to Dershowitz and Silverglate, the two friends had a decision to make. "[Harvey] and I agreed that [Shelley] had been taken advantage of, and that he desperately needed legal assistance," says Dershowitz. "With some hesitation about representing a double agent who had deceived us for so long, we agreed to remain in the case."

Shortly thereafter, Seigel's prospects were improved when it was disclosed that the FBI had planted wiretaps in the offices of the JDL and on Seigel's home phone. That was how they had originally gotten to him. These wiretaps had been placed without a warrant, which was in direct violation of a 1967 Supreme Court decision *Katz v. United States*.

Dershowitz, Silverglate, and Jeanne Baker wanted to use this incriminating fact to Seigel's advantage. "The first problem we encountered was that there was no established mechanism by which a witness—as distinguished from a defendant—could raise such charges and put the government on trial," Dershowitz said. "A defendant could move to exclude the incriminating evidence that the government was seeking to introduce against him at his trial. But Seigel himself would not be on trial in the [Hurok bombing] case; there would be no evidence introduced against him; he would be called simply as a witness against others, and asked some questions. Seigel would actually have been in a better position had he been a defendant on trial for murder in the [Hurok bombing] case than he was as a witness with immunity from prosecution."

As the trio considered their options, they hit upon an unorthodox approach. "Instead of simply waiting for the government to call Seigel as a witness—which is what the government expected us to do—we went on the offensive and brought a lawsuit against the government," explains Dershowitz. "We decided to try something that had never been tried before: we would ask the court to put Seigel on trial for murder."

Although this move was fraught with risks, Dershowitz said they were "confident that the evidence of Seigel's complicity in the [Hurok bombing] had been secured by illegal means and that without it he could not be convicted of murder." The trial for the Hurok bombing was set to begin in February 1973, and the trio prepared to bring their proposal before the judge.

The case proceedings took Dershowitz away from home for half of each week. He spent Mondays through Wednesdays teaching at Harvard and the rest of the time in New York. It was a rigorous schedule, and Dershowitz often found himself driving back and forth to Massachusetts bleary-eyed in the middle of the night. Despite his hectic schedule, Dershowitz continued creating a new course at Harvard each year, including "Legal Ethics," "Law, Mathematics, and the Talmud," and "Advanced Constitutional Litigation."

* * *

When it became public knowledge that Dershowitz had decided to represent Shelley Seigel, certain members of the Harvard faculty treated Dershowitz with disdain. In those days, it was frowned upon for a Harvard law professor to take on clients, instead of focusing one's attention on teaching legal theory. "One of my colleagues approached me, upon hearing that I had taken on a case, and said, 'At Harvard Law School, we don't have *clients*,'" says Dershowitz. "His voice dripped with contempt as he uttered the word 'clients.'"

Dershowitz was pressured by the upper echelons of the university to drop Seigel's case. The brother-in-law of the young woman killed by Seigel's bomb was immensely wealthy and a Harvard donor. Harvard president Derek Bok called Dershowitz into his office to inform him that the uncle was threatening to stop all his donations to the school unless Dershowitz was fired. He had also promised to sponsor a brand-new, beautiful building for the campus. Thankfully for Dershowitz, the university refused to fire one of its tenured professors.

Dershowitz was not dissuaded by the pushback from his school. "I wanted to make legal history, rather than just write about others who did," he says. "I needed to know what it felt like to have flesh and blood clients whose lives would be affected by the law, rather than merely reading about abstract cases with faceless names."

In February, Dershowitz, Silverglate, and Baker headed to the federal courthouse in New York for the start of the Hurok bombing proceedings. As planned, they asked the government to put their client on trial for murder. Somewhat perplexed, Judge Bauman allowed their request to move forward, and the trio got down to work determining the best strategy for holding the government's feet to the fire. A member of the JDL allowed them to use his town house on 38th Street in Manhattan as a makeshift office, where they set up a typing area, library, interview room, and cassette-tape center. "It was a dilapidated old mansion and quite spooky—we had to use lamps to light the rooms," comments Silverglate.

Seigel had given them the recordings of his conversations with the cop Parola, and Baker began listening to each tape. One night, Dershowitz and Silverglate were woken at 4:00 a.m. by Baker shouting excitedly upstairs. Hurrying to her room up the stairs, they found Baker on her bed holding one of the tapes. "I found it," she said. When they questioned her, she explained, "I found proof that the government first learned about Seigel from the wiretaps." She played the tape, and the trio carefully listened to the critical portion:

PAROLA: If we wanted to prosecute the first case, don't you think we got a good chance of knockin' you over if we really push?
SEIGEL: Not much.
PAROLA: Supposing I decide to testify. You know . . . how we came to get all this information. You know it's [*done?*] on wiretaps.
SEIGEL: What's that have to do with the first case?
PAROLA: 'Cause that's how we stumbled onto you. [Who] do ya think fingered ya? We did.

Silverglate and Baker were thrilled. Here was Parola admitting that the government's surveillance had been illegally "*done* on wiretaps." Dershowitz was not so sure. The pivotal word was garbled, and it sounded to him like Parola had said: "You know it's *not* on wiretaps." "What, are you deaf?" scoffed Silverglate and Baker simultaneously. "It says, 'You know it's *done* on wiretaps.'"

With this incriminating tape in their possession, the team decided on a twofold strategy. In addition to exposing the government's illegal use of wiretaps, they wanted Parola to confess he had promised Seigel protection from being called as a witness against his friends. "But that crucial promise was not on tape," laments Dershowitz. "We had to get Parola to admit on the witness stand that he had made it." After careful consideration, Dershowitz and Silverglate decided upon a little trick.

On the day Parola was to be called as a witness, Silverglate went to a record store in New York and bought several blank cassettes. Upon entering the courtroom, he placed them on the defense counsel's table for Parola to see once he took the stand.

It had been decided that Dershowitz would cross-examine Parola. A bit self-assured, Parola took the witness chair as Dershowitz stood up at the lectern with transcripts of Seigel's tape recordings. After asking the court for permission to quote obscenities, Dershowitz asked Parola if he had ever exchanged the following words with Seigel: "You're not going to jail on either one of them, and if you ever say that I said it, I'm gonna deny it and I'm gonna meet you some fuckin' night, and I'm gonna run you over with a truck." Unsure of what was going on, Parola denied saying this.

"You are certain that you never said anything about running him over with a truck?" pressed Dershowitz. "I never said anything like that," Parola lied. As Dershowitz continued rattling off lines from the tape transcripts, Parola's tough exterior broke down, and he noticed Silverglate's cassette tapes on the defense table. He became pale and sweaty and asked for a glass of water.

A recess was called, and Dershowitz's mother, who was visiting the courtroom to watch her son in action, marched up to the defense table. "Where did you learn that word [fuck]? And who gave you permission to use it?" she sternly demanded. Dershowitz tried to explain he was simply quoting Parola, to which Claire Dershowitz countered: "Does his mother know that he uses words like that?"

When Dershowitz and Parola resumed their positions, Dershowitz implemented the next phase of their strategy. Using a fabricated transcript that he and his team had written, Dershowitz began to read as though it was simply a continuation of earlier transcripts:

> **PAROLA:** I promise you, Shelley, just give us the names and leave the rest to us. If we can't prove it without ya, then we can't prove it.
> **SEIGEL:** What if someone finds out?
> **PAROLA:** No one's going to find out. You won't even have to go to the grand jury in this one. . . . We ain't going to use you. We just ain't. We won't have to. We can make the case without you.

Judge Bauman was intrigued by the exchange. "Did you say that to him?" he asked Parola. "That sounds familiar to me, Your Honor," replied Parola, "I don't recall exactly if those words are the words." Fuming, the judge barked, "I take it when you say 'that sounds familiar,' that that means that you recollect that in substance, if not in those words?" Parola acknowledged the judge's point, thereby admitting his promise to Seigel.

Soon after this momentous day in court, the *New York Post* ran an article titled "Tapes Jeopardizing Hurok Bomb Case?" which described Dershowitz and his team's brilliant tactics. The victory was short-lived, however. The prosecutors requested the tapes of Parola and Seigel's conversations, and Dershowitz's team was obliged to hand them over. After listening to them, the prosecution called Dershowitz and congratulated him on his brilliant ruse, while also berating him—ironically—for his deceitfulness.

After two months of deliberation, Bauman released his thirty-eight-page opinion. Despite the trio's best efforts, the judge ruled that Seigel would be required to testify in the Hurok bombing case, partly on the ground that Parola had no authority to promise Seigel otherwise. When Seigel was called before the court, he refused to testify and was held in contempt. Dershowitz, Silverglate, and Baker turned to their last, desperate option. They appealed the contempt ruling for review and sent the Parola-Seigel tapes to the appeals court. The Hurok trial was postponed while all the participants awaited the decision.

"It is a fundamental rule of appellate review that findings of facts made by a district judge cannot be overturned by a court of appeals except in extraordinary situations," says Dershowitz. The likelihood of the appeals court reviewing any of the contested facts of the case was slim, and Seigel's fate hung by a thread.

Two weeks passed before Dershowitz received word of the ruling. A clerk at the appeals court called him at Harvard and said that the judges had decided to overturn Seigel's contempt conviction. Exhilarated, Dershowitz obtained a copy of their written opinion. "We have concluded, without the slightest doubt, ambiguity or uncertainty," it read, "that Parola related to Seigel: 'You know it's *done* on wiretaps.' . . .

"If the New York City Police Department did learn of Seigel's involvement from a wiretap lead, the contents of those wiretaps, in the hands of Seigel's counsel at the taint hearing, may have dealt a shattering blow to the Government's proof of independent source. For if wiretaps were indeed involved, Parola's in-court testimony on independent source, undermined on this critical point, would clearly have counted for little thereafter. . . .

"Of course, we all suffer when, in Cardozo's classic phrase, the criminal goes free because the constable has blundered, there are those who argue that on occasion illegal methods must be employed to preserve the rule of law. Justice Brandeis responded eloquently to that argument: 'Our government is the potent, the omnipresent teacher. For good or for ill, it teaches the whole people by its example. Crime is contagious. If the government becomes a lawbreaker, it breeds contempt for law; it invites every man to become a law unto himself.'. . . Accordingly, the order of civil contempt against Seigel is reversed and vacated."

"It was an incredible success," notes Silverglate, "because it was so unusual to have a court of appeals reverse the fact finding of a federal district judge." Without Seigel's testimony, the government's case in the Hurok bombing trial fell apart. When the Hurok proceedings were reconvened, Bauman was forced to dismiss the case against Seigel and the JDL. As Seigel and his friends left the courtroom celebrating, the judge angrily called after them, "Do you know who isn't in court today? Iris Kones."

"His words went through me like a knife," Dershowitz says. "Never had I been so uncomfortable as I was then, with the case over and my client entirely victorious. He was right. . . . I sat in court for a full hour after everyone else had left. I wanted no part of the victory celebration. I could not forget Iris Kones."

A young Jewish girl going about her day in the office had been suddenly engulfed in hot smoke and breathed her last while choking on the deadly air around her. The young Jewish man who had created the bomb which caused her painful death was now free to live his life however he wanted. This was the outcome of the first major case Dershowitz spearheaded as a lawyer.

To some, Seigel's defense team had made a mockery of justice, but that is not how Dershowitz saw it. "Every decision like that rendered in Seigel's case must be seen as a victory for the United States Constitution," he says. He and Silverglate believed that because the government had been held accountable for its illegal wiretaps and the defense had been allowed to present damning evidence in court, both the Fourth and Fifth Amendments had been upheld.

In 1972, Dershowitz had given an interview in which he acknowledged: "I would represent anybody, literally anybody, once, for a crime for which he couldn't get representation. I would not, however, represent the American Nazi Party on a continuing basis, I would not represent the American Communist Party on a continuing basis. . . . I think when you represent somebody on a continuing basis, you do commit yourself, kind of, to some degree of association with that person's position."

"You wouldn't ask this question of a cardiac surgeon, would you: 'How could you do open heart surgery on such an awful human being?'" says Silverglate. "A defendant in a criminal case has a constitutional right to a lawyer. So my obligation is even stronger than that of the doctor who takes the Hippocratic oath. . . . It's written in the Constitution: the right to effective assistance of counsel. You're not only entitled to a lawyer, but an effective lawyer."

* * *

Seigel's case gained Dershowitz some attention in the newspapers, and his phone began to ring with calls from people desperate for representation.

Dershowitz's brilliant strategic mind, combined with Silverglate's courtroom experience and Baker's tireless work ethic, had been a major factor in their victory over the government. "Alan was energetic," remarks Silverglate. "He was very bold and unafraid."

"Alan's career as a lawyer took off after Shelley's case," says Dershowitz's cousin Norman Ringel. "That was when he realized he was smarter than the judges."

Dershowitz's hectic work schedule on behalf of Seigel was too much of a strain on his marriage. During the case, he and Sue finally separated and began making plans for a divorce. Alan moved into a small apartment on Concord Avenue, where he spent the first night sleeping on the floor with just a pillow, since no furniture had yet been purchased. Shortly after separating from Sue, Alan started a romantic relationship with Jeanne Baker, who was attractive, smart, and energetic. Sue became extremely jealous and grew to despise her husband's girlfriend.

As his marriage disintegrated, Dershowitz's relationship with a renowned academic ally from the Vietnam days fell apart. In the spring of 1973, Noam Chomsky publicly supported an enemy of Dershowitz named Israel Shahak, a Jewish academic from Israel who chaired the Israeli League of Human and Civil Rights.

Dershowitz had written an academic article in 1970 concerning Israel's preventive detention of suspected terrorists. While criticizing certain elements of the country's approach, Dershowitz argued that Israel generally upheld civil liberties. Shahak attacked Dershowitz and his article in the Jewish magazine *Commentary*, concluding with this parting shot: "Although I could cite many more examples of Mr. Dershowitz's hypocrisy, lack of knowledge, and even outright distortions, I shall end my rebuttal here. Mr. Dershowitz is not really important in himself, but unfortunately his attitude is typical of several American Jews I have encountered in Israel; their liberalism is, and always was, a fake."

So, when Shahak gave an interview to *The Boston Globe* in early 1973 claiming Israel was a racist country because it designated citizens as either Jewish or non-Jewish, Dershowitz pounced. "Let no one believe that Shahak is a civil libertarian. He is the furthest thing from it," he replied in *The Globe*. "A civil libertarian defends the rights of those with whom he disagrees as vehemently as those with whom he agrees. . . . Shahak has never defended the rights with whom he disagrees politically; nor has he ever attacked the practices of those with whom he agrees politically."

Chomsky, a friend of Shahak, saw Dershowitz's article and wrote a deft rebuke in *The Globe*. "'Shahak has never defended the rights of those with whom he disagrees politically.' The facts are quite different," he declared. "He has courageously defended the rights of the oppressed and under-privileged: Arabs, Oriental Jews, political dissidents, and others who differ from him markedly not only in political belief but also social status. He is a man of honor and principle who needs no lessons from Alan Dershowitz or anyone else on what it means to be a civil libertarian."

Dershowitz was undeterred. "Though Chomsky and I have been allies in numerous cases, I have seen over the years that Chomsky will stop at nothing in attacking those who support Israel or in defending those who attack it," he shot back in *The Globe*.

A final letter from Chomsky ended the exchange. "Dr. Shahak and the Israel League, acting with courage and honor, have produced substantial evidence on violations of human and civil rights by the Israeli government, avoiding no relevant instances to my knowledge," he wrote. "Apparently unable to refute the facts, Dershowitz has chosen to defame the man, in a manner which is as familiar as is deplorable."

Whatever cordial relationship Dershowitz and Chomsky previously had was over. At the same time he cut ties with Chomsky, Dershowitz formed a bond with a young man who was destined to shape Israel's destiny. In 1973, Benjamin Netanyahu was a twenty-three-year-old student at MIT, just down the road from Harvard. A celebration of Israel's twenty-fifth anniversary was held at MIT that spring, and both Dershowitz and Netanyahu attended.

Netanyahu was born in Israel but spent part of his youth in the United States. He joined the Israeli Defense Forces in 1967 and became a member of the Sayeret Matkal, an elite special operations unit. In 1972, Palestinian terrorists slaughtered Israeli athletes at the Munich Olympics and also hijacked a civilian airplane bound for Tel Aviv. After it landed, Netanyahu and his highly trained comrades broke into the plane, and Netanyahu helped remove one of the terrorists with his bare hands. Soon after this rescue mission, he left the military for a time and headed to the United States to begin working toward a doctorate in political science at MIT.

Netanyahu and Dershowitz struck up a friendship during Israel's twenty-fifth anniversary celebration. "Bibi was very charming and very handsome," says Dershowitz. "At the time, I didn't have any idea he was conservative. I just knew him as a supporter of Israel."

A few months after meeting Dershowitz, Netanyahu was called home to take up arms in defense of Israel. Once again, the country was in peril. Some of the Arab nations had grown increasingly agitated by Israel's occupation of the Sinai Peninsula, Golan Heights, West Bank, and Gaza Strip and initiated a full-scale attack against Israel. On Yom Kippur in 1973, while all operations inside Israel were shut down for the holiest day of the year, Egypt and Syria launched swift invasions into the Sinai Peninsula and Golan Heights, catching Golda Meir's government totally off-guard. As the Arabs advanced toward the heart of Israel with military aid from the Soviet Union, America hurriedly sent supplies to help protect Israel.

On that fateful Yom Kippur, Dershowitz was preparing to attend a religious service at Harvard's Hillel, a nationwide campus organization that sponsored Jewish activities. When he heard the news, he joined his fellow congregants at the Hillel building and uttered a prayer for the Israeli soldiers.

In the coming weeks, Israel pushed back the Egyptians and Syrians and ultimately drove them out of the occupied territories, resulting in heavy casualties. The Yom Kippur War came to a quick end on October

26, and all three countries signed cease-fires. The war had shattered the belief of some Jews that the nation was invincible. Due to the destruction of Israeli defense fortifications along the Suez Canal, it also became clear that Israel's occupation of the Sinai Peninsula was not a viable long-term option.

The war prompted an in-person debate between Dershowitz and Chomsky. Sponsored by the American Friends Service Committee, the two professors met at Old South Church in Boston in front of several hundred audience members, who were a mix of Israel supporters and anti-Israel advocates.

Although both men were Jewish and highly intelligent, they had anti-thetical views of the world and of Israel in particular. As scholar James McGilvray points out, Chomsky regarded "the domestic political scene of the United States and other major capitalist countries as theatres in which major corporations and their elite managers strive to protect and enhance their economic privileges and political power."

Dershowitz did not share Chomsky's worldview. He saw America and Israel as flawed countries, but believed that the ideologies of both nations generally leaned toward peace, freedom, and civil liberties.

As far as the Israel-Palestine conflict was concerned, both Dershowitz and Chomsky had expressed sympathy for the plight of the Palestinian refugees. Chomsky blamed their suffering on Israel, partly because Israel expanded its borders in the Six-Day War and thereby caused the flight of the refugees. Taking the opposite view, Dershowitz laid responsibility at the feet of the Arab nations for failing to create a Palestinian state in 1948 and neglecting to provide care and housing for the refugees of the Six-Day War.

These opposing views were on full display in their debate at Old South Church in Boston. Speaking in a polished style, Chomsky argued that the idea of a "Jewish state" was inherently discriminatory toward non-Jewish citizens, and he proposed the creation of a binational state in which Jews and Arabs could live side-by-side with equal rights before the law. Dershowitz dismissed this proposal as unrealistic and said it was reasonable for a Jewish nation to exist, especially after the Holocaust and centuries of suffering experienced by Jews around the globe.

"I want to see self-determination," said Dershowitz. "Israel should of course recognize the Palestinians and should recognize the legitimacy of their claims for what they are: legitimate, not all that pressing; substantial, not overwhelming; justifying compensation, justifying some attempt to reintegrate as many as possible safely within the community. But they do not justify terrorism"—referring to the massacre of Israeli athletes in Munich and the recent assassination of Cleo Noel, US ambassador to Sudan.

Responding to the Palestinians' claims of being expelled from their homeland, Dershowitz stated that "armed violence is not an appropriate response to expulsion. I am not, as some of you are, a pacifist. I believe that killing to save life is sometimes appropriate. I also believe that on rare occasions, armed violence to secure liberty is appropriate. But I can never," and at this point he raised his voice slightly, "under any circumstances justify *killing* to secure property, even when that property is one's birthplace, one homeland."

Chomsky responded calmly. "So, what is happening here is a balance against an alleged moral wrong of some value, versus the amount of violence that's undertaken in response to it," he commented. "Now what I'm saying is that if we look at the situation, not the way he did, but as the facts indicate, we will see that the overwhelming mass of violence throughout this period [1947–present] was conducted by the Israeli state, precisely because it had the most power." During a question-and-answer period, Chomsky was pressed by a pro-Israel audience member about this point, and he conceded that the Arabs were the ones who had first initiated violence between themselves and the Jews in Palestine before the creation of Israel. This prompted a chorus of derisive laughter from the pro-Israel audience members.

Chomsky, meanwhile, embarrassed Dershowitz twice during the debate: once by pointing out that Dershowitz had violated the "standard ethics of debate" by using part of his opening statement to respond to Chomsky's opening statement, an unfair advantage; and a second time by displaying at the podium physical documentation of a quote which Dershowitz had called into question.

It was only a short time after Dershowitz debated Chomsky that he gave an address at MIT and called on Israel to give up Arab land. "[Dershowitz has] advocated the gradual return of Palestinian territories now occupied by Israel as a solution to the problem of Palestinian refugees in an address last night at MIT," reported *The Harvard Crimson*. "He said the Israeli government, over a period of 'perhaps twenty years,' should gradually return the territories, 'not in return for paper but in return for a guarantee of security.' . . . 'The Palestinians,' he said, 'were wrongly expelled, but it does not follow that they should take back their lands by violence.'" By the end of the decade, Israel would in fact follow this proposal and forever change their status in the Middle East.

"I am following the liberal light," Dershowitz declared to *The Crimson*. "No liberal should be anything but pro-Israeli."

* * *

The courtroom was packed. Thousands of miles from the United States, a small group of Jews awaited their sentencing from a panel of Soviet judges. Mark Dymshits, Eduard Kuznetsov, and Eduard's wife Silva were facing charges of treason. Their crime was attempting to emigrate to Israel. Along with several friends, they had tried to fly a small plane from the Soviet Union to Sweden, where they could claim political asylum and go on to Israel from there. But on the day of their planned takeoff, KGB agents—tipped off about the scheme—arrested the group before they could even reach the plane.

Since the Six-Day War when the Soviets had sided with the Arabs against Israel, the conditions for Soviet Jews had worsened. The government relished opportunities to twist the law in order to "get" Zionists. As Mark, Eduard, and Silva huddled together in the courtroom, they found themselves surrounded by hundreds of Communist Party members, who had been brought in by the government to voice support for the decision of the judges. When the guilty verdict rang out, cheers erupted from the Party members. Silva was to be sent to a labor camp, and Mark and Eduard were sentenced to death.

Fortunately, by 1973, Mark and Eduard's death sentences had been commuted to several years in a labor camp, but this itself was condemnation to a living death. Eduard kept a diary during his time in the Soviet camp, and the following account of despair and self-mutilation is part of what he recorded:

I have seen convicts swallow huge numbers of nails, quantities of barbed wire, mercury thermometers. . . . I have seen convicts cut open the skin on their arms and legs and peel it off as if it were a stocking; or cut out lumps of flesh (from their stomach or their legs), roast them and eat them; or let the blood drip from slit vein into a tureen, crumble bread crumbs into it, and then gulp it down like a bowl of soup.

The plight of his Jewish brothers and sisters in the Soviet Union came to Dershowitz's attention in the early 1970s. During Seigel's case, he rubbed elbows with supporters of the JDL who chastised him for doing nothing to help alleviate the suffering of Soviet Jews. "They're being annihilated, spiritually and physically. And what are you fancy liberals doing about it? Nothing, that's what," Dershowitz was told by Meir Kahane, the controversial leader of the JDL. "You're no different from the American Jews who stood by silently while six million of your brothers and sisters were being gassed by the Nazis."

These diatribes began to make Dershowitz feel physically sick. "Some of my own family—like many American-Jewish families—had emigrated from what is currently the Soviet Union," he says. "As I thought about these alternatives, I began to feel a bond with Soviet dissidents. There but for the grace of God, and the foresight of my great-grandparents, go I."

Simultaneously, Dershowitz started receiving mail from organizations spreading word of the persecution of Soviet Jews. "Leonid Rigerman is one person, but 'he who saves even one life has saved the world' (The Talmud)," read one pamphlet highlighting the plight of a particular Jew. "WE CALL UPON PEOPLE EVERYWHERE to raise their voices against persecution of Soviet Jewry and demand that the Soviet authorities cease depriving three million people of their rights as a people to exist."

The final straw came from a man who had seen with his own eyes perhaps the greatest evils ever committed by one race against another. Like Dershowitz's great-grandfather Zecharia, Elie Wiesel grew up in a peaceful Hasidic community in Eastern Europe. When the Nazis took over his home country of Hungary in 1944, Wiesel's happy life was torn apart as he and his father, mother, and three sisters were transported to the

Auschwitz concentration camp. Wiesel's mother and one of his sisters were murdered by the Nazis, and Wiesel was sent to a slave labor camp with his father. While being deprived of any comfort and forced into excruciating "living" conditions, Wiesel watched his aging father die of exhaustion after receiving painful beatings.

Miraculously, Wiesel survived the camp, and at the time of his liberation by the Allies, he was no more than a walking skeleton. He managed to start a new life in France as a journalist, and a friend urged him to write about what he had experienced in the Holocaust. His first book, *Night*, was the sobering, shocking result. As his fame grew, Wiesel began raising awareness for suffering Jews around the globe. His book *The Jews of Silence* drew attention to the increasing marginalization of Soviet Jews, along with the Soviet government's refusal to allow many Jewish citizens the right to emigrate to Israel. When Dershowitz read *The Jews of Silence*, he was stricken with guilt for not previously giving thought to the millions of Soviet Jews, who were not free to celebrate their heritage and live out their Jewish identity as he was in America.

In 1973, through a mutual friend, Dershowitz arranged a meeting with Wiesel in New York City, where Wiesel was working as a professor at the City College. "He urged me to travel to the Soviet Union to defend refuseniks—Jews who were refused exit permits," says Dershowitz. Soon after this call to action, Dershowitz started the Soviet Jewry Legal Defense Project in collaboration with some of his lawyer friends, including Jeanne Baker, who also sympathized with the cause. Their goal was to investigate instances of legal injustice toward Soviet Jews and try to provide them with some form of representation inside the Soviet Union.

Dershowitz and his friends in the Project wanted someone with international influence to head their team. They found the perfect man in Telford Taylor, the US chief prosecutor at Nuremberg and Dershowitz's former professor at Yale. During the Nuremberg trials, Taylor had become close friends with the chief prosecutor from the Soviet Union, Roman Rudenko. Fortuitously, Rudenko was currently serving as the Soviet Union's procurator general, a position similar to the US attorney general. In this capacity, Rudenko had the power to protest—and thereby potentially overturn—criminal sentences.

Taylor agreed to head the project and tasked Dershowitz with supervising all brief-writing and legal research.

Legal representation of Soviet prisoners by a group of foreign lawyers had never been attempted before. Taylor's team began preliminary research into the cases of several refuseniks, including the three who had attempted to fly a plane to Sweden. They were sent copies of Eduard Kuznetsov's harrowing diary, which had somehow been smuggled out of the Soviet Union. Together with a visiting professor at Harvard named George Fletcher, Dershowitz prepared a bulk of memoranda on the Soviet legal system, attempting to discover instances where the Soviets had violated their own laws while prosecuting the refuseniks.

In the winter of 1973, Taylor's team went to Israel to interview relatives of the refuseniks, who had been permitted to leave the Soviet Union. Dershowitz and Jeanne Baker traveled together and stayed at the Plaza Hotel on the beach in Tel Aviv. During the ten-day trip, the team conducted interviews with several relatives and gained detailed information about the refuseniks' arrests, trials, and punishments. The picture that emerged of the Soviet government was deplorable.

Across many regions of the nation, Jews were arrested simply for possessing Zionist literature, which had been deemed a threat to the state. Using the press as a formidable ally, the government stirred up public opinion against Jews and rigged the justice system to produce automatic convictions. During a trial, defendants were regularly denied the opportunity to call witnesses or introduce documentary evidence in their favor. "Soviet law gives defendants the right to counsel of their own choosing," noted Telford Taylor. "But when the prisoners' relatives set about finding counsel, they soon discovered that in 'political' cases—as these were officially regarded—lawyers would not be allowed to act as defense counsel unless so authorized by a special permit, called a *dopusk*." Thus a defendant was trapped, since their own defense attorney was appointed by the government. As Dershowitz and his coworkers discovered in their research, these despicable tactics were violations of the Soviets' own law, which required a zealous legal defense for all citizens brought to trial.

The prisoners' relatives in Israel granted Taylor's team powers of attorney to represent their family members trapped in the Soviet Union. Once the team arrived back in the United States, they prepared affidavits and documents certifying their representation of the prisoners—nineteen in all. Dershowitz made a handwritten list of the prisoners on a long piece of yellow legal pad, which he was fond of using. "We were now armed with the information we needed: eyewitness accounts, affidavits, documents, diaries, and physical evidence," he reports.

In the spring of 1974, Taylor and George Fletcher traveled to the Soviet Union on business-trip visas. Upon arrival, they sought a meeting with Taylor's old friend Rudenko. Coming in separately, Dershowitz flew to Moscow with his twelve-year-old son Elon under the auspices of a tourist visa. His real purpose was to meet members of the Zionist community in Moscow to gain their opinions on the project and to gather any information about their clients that might be available.

One of the Jews Dershowitz met was a tiny, motherly woman named Ida Nudel, who had somehow managed to obtain information on the conditions of many Jewish prisoners and who was herself about to be sent to prison for her work as a refusenik. Sitting on a park bench within eyeshot of the multicolored St. Basil's Cathedral, Nudel told Dershowitz through tears that in the Soviet Union, "The Jews . . . are blamed for everything."

Dershowitz asked her whether the involvement of American lawyers might help Soviet Jewry. "Definitely, most definitely," she answered. "Outside intervention is what is needed. The Soviet authorities must be told that this is not merely a local problem. They must understand that the world cares about our prisoners." Dershowitz surprised Nudel and some of her friends with copies of *Exodus*, a worldwide bestselling novel about the founding of Israel. The book was banned throughout the Soviet Union, but that did not stop Dershowitz from smuggling several copies inside briefcases he had packed.

Meanwhile, after days of hearing nothing from Rudenko's office, Taylor and Fletcher were told he was feeling "unwell," but that his assistant Malyarov would meet them. Taylor explained the reason for their visit and noted the grievances committed against their nineteen clients. A back-and-forth ensued between Taylor and Malyarov, who was reluctant to allow American lawyers to petition the Soviet government. After persistent efforts by Taylor, though, Malyarov granted his team permission to submit petitions for the prisoners and said the Soviets would "receive and consider them."

* * *

Back in the United States, political chaos had ensued. Richard Nixon, reelected in 1972 by a total of forty-nine states, was headed for impeachment. An investigation into the Watergate break-in had revealed that members of Nixon's cabinet attempted to hide their involvement from the American people. Many surmised the president had covered up the burglary to preserve his chances in the 1972 election. Nixon's enemies were determined to make him the first president ever removed from office. All around him, cabinet members were jumping off the sinking ship, including his attorney general, Richard G. Kleindienst.

Dershowitz was a vehement opponent of Nixon. As far back as November 1970, he had engaged in a public debate at Harvard with Attorney General Kleindienst over the government's use of preventive detention toward "dangerous" persons. In September 1972, he had written a scathing article for *The Boston Globe* titled "The Erosion of Our Rights," which accused Nixon and his administration of trashing the Bill of Rights. "The civil liberties of all Americans—the right to be free from unwarranted government intrusion, to speak critically of those in power, to be treated fairly and with due process—have been seriously curtailed over the past few years," he declared, citing violations of the First, Fourth, and Eighth Amendments.

Despite his profound dislike for Nixon, Dershowitz was initially hesitant to support his impeachment. Even as investigations ramped up in 1973 and into 1974, there was no hard proof that Nixon had covered up the Watergate break-in. It had become common knowledge that tape recordings existed of all conversations inside the Oval Office, but the tapes had not been released to the public. Near the end of 1973, Dershowitz appeared on a public television station in Boston to discuss the constitutional justification for impeachment. The president of the ACLU, Aryeh Neier, appeared along with Dershowitz and clamored for Nixon's impeachment. Dershowitz, sitting calmly under his mop of curly red hair, took a pragmatic position. "I think the Constitution on this issue is quite ambiguous," he told viewers. "I don't think anybody could say with certainty that the Framers intended there to be a crime or it to be a complete power play [by the House]. . . . I have my own views on how the Constitution should be construed, but I state them without any confidence that they have any real basis in history, and I come somewhere between the extremes. I don't think we should require an indictable offense, but I don't accept the forward view that it should be a simple exercise of naked power."

Dershowitz argued that, moving forward, Congress should "begin the process of articulating what the grounds of impeachment are, and in doing so, they should set out neutral principles which are equally applicable to all people—whether they be Democrats or Republicans, liberals or conservatives."

This principled argument masked Dershowitz's contempt for the president. Soon after this TV appearance, he was interviewed by the campus newspaper of MIT and explained, "I do not try to equate impeachability with deplorability." The article stated, "Dershowitz believes that President Nixon should be impeached only if he has committed any impeachable offenses. Among these impeachable offenses, he said would be if the President had been aware of the Watergate coverup or if he had known of Watergate in advance. . . . Dershowitz believes that impeachment should not be a political move, and that it ought to be used very sparingly."

In the summer of 1974, the final blow fell on the president. On July 23, the Supreme Court ordered him to release his Oval Office tapes, which confirmed he had aided in the Watergate cover-up and lied to the American people about doing so. After this, Dershowitz joined his fellow liberals and a host of Republican Representatives in supporting the president's impeachment.

Rather than face this ugly proceeding, Nixon resigned the presidency. His vice president, Gerald Ford, assumed the mantle of power on August 9, as Nixon left Washington, DC, and politics—for good.

* * *

Throughout the spring and summer of 1974, Dershowitz and his friends in the Soviet Jewry Project had taken over several rooms at Harvard and produced the necessary legal documents to file petitions to Rudenko's office. During the research process, they discovered that under Soviet law, all of their clients—even Mark, Eduard, and Silva—should have only received a maximum of three years in prison. "It was plain enough that the accused were not seeking to weaken the Soviet regime, but rather to practice their religion, to deepen their knowledge of Jewish culture, and to join their fellow Jews in what they regarded as their homeland," comments Telford Taylor. "Soviet law explicitly guarantees defendants the right to counsel of their own choosing . . . but in virtually all of our cases this basic right was flagrantly violated by the requirement that only [lawyers] with the *dopusk* (i.e., permit or clearance) could be retained."

The team completed forty-six hefty documents citing all the incidents where Soviet law had been violated. They included a specific plea for the immediate release of Silva, who according to reports had contracted an ulcer and tuberculosis in prison and was also suffering psychologically. Taylor flew to Moscow and this time met with Rudenko himself. After reminiscing about old times at Nuremberg, the two legal giants got down to business, and Rudenko ultimately gave Taylor a noncommittal response, telling him that his office would examine the documents and get back to Taylor with an answer.

It appeared the Soviets were going to simply ignore the petitions, and Taylor's team became discouraged. Then, a glimmer of hope came in August when Silva was freed by the Soviet authorities and allowed to emigrate to Israel. The Soviets did not acknowledge if this came as a result of the plea from the Americans, but nevertheless the team was thrilled. Soon after settling and receiving medical treatment in Israel, Silva came to America, where she met Taylor, Dershowitz, and the other lawyers that had worked to gain her freedom. The group had an emotional lunch at a kosher restaurant in Manhattan, and Dershowitz ordered a piece of rare roast beef as a special treat for Silva.

Months passed after Silva's release, and no word came from Moscow on the other defendants. Dershowitz and his coworkers were restless for additional information about the prisoners. Near the end of 1974, they traveled to Israel once again to catch up with their clients' relatives and to interview other prisoners who had since completed their sentences in the

Soviet Union and made *aliyah*. Unfortunately, the prisoners' relatives had little information about how their family members were faring.

During the trip, Dershowitz and Jeanne Baker, who had accompanied him, bumped into a middle-aged woman named Yalta Pinkhasov, whose husband, Pinkhas, was being held in a Soviet labor camp. Pinkhas was a Jewish carpenter who had lived with his family by the Caspian Sea in the Soviet region of Dagestan. He had lost a leg in an accident but rose above the disability to become a respected member of his community and a skilled craftsman. The government came after him when he became the first citizen of the Dagestan area to request permission to move to Israel. They allowed his family to go on without him, but they arrested Pinkhas on a bogus accusation that he had overcharged his clients for carpentry services. He desperately tried to defend himself in court, since he was unable to secure the help of a lawyer, but it was no use. The rigged court system found him guilty and sent the one-legged carpenter to a labor camp.

Pinkhas's wife, Yalta, was adamant her husband never overcharged for his services. "If you don't believe me, ask the judge," she said to Dershowitz. When he asked what she meant, Yalta explained, "One of the judges that sat on my husband's case is here in Israel. She is a Jew, and several months after my husband's conviction she herself emigrated." The judge in question was Riya Mishayeva, who was then living in Sderot near the border between Israel and the Gaza Strip. Dershowitz and Baker decided to track her down and headed south from Tel Aviv to Sderot.

Stopping citizens in the town's market, they eventually found a man who knew where Mishayeva lived. After being taken to her apartment and introducing himself, Dershowitz asked Mishayeva to share what had happened in Pinkhas's case. Mishayeva was somber and reluctant to speak. "What you tell us could save his life," Dershowitz calmly explained. "Don't you think, perhaps, you owe him the truth at this point?"

At last Mishayeva explained that, although she had been a communist sympathizer in the Soviet Union, she had discreetly maintained her Jewish identity and stayed on the bench to help her fellow Jews receive lighter punishments. When Pinkhas was brought before the court, the other judges wanted to give him seven years in prison, but Mishayeva held out for a shorter sentence of five years. "There was absolutely no evidence that he overcharged," Mishayeva told Dershowitz while crying. "The whole case was a fabrication. We were under instructions to find him guilty unless he renounced his application to emigrate."

Dershowitz got the middle-aged judge to sign an affidavit which attested to Pinkhas's complete innocence of the charges brought against him. "I believe that Pinkhasov was prosecuted because he had made an application to emigrate to Israel," it clearly stated. After returning to the United States, Dershowitz forwarded Mishayeva's affidavit, along with a petition on behalf of Pinkhas, to the Soviet authorities. Months went by as Dershowitz wrapped up another year at Harvard and Pinkhas remained in prison thousands of miles to the east.

Then, in the fall of 1975, Yalta Pinkhasov received a letter from the Soviet government. "The Presidium of the Supreme Court of the Dagestanskaya Autonomous Socialist Soviet Republic has decided on the 24th of September 1975, to reduce the sentence of your husband to two years of deprivation of freedom and to release him from his place of detention following the completion of his term of punishment." Since he had been sentenced in September 1973, his prison term was now over, and he was granted permission to reunite with his family in Israel. Pinkhas was free.

FOR ME BUT NOT
FOR THEE

Pinkhas and Silva were finally settled in Israel, but Mark Dymshitz and Silva's husband Eduard were closing in on seven years of nightmarish imprisonment and hard labor. Dershowitz and the other members of the Soviet Jewry Legal Defense Project waited anxiously for news of the two men, but none was forthcoming.

During this time, Dershowitz's own family was irreparably ripped apart. Depressed with longing for a past life and bitter at Alan's relationship with Jeanne Baker, Sue had finally filed for a divorce after months of child custody hearings. The ugly proceedings began in late 1975. During the proceedings, Alan's blood pressure increased, and he had to live on a tight budget due to Elon's medical bills and the funds he was giving to Sue as part of the divorce.

Alan turned to his brother to help negotiate a fair settlement. "Sue was having difficulty with the whole notion of divorce," says Nathan Dershowitz. "I was asked to mediate the resolution of the marriage. Alan was reasonable in terms of what he was requesting. Unfortunately, Sue was incapable of having rational discussions because she wanted to go back to the way the marriage was initially. And you can't go back."

For the in-court proceedings, Alan reached out to Harvey Silverglate, who at first refused to participate, saying that he was a criminal defense attorney, not a divorce lawyer. "But in the end I agreed," says Silverglate, "because I thought it imperative that Alan get custody of his sons."

Alan asked for half-custody of the children and offered to give Sue most of their money. Unfortunately, Sue was starting to manifest serious psychological problems, and the court called in a social worker, who confirmed this.

In addition, Alan asked Silverglate to question Sue and her sister, Marilyn. "I thought Alan's calling of my wife was outrageous," comments Nathan. "Marilyn wanted to testify for the sake of the children, whom she loved," Alan states.

Silverglate found the process excruciating because he was a friend of Sue, and his wife, Elsa—a professional photographer—had taken family portraits for Alan, Sue, and their sons. "It was a very difficult and very sad case," says Silverglate. "The issue was child custody. At that time, it was virtually unheard of for the husband to get custody of young children. It was always the wife who got custody, but Sue was mentally ill. She was not fit to raise those kids."

The judge ultimately sided with Alan and awarded him full custody. Their divorce was finalized in early 1976, and Alan found himself a single parent with two young men to raise. Sue faced a future without her children and eventually had to be institutionalized.

"It was traumatic for my family," Alan says. "It was very painful, but it was necessary."

* * *

Two years before Dershowitz's divorce, a young Jewish man named Herbert Streicker was woken early in the morning by a knock at the door of his New York City apartment. He opened up to an FBI agent, who informed him that he had been federally indicted for participating in a conspiracy to transport pornographic materials across state lines. His presence was required in Memphis, Tennessee, for the indictment before a grand jury.

A college dropout, ex-Marine, and onetime Shakespearean actor, Streicker eventually found easy work making porn movies. His big break came in 1972 while working as a lighting technician on a major new film titled *Deep Throat*. When the lead actor failed to show up for work, Streicker was asked to take on the role of "Dr. Young," which he did under the pseudonym of Harry Reems, performing acts of oral sex with his costar Linda Lovelace (hence the name, *Deep Throat*).

Deep Throat became a cult classic and quickly faced the ire of the religious community, who condemned the film and its creators. In 1974, a Bible Belt prosecutor named Larry Parrish—nicknamed "Mr. Clean"—launched an indictment against 117 people for supposedly coordinating a nationwide "conspiracy" to distribute obscene content across state lines. Reems was included in this net, and following his early morning call from the FBI, he went to trial in Memphis for the grand jury indictment. Even though he had not contributed in any way to the marketing or distribution of *Deep Throat*, he was informed by Larry Parrish that "once a person joins a conspiracy, he is liable for everything that happens in that conspiracy until it is ended." At twenty-seven years old, Reems had just become the first actor in American history to be indicted on obscenity grounds. In early 1976, he was convicted of the conspiracy charge and was staring at a sentence of five years in prison and an $810,000 fine. He began looking for an appellate lawyer to rescue his future.

Reems had first heard about Dershowitz during the *I Am Curious (Yellow)* case. He contacted Dershowitz to ask if he would be willing to take the case, and Dershowitz agreed to meet him at Harvard. In May 1976, Reems showed up to Dershowitz's office in a suit and tie and shared his life story with Dershowitz.

Though he had not gone to see *Deep Throat*—nor any hard-core porn films for that matter—Dershowitz decided to take on the case because of the nefarious "conspiracy" charge Larry Parrish had leveled against Reems. Dershowitz knew Reems was simply being made an example of and believed he would be easy pickings for Parrish, who had won forty previous porn cases. "I explained to Reems that we could no longer expect to convince any court to accept our broad constitutional attack on movie censorship," says Dershowitz. "Chief Justice Burger had put that argument to rest [in the *I Am Curious (Yellow)* case], at least for the present. . . . As I laid out the arguments pro and con, it became clear that a decision on this issue could go either way; there were plausible arguments on each side. In the prevailing mood against obscenity, I could not afford to place all my reliance on a technical, legal argument. We had to persuade the media, the public, and the courts that the conviction of Harry Reems was an outrage."

Dershowitz began making the media rounds to publicly decry Reems's prosecution, against the opposition of his Borough Park family, who found Reems's lifestyle distasteful. He even once overheard a family friend from Borough Park refer to him as "Harry and Claire's older kid. . . . You know, the one who used to be the troublemaker and now is the lawyer for the troublemakers."

At the same time, Reems, whom Dershowitz called "Herb," used all his connections in the media and film industry to whip up support and convince the acting community that if the government came after him today, it would come after them tomorrow. He could not afford to pay his travel expenses, let alone any legal fees to Dershowitz, and as a result, he set up the "Harry Reems Legal Defense Fund," which began receiving significant contributions.

"[Mr. Reems] has the support of some of the country's best-known entertainers. Tonight Colleen Dewhurst, Ben Gazzara, Mike Nichols and Stephen Sondheim will be hosts at an invitation-only party at Ted Hook's Backstage to raise money for Mr. Reems's legal defense," wrote a *New York Times* reporter in June 1976, who also noted that he had "some of the country's most impressive legal talent working on his appeal. . . . Mr. Dershowitz's position is that Mr. Reems did not participate in the final editing or production of the film, and at the time he acted in it, he had no way of knowing what the final product would look like. Nor did he have any way of withdrawing from the alleged conspiracy, Mr. Dershowitz said."

Dershowitz's phone rang off the hook with journalists seeking his comments, and together, he and Reems barnstormed the country. Over the next several months, they appeared with politicians at fundraisers, participated in forums on college campuses, and made the rounds of radio and TV shows. A barrage of articles appeared with titles ranging from the academic—"Harry Reems, Cinema Sex Star with Alan Dershowitz, Defense Attorney 'Can Morality Be Legislated?'"—to the humorous— "Reems Shafted in Bible Belt." One unfriendly reporter bemoaned the fact that after centuries of heroes like Thomas Paine, Jefferson, and Eugene V. Debs, "we are now asked to fight for the right of Harry Reems to be a public creep. . . . Anybody who contributes to his defense fund is a mental moonbeam."

"The media were writing and distributing our briefs for us," notes Dershowitz. "The publicity was having its intended effect on the public, on the Justice Department, and on the courts. We began to get the message that the Reems conviction was an embarrassment. This was exactly what we had hoped would happen." Despite being pelted with hateful comments such as "Jews are loudmouths" and "Yids run the pornography business," Dershowitz thoroughly enjoyed the struggle to defend Streicker. He admitted once that "battling the religious right is just a lot of fun."

Dershowitz had a superb occasion to do just that when he and Reems jointly appeared on William Buckley's PBS program *Firing Line*. Founder of the influential conservative journal *National Review*, Buckley was a Yale graduate, devout Catholic, and one of the most well-respected members of the religious right by the time Dershowitz and Streicker came on his show.

Seated in uncomfortable-looking black office chairs in front of a small audience of young people, Buckley, Reems, and Dershowitz were all dressed in suits and ties. The most bemusing physical characteristic of the three participants—beyond Buckley sticking a pen in his mouth like a pipe—was Dershowitz's poofy red hair, which had now taken on Afro-like proportions. According to Dershowitz, it was a deliberate attempt to appear more radical.

Despite his radical viewpoints, Dershowitz maintained a calm demeanor throughout the debate and seemed to enjoy moments where he could find a point of agreement with the conservative Buckley. They both shared similar beliefs about what kind of sexual acts should and should not be encouraged, but Dershowitz took the libertarian view that it was not the government's role to regulate people's sex lives nor the type of media they could consume. "If we simply passed a law saying from now on films are not covered by the First Amendment, that wouldn't convert us into a totalitarian society automatically," Dershowitz argued to Buckley. "But it's a better society which has a vigorous support of any media of any film no matter what its content."

"Well, I don't think it's necessarily a better society," countered Buckley in his distinct drawl. "Surely a society which condones . . . the reduction of sex to its exclusive biological dimensions is no more commendable than a society that reduces liquor to its pure alcohol effect."

"See, here's the essential fallacy of your view, I think," stated Dershowitz. "Your view suggests that by allowing something under the First Amendment a society condones it. My view is that society does not condone something just because it permits it. . . . We live in a world where most countries now ban most free speech. I think Senator-elect Moynihan has been right: we have a society where we constrain free speech so much [that] it's in diminishing quantity. And for us in this country who have the most robust free speech in the world, bar none—those who call us a repressive society don't understand what a repressive society is," at which point Buckley voiced agreement, "to give up that valuable commodity because we are afraid that maybe it would degrade the quality of life somewhat . . . is I think to give up a very unique thing."

While Dershowitz and Buckley debated, Reems mostly remained quiet, answering questions only when specifically addressed by Buckley. Although he did not stoop to personal attacks, it was clear Buckley had disdain for Reems and the profession he had chosen. When Reems tried to use statistics from a 1968 study on pornography to his advantage, Buckley waxed eloquent.

"We know that the incidents of profligate sex have greatly increased during the past five, six, seven years," he began. "Now it's increased on account of something. We are all biologically the same as we were twenty, thirty, forty years ago. Question: does profligate sex have a weakening influence on the institution of the family? Does it breed an end to that sense of shame which I think Professor Walter Burns so rightly points out is an aspect of our Western culture and the free man? . . . I don't see that the . . . 1968 commission exhausted those questions with anything like the finality that justifies us in dealing with sex as though it was simply an extra cup of tea in the afternoon."

Shortly after their TV appearance with Buckley, Reems wrote a letter to Dershowitz, which included this note: "Can't tell you how glad I am that Buckley directed most of his semantic bull to you. His mental gymnastics far exceeded my own abilities, but he met his match in you."

Despite their political differences, Dershowitz and Buckley formed a friendship, occasionally going out for drinks after an appearance together. Looking back on their debate over *Deep Throat*, Buckley conceded decades later: "In a way, Dershowitz had it right. A truly civilized society is judged by the extent that it succeeds in governing its own appetites without the need of the law."

In early 1977, the Justice Department dismissed the indictment against Reems. Considering the fact that his "crime" was not very different from the other defendants who had been indicted, Dershowitz assumed the government had caved to the public furor they had drummed up. "Chief Justice Burger may have won in the courthouse in the *I Am Curious (Yellow)* case, but we won in theaters and on television sets throughout the nation," notes Dershowitz.

Through the help of fans and his radical lawyer, Reems had escaped a prison sentence. He eventually retired from the porn business and ironically converted to Christianity, settling down in Utah as a real estate agent. As a memento of their time together, he sent Dershowitz an auto-graphed picture, which Dershowitz proudly hung in his office at Harvard. Beneath Reems's mustached face, a humorous inscription said: "To Alan Dershowitz—You taught me everything I know."

* * *

Right around the time Dershowitz won the *Deep Throat* case, in March 1977, headlines across the West flashed the news that Natan Sharansky, one of the most famous dissidents in the Soviet Union, had just been arrested by the KGB and was currently being held in Moscow's notorious Lefortovo Prison, which had been used under Stalin as a place of tor-ture and mass execution. The Soviet authorities saw Sharansky as a greater threat than most dissidents because he spoke fluent English, possessed a charismatic personality, and had a network of contacts in the media and worldwide human rights movement. When Sharansky and his sweet-heart Avital applied for a visa to Israel in 1973, the government denied Sharansky permission, but allowed Avital to leave the country. The night before Avital's departure to Israel, the couple were married in a clandestine Jewish ceremony.

A year passed, and still Sharansky had not been granted permis-sion to join his wife in Israel. Sharansky became the unofficial leader of Jewish *refuseniks* and he reported on human rights violations taking place throughout the Soviet Union. In early 1977, the government broadcast an hour-long documentary around the country which portrayed Sharansky and his friends as fat, money-grubbing Jews who were "soldiers of Zionism inside the Soviet Union." Shortly after, Sharansky was betrayed to the KGB by his roommate, who was pressured into saying Sharansky was an agent of the CIA. Sharansky was charged with treason and spying for America, both of which carried the death penalty.

Sharansky's arrest flashed in newspapers around the world, and Avital immediately began searching for a lawyer to be her husband's advocate outside the Soviet Union. She asked her friend Elie Wiesel who he would recommend, and he advised her to call Irwin Cotler, a young Canadian attorney and human rights advocate, and Alan Dershowitz.

Soon after, Dershowitz received a call from a woman speaking broken English who introduced herself as Sharansky's wife. She was frightened her husband would starve to death in prison or languish long enough that she would grow too old to bear children while waiting for him. Dershowitz was aware of Sharansky's case, having followed it in the newspapers. He told Avital it would almost certainly be impossible for him to travel to the Soviet Union to represent Sharansky in his trial, but he eagerly agreed to work *pro bono* as Sharansky's prime advocate in the United States.

Because Sharansky had been slapped with the phony charge of spying for America, Dershowitz decided the first thing which needed to happen was for the US government to deny this charge. "I knew this would be difficult, since it is the policy of both the State Department and the CIA not to issue denials in spy cases," says Dershowitz. "The logic is that if denials are issued in some cases, the world will know that the charge is true whenever there is no denial. . . . Nonetheless, I decided to try. . . . I did some research and discovered that at least in one prior case, a President—John F. Kennedy—had issued a specific denial that Professor Frederick Barghoorn of Yale University was a CIA agent."

Dershowitz decided to take his petition straight to the White House, arranging a meeting with his former student Stuart Eizenstat, who had become Jimmy Carter's chief domestic policy adviser and had an office down the hall from the Oval Office. Dershowitz told Eizenstat and Robert Lipshutz, the president's counsel, that Carter's recent statements defending human rights could work against the very causes he was trying to help. "If he keeps it up it will be constructive," Dershowitz said, "but if he lets up now it might be worse than if he had done nothing."

Eizenstat and Lipshutz asked Dershowitz what specific action he would recommend the president take. "The President should issue a direct statement categorically denying that Sharansky is an American spy or that he has ever provided any information to American intelligence," said Dershowitz. They assured Dershowitz they would mention his suggestion to the president.

Despite pushback from the State Department and the CIA, Carter did just what Dershowitz had advised. Two months after Dershowitz's meeting with Eizenstat, Carter released the following public statement: "I have inquired deeply within the State Department, and within the CIA, as to whether or not Mr. [Sharansky] has ever had any known relationship in a subversive way, or otherwise, with the CIA. The answer is 'no.'"

"The Soviets could not now charge [Sharansky] with spying for the United States without, in effect, calling President Carter a liar," said Dershowitz, who was gleeful at Carter's decision. "Shortly after this statement was made, the Soviets stopped referring to that charge."

In the summer of 1978, Sharansky was put on trial in Moscow for "high treason." Avoiding mention of the CIA accusation, the Soviets claimed he had passed along state secrets to "Western Diplomats, intelligence, as well as an agent of a foreign military-intelligence service who worked under the cover of a journalist in Moscow." Dershowitz and Irwin Cotler tried to gain permission to attend the trial, but their requests went unanswered by the Soviet authorities.

"How does the trial for treason in the Soviet Union compare with one here?" Dershowitz was asked by Barbara Walters during an interview on ABC.

"The investigation that occurs in secret is the basic trial," answered Dershowitz. "Sharansky, therefore, has [already] been tried [and] has been found guilty. Now there's a public trial, the purpose of which is simply to decide whether the earlier trial was accurate or inaccurate. He can, under Soviet law, have a lawyer, but the lawyer has to have KGB approval. And he refused to accept the lawyer that was appointed for him, and he can't have witnesses unless the court agrees to call them."

"Professor, is this trial a farce?" asked Walters.

"This trial is a farce," answered Dershowitz calmly. "There has been no case in the history of the Soviet Union where a dissident who has been accused has been found innocent. This is an even greater farce because Sharansky stands alone, without even the assistance of counsel."

The Soviet judges ultimately refrained from ordering Sharansky's execution, but they sentenced him to thirteen years in prison. When Sharansky was given a chance to speak, he turned his back to the judges and declared to the courtroom attendees: "Now, when I am farther than ever from my people and from my Avital, when I face many difficult years of imprisonment, I say, addressing my people and my Avital: 'L'shana ha-baah b'Yerushalayim!' 'Next year in Jerusalem!'"

* * *

At the same time Dershowitz was desperately fighting for Sharansky, his commitment to the First Amendment was put to the ultimate test. In 1977, members of the National Socialist Party of America had begun conducting mini-parades down the streets of Skokie, Illinois, wearing brownshirt uniforms and brandishing swastika banners. Skokie had been specially selected because it had the largest percentage of Holocaust survivors of any town in America. "My dad was going nuts about this when it would come on TV," said Howard Reich, son of a Skokie Holocaust survivor. "My dad would turn ashen pale, and the relatives would be calling each other on the phone: 'The Nazis are coming back! They're coming again!'"

When the Nazis petitioned to stage a full-scale march through Skokie, the authorities faced pressure from the community to deny them permission, and they did so, reasoning that violence would erupt if their march took place. The Nazis sued the town, and the case became national news, with the ACLU stepping in to provide recommendations as to which side was in the right.

Dershowitz urged the ACLU to support the right of the Nazis to march through Skokie, voicing his opinion on television and privately lobbying ACLU members at board meetings. "I understood why the Holocaust survivors would be deeply offended, even possibly traumatized, by being

forced to reexperience the spectacle of brown-shirted Nazis wearing swas-
tikas," says Dershowitz, some of whose relatives had been killed in the
Holocaust. "But I worried about the implications of a judicial decision
authorizing censorship."

Claire Dershowitz was furious. "Whose side are you on?" she demanded
of her son on a phone call. "Ma, I am simply defending free speech," he
tried to explain. "Don't give me that!" retorted Claire. "I'm your mother.
Free speech—free smeech. Are you for the Nazis or the Jews?"

Ironically, Dershowitz's stance on the Skokie issue also earned him
hate mail from the very people whose rights he was defending. "[Jews]
should all go back to the African Jungle and bring your Black brothers," read a letter postmarked Skokie, Illinois. "Who needs you crooks?
Madmen . . . Yiddish lies!! Kill! Kill! Kill! Money! Money! Money! (Other
peoples). Greed! Greed! Greed! Busy bodying in others affairs!"

Dershowitz's response to these attacks was to stand his ground. "I wish
I could limit my defense of civil liberties to those people with whose views
I agree," he confessed on a Boston radio program. "[But] in every society
that I know of which censors, the corollary of the statement 'You may not
read certain books,' is the exact opposite: 'You *must* read other books.'"

The Supreme Court ultimately decided in favor of the Nazis, to the
outrage of many. In the summer of 1978, Dershowitz appeared on *Firing
Line* with William Buckley once again to discuss the controversy. "The
power of discrimination in speech is the most dangerous power of all," he
declared. "It's a power that we have as individuals, but a power that must be
denied the government, or else in a democratic society every single interest
group will ask that that power of discrimination in thought be exercised in
their direction. I have no doubt that had the Nazis been banned in Skokie,
the next step would have been to ban the Ku Klux Klan in Mississippi.
The step after that would have been to ban the Communist Party in other
parts of the world. Then there would have been a movement to ban the
Manchester Union leader growing out of Boston, Massachusetts, looking
up north to—"

At this point, Buckley interrupted. "I really think that is hysterical," he
said. "I honestly do . . . if the Communists were banned in every state of
the union, I don't think that liberties would be lessened."

"I despise the Communist Party," replied Dershowitz. "I think they are an evil in this world, and yet they have their own definition of freedom which I can't dismiss as absolutely frivolous. They talk about economic freedoms, they talk about social freedoms. They think that the kind of freedoms we all agree with are bourgeois freedoms. Now surely we would not accept a communist regime which banned everybody from speaking except those who agree with their definition of freedom. In fact, that's what the Communists do, and that's why we're so opposed to them. But I don't think that a single definition of freedom—whether it be our definition or their definition—should be the hallmark of free speech."

* * *

In public, Dershowitz was becoming a sought-after lawyer and respected news contributor, but in private, he was a single parent living a bachelor's life. Although he had a fairly close relationship with Jeanne Baker, she did not live with Alan, Elon, and Jamin, and the three guys decided to set up bachelor-like living quarters. Alan was able to rent a large, 150-year-old house on Elmwood Avenue in Cambridge for a song, and he and his sons decided to call the mansion "Camp Dersh."

Camp Dersh became a local watering hole for Alan's colleagues and his sons' friends. The premises were packed with a ping-pong table, pinball machine, and sauna, among other accoutrements. Alan hired a cleaner to come in once a week and do some household chores and tidy up the home's twelve rooms. He came home in the afternoons to play basketball with his sons and cook dinner. He had no aptitude for the latter, once accidentally incinerating a pot until all that was left was a small piece of metal.

Alan devoted part of his energy to ensuring Elon received the best radiation treatment possible. "Dear Senator," he once wrote to Ted Kennedy, "I'm really sorry to have had to miss the dinner at your home tonight. . . . I just learned that my son Elon—who sends his regards—has to go into Children's Hospital tomorrow morning for some minor surgery. . . . I don't feel comfortable leaving him alone tonight, and I would like to take him to the hospital tomorrow first thing in the morning."

Alan's efforts paid off. Nearly a decade after his surgery, Elon was declared free of all cancer and began his career. In 1979, Alan helped secure him jobs in Washington, DC, where Elon worked in Ted Kennedy's office as an intern.

Elon's younger brother, Jamin, inherited his father's personality. Unlike the home Alan had grown up in, there were no weekly Shabbat dinners and no kosher observance, but Alan did take his boys to the synagogue at Harvard Hillel for major holidays. One Yom Kippur when he was thirteen, Jamin got upset with Alan for making him attend services. Alan insisted, since it was a focal point in the life of the Jewish community at Harvard, drawing many teachers and students. During the service, Rabbi Ben Zion Gold began taking questions from the congregants as per custom, and Jamin raised his hand.

"Rabbi," he began, "is it not true that under the Jewish religion, when a boy turns thirteen, he becomes responsible for his own religious observance?"

"Yes, [Jamin]," Rabbi Gold replied. "You learned your Bar Mitzvah lessons very well."

"Then why does my father have the right to make me go to services if I don't want to?" A gasp went through the crowd. Alan overheard one person comment: "That's Dershowitz's kid."

Alan remained close to his parents, financially supporting them as much as he could. "Alan treated his parents very, very well," says his aunt Shirley Ringel. Unfortunately, his father's memory had been deteriorating, and he was eventually diagnosed with Alzheimer's. "It is such a pity to see a wonderful man begin to disintegrate before the eyes of his family," Alan wrote to Arthur Goldberg. "Life can be kind and cruel at the same time. It is not nearly as hard on my father as it is on my mother." One day, Harry Dershowitz disappeared in the middle of New York City, and his frightened family enlisted the help of several police departments throughout the city to find him. At last, he was located, and Alan wrote a profusely thankful letter to Mayor Ed Koch, praising the city's police force.

Harry was not the only family member in decline. Sue Barlach was distraught after the divorce and loss of her sons and began a long decline into depression. Her psychological issues compounded her troubles. "She was really bitter," notes Judy Beck, wife of Alan's friend Bernie Beck, who remained close to Sue after the divorce. "There was a lot of status being Alan's wife, and I think she had liked that."

Sue spent a period with relatives in Colorado, but eventually settled back in her home state of New Jersey, where she and Alan had dated those many years ago. Even with her difficulties, Sue managed to go back to college, attending Rutgers University and finding work as a librarian. "She was really quite smart," says Judy, "but I don't think she ever got over the divorce."

ON THE THRESHOLD

Dershowitz's fame as a lawyer was growing. September 1978 found him celebrating his fortieth birthday, and Jeanne Baker had arranged a surprise meeting with Woody Allen as his birthday gift.

Dershowitz was a Woody Allen aficionado. He had gone to see every film Allen made and constantly quoted his jokes. Whenever one of Allen's films was released, he and his sons tried to be first in line at the theater.

Baker came from a prominent left-wing family and knew the communist screenwriter Walter Bernstein, who worked with Allen and arranged a lunch between him and Dershowitz. While Allen was filming *Manhattan*, Dershowitz went to New York City to have lunch with him at a restaurant across the road from the Metropolitan Opera, "I was aware even then of what a brilliant lawyer Alan was," says Allen. At one point during their lunch, Allen asked Dershowitz whom he would choose to represent if he could go back in time.

"Jesus," Dershowitz quickly replied. "Imagine how different history would be if a Jewish lawyer saved Jesus. They couldn't accuse us of killing their Lord."

"But he wouldn't have been their Lord, if you had won," replied Allen. "He wouldn't have been crucified. And without crucifixion, there's no Christianity, so if you had won they'd be blaming the Jews for destroying Christianity."

"But there wouldn't be any 'they' to blame us," noted Dershowitz.

"There's always a 'they,'" said Allen with a smile.

The two men parted as friends, and Dershowitz's only surprise at meeting his idol was how serious Allen was in person.

* * *

Nearly a decade had passed since Dershowitz began fighting for Mark Dymshitz and Eduard Kuznetsov to be freed from their imprisonment in the Soviet Union and have the freedom to live in Israel. Although Eduard's wife, Silva, had been released, for several years the authorities refused to budge on Mark and Eduard's sentences.

In 1979, Dershowitz and the other members of the Soviet Jewry Legal Defense Project decided to ratchet up the pressure. The Soviet Communist Party was exerting considerable influence over European politics, and at the time, they were particularly interested in securing seats for Communists during the upcoming elections to the Italian Parliament. Dershowitz flew to Rome in an attempt to find sympathetic ears for their clients. He met with Pope John Paul II's assistant on human rights matters and also with Senator Umberto Terracini, a high-ranking member of the Italian Communist Party.

As a young man, Terracini was an active supporter of communist organizations, and during Mussolini's reign, he was imprisoned for two decades for opposing the dictator's Fascist ideology. After the country was liberated by the Allies during World War II, Terracini was set free and helped draft a new constitution for Italy, eventually being elected to both houses of Parliament. By the time Dershowitz met Terracini in 1979, he was one of the most powerful Communists in Italy.

"He was a wonderful, wonderful old man," says Dershowitz. "I was always brought up to hate communists, but I loved this guy. He was so nice." Terracini was appalled at the Soviets' treatment of Mark and Eduard and immediately got on the phone with the Kremlin. "To get phone calls from both the Communist Party of Italy and from the Vatican at the same time—it was incredible," describes Dershowitz. "The Soviets had to listen to them because they were trying to win elections in Italy, and so they couldn't present the face of repression."

Soon after, a Soviet airplane landed at JFK Airport bearing five tired, pale prisoners. "FLIGHT FROM THE GULAG" reported *The New York Times*. "On April 27, 1979, the Soviet Government released five prominent dissidents and flew them to America, in exchange for two convicted

Soviet spies. One of the five Russians was Eduard S. Kuznetsov (the others were Aleksandr Ginzburg, Valentyn Moroz, Mark Dymshitz and the Rev. Georgi Vins)." For the first time in history, America and the Soviet Union had exchanged a group of Soviet citizens without any Americans being included in the deal.

Eduard traveled to Elmwood, Massachusetts, to recuperate at the home of Andrei Sakharov's stepson, and Dershowitz arranged a meeting with the client he had represented *pro bono* for nearly ten years. Eduard thanked Dershowitz for all his work and told him that the Project had probably discouraged the Soviets from bringing prosecutions against hundreds of other Soviet Jews. "Publicity is the air and water which keeps the prisoners alive," Eduard told Dershowitz. "Unknown prisoners die every day in the camps. But they do not dare let a prisoner die if he is known in the West."

Following their warm reception in the United States, Mark and Eduard made *aliyah* and restarted their lives in Israel, where Eduard was reunited with his wife, Silva.

Pinkas Pinkhasov, Mark, Eduard, and Silva had been saved, but Dershowitz's mind often turned to Natan Sharansky and also to Moishe Catz, the professor he had met at Stanford back in 1971 whose family was trapped in Romania under the anti-Semitic regime of communist ruler Nicolae Ceaușescu.

To get out of Ceaușescu's country legally was a tall task. Moishe and his family bided their time until the early 1970s when a job opportunity in America arose for Moishe. He was offered a position with the World Bank, which would enable him to live in the United States. Moishe and his wife arranged separate trips out of the country, and once they had left Romania, they both sought asylum at an American embassy and declared they were permanently leaving Romania. They had been unable to travel together as a family and were forced to leave their two children behind for the time being. When Moishe and Dershowitz met up in the States, Dershowitz said to him: "Moishe, I will do everything within my power. I promise that your kids will join you here, no matter what it takes."

Throughout the mid-1970s, Dershowitz reached out to members of Congress, the Red Cross, and even the White House, trying to find someone who was in a position to help. It so happened that at one point, Ted

Kennedy was scheduled to have a call with Nicolae Ceaușescu, who was trying to build relationships with the Western powers while simultaneously staying within the good graces of the Soviet authorities. Dershowitz got wind of this and arranged a meeting with Kennedy to explain the situation of Dana and her brother, Andrei. He asked Kennedy to mention the teenagers during the phone call, but Kennedy was initially hesitant to raise the matter with Ceaușescu. Dershowitz pleaded with Kennedy to save Dana and Andrei and left a paper for Kennedy which outlined the siblings' names and situation.

Soon after, Kennedy had his call with Ceaușescu, who was eager to please the powerful senator. As they were about to hang up, Kennedy noticed the paper from Dershowitz on his desk. "You know, I have one more request for you—I hope you can fulfill it," he said to Ceaușescu. "I need two kids for a couple who are now living in the United States—their kids are in Romania. Just two kids in Bucharest." Without hesitation, Ceaușescu replied, "They're yours. Send on the names to my administrators, and they should be out within forty-eight hours."

And that is exactly what happened. Dana and Andrei were flown to Amsterdam, where they waited for almost a month while Dershowitz pulled strings to secure them green cards. After reaching America, Dana and Andrei reunited with their parents. Dana decided to pursue a medical career, and as part of her master's program, Dershowitz helped her gain admittance to Brandeis University, where she earned a scholarship to study medicine. When she came to Massachusetts to begin her stint at Brandeis, Dana moved in with Dershowitz and his sons at Camp Dersh. "It was the most natural thing in the world," says Dershowitz. "Dana had no place to go and no friends in the area." The house was large, and Dana was able to have most of the first floor to herself.

The Catz family had all successfully begun new lives in America. "Alan never asked for money for helping us—he wasn't doing it for money," says Dana. "He was very kind, but the thing that always struck me the most when I was a kid, was his can-do attitude. There was nothing that he would say could not be done—no matter how complicated, hard, or impossible it was."

* * *

In 1979, *Time* published a magazine titled "50 Faces for the Future." Number fourteen was thirty-two-year-old Arkansas governor William J. Clinton. Just below Clinton, at number sixteen, was Dershowitz. "The student editors of the Harvard Law School *Bulletin* seldom lavish praise on the faculty, but for Dershowitz they made an exception," reported *Time*. "As the *Bulletin* put it, 'He energetically attacks discrimination, represents criminals and defends the rights of others to defend themselves.'

"The onetime boy wonder from Brooklyn (he was a full professor at Harvard at 28) admits to being 'an extremist' on civil liberties. His credo: 'If there is discrimination against anybody, there is discrimination against everybody.' He has fought for the rights of American Nazis to speak and assemble, and successfully defended actor Harry Reems, the lead in *Deep Throat*, against obscenity charges."

Around the time that article was released, Ted Kennedy asked Dershowitz to travel to China on his behalf. Three years after Mao's death in 1976, Mao's successor, Deng Xiaoping, had decentralized much of the economy and opened new doors for cultural exchanges with foreign nations. Kennedy was interested in showing China that Americans cared about establishing a good relationship between the two nations, but was also interested to know whether the government was treating its people fairly. He asked Dershowitz to report on the current state of human rights in the country, but they agreed the public explanation for his visit would be that he was visiting the country in order to help the Chinese draft a new criminal code.

After all the necessary arrangements for the trip were completed, Dershowitz flew to Hong Kong in early January 1980 with his son Elon and Jeanne Baker. They journeyed to Shanghai, where Dershowitz spent time visiting the large Shanghai Prison and making detailed, handwritten notes in a red-leather notebook which he used throughout the trip. "During my visit to several prisons, I learned about a practice that seemed unique to China," Dershowitz says. "When the sentence of death was imposed for certain types of crimes, the condemned prisoner was sent to a particular institution to await execution. After about a year, half of the condemned would actually be executed, while the other half would be spared. All the condemned were competing against one another in a zero-sum game, in which the stakes were life and death."

During one of his visits to a Chinese prison, Dershowitz bumped into a Chinese defense attorney outside. He struck up conversation with the woman, asking how she went about defending her clients in court. "Well, I just beg the government to have mercy on my client," she replied to a slightly stunned Dershowitz.

While in Shanghai, Dershowitz delivered a guest lecture at the city's Law Institute to a packed audience of Chinese lawyers. "After the end of the Cultural Revolution, these lawyers were hungering to learn about Western ideology," notes Dershowitz.

"The American legal system is called an adversary system," he told his attentive listeners at the Shanghai Law Institute. "We have decided after years of experience, that for our purposes, the best way to achieve the truth is to have a prosecuting attorney and a defense attorney opposed to each other in the courtroom with a judge in the middle trying to resolve the dispute. . . .

"One of the most important statements of our legal system is the following: it is far better that ten guilty people should go free than that one innocent person should be wrongly convicted. Of course we would all prefer if no guilty people went free and if no innocent people were convicted, but that isn't always possible. We understand that mistakes will be made, and it is our philosophy that if there is going to be a mistake, it's better that a mistake result in a guilty person going free than an innocent person being wrongly confined."

After traveling back home, Dershowitz met with Ted Kennedy and reported on what he had seen in China, particularly the fate of death-row inmates.

During his decades-long tenure as a senator, Kennedy frequently consulted Dershowitz, whom he called "Al." Kennedy's assistant Ken Feinberg noted that the senator would tell him to "Run it by Al" when a constitutional question came up. By 1980, eleven years had passed since the notorious Chappaquiddick incident, and Kennedy's demons had been exorcised enough for him to challenge Jimmy Carter for the Democratic nomination in the upcoming election.

Dershowitz decided to support Kennedy over Carter, in part because of Kennedy's staunch commitment to Jerusalem being recognized as an "undivided" city with "millennial" ties to the Jewish people, as opposed to an official statement by the Carter administration which labeled East Jerusalem "occupied territory." Dershowitz threw whatever weight he had behind Kennedy, volunteering to help his campaign. He gave many speeches on behalf of Kennedy and also spent weeks traveling to California and several other states on the campaign trail with Kennedy. During this invigorating time, Dershowitz met Joe Biden, a senator from Delaware and a friend of Kennedy's. Dershowitz also got to know Kennedy on a more personal basis, even learning they were both ice cream fanatics. "Ted could never pass by an ice cream place without going in," says Dershowitz.

Kennedy ultimately fell short of receiving the necessary delegates at the 1980 DNC convention. It had been a hard-fought battle, but he had been plagued by issues from the start, including his bumbling answer when a CBS reporter asked him, "Why do you want to be president?"

After Carter secured the nomination, Dershowitz and some of his Harvard colleagues issued a public statement supporting Carter over Republican candidate, Ronald Reagan, based on Carter's policies on the environment, the Equal Rights Amendment, women's and minorities' rights, and healthcare.

It was to no avail. Reagan summoned all his skills as a former Hollywood actor turned California governor to devastating effect. "Are you better off than you were four years ago?" he poignantly asked viewers during a debate with Carter. The citizens of forty-four states answered "no." When Carter lost the election, Dershowitz received a note of condolence from his former research assistant Rob McDuff, who had become a public defender in Texas and an avid supporter of Carter. In January 1981, Reagan became the fortieth president, and a new age of conservatism descended upon the land.

* * *

In the months after Reagan's inauguration, both he and Pope John Paul II narrowly escaped death after being shot, and Dershowitz wrote an article bashing the assassins, particularly terrorist Mehmet Ali Ağca, who had shot the Pope.

Despite his disgust with murder and murderers, Dershowitz remained as vehemently opposed to the death penalty as when he helped Arthur Goldberg begin the process of its abolition. In the summer of 1981, he was anxiously awaiting a decision from the Arizona Supreme Court about whether two of his clients would live or die. The story of his involvement with these young men was long and sordid.

Back in 1979, Dershowitz had appeared on *The Advocates* to debate the question, "Should Your States Carry Out Death Sentences?"

"We execute people because they murder certain kinds of people," Dershowitz declared passionately to the audience. "We execute Black people because they murder whites. We *don't* execute white people because they murder Blacks. We execute because people will not cooperate with the government and become finks and support the government's side of the story. . . . The reality is you will *die* if you kill the wrong victim. You will *die* if you hire the wrong lawyer. You will *die* if you refuse to cooperate with the government. . . . That's the reality today in 1979."

Sitting in prison far away in Arizona, Ricky and Raymond Tison watched the program with rapt interest. The brothers were facing the possibility of execution for their complicity in one of the most appalling crimes in Arizona history.

Ricky and Raymond had received both a blessing and a curse by being born to Gary Tison. Gary was a known killer who spent most of his sons' childhood behind bars. When the boys came for visits, though, he showered them with thrilling stories and affection, and the boys developed a deep attachment to their father. In mid-1978, when Gary informed them of an escape plan he had hatched, his sons agreed to help put it in motion. Their condition was that no one would be shot in the process, which Gary assured them would not happen.

After breaking Gary out of prison, the group made a dash for the Mexican border. When two of their tires became flat, Gary waved down a passing car. John Lyons and his wife, teenage niece, and infant son were on a family trip through Arizona and decided to pull over to help the travelers stranded on the side of the road.

It was a terrible mistake. Gary pulled a gun on the Lyonses and forced them to trade their Mazda for his broken-down Ford. After moving the cars down a desolate side road, Gary told his sons to go to the Mazda and bring back some drinking water. As the boys did so, they suddenly heard gunshots back at the Ford. When they turned around, they saw their father shooting the Lyons family at point-blank range. Gary had apparently changed his mind about their fate.

The bodies of the Lyons family were eventually found, and the biggest manhunt in the history of Arizona commenced, with hundreds of law officers using communication networks, helicopters, and roadblocks to find the Tisons. The Tisons eventually ran into a police roadblock as they neared the Mexican border. Ricky and Raymond were captured, but Gary—who had fled the scene and managed to escape—was found dead in the wilderness several days later.

The public outcry at the death of the Lyons family was fierce. During their trial, Ricky and Raymond tried to convince the court that they had never intended for anyone to be killed during the prison break. Although they had not personally committed the murder of the Lyons family, the Tison brothers absorbed the full wrath of the media and parents throughout Arizona. "We were some of the most hated people in Arizona," says Raymond.

In early 1979, the brothers appeared before Judge Douglas W. Keddie for their sentencing. Under the laws of conspiracy and felony-murder, the judge imposed the death penalty and ordered Ricky and Raymond to be executed in a gas chamber.

"For a lot of people that sit on death row, it doesn't become real until you actually get put in a cell next to the death house a couple of days before you're going to get executed," says Ricky. "Then it gets real very fast."

The brothers appealed the decision, and when they saw Dershowitz on *The Advocates* arguing forcefully against the death penalty, they reached out to him and asked if he would take their case. As Dershowitz reviewed the details of the case, he was appalled by the use of the felony-murder rule to convict the brothers. According to this rule, "anyone who intentionally commits a serious felony, such as breaking someone out of prison, is deemed to have 'intended' any death that results from the felony, even if he actually intended that no one should die," reports Dershowitz. "I could not turn down the request of these young men to help save them from the gas chamber."

"[This was] an opportunity to persuade the courts not to permit the commission of judicial murder on two defendants who did not deserve to die," notes Dershowitz. "I felt that if the case was to reach the U.S. Supreme Court, we would have a chance of getting the death sentences overturned."

It was not until the fall of 1980 that the Tison brothers' appeal came before the Arizona State Supreme Court. Dershowitz filed a brief in which he emphasized the importance of proportionality between a crime and its punishment. He also made sure to point out that it had been a quarter of a century since a state had executed a defendant in a murder trial who had not personally committed the murder. "I hoped that the Arizona Supreme Court would be reluctant to have its state become the first to execute a defendant under these circumstances," says Dershowitz.

Leading up to his court date in front of the Supreme Court, Dershowitz pored over the Arizona statute books in between his teaching duties at Harvard, examining dozens of death penalty cases and also studying the decisions of the judges whom he would be arguing before. On the eve of Halloween, he flew out west.

Before his court appearance, he traveled to death row to meet Ricky and Raymond, who were being housed in high-security prison in the middle of the desert in Florence, Arizona.

At the time, Ricky was twenty-one, and Raymond was just eleven months younger than his brother. "When you meet criminals individually, they almost never look like criminals are supposed to look," said Dershowitz. "Raymond and Ricky appeared to be typical small-town teenagers."

"I was expecting a stereotypical attorney in a three-piece suit to walk in," says Ricky. "But that wasn't what we got in Professor Dershowitz! He was wearing jeans and was much more of a real-life person than many lawyers you'd meet."

Upon meeting Dershowitz, Raymond whipped out documents and press clippings and began sharing their side of the story. "We told Dad, we'll do this on one condition—that no one gets hurt," said Raymond. "He was the most efficient and determined person we ever knew," chimed in Ricky. "He had a magnetic power. He could influence people without their knowing it."

Dershowitz asked the brothers if they had at any point considered separating from their father. "Near the very end," answered Raymond. "Just before the roadblock, we talked about it. It was clear that Dad was losing control. We discussed splitting up and going off separately, every man for himself. We had become a burden on Dad. He couldn't move as quickly with us as he might without us. He had to take care of us. After all, we didn't know what to do or where to go without him."

"I can still hear the shots," said Ricky, his dimples twitching. "We felt helpless and terrible. We couldn't believe something like this could happen."

"Especially the baby," Raymond interjected. "Why the baby? He couldn't have identified anyone. He probably would have died anyhow, but why did they have to shoot the baby?"

Facing the ground, Ricky said, "Some people think we should have killed our dad after the [Lyons] shootings. But I couldn't kill my own dad, no matter what he did. I couldn't put a gun to his head and pull the trigger. He was my father and I still loved him and respected him."

Dershowitz sat amazed at the level of devotion the brothers retained toward their father. "Are we going to die in here, or will you save us?" Raymond asked him as their meeting came to an end. "There are no guarantees in the law," Dershowitz replied safely, as the two young men looked earnestly into his eyes. As Dershowitz left, Ricky somberly told him, "We're counting on you. You're our only hope of ever getting out of here alive."

On that note, Dershowitz left to make final preparations for his argument. During the court hearing, Dershowitz's intensity contrasted to the quieter styles of the lawyers who preceded and followed him. He maintained a demure posture when being questioned by the judges, but made fast-moving hand motions and spoke fervently when arguing his points. He declared to the judges that Arizona law did not mandate the death penalty in this case, since the Tison brothers did not have any serious criminal records, nor did they have control over the killing of the Lyons family. The chief justice fired back, asking Dershowitz what the brothers' intent was by bringing guns during the prison breakout. "The intent was to break their father out of prison," Dershowitz replied, pointing out that this was not a capital crime in Arizona.

When the hearing ended, Dershowitz was swarmed by the press. "Why did you come all the way from Massachusetts to argue for these two boys?" asked one reporter. "Do you make it a habit to defend baby-killers?" sneered another.

After arriving home, he spent the first night tossing and turning in his bed. What scattered sleep he had was filled with nightmares of the Lyonses' infant or Ricky and Raymond being led to the gas chambers.

Over half a year passed, and in the summer of 1981, mere weeks after the shootings of Reagan and Pope John Paul II, Dershowitz received the decision of the Arizona Supreme Court. The Court had determined that even though Ricky and Raymond had not actually pulled the triggers, they had willingly aided known killers and were thus liable for the death penalty under Arizona law. The brothers' sentence was affirmed, and the two boys were to be gassed as originally ordered.

Dershowitz's only option was to appeal the case once again. He tried unsuccessfully to gain relief from several Arizona state courts, and ultimately petitioned the highest court in the country. The process of bringing a case to the Supreme Court required considerable time, and Dershowitz was forced to bide his time while Ricky and Raymond waited anxiously in prison.

* * *

When he was not teaching, litigating, or spending time with his sons, Dershowitz maintained an active social life, attending Celtics games on Saturday nights and having weekly dinners on Thursdays with his colleague Robert Nozick at a popular restaurant in Harvard Square called Harvest. After 1981, when he and Jeanne Baker amicably ended their eight-year relationship, he was "very active sexually," as a close family member reports. He dated a colleague in the ACLU, an employee at a resort in Guadalupe, and a number of women in Cambridge.

Apparently, he was not the suavest of romancers. "I helped Alan pick up some of the most beautiful women I knew when he was single," says his colleague Susan Estrich. "They would tell me that all he did was talk."

Once, he was on a date with an attractive and quite wealthy young woman. They had just about made it through the first course when the woman started railing against Israel, and Dershowitz could not take it. "Look, why don't we end this amicably?" he politely suggested, where-upon they unceremoniously parted ways.

For Dershowitz, supporting Israel was an integral part of his being. In his view, Israel was "the Jew" among the nations, and to attack Israel was, in a sense, to attack the Jewish people. "I'll never do anything that would hurt Israel," he once told Stuart Eizenstat. "I believe it's the Holy Land. I believe that the Jewish people have a God-given right to a state."

By 1982, Dershowitz was entering his seventh year as a bachelor and had gone from one date to the next. When the Combined Jewish Philanthropies of Boston invited Dershowitz to give a talk to a Jewish singles' brunch in Newton, Massachusetts, he decided to accept. "I was really there to pick up girls," Dershowitz admits.

During his talk on Israel and human rights, his eye was caught by a blond in the back, and he could not stay focused on his speech. This woman was nodding at all his arguments, and as soon as he finished, Dershowitz navigated through the crowd and walked up to the woman. "Don't I know you from somewhere?" he said rather awkwardly. When she replied in the negative, he properly introduced himself, and she then told him her name was Carolyn Cohen. "Carolyn was strikingly beauti-ful when I first saw her," says Dershowitz, who asked if she needed a ride home. Carolyn politely declined, saying that she already had a car, and the two parted ways. Alan rushed home to look up her number in a phone book.

Carolyn was smitten by Alan immediately. "I thought he was really cute," she says. After getting home from the event, she called up a girl-friend to tell her about the wonderful man she had met. When Alan found her number in the phone book and invited her out for dinner, Carolyn broke a previously scheduled date for that evening and met Alan at a Chinese restaurant in Cambridge. They hit it off. "I felt like I'd known him all my life," says Carolyn, who found Alan attractive in his poufy red hair, mustache, and glasses. "I had this overwhelming feeling when Alan was talking. I liked his sense of humor. I liked his energy. I felt like this was a guy I could settle down with."

Following their date, Carolyn was so excited that she could not fall asleep. At the time, she was working at Boston Children's Hospital as part of a PhD program in psychology, and on Monday morning, she went to work at the hospital. Partway through the day, she got a call from Alan, who asked if she wanted to go out that night instead of waiting until Saturday, as they had planned.

"Alan hunted me down," Carolyn says. "I hadn't given him my work number." Carolyn told Alan she was physically unable to go out that night because she was so exhausted from being up all night. They met on Tuesday night instead and continued to meet every night after.

Carolyn was thirteen years Alan's junior. Born in 1951 and raised in Charleston, South Carolina, Carolyn was the younger of two siblings and grew up in a non-Orthodox Jewish family. Although her father was a businessman and had conservative views on the economy, her family was liberal on social issues and supporters of Israel. Like Alan's ancestors, Carolyn's paternal grandparents had emigrated to the United States from Poland, while her maternal grandparents had escaped the rule of the tsar in Russia in the early twentieth century.

Alan and Carolyn bonded over a shared connection to their Jewish identity and heritage. "We also just had a great chemistry and were interested in similar things," says Carolyn. "We both like music and theater and were both curious people. And we got along."

Soon after meeting Carolyn, Alan called Susan Estrich and said he had found the woman he would marry. Excitedly, he told her: "She's tall, blond, blue-eyed, *and* she's Jewish!"

* * *

In April 1981, Dershowitz had been featured on the cover of *NEXT* magazine as one of the "100 Most Powerful People for the 80s."

"Full professor at Harvard Law at 28, Dershowitz, now 42, is the nation's most dedicated defender of civil liberties," read his entry. "When

Harry Reems, leading actor in 'Deep Throat,' was tried on obscenity charges, Dershowitz won his acquittal. A Jew, he battled for First Amendment rights of American Nazis. 'The fight for human rights has now fallen to the private sector,' says Dershowitz. 'I would like to build an advocacy movement, ready to take legal action to defend human rights around the world.'"

In the pages following Dershowitz's were entries for thirty-three-year-old Tennessee congressman Albert Gore, thirty-eight-year-old Senator Joe Biden, and thirty-four-year-old Manhattan developer Donald Trump, whom the magazine reported "wants to be immortal."

One year after this article was published, Danish aristocrat Claus von Bülow was convicted of murdering his wife, Sunny, in a trial that had sensationalized the nation and made the front page of *The New York Times* in early 1982. He was likely to be sentenced to thirty years in prison. At fifty-five years old, Bülow had no intention of spending the rest of his life behind bars. He sent a memo outlining the major points of his case to his friend Abe Fortas, who had filled Arthur Goldberg's vacant seat on the Supreme Court and had since left the Court to open his own law firm. Fortas, who was incidentally just days away from death, reviewed the memo from Bülow and sent it back with the following handwritten note in the margins: "There's only one appellate lawyer who can win this case for you."

When Dershowitz was contacted by Bülow and reviewed the facts of the trial, he agreed to become Bülow's appellate lawyer. "I was fascinated by the law's relationship to science," says Dershowitz. "This case promised to be a great intellectual challenge, as well as a fascinating, real-life whodunit."

The media came out swinging against Dershowitz and Bülow. One commentator declared that Bülow's selection of Dershowitz showed he was "no longer protesting his innocence, merely the methods used to catch him. Dershowitz enjoys a wide reputation as a last resort for convicted criminals, being especially keen at finding legal loopholes that render his clients' convictions unconstitutional." Citing the opinion of a leading criminal defense lawyer, *New York Magazine* predicted: "He'll add something useful and do a brilliant analysis of the record. He isn't going to make it. Of some [clients] you can say, 'That's a patient he isn't going to save. He can only make him more comfortable.'"

Family members, friends, and colleagues told Dershowitz he was making a mistake in helping Bülow.

"I love cases where everybody says I'm going to lose," says Dershowitz. And so, with the odds stacked against him and his national reputation as a lawyer on the line, Dershowitz set his sights on the salvation of his client.

PART TWO

GLORY DAYS

OUTNUMBERED

It was a sunny April day in New York City, and Dershowitz found himself on Fifth Avenue in Manhattan going to meet Claus von Bülow for the first time. Before agreeing to take the case, Dershowitz had decided to meet Bülow in person. Like many Americans, he had followed the "case of the decade" from his TV screen, and when the guilty verdict rang out, he felt that justice had been served. As Dershowitz knew well, a majority of people charged with a crime in America were, indeed, guilty.

Dershowitz knew little about the mysterious defendant, a Danish aristocrat charged with killing his wife, Sunny, by injecting her with insulin. As he walked through the maze of skyscrapers of the city, Dershowitz found his thoughts turning to his home across the East River in Brooklyn. "For my parents from Brooklyn, Fifth Avenue was a tourist attraction, a part of New York City's culture—to be viewed and appreciated, but not touched or partaken of," says Dershowitz. "Though I had passed by many of the elegant mansions along Fifth Avenue on my way to and from the museums, I had never actually been inside one."

A doorman gave him directions to Bülow's condo, and after ascending in the elevator to the correct floor, Dershowitz watched as the door opened to a magnificent home bedecked with gold and marble, tall ceilings, and open spacing.

Bülow came out to meet Dershowitz donned in clothes that seemed to have been over-tailored to appear casual on his six-foot-three frame, which loomed half a foot taller than Dershowitz's. "Professor, how nice of you to come," said Bülow in his upper-class British accent.

Bülow was born to an aristocratic Danish family and spent part of his childhood in England, where he attended the University of Cambridge and obtained a degree in law. In the early 1960s, while at a dinner party in London, he met the beautiful, blond-haired Martha "Sunny" von Auersperg, who became smitten with Bülow. Sunny was fabulously wealthy, having inherited a fortune worth hundreds of millions of dollars from her father, who had founded the Ohio Fuel Supply Company. Sunny decided to leave her husband, Prince Alfred von Auersperg, for Bülow, and they eventually married and had a daughter named Cosima.

The Bülows moved to fashionable Newport, Rhode Island, a seaside watering hole for the super rich. Sunny's two children from her first marriage, Alexander and Annie, periodically visited their mother, stepfather, and stepsister at their enormous white mansion in Newport, Clarendon Court. Unfortunately, Claus and Sunny grew apart as the years went by. Though a gracious and charming woman, Sunny thought often about death, and during the 1970s, she retreated into herself, becoming a homebody and occupying herself with menial, day-to-day affairs. In the absence of a physical relationship with Sunny, Bülow turned to other women for sex, visiting prostitutes and also starting an affair with soap opera star Alexandra Isles, who began to pressure Bülow to divorce Sunny and marry her instead. Bülow was noncommittal. If he were to divorce Sunny, he would lose access to his wife's fortune and the lavish Newport lifestyle he had become accustomed to.

It was all a perfect storm. When Sunny experienced two life-threatening comas, her children, Alexander and Annie, suspected foul play on the part of their stepfather. The first coma seized Sunny during the Christmas holidays in 1979. Her breathing became heavy, and her body went virtually limp. Bülow astonished Sunny's maid, Maria, by not calling a doctor, insisting that neither of them had slept the previous night and that Sunny had also been drinking. Eventually, though, after many hours, Sunny's breathing started to rattle, and Bülow phoned a doctor, asking him to come immediately. After receiving CPR, Sunny was rushed to the hospital, where she regained consciousness the following day.

Not long after this coma, Sunny became sick again while at her and Bülow's Fifth Avenue apartment, and after going in for tests, it was discovered that Sunny suffered from reactive hypoglycemia, which lowers one's blood sugar after the consumption of carbohydrates. It turned out that Sunny had drunk eggnog on the night before her first coma and had eaten a greasy hamburger the day before she fell ill at their Fifth Avenue apartment.

Even with this diagnosis, Sunny was not as careful with her diet as she should have been. She gained a lot of weight, and in early December 1980, she suffered from an aspirin overdose. During the Christmas holidays, while her entire family was home at Clarendon Court, she once again lapsed into a coma. This time, she never came out.

On the night of her coma, she had eaten a large ice cream sundae with caramel sauce and was carried to bed by her son, Alex. The next morning, Bülow took a stroll by the ocean, and after coming in for a late breakfast at 11:00 a.m., he told the children that he was surprised Sunny was still sleeping. Together, he and Alex went into Sunny and Claus's bedroom and found her body ice-cold and unconscious on the bathroom floor, but still breathing. Sunny was again taken to a hospital and treated for the symptoms of a deep coma. The doctors told her family and her maid, Maria, that there was no hope. She would live, yes, but in a permanent vegetative state.

Amid their grief, Alex and Annie's minds turned to dark thoughts. They had never been as close to "Uncle Claus" as their mother, and they were aware of the motives their stepfather had for killing Sunny, including his extramarital relationship with Alexandra Isles. They hired a private investigator named Richard Kuh, former DA of Manhattan, who conducted clandestine interviews with Bülow's stepchildren and Sunny's maid, Maria—all of whom shared a dislike for the rather pompous and stiff Bülow. Kuh also conducted a secret search of Clarendon Court while Bülow was away from home. He and the stepchildren raided Bülow's study and found a small, zippered black bag with some liquid, pills, and three hypodermic needles—one of which was loose. They sent the loose needle to a lab for testing. When they received a report back that the needle had been used and also contained a high level of insulin, a hormone which lowers the body's blood sugar, they decided to go public with their suspicion.

The whole story was like something right out of a mystery novel, and the trial—nationally covered on television and in the papers—became a soap opera. Although Bülow steadfastly maintained his innocence, the prosecution masterfully presented Bülow's motives and the circumstances around both of Sunny's comas to make him appear guilty as sin. The stepchildren hired expert medical doctors to give their input based on Richard Kuh's findings, and Bülow's entire circle testified against him, including Sunny's financial adviser, Maria the maid, and even the emotional Alexandra Isles, who had grown impatient waiting for Bülow to leave Sunny for her. Unfortunately for Bülow, he was unable to access the notes Richard Kuh had taken from his clandestine interviews and investigation, since the trial judge had ruled that they were protected by lawyer-client privilege.

Bülow was wildly outmatched. After the jury found him guilty, Bülow sought out an appellate lawyer who could save him from spending the rest of his life in jail.

Dershowitz was soon to become aware of all these facts. "It's nice to meet you, Mr. von Bülow," he said to Bülow upon entering his Fifth Avenue apartment. "Shall we go to lunch first?" suggested Bülow. "Then after we've gotten to know each other a bit better over a glass of wine, we can come back here and talk business."

Bülow took Dershowitz to the ritzy Carlyle Hotel, where they dined on cold poached salmon. After engaging in small talk, toward the end of the meal, Dershowitz noticed Bülow seemed to be letting down his guard and opening up. "I need the best lawyer I can get. I am absolutely innocent and my civil liberties have been egregiously violated," he said. "I need someone who will always be straight with me."

"Mr. von Bülow, I'm sorry, but I can't be both your friend and always straight with you," remarked Dershowitz. "A friend sometimes has to put up an encouraging façade. A lawyer has to be brutally honest."

In advance of their meeting, Dershowitz had sent Bülow galley proofs of a memoir he had recently completed called *The Best Defense: The Courtroom Confrontations of America's Most Outspoken Lawyer of Last Resort*.

Originally titled *The Best Defense Is the Best Offense*, the book was partly autobiography and partly a manifesto for Dershowitz's controversial legal philosophy: that guilty people sometimes getting off is the price that must be paid for a fair legal system. "Once I decide to take a case, I have only one agenda: I want to win. I will try, by every fair and legal means, to get my client off without regard to the consequences," he wrote. "The question I am most often asked—by students, lecture audiences, friends, and even my parents—is how can you defend a client when you know he is guilty of a despicable crime? . . . Almost all criminal defendants—including most of my clients—are factually guilty of the crimes they have been charged with. The criminal lawyer's job, for the most part, is to represent the guilty, and—if possible—to get them off."

Dershowitz had been asked to write the book by Robert Bernstein, head of Random House, one of the country's leading publishers. "I thought I had a different approach to defending people accused of crime than other lawyers," says Dershowitz, "and I thought it was a good thing for me to present that approach—which was to be offensive." When Dershowitz was considering whether to take Bülow's case, he wanted to ensure his prospective client understood his controversial legal philosophy. "I have several problems about retaining you," said Bülow during their first meeting. "But they're my problems, not yours."

Dershowitz inquired whether the book had made Bülow leery. "To the contrary, the book is a big plus. I like your directness and honesty," replied Bülow. Delicately, Bülow explained that some of his highbrow friends did not like the idea of him bringing on an "aggressive Jew" to defend him. "Mind you, I don't buy any of that for one minute," said Bülow. "My boss . . . is Mark Millard, a brilliant Russian Jew who is a master at finance and a true gentleman. I don't have an ounce of the anti-Semite in me."

The other issue Bülow raised was that, although he wanted Dershowitz to come on as his appellate lawyer, he felt he had to keep his trial lawyers, Herald Fahringer and John Sheehan, on the defense team as well, for the time being. "Nobody will listen to a word you say, unless you have the right people behind you," Bülow explained to Dershowitz. "It's the only way to practice law in Rhode Island." When Dershowitz brought up the obvious fact that Fahringer and Sheehan had lost the first trial, Bülow held his ground, saying, "I can't take any chances, especially not now."

The challenge of winning Bülow's appeal was too great an opportunity for Dershowitz to pass up, and he agreed to take the case. The likelihood of Dershowitz winning the case was slim to none. The prosecution had vast resources: seemingly credible witnesses, implicating motives, and lots of money. The defense had a statistic staring in its face: less than 6 percent of criminal appeals ended in victory.

Dershowitz got down to work. The first task was to file a bail application so that Bülow could remain out of prison during the appeal. "I quickly assembled my support team," says Dershowitz. "My secret weapon is that I never work alone. I always assemble my team, consisting of some junior colleagues and students. Whenever I put a team together, I always think of . . . *Mission: Impossible.*"

In a move atypical for a convicted criminal, Bülow asked Dershowitz to find a quality investigator to thoroughly examine all the evidence with no stone unturned. Meanwhile, Dershowitz called Jeanne Baker, Baker's new partner David Fine, and his colleague Susan Estrich to bring them onboard the defense team. He also recruited several bright young students of his, including young Jim Cramer, destined for fame as the host of a popular financial show on NBC.

"It was unusual for a law professor to put together such a large team," says Dershowitz. "But it was such a complicated case involving so many facets that I needed to create a team. I picked the students based on their level of interest and background (science was a priority). These students were actually interested in working on the case, rather than just making money."

Dershowitz arranged group sessions with his entire team to begin brainstorming about how to win the case. "At these sessions, we were all equals; ideas rose or fell on their own merits or demerits, not their source," he said. "When it came to writing the final brief, I would have to make the tough decisions about what to include and how to frame the argument."

In May 1982, Bülow was sentenced to thirty years in prison. The defense submitted the bail application prepared by Dershowitz and his team, and Bülow was given bail of one million dollars, which his millionaire friend J. Paul Getty Jr. covered.

"In an attempt to appear sympathetic to the thirty-year sentence, I remarked, almost automatically, how unfair the long sentence was," Dershowitz says. "[Claus] looked down sharply and rebuked me: 'A thirty-year sentence is entirely fair for a man who twice tried to murder his wife.

Anything less would be monstrous.' As I wondered what he was trying to tell me, he quickly added in an assertive voice: 'But for me any sentence would be unfair, because I never tried to harm my wife.'"

As the appeal got underway, Bülow grew tired of Herald Fahringer, who was known as a media hog, and dismissed him as chief counsel. In his place, Bülow made Dershowitz head of the defense, which now consisted of Rhode Islander John Sheehan and Dershowitz's band of young lawyers.

The 1982–1983 year became so hectic for Dershowitz that he took a sabbatical from Harvard. At the same time he was preparing Bülow's defense, he was actively working for the release of Natan Sharansky, who remained imprisoned in the Soviet Union, virtually unable to communicate with the outside world. Together with Irwin Cotler and Sharansky's steadfast wife, Avital, Dershowitz traveled around the world for meetings and rallies. Flying on the cheapest airfare possible and staying at the homes of hospitable locals, they traveled to New York City, Madrid, London, Paris, Washington, DC, and Israel. He kept a "Sharansky calendar" to keep track of all his Sharansky-related events, which included benefit concerts, luncheons at Harvard, and rallies. During one rally in New York, Dershowitz addressed a crowd of thousands jammed into Dag Hammarskjöld Plaza on 47th Street. He and Cotler also appeared on multiple TV programs and prepared a five-hundred-page legal brief to send to the Soviet authorities overseeing Sharansky's case.

"We tried our best to keep [Sharansky's] name and face in the forefront of the media," says Dershowitz. "This, we were assured, was the best life insurance we could buy on his continued health and welfare."

Dershowitz attempted to correspond with Sharansky, but his messages were never sent through. "Nonetheless, I monitored his every move from prison, to camp, to hospital, to solitary confinement," said Dershowitz. "I knew what he was being given, and not given, to eat. I followed his medical condition (he had headaches, vision problems, and chest pains) and arranged for American doctors to diagnose him on the basis of our incomplete information. . . . Occasional visits from his mother provided the most reliable updates."

"The reason I so closely [identified] with Sharansky is that there, but for the grace of God and the luck of having grandparents and great-grandparents with the foresight to leave Eastern Europe, go I," Dershowitz once explained. "If Sharansky's grandparents had come to America and mine had remained in Europe, our roles could easily have been reversed."

Working behind the scenes, Dershowitz traveled to Madrid to testify before the Helsinki Commission on Security and Cooperation in Europe, and he provided detailed reports and witness accounts to the "Ad Hoc Commission on Justice for Anatoly Sharansky" in Washington. He also aided Avital Sharansky in lobbying cabinet members and arranged a meeting with his friend, Ted Kennedy. Avital was a demure woman, but her passionate love for her husband, beautiful countenance, and ironclad spirit inspired hundreds of thousands of supporters and opened doors with prominent people. She met with Shimon Peres, French president François Mitterrand, Margaret Thatcher, and even President Reagan. After meeting with Avital and hearing of Sharansky's treatment by the Soviets, Reagan wrote in his diary: "D–n those inhuman monsters. . . . I promised I'd do everything I could to obtain his release & I will."

* * *

Inevitably, as Dershowitz struggled to fight for Jewish rights, he received a steady stream of hate mail. One "Rabbi Balfour Brickner" sent a hand-drawn picture depicting Dershowitz as a cartoon character with the words "I am a whore" coming out of his mouth. Above the cartoon figure was written: "Shyster. 'I take Nazi Van [sic] Bulows Money.'"

But his public advocacy did not always garner him hatred. In 1983, Dershowitz received another thrill when Woody Allen attended a debate Dershowitz was participating in concerning the controversial 1953 electrocution of alleged Soviet spies Julius and Ethel Rosenberg. Allen brought along his girlfriend, Mia Farrow, and after the speech, they visited Dershowitz backstage and debated his argument that Julius Rosenberg had truly been a spy for the Soviets, despite theories to the contrary. Dershowitz remained in touch with Allen and Farrow, and occasionally, Farrow called Dershowitz to chat about political goings-on.

At this same time, Arthur Goldberg formed a committee consisting of many of Dershowitz's family and friends—including Woody

Allen, Dershowitz's brother Nathan, his colleague Larry Tribe, Telford Taylor, Jeanne Baker, Susan Estrich, Aharon Barak, Stuart Eizenstat, Ted Kennedy, and Elie Wiesel—to arrange a ceremony to honor Dershowitz's achievements.

At a fancy dinner in Boston, with Carolyn and Dershowitz's relatives looking on proudly, the Anti-Defamation League presented Dershowitz with its prestigious First Amendment Freedom Award. Dershowitz's friend Elie Wiesel delivered the keynote speech. "When Alan Dershowitz is fighting anti-Semitism, he is also fighting for human rights everywhere," Wiesel told the gathered audience. "If there had been a few people like Alan Dershowitz during the 1930s and 1940s, the history of European Jewry might have been different."

As he advocated on behalf of Sharansky, Dershowitz was in the fight of his life trying to defeat the government's case against Bülow. The appellate hearing in front of the Rhode Island Supreme Court was coming up, and Dershowitz's team was tasked with writing a brief that would be submitted to the Court.

"After they have been convicted, defendants on appeal are presumed guilty," noted Dershowitz. "And this presumption is much harder to overcome than the pretrial presumption of innocence—because it is even more firmly grounded in reality. . . . I am a firm believer in interjecting claims of innocence into any appeal where appropriate. The trick is to try to find legal issues in the case that implicitly make the claim of innocence for the defendant."

Dershowitz developed a hunch that investigator Richard Kuh's notes contained incriminating material against the prosecution. His interviews and searches were conducted with distraught people, and beyond this, Dershowitz understood well from years of experience that people's memories of minute details often get mixed and blurred in times of great emotion. Attempting an aboveboard approach first, Dershowitz wrote a cordial letter to Kuh asking to obtain his notes. "Dear Alan," replied Kuh, "your superlative academic credentials are such that you, of all persons, know that privileges and other exclusionary concepts may on occasion keep highly relevant information from the eyes of those not privy to the privilege. . . . Happily, that is not here the case. I am satisfied that there is not a scrap of paper in my files that might even arguably be viewed as exculpatory."

Not dissuaded, Dershowitz and his team filed a motion to the Rhode Island Supreme Court asking the justices to instruct Kuh to hand in his notes. When the Court declined the motion, Dershowitz was forced to turn to a multi-pronged attack instead (he would not learn until the end of the case that Kuh's notes did, in fact, contain damaging information concerning the prosecution's side of the first trial).

Luckily for the defense, incriminating details about Bülow's family began to surface just when they were most needed. Dershowitz discovered that the celebrated author Truman Capote had given an interview to *People* magazine in which he had discussed his friendship with Sunny von Bülow. He contacted Capote and arranged a meeting in New York. It turned out that Capote had known Sunny for thirty years. While she was a charming woman and a good friend, Capote told Dershowitz she had a decades-long drug addiction. In his high-pitched voice, he described one episode that occurred while he was writing *Breakfast at Tiffany's*. During a lunch with Sunny, they were both discussing their individual weight and health problems, and Capote told Sunny that regular visits to a doctor to receive mood drugs were distracting him from writing. Sunny told Capote that he should inject himself instead of going to a doctor.

"It's the simplest thing in the world," said Sunny. "Once you do it, there's nothing to it at all." She proceeded to show Capote a small, zippered black bag with hypodermic needles inside that she used for self-injections.

Another seemingly lucky break fell in the defense's lap when an anonymous man called Dershowitz and asked if he would like information about his stepson's drug use. Dershowitz decided to follow the lead and arranged a meeting with the man, who told him that Dershowitz could come to his home as long as he was alone and possessed no recording devices. "I had no desire to meet alone with a drug dealer," says Dershowitz. "But those were his conditions and I had little choice but to accept."

On the night Dershowitz went to the man's house, he had an armed private investigator wait in the car outside with instructions to enter the house if Dershowitz was not out within an hour.

The man turned out to be a tall, handsome young man in jeans. His name was David Marriott, and it quickly became obvious that he was a homosexual drug dealer. "There's somebody on the North Shore I talked to," Marriott told Dershowitz. "He's a politician and a lawyer. He said it would be all right to talk to you, but only for the purpose of giving you some leads. I'm not going to testify or anything like that." Moving his finger across his throat, Marriott said, "I could get my throat slit or my head blown off. What I have involves some people pretty high in the drug business." He proceeded to tell Dershowitz about his relationship with a pimp and drug dealer named Gilbert Jackson. Marriott and Jackson had often traveled to fashionable Newport, and while there, Jackson had become smitten with Sunny's handsome son, Alex. According to David, Jackson began delivering presents (drugs) to Alex. Once, Marriott had seen a large quantity of drugs in Alex's possession and remarked that it was "an awful lot for one person."

"Oh, I give some to my mom to keep her off my back," replied Alex.

Marriott went on to tell Dershowitz that Gilbert Jackson was eventually found murdered by his associates in the drug ring. All of these details were sad and juicy, but Dershowitz knew that the justices would find Marriott and his account highly suspect. "His motive to come forward, at so great a risk to himself, simply to help a wealthy man in trouble, would raise the suspicion of a payoff," said Dershowitz. With help from his team and his son Jamin, who set about investigating archives of local newspapers, Dershowitz began digging up information to corroborate Marriott's accounts about Jackson. At one point, the defense received yet another anonymous phone call. Without introducing himself, the caller told Dershowitz, "I hear you're interested in Gilbert Jackson." In a devious tone, he asked Dershowitz, "Do you know what a keg of dynamite you're playing with?

"Let me caution you, because I respect you as a lawyer, that Jackson was only a small fish, a front for a much bigger, and much tougher, organization," the caller continued. "And he wasn't the only one killed." When Dershowitz asked him to elaborate, the caller said that he would do so— but only in person. "I asked if I could bring my student research assistants along to take notes," says Dershowitz. "I made this request as much out of fear as out of the need for note-takers."

One of the research assistants Dershowitz brought along to this frightening meeting was twenty-three-year-old Eliot Spitzer. Born and raised in the Bronx, Eliot attended both Princeton and Harvard. "[Eliot] was the quiet one, the behind-the-scenes guy, the library guy," says Dershowitz, who picked Spitzer as his research assistant and invited him to join the defense team for Bülow.

Together with Spitzer and Spitzer's fellow research assistant Cliff Sloan, Dershowitz traveled to the arranged meeting location one afternoon. The three lawyers were shocked when they found themselves inside a gay bathhouse that catered to the rich and intellectual. After passing through the musty hallways, they made it to an office where a thirtysomething man introduced himself as the man who had called. He asked to remain anonymous in the case dealings.

"How did you know we were interested in Jackson?" Dershowitz inquired. "I work with cops, and you were snooping around the Jackson police files," the man replied. "There aren't many secrets between me and my police friends." Dershowitz wanted to know why this man had agreed to help Bülow's defense. "Lots of reasons. Maybe if I help you, you'll feel indebted to help me if I ever need you." Dershowitz immediately interrupted and said, "Look, you have to understand, that's not the way I play the game. I don't want to feel indebted to you. If you have any information you want to give me, fine, but don't expect anything in return." The man relayed his information about Gilbert Jackson and his circle—nasty tales of murders, molestations, and drug cover-ups. Specific details related to Gilbert Jackson were consistent with accounts Dershowitz had heard from David Marriott.

Soon after this bathhouse meeting, David Marriott began receiving death threats and was physically assaulted. Unfortunately for the defense, he turned out to be something of a liar and a press-hungry narcissist, and Dershowitz was unable to rely on his testimony. "Nor could I count on Truman Capote," says Dershowitz. "The idea of putting on a case consisting primarily of a man who would admit carrying drugs for a gay interior decorator, an author with his own drug problems, and the operator of a bathhouse would not bring joy to the heart of any lawyer."

And so, Dershowitz and his team went after the scientific and medical elements of the case. They compiled all the evidence regarding the insulin-encrusted needle as outlined at Bülow's trial, and they sent it to some of the world's most renowned forensic experts. Each and every one of them gave a variation of the following statement: "The needle alleged by the State of Rhode Island to have been injected into [Sunny] von Bülow was not, and could not have been, injected."

Dershowitz got chills when he realized the implication of this statement: if the needle had not been injected into Sunny's body, the only way it could have been encrusted with solution is if it had been dipped into a solution. After consulting the chief medical examiner for New York City and a chief toxicologist in the state, Dershowitz's hunch was corroborated. They declared that the outside of the needle's tip was "inconsistent with injection," and that the only possible reason why solution existed on the needle's tip—rather than further up on the needle's shaft—was that the needle had been "dipped into solution."

In addition to this finding, Dershowitz and his team also investigated the claims that Sunny had been injected with insulin. "The only scientific evidence of insulin had come from a test conducted by a laboratory called BioScience, an internationally used and highly reputable testing service," says Dershowitz. He and his team sent the data from BioScience for lab testing and review by prestigious scientists who specialized in insulin readings. The feedback was momentous: the BioScience reading of insulin had been false. The needle washings they had tested contained amobarbital and Valium, which together produce a false positive for insulin when the needle was dipped into a saline solution.

After all this evidence was gathered, Dershowitz's team worked feverishly to compile the brief for the Rhode Island Supreme Court. "We decided to convert my house into a combination law office, dormitory and restaurant," said Dershowitz. "There were so many teams working, and so many issues to be covered, that I wanted everybody under one roof during the final writing phase." He divided his students and friends helping on the case into several different teams, like the black bag team, self-injection versus other-person-injection team, the needle team, the private search team, among others. Elon and Jamin were off at college for most of the year, and the house filled to overflowing with a constant buzz of activity. "The house was crazy noisy, my god," says Dana Cernea, who was staying at Camp Dersh for a time while she finished her medical degree. "People were working around the clock—thumbing through law books, making calls, and even falling asleep in the corners of rooms."

The tasks of food and beverage delivery were shared between the team members, so that someone was always brewing coffee, making bagels for breakfast, or ordering take-out Chinese food for dinner. The teams relieved their stress on the basketball court and at the ping-pong table. "It was like a huge legal frat house," says Cernea. "It was a constant, controlled, creative chaos. Alan was always running around in casual clothes, encouraging the teams. He would be teaching on-the-go during the whole process, helping the students dissect the case, versus just learning by rote from a textbook."

Eliot Spitzer somewhat jokingly remarked that Dershowitz was a "terrible" boss. "He would call at 10:00 p.m. and say he needed a document the next morning," he describes. "But then he'd give us Celtics tickets as recompense, which was nice.

"Alan was rigorous," he continues. "He was brilliant. He was creative. The case was great fun, and it was challenging—I thought it was winnable, but nobody was betting our way."

As the brief was being compiled, Dershowitz had to sift through the numerous legal arguments his team had crafted and decide which components would be included in the final document. "The most difficult job was deciding which arguments to omit," he says. "That's the kind of decision that really keeps you up at night."

One of the arguments that Jeanne Baker and Susan Estrich were jointly working on was a technical, constitutional point. Richard Kuh had sent the findings from his clandestine search of Claus's home to the police, who had submitted articles for lab testing without a warrant. Baker and Estrich argued this had violated the "search and seizure" clause of the Fourth Amendment as interpreted by a recent Supreme Court decision titled *United States v. Chadwick*, which forbade a warrantless search of luggage.

Bülow initially wanted to forgo this argument and stick with ones that would show his factual innocence, but Baker was convinced it was an "absolutely solid argument," as she says. She insisted to Dershowitz that they keep it in, and it ultimately was.

Dershowitz kept in regular contact with Bülow by phone and letters, providing updates and asking for his client's opinion on aspects of the defense. Dershowitz and his team completed the brief and delivered it to the courthouse in Providence mere minutes before it was due on March 15, 1983.

Since the brief was made public, the press was able to pore over the thrilling new details revealed inside. "QUESTIONS ARE RAISED ABOUT NEW EVIDENCE IN VON BÜLOW CASE" read one headline.

The media and its consumers eagerly followed the case. From the Agatha Christie–like plot to the physically attractive cast of characters involved, it became known as "the case of the decade." At various points, Bülow or his stepchildren graced the covers of *People*, *New York Magazine*, and *Vanity Fair*. Updates about the case were circulated in tabloids and newspapers around the United States from the *Los Angeles Times* to the *New York Post*. Significantly, the mid-1980s represented the peak of newspaper use in America, with nearly sixty-five million newspapers in daily circulation. Articles highlighting Dershowitz's role in the case appeared in the *Evening Bulletin*, *USA Today*, and the *New York Times*. "Alan Dershowitz for the defense: Once Harvard Law's youngest professor, he loves to fight people in power" read one headline.

"Alan would do interviews whenever anybody asked," says Susan Estrich. "What he taught me was that in a high-profile case, it wasn't enough just to get the best brief or just to write the best grades. If you weren't out there fighting for your client in every arena that you could and changing the atmosphere around your client, you weren't doing your full job as a lawyer."

Amid all the hubbub, Dershowitz remained pragmatic. "I thought we were probably going to lose," he admits. "The odds of winning were less than 10 percent. I was anticipating a loss before the Rhode Island Supreme Court and was always prepared for the next step."

Months passed as the case proceedings dragged on, and in October 1983, Dershowitz traveled to Newport to deliver the most important oral argument of his life. In preparation, he had read his proposed argument in front of a moot court consisting of friends—including John Kerry—and students, who carefully critiqued Dershowitz's points and delivery style.

The oral argument was held on October 17, as press and attendees filled the courtroom. Dershowitz had traveled with Susan Estrich and a former student named Sandor Frankel, now a lawyer in his own right whom Dershowitz had consulted on various aspects of the case. Bülow himself stayed away from the courtroom and planned to watch Dershowitz's argument from a TV in his hotel.

As Dershowitz rose to deliver his argument inside the mahogany-walled courthouse, the courtroom was quiet, and Dershowitz found himself alone at the lectern before five robed justices staring down at him. "There was a lot of cynicism and skepticism about Claus and his high-priced, media-hungry lawyers," says Estrich, who sat near Dershowitz's side at the defense table.

Dershowitz's argument was being broadcast live on stations throughout the Northeast. As he stood in front of the cameras at the lectern with his thick hair, large oval glasses, and small mustache, he methodically and fervently made his case. As he touched on each grievance toward his client, his hand motions grew more vigorous, his speech more pronounced, and his energy level more fiery. When the justices interrupted him with questions, he was quick on his feet and answered articulately, drawing on his vast knowledge of the case and of legal history.

In a hypothetical reminiscent of his classes at Harvard, Dershowitz said to the justices: "Imagine a case where a woman with reactive hypoglycemia deliberately sets out to commit suicide. So she swallows one hundred barbiturates and decides as her last meal she was going to have an ice-cream sundae. What would happen in that case is that the ice-cream sundae would knock down her blood sugar. The barbiturates would put her in a coma. She would be in a coma. She would have low blood sugar. The barbiturates would have caused her coma. The ice cream would have caused her low blood sugar."

The chief justice, John Kelleher, evidently wanted to show up this out-of-town lawyer. He took Dershowitz to task for discussing the facts of Bülow's case, which were supposed to have already been covered at trial. Dershowitz stuck to this line of argument, though, and while in the middle of discussing Richard Kuh's clandestine investigation, Kelleher suddenly interrupted, raising his finger and saying loudly: "Don't talk to me like that!"

The courtroom became silent. Watching from his hotel room, Bülow felt his heart sink into his stomach.

"Your Honor, I'm not meaning any disrespect," Dershowitz said demurely with a smile, trying to recover.

"I'm sorry. I—okay," Kelleher began and then ended awkwardly. Meanwhile, the other justices glanced at each other and then stared down at their notes.

"I'm not meaning any disrespect and I apologize," reiterated Dershowitz. "That's simply my style of argument—I was simply trying to engage the court as the court was trying to engage me."

"You know, argue it any way you want," said Kelleher in an annoyed tone. "You've got a half an hour, you've been on this twenty minutes."

"I intend to continue on this point, you Honor," replied Dershowitz calmly, but firmly.

Having watched it all unfold, Sandor Frankel noted that Kelleher's words came "out of left field—out of the left field bleachers! Alan skillfully parried the comment, though."

Dershowitz managed to recover from this setback and declared near the end of his time: "We are talking about a case here which has been very, very short on hard facts, very, very tall on long inferences, and very wide in the gaps created both by what remains in the prosecutor's files and what was destroyed during the course of the private search. . . . And the Fourth Amendment and the rules of Rhode Island provide . . . for making sure that the proper procedures of neutrality are carried forward in the search itself."

Dershowitz sat down back down at the defense table, and when the prosecutor, Stephen Famiglietti, rose and declared that he was not "prepared to stand here and argue the guilt of Mr. von Bülow," Dershowitz felt pleased with the job he had done. He had clearly made the case for Bülow's innocence, instead of merely arguing a technicality like the press had predicted he would several months previously.

"The tone had been set and the court continued to question Famiglietti about the facts," says Dershowitz. "It was obvious that at least several of them were concerned that a possibly innocent man had been convicted. . . . Famiglietti went on for nearly an hour, but he was plainly on the defensive both legally and factually."

When Famiglietti was finished, the justices asked Dershowitz if the defense had any final comments. As Dershowitz started to stand up, he felt Susan Estrich tugging on his gray striped suit. "I know how difficult it is for you to keep quiet, but if there ever was a good time, this is it," she whispered. As she pulled him back down into his seat, Dershowitz looked at the justices and said simply, "Unless the court has any questions, we will rest."

Months passed as the justices deliberated. During this time, Dershowitz's girlfriend, Carolyn Cohen, was a great source of support. While Camp Dersh was packed with his team of lawyers, Alan and Carolyn lived separately, but they slowly hunted for an apartment they could share once Alan's work on the case died down.

Carolyn had a warm, motherly personality. Although they had an occasional scuffle (Carolyn found Alan to be an extremely messy person), they formed a steady relationship. "It was a fantastic dating relationship," says Dershowitz. "I was so happy I had met someone who was kind and Jewish and who had a good family. Even though she came off as a sweet Southerner, she was as tough as anybody from Brooklyn if she needed to be."

Carolyn helped Alan learn to relax more often. Instead of working seven days a week, she urged him to slow down over the weekends. Together they went to plays and basketball games, and they took walks and bicycle rides. In December 1983, while still awaiting news of the justices' decision, they took a vacation to the Caribbean and then flew right to Massachusetts for Alan's annual New Year's Eve get-together with his "Big 8" friends from childhood. "I liked them all immediately," says Carolyn, who had first met them the year before. "She was easy to get to know and instantly became one of the group," says Carl Meshenberg.

During these get-togethers, conversation between the Big 8 and their wives flowed just as easily as it had in decades past. But on this New Year's Eve in 1983, tragedy struck. As they were eating and laughing, Alan received a telephone call from his son Jamin, who told him Sue Barlach was missing.

Alan immediately left the get-together and traveled to New York, where Sue had last been living and where Jamin would periodically visit her. Sue had occasionally called Alan for financial and legal advice, and he knew she was struggling psychologically. "Avi was very concerned," says Meshenberg. "He was very stressed when he got the news."

Jamin put out a police report for Sue, and soon after, a body was discovered in the East River, which Jamin identified as his mother.

Alan's sons were distraught, and he stayed close to them for a time. Whether Sue deliberately killed herself or not was never clearly determined.

"I just don't know whether she ever made the decision to be or not to be," says Dershowitz. "It's possible that she walked towards the river and just didn't stop. I didn't know her well at that time, but it was terrible because she drifted into paranoia and schizophrenia."

Alan felt honor-bound to attend Sue's funeral, but stood off to the side out of respect for her relatives.

"I think as Sue got older, she felt we were friendlier with Avi than her," comments Joan Meshenberg, Carl's wife. "She thought we were taking sides, although many girls in the group were calling her and trying to keep her part of everything. I think her perception was that she was an outsider. We were all shocked by her death. I think that she probably had anger and resentment, but there was no way of knowing what pushed her over."

"Sue was really quite a smart woman, and she was pretty," says her friend Judy Beck. "I thought she did a wonderful thing by going back to school and becoming a librarian. She went to Rutgers to obtain a degree in library science. But I think that the loss of status as Alan's wife was very difficult. We had conversations, as well, about his relationship with Carolyn. She thought Carolyn was a good person, but I think the idea of Alan potentially getting remarried was very hard for her.

"She never got over her divorce. That was something she could never, never get over. I think that pretty much destroyed her."

Carolyn did what she could to help comfort Alan's family. "Alan's reaction to the whole situation was centered around his kids," she says. "I mean, he just wanted to make sure they were okay." For a time, Alan thought that Jamin, who had identified Sue's body, might drop out of college from grief, but he made his mother proud by sticking to it and ultimately finishing near the top of his class at Yale Law School.

As though his family had not endured enough grief, in the spring of 1984, Harry Dershowitz finally succumbed to Alzheimer's. Alan and his brother Nathan traveled to Borough Park to be with their mother, and per Orthodox custom, they sat *shiva*, a seven-day period of mourning. As friends and relatives stopped by their home on 48th Street, Alan, Nathan, and Claire sat on the floor to symbolize how far they had fallen because of their great loss. As they were in the middle of *shiva*, on April 27, Alan received startling news from the staff in his office back at Harvard. The justices had at last come to a decision in Bülow's case. The defense had won the appeal.

Alan began receiving calls from the press off the hook. "Typically, one is supposed to remain separate from the outside world during *shiva*," said Alan's uncle Zecharia, who had traveled from Israel to mourn the loss of his older brother. "But Alan felt it was extremely important to explain to the press why he had won the appeal."

As Dershowitz drove the half hour to Bülow's condominium on Fifth Avenue, he entered a whole different world of cameras and mics and reporters shouting: "When will Claus be down?" "Can we come up with you?" and "What is Claus going to do now?"

"No comment until I see, or hear, the opinion," Dershowitz said as he strode through the gaggle and rode the elevator up to Bülow's condo. Bülow was on the phone listening to the justices' opinion being read off by Terry MacFayden, one of the lawyers on Bülow's defense team. Bülow signaled to Dershowitz to pick up another receiver. "Bottom line, what did they do?" Dershowitz interrupted MacFayden, who told Dershowitz that they had totally reversed the conviction. It turned out that the primary grounds for the justices' decision was the Fourth Amendment argument drafted by Baker and Estrich—the argument Bülow had initially wanted to drop.

The decision made the front page of *The New York Times*. Next to a headshot of Bülow, a headline declared: "VON BÜLOW'S 2 CONVICTIONS VOIDED ON APPEAL." "The private laboratory tests conducted from the needles and drugs discovered in a black bag found in the closet were admissible, the court ruled," the article read. "But when those objects passed into the hands of the public authorities in Rhode Island, the justices wrote, the search warrant was required under both the United States Constitution and the Declaration of Rights in the Rhode Island Constitution."

"Professor Dershowitz applauded the court's ruling against such activity," reported the article, who quoted him as saying: "'Police work has to be left to the police. . . . The big lesson is that you can't have it both ways. You can't try to circumvent constitutional constraints by having private investigators do the work for you.'"

"We won the appeal on a technical ground," states Susan Estrich, "but the significance of telling the facts of the whole story was to give the justices some comfort that they weren't letting off a guilty man. Alan used to talk with me about the facts because it was his view that if you don't grab the justices by the facts—and at least introduce a reasonable doubt in their mind—they won't be open to your legal argument. So as important as our technical legal argument was, equally important was telling the facts and the story in a way that gave rise to at least reasonable doubt as to whether Claus was guilty."

"Alan deserves the credit for the victory because he was the mastermind of the whole appeal," Jeanne Baker notes. "And although the particular argument that Susan and I wrote is what the Rhode Island Supreme Court hung its reversal on, if Alan had not orchestrated the entire appeal, there's no way that argument would have even gotten to the Court."

"My dad is the ultimate creative thinker," says his son Elon. "For example, he doesn't know higher math, but he figures out the concepts behind it. He's a genius at doing an analysis of trial transcripts. I've heard him look at a transcript and say, 'But I don't understand, why didn't they say such-and-such?' Dad has a unique ability to come up with creative ideas and turn a situation on its head."

The Claus von Bülow saga dragged on for one final year, as the government—granted a retrial by the Rhode Island Supreme Court—sought to put Bülow behind bars. Bülow found himself opposed by his stepchildren, Sunny's maid Maria, and his former lover, Alexandra Isles, who all lined up to testify against him. Besides Dershowitz and his other lawyers, Bülow's main supporters were his outspoken, fiercely loyal new girlfriend, Andrea Reynolds, and his daughter by Sunny, Cosima, who steadfastly stood by her father's side even when her maternal grandmother disinherited Cosima from any portion of her $100 million estate. To help his daughter, Bülow renounced his claims to any of Sunny's fortune in exchange for Cosima receiving a portion of her grandmother's estate.

Dershowitz took a back seat during the second trial, surrendering leadership of the defense to former prosecutor Thomas Puccio, an acquaintance of Dershowitz's who had grown up in an Italian neighborhood in Borough Park. "A trial lawyer would miss classes, and I don't miss classes," explained Dershowitz to *The Harvard Crimson*. Puccio dismantled the government's original case and the testimony of its chief witnesses. He was greatly assisted by the multitude of information dug up by Dershowitz and his team, along with the notes from Richard Kuh's clandestine investigation, which had at last been released. Just as Dershowitz had suspected at the beginning of the case, they revealed fundamental contradictions between the original testimonies that witnesses privately gave to Kuh and the memories they recounted in public at the first trial.

When on June 10, 1985, the jury announced a verdict of "Not Guilty," cheers rang up from many of the court attendees, Bülow's head dropped with relief, and Dershowitz leaned over to his client and whispered, "Congratulations. Now the world knows you are an innocent man."

Indeed, the world knew. Beyond filling the papers and TVs of the United States, Bülow's case had been covered throughout Europe, including in England and Germany, where the aristocratic Bülow family was well known.

In an interview on NBC following the verdict, Bülow made special reference to Dershowitz, stating in his upper-class British accent that "without [Alan] there wouldn't have been a case."

The case brought Dershowitz into the national spotlight. *The New Yorker* published a cartoon poking fun at his frequent commentating on legal issues, but *The Boston Herald* focused on his brilliance by including a cartoon of Alice in Wonderland receiving death threats from the Queen of Hearts and dialing a friend to say, "Quick—Get Me Von Bülow's Lawyer!"

Newsday ran a feature article on Dershowitz titled "The Lawyer of Last Resort" and placed a full-body picture of him on the cover. In addition to highlighting his major cases from Harry Reems to Sharansky and the Tison brothers, the article included personal details about Dershowitz's life and his new girlfriend, along with input from his friends. One revealing comment from Harvey Silverglate stood out. "Underneath it all, Alan is very insecure," he told *Newsday*. "He worries an awful lot about what people think of him."

The case brought Dershowitz a whopping $100,000 in legal fees. Compared to his annual salary from Harvard of $90,000, it was a windfall, but Dershowitz only kept a portion of it. The rest he divided up between his fellow lawyers and research assistants who had worked on the case, paying them out of his own pocket rather than having Bülow make numerous separate payments.

That was not the only windfall from the case. Impressed by Dershowitz's readable, polished writing style in *The Best Defense*, Robert Bernstein of Random House offered Dershowitz a $100,000 advance to write a book about the case. Dershowitz rented a house with Carolyn in the quiet, beautiful neighborhood of Chilmark on Martha's Vineyard while he wrote a memoir of the case using a pen and his beloved yellow legal pad.

"Although our legal system proudly proclaims its commitment to this principle of super-certainty, many Americans have difficulty understanding why we go so far in resolving doubts in favor of those accused of crimes," he wrote in the book's conclusion. "What about the victims? Wouldn't it be better for a few innocent defendants to go to jail so that some innocent victims might be saved from suffering?

"But history teaches that countries that trample the rights of those accused of crime tend also to ignore the rights of persons victimized by crime; and that countries that respect the rights of the accused also promote the rights of victims. The manner in which a government treats all of its citizens—whether victims of injustice or victims of crime—is what distinguishes democratic nations from repressive ones."

Once he finished writing, Dershowitz sent his yellow pages over to his assistant, Maura Kelley, who had the somewhat challenging task of deciphering Dershowitz's handwriting and typing the manuscript. "Personally, Alan was very shy," Maura recounts. "When he was working at Harvard, he would come out to my desk and, with his fingers together, gently ask if I could please take care of something. But that's Alan as a person. As a lawyer, he's a barracuda."

Dershowitz's book on the Bülow case was eventually published as *Reversal of Fortune*. During an interview on NBC following the book's release, Dershowitz was his usual red-haired, bespectacled self, but rather than being feisty and belligerent, he had an air of self-satisfaction. "You are by all accounts a brilliant attorney," began reporter Bryant Gumbel. "What did you do that was so brilliant the second time that wasn't done the first?" "It was all hard work," answered Dershowitz with a smile. "I had my secret weapon: my eighteen students scurrying around all over—the Harvard Medical School, the town of Newport—finding every possible piece of evidence that was simply not uncovered at the first trial, and I think we just persuaded the court by overwhelming evidence that Claus von Bülow didn't do it."

"You have your own theories about who did it?" inquired Gumbel. "I have my own theories," said Dershowitz. "And they include?" asked Gumbel. "They include the possibility that his children honestly believed that he did it, but also believed that they couldn't convict him of it," replied Dershowitz. "And so, they may have remembered certain things and forgotten certain things and made it easier for him to be convicted the first time around."

Larry King invited Dershowitz on his radio show, and as they discussed the case, Dershowitz curiously failed to give credit for the victory to his entire team, stating simply: "I argued and worked very hard on a brief" and "I prepared almost all the evidence for the second trial."

In addition to questions about the case, they discussed Dershowitz's negative views of judges throughout America. "I look beneath their robes," Dershowitz said, referring to what he saw as the corrupt, selfish ambitions of many judges, who were seeking promotions. "It's very hard for me to utter the words 'Your Honor, may it please the court.' I had that trouble with rabbis when I was a kid, too. It's an authority problem."

Larry took calls, and some of the callers were Democrats eager to get Dershowitz's take on recent decisions by President Reagan. When asked about Reagan's Supreme Court nominee, Antonin Scalia, Dershowitz replied facetiously that Scalia was one of the great minds "of the eighteenth century," referring to Scalia's "originalist" legal philosophy.

At another point, Dershowitz touched on his relationship with perhaps America's most despised attorney of the day: Roy Cohn. Dershowitz noted that he "fundamentally" disagreed with "all" of Cohn's politics, but that he believed recent attempts to disbar him were politically motivated and wrong. "I am just as offended if a conservative is politically attacked because of his politics as if a liberal is politically attacked," Dershowitz told listeners.

Roy Cohn burst onto the national scene when he successfully prosecuted Julius and Ethel Rosenberg in 1953, and soon after, he served as chief counsel to Joseph McCarthy during the notorious communist hearings. Over the coming decades, Cohn became a prominent power broker in New York and served as a personal attorney to Donald Trump, as well as Mafia bosses. Cohn supported many Republican officials and maintained ties to prominent conservatives from William Buckley all the way to Reagan.

Dershowitz and Cohn had met during the Bülow case, during which Cohn served as counsel to Bülow's daughter Cosima. Twice they engaged in public debates, the first in 1982 in New York. "Mr. Right vs. Prof. Left," summarized an article in *The National Law Journal*. Although the article highlighted the difference in their political philosophies, it also reported a telling quote from Cohn. "[Alan and I are] both iconoclasts, we've both spoken out against the system," Cohn had told the audience. "We both dislike the establishment."

Three years later, they met once again during a debate on CBS over freedom of the press. Dershowitz advocated total freedom for the press and vehemently argued against bringing lawsuits even when outrageous statements are published, while Cohn demanded the press be held legally accountable when they reported damning information without proper research.

Dershowitz was asked to comment on a recent suit brought by Jerry Falwell against *Hustler* magazine for supposedly inflicting "emotional damage" on the reverend. In a mocking reply, Dershowitz called it a "terrible" lawsuit. "Under the First Amendment is the right to inflict emotional damage on people," he said. "When I write an article critical of President Reagan, I *want* to inflict emotional damage on him. I want to make sure he sits there and says, 'Oh my God, they're discovering what I'm really doing with the Star Wars phenomenon.' If people who don't have thick enough skins to be able to tolerate the infliction of emotional damage on them when we tell the truth about them, as Harry Truman once said, 'They ought to get out of the kitchen and out of the White House.' And I'm hoping we can get him out of the White House."

"I must say," interjected Cohn, "in his crusade against President Reagan, as he's outlined, [Alan] did a great job in Minnesota and the District of Columbia," referencing Reagan's landslide in the 1984 election. With a smile, Dershowitz good-naturedly replied, "Next time we're gonna get three or four more, you'll see."

Despite their substantial disagreements, Dershowitz and Cohn had a friendly personal relationship. One of Dershowitz's public outings with Carolyn was at a party Cohn invited them to at the Studio 54 nightclub. "Roy was very smart, very quick, and very loyal," says Dershowitz. "If you were his friend, he would do anything for you. If you were his enemy, he would do anything to get you." Although he did not meet Donald Trump through Cohn, he was aware of their relationship and the similarities in their philosophies: never surrender and take fights to your enemy.

Cohn's ties to Joe McCarthy and his belligerent legal mindset made him a host of enemies. In 1986, he was disbarred in a unanimous decision by a New York appellate court for "attempting to defraud a dying client by forcing the client to sign a will amendment leaving him his fortune," as the *New York Times* reported. *USA Today* reported the disbarment and referenced Dershowitz. "Alan Dershowitz said the charges were unfair, out of date and shouldn't be pressed against a terminally ill man. Dershowitz Monday called the disbarment 'belated revenge for Cohn's actions during the McCarthy period. It's a political act.'"

Compounding his already controversial life, Cohn was terminally ill with AIDS, a fact he tried to conceal from a 1980s public that was none too welcoming to homosexuals. Just over a month after being disbarred, Cohn succumbed to the disease, leaving a legacy of controversy behind.

The response to the AIDS crisis was just one issue Dershowitz had with America's reigning conservative government. He saw the gay community as a persecuted minority. "My private preference [runs] against homosexuality, but I have no religious or moralistic views about the subject, any more than I do on other matters of taste and lifestyle among consenting adults," he once wrote. Around the time of Cohn's death, Chief Justice

Warren Burger wrote an opinion in favor of a Georgia law condemning homosexual acts between consenting adults, writing that "sodomy" was "of deeper malignity than rape."

Soon after, Dershowitz spoke on Soviet Jewry at a gathering of the American Bar Association at the Hilton Hotel in New York, and partway through the event, Burger arrived as a surprise guest speaker. Dershowitz refused to share a table with him, and when Burger was introduced at the podium, Dershowitz got up and silently exited the hall. Outside was a group of gay rights activists protesting Burger's appearance, and Dershowitz made a stump speech in support of their protests and gave a few comments to the press. Somehow, his mother saw Dershowitz's comments in the paper and called him to say: "Now I know why you got divorced. We'll get you the best medical attention."

Dershowitz fought against the Reagan administration in a variety of ways. Together with his colleague Larry Tribe, he publicly opposed Reagan's Supreme Court nominee Robert Bork, who was ultimately blocked by a Joe Biden–led Senate Judiciary Committee.

Dershowitz used his weekly syndicated column to attack Reagan's conservative decisions on abortion, Supreme Court nominees, the AIDS crisis, the death penalty, and the relationship between church and state. Despite his vehement opposition to Reagan's policies, Dershowitz opposed calls from certain liberals to impeach Reagan during the Iran-Contra affair. "[1988] is just around the corner and the presidential campaign has already begun," he wrote in a 1986 article. "Those who invoke the cumbersome and extraordinary process of impeachment and removal should, instead, focus their energies on the ordinary political process. It really does work. Impeachment and removal are important parts of our constitutional self-defense system. However, they should generally remain behind a window with a sign that reads, 'Break glass only in case of constitutional emergency.'"

It was at the height of the Reagan Revolution that Dershowitz taught three students who would one day have significant influence on the liberal side of the political aisle. A descendant of Jewish immigrants from Russia, Jamin "Jamie" Raskin was a Phi Beta Kappa student at Harvard College before enrolling at HLS in the mid-1980s. His father, Marcus, gained notoriety in the Vietnam era as a member of the "Boston Five" draft dissenters and became acquainted with Dershowitz through lawyer Leonard Boudin, a mutual friend.

"I remember Professor Dershowitz calling on me when he talked about the famous Boston Five trial, because my father was one of the defendants," says Raskin. "I always appreciated Professor Dershowitz's activist and engaged approach with the law. I could tell early on we were going to have some political differences. When I was in law school, the students were very up in arms about corporate investment in apartheid South Africa, and we were involved in the divestment movement. We had tried to get various professors to side with us. A number did, but Professor Dershowitz did not. I remember one discussion where he asked why nobody was talking about divestment from North Korea? One reason for that certainly was that a number of American corporations were invested in North Korea."

Around the same time as Raskin, two students named Elena Kagan and Jeffrey Toobin also arrived at Harvard and became fast friends, sitting together in the front row of Dershowitz's classes. Kagan was raised in New York and eventually obtained degrees at both Princeton and Oxford before moving on to HLS. "I remember thinking I was the luckiest person in the world to have [Alan] as a criminal law professor," says Kagan, who also noted: "Underneath that public persona [was] one of the most caring, generous, genuine people I have ever met."

Jeffrey Toobin displayed a flair for the media early on, becoming a freelancer for *The New Republic* during his time at Harvard. "When I was an undergraduate at Harvard, I [also] worked on *The Harvard Crimson*," says Toobin. "Alan was frequently in the news in those days. His Criminal Law class was on my first day at Harvard. He had this great way of integrating contemporary issues, including his own cases, into the more timeless lessons that you had to teach in a criminal law class. Once he played some undercover tapes between cops and suspects, and I remember thinking it was really great to hear how police actually do their work, as opposed to second- or third-hand descriptions of it. Alan's dual work as a scholar and practitioner gave a depth to the class it wouldn't have had if he had just been one or the other."

One of Dershowitz's idiosyncrasies which left a mark on Toobin was Dershowitz's posting of hate mail he received onto the door of his office. Full of rabid anti-Jewishness and, at times, foul language, the notes had come in response to a variety of episodes from Dershowitz's career. They included messages like:

The Jews are Communist. They are the sons of Satan.

Nothing is lower than a Jew.

Do I wish I could make you experience the Nazi period in Europe, how do I wish.

You're the best argument for abortion one could present.

Dershowitz instructed Maura Kelley that if she opened any piece of hate mail, she was to apply Scotch tape and place it on his office door for students to see as they walked in. "I thought that students who grew up protected from this kind of thing should see what they would encounter if they defended Jewish values," says Dershowitz.

"I remember Professor Dershowitz used to say that he was not the first Jewish law professor at Harvard, but he was the first Jewish Jewish law professor—in that he was unabashedly Jewish and talked about what that meant," says Jamie Raskin.

* * *

While Dershowitz received hate mail for speaking his mind, people like Natan Sharansky in the Soviet Union received prison sentences. It had been nearly a decade since he had been arrested for "treason" and supposedly spying for the United States. Though he remained strong in spirit, years of malnourishment, punishment cells, freezing Russian weather, hunger strikes, and solitary confinement had taken their toll on his body. His dream was to start a family with his wife in Israel, but Avital's years of fertility were dwindling. If Sharansky was not released soon, they would be unable to have children.

A ray of hope appeared when Reagan forged a cordial relationship with the Soviet Union's new leader, Mikhail Gorbachev. During a summit in Geneva in late 1985, Reagan had mentioned Avital's efforts to free her husband. Gorbachev repeated the old Soviet line that Sharansky was a spy for the CIA. "You can keep saying that Sharansky is an American spy," replied Reagan, "but my people trust that woman. And as long as you keep him and other political prisoners locked up, we will not be able to establish a relationship of trust."

Dershowitz sought to drum up support for Sharansky's cause in the press. In an article for *The Boston Herald*, he declared: "At the very least, Gorbachev should release the one Jew who has been denied all of his rights, who, for the past eight years, has been languishing in the Gulag for the 'crimes' of wanting to join his wife in Israel and speaking out on human rights!"

Behind the scenes, Dershowitz and Irwin Cotler worked through back channels to negotiate a prisoner swap with the Soviets. They were able to connect with a mysterious East German lawyer named Wolfgang Vogel, who had negotiated the swap of American spy Francis Gary Powers in the notorious U-2 spy plane incident in the early 1960s. Vogel had been previously aware of their work on behalf of Sharansky, and after discussions with Dershowitz and Cotler, Vogel arranged a swap for Sharansky. Gorbachev himself ordered Sharansky to be set free, making Sharansky the first political prisoner Gorbachev had ever released.

The Americans and Soviets had agreed to swap four Eastern spies in exchange for three Western spies and Sharansky. On February 11, 1986, representatives of both nations gathered with their prisoners on either end of the snow-covered Glienicke Bridge, which stretched over the border between East and West Germany. Sharansky insisted on walking separately from the three Western spies to emphasize he had not worked as a spy, but as a spokesman for human rights. Vogel drove Sharansky to the middle of the bridge, and from there, with a smile on his face and his Book of Psalms in hand, Sharansky crossed the border and was a prisoner no more. Watching live on television back in the United States, Dershowitz started to cry.

Soon after his release and arrival in Israel, Sharansky traveled to New York to thank his supporters in America. Through all his time in prison, Sharansky had been kept in the dark by his Soviet captors about the efforts being made to free him, but upon his release, he soon learned the depths of love shown to him by so many, including Dershowitz. When they saw each other for the first time, Dershowitz and Sharansky cried softly and hugged each other. Sharansky told Dershowitz he had said a blessing for him at the Western Wall in Jerusalem: "*Baruch matir asurim*"—"Blessed are those who help release the imprisoned."

Looking back on his time in prison, Sharansky comments, "I spent 405 days in a punishment cell, which was kind of a record at that time. I spent more than four years in solitary confinement, and I spent a year and a half facing interrogation under the threat of capital punishment by the KGB. Although physically it was a very, very difficult time, morally it was a very easy time. In prison everything was clear—here is light, here is darkness; here are friends, here are enemies; here is truth, here are lies. In prison, you say no to the KGB. Of course, it took some weeks to get used to the fact that for this you can be sentenced to death, but every Jew has commandments—*mitzvah*—and my duty was to fulfill my *mitzvah*. In prison, I learned there are more important things than one's personal survival."

As to why he was never executed by the Soviets, Sharansky replied, "Because it was not Stalin's time. His regime killed tens of millions of citizens to keep everybody under control—why not kill another 1,000 Jews who started this movement for human rights? But from the moment I was arrested, world Jewry was mobilized to save me and organized unprecedented pressure on all levels. In the beginning, that stopped the Soviets from sentencing me to death. The Soviets lived under this constant pressure—from President Carter's statement to public trials to lobbying world leaders. The work of the Jewish lawyers was very important, and Alan played a very special role in this."

Just months after Sharansky met Dershowitz for the first time, he and his wife received joyous news. Avital was going to have a baby.

* * *

After four years of dating, Carolyn was ready to take her union with Alan to the next step. "I was very clear that I wanted to get married and have kids," says Carolyn. "I had never been married before. Although Alan was clear he wanted to be with me for the rest of his life, he had experienced a difficult divorce and was gun shy of getting married. It took him time to understand I was a genuine, non-manipulative person. And there were some things he feared giving up. When I first met him, he had just been voted one of the top ten most eligible bachelors of Boston. It was somewhat hard for him to give up that reputation. He had a lot of contradictions that he had to figure out about himself. He was not the most mature person when I met him."

"I was reluctant to marry again," admits Dershowitz, "but I always wanted to commit to Carolyn." By 1986, he had moved out of Camp Dersh and into a small apartment on Brattle Street in Cambridge he and Carolyn had chosen together. Now thirty-two years old and tired of waiting, Carolyn gave Alan an ultimatum: marry me or I leave.

He chose the first option. Near the end of August 1986, the Dershowitz and Cohen families gathered in Carolyn's hometown of Charleston, South Carolina, for a memorable wedding. Everyone from Alan's immediate family was there, along with the Big 8 and many other friends of Alan. "I found it interesting," says Joel Klein, Alan's research assistant at Stanford back in the early 1970s, "that before the actual wedding—which took place in a Reformed synagogue—we went to a much smaller Orthodox synagogue, which is where Alan was comfortable."

After the wedding, Alan and Carolyn headed to the Vineyard for a honeymoon before returning to Cambridge for the fall semester at Harvard.

"Carolyn changed my life in every possible way," says Dershowitz. "Even though we didn't always agree, I never wrote a column, delivered a speech, or made a major decision without checking with her first. She became a full partner in everything I did."

Less than three months after their marriage, Carolyn was by Alan's side for one of the most high-stakes court arguments of his life. The Tison brothers' case had finally made it to the Supreme Court, who would be deciding whether to vacate, remand, or affirm their death sentences. It could not have come at a worse time. William Rehnquist, who had been made chief justice by Reagan after the retirement of Warren Burger, was a proponent of capital punishment. Sandra Day O'Connor, another Reagan nominee, had been appointed to the high court from Arizona, where she had observed the terrorizing breakout and murders unfold in the media back in the late 1970s.

But the most formidable justice awaiting Dershowitz was a brand-new Reagan appointee: Antonin Scalia, destined to become a pillar of conservatism. Dershowitz had known Scalia's father Eugene, a Sicilian immigrant, during his time at Brooklyn College, where the elder Scalia had stood on opposite sides from Dershowitz over the firing of allegedly communist professor named Harry Slochower.

Dershowitz decided to base his oral argument on a 1982 case, *Enmund v. Florida*, in which the Court had reversed the death penalty of Earl Enmund, who had driven the getaway car during the murder of an elderly couple, but had not actually fired the weapon. "We hoped the justices would simply 'remand the case for reconsideration in light of *Enmund*,'" says Dershowitz. "In other words, that they would send the case back to the Arizona courts so that those judges could apply the *Enmund* precedent to the facts of the Tison case."

Before he had sent the case up to the Supreme Court, Dershowitz had been called by several anti–death penalty advocates who begged him not to do it. "Count the noses," said one. "You may not have five anymore. We have *Enmund*. Most courts will follow *Enmund* and reverse felony-murder death sentences. But if the Supremes take your case and reverse or limit *Enmund*, people will die because of you."

Dershowitz would not back down. "It was an excruciating emotional conflict, but not a difficult legal or ethical decision," he says. "I had two actual clients on death row. I was their lawyer, not the lawyer for the many other death row inmates whose fates could be adversely affected by a negative ruling in our case. I cared deeply about every inmate facing the death penalty, as I did about the issue itself. But I could not allow these strong feelings to influence my decision regarding my clients."

Sitting in prison in Arizona, the Tison brothers had great faith in their star lawyer. "We had high expectations," says Ricky, the older of the two. "We didn't have the money to pay anybody at that time. The only people that got involved were the people Professor Dershowitz brought on board.

"One thing I always appreciated was his meticulous nature when it came to the briefs that he wrote. He's the only person I've ever known to write a brief that is concise and always on point. Most attorneys don't do that. They fill the briefs with large amounts of case citing—almost like they're trying to drown you in legal research. I've read a lot of briefs, and his were the only ones that ever actually made sense."

As Dershowitz readied his argument for the Supreme Court, he brought it to class and read it aloud to some of his students, getting their criticism just like in the Claus von Bülow case. After traveling to Washington, on November 3, 1986, Dershowitz walked into the Supreme Court, where he had spent so many hours working for Justice Goldberg nearly a quarter century before. Jamin, nearly completed with his education at Yale, had come along, as had Carolyn, who was about to watch Alan argue in court for the first time. "It was so overwhelmingly scary because of its importance," says Carolyn. "I was feeling so anxious for him that I was practically nauseous. He, on the other hand, didn't appear nervous at all."

"I was only nervous for the Tison brothers, not for myself," says Dershowitz. "I knew that if I lost the case, they could die."

After taking his seat in the grand, marble-pillared courtroom, Dershowitz eventually heard his name called by Chief Justice Rehnquist. As Dershowitz rose to the lectern, he scanned his eyes over the nine justices seated at the raised mahogany bench. His normally bushy hair had been trimmed, and his oft-worn sport jacket had been replaced with a conservative gray suit, according to the rules of decorum in the high court. With a firm voice, Dershowitz declared into the microphone: "The State of Arizona seeks to execute two young men who had no specific intent to kill. . . . There was a careful plan in the case to avoid firing the weapons. It worked [during the escape itself]. We're arguing that this court has established a clear test—purposefulness—as defining specific guilt. . . . [The Tison brothers] intended specifically that nobody should be harmed."

At this point, Justice Scalia interjected and threw a hypothetical at Dershowitz. "What about someone who tosses a gun to a triggerman, who kills a policeman?"

Dershowitz later remarked, "I had prepared for every likely question I might be asked by the justices, but the idea of a gun being thrown by one robber to another had never occurred to me." Dershowitz sidestepped Scalia's hypothetical, but Scalia pulled him back. "Please answer my hypothetical," he demanded. "The theory of intent is that, for a non-triggerman, that's not enough for specific intent," Dershowitz answered. "To throw a hypothetical at you—which I'm not entitled to do, so I'll throw it at myself—anyone who provides a gun to someone wherein death results is guilty of first-degree murder. I don't think that's supportable."

"But the triggerman asks for a gun," continued Scalia. "Toss me a gun. He tosses him the gun. . . . That wouldn't be enough?" As Dershowitz pondered how to answer, his mind drifted back to the *I Am Curious (Yellow)* case when Warren Burger had asked him a seemingly nonsensical hypothetical about bear-baiting. "No. That wouldn't be enough," Dershowitz said to Scalia. "And that is not this case in any event. This case is handing guns over, under an agreement that no shooting would take place. In *Enmund* the guns were also provided. What Your Honor, Justice Scalia, is asking for, in a sense, is a return to the felony-murder rule where guns are provided."

"Alan doesn't like having to say, 'Your Honor,'" notes Carolyn, who observed the back-and-forth between these legal titans. "It didn't come out well from his mouth." Carolyn noticed that during Scalia's exchange with Alan, Thurgood Marshall, an acquaintance and admirer of Alan, grew increasingly angry.

When Deputy State Attorney General William Schafer stood to argue the state's case, Marshall questioned him about the Tison brothers' well-documented attempt to grab water for the Lyons family right before the shooting started. "If you're going to shoot a man, would you get him a drink of water?" said Marshall. "I don't know, I can speculate," replied Schafer. "Would you speculate on a man's life?" fired back Marshall.

After the momentous proceedings adjourned, Dershowitz was satisfied that he had held his own. "The only advantage a lawyer has over the judges in arguing on appeal is superior knowledge of the facts of the case," he says. "That's why I always immerse myself in these facts before arguing."

Half a year went by, as Dershowitz rolled through semesters at Harvard and the Tison brothers basically sat on their hands in prison. In April 1987, the decision at last came down. It turned out to be somewhat of a Pyrrhic victory. The Court had not affirmed the brothers' death sentences, but it also had not vacated them. As well, the conservative justices had taken the opportunity to expand the scope of the death penalty—a move that was angering, but not surprising, to Dershowitz. "The Court stopped short of directly upholding the death sentences imposed on the two brothers, Ricky W. and Raymond C. Tison, and sent the case back [to Arizona] for further proceedings," reported the *New York Times*.

The *LA Times* quoted Sandra Day O'Connor, who had written the majority opinion: "'Without officially reversing the earlier [*Enmund*] decision, we simply hold that major participation in the felony committed, combined with reckless indifference to human life, is sufficient grounds for sentencing a person to death,' O'Connor said.

"Death penalty foes said they were distressed by the ruling, saying it appeared to strip away a key defense in many capital punishment cases," the *LA Times* continued. "'This not only takes away a shield used by the defense, but gives a sword to the proponents of the death penalty,' said Harvard University Prof. Alan Dershowitz, who defended the two brothers tried in the Arizona case in question. 'This decision seems to encourage states to enact a more aggressive penalty.'"

Although frustrated at the conservatives' affirmation of the death penalty, Dershowitz was relieved they had not explicitly approved the Tison brothers' execution. "[The justices] remanded the case back to the Arizona courts 'for determination' whether the Tison brothers met [the justices'] new criterion," he notes. "Had they simply 'affirmed' the judgment—the death sentence—the case would have been over, and the Tison brothers would have been gassed to death, but by 'vacating' the death sentence, the justices gave us a new beginning."

Pouncing on the justices' new criterion for execution, the State of Arizona asked the original trial court to affirm that the brothers had acted with "reckless indifference to human life" and were, therefore, eligible for the death penalty.

As the case dragged on and the 1980s came to a close, little did Dershowitz know that America's elite would soon be knocking at his door.

HELP WANTED

On a wintery day in January 1990, a private 727 descended into Massachusetts. The plane had a glossy-paneled living room filled with posh furniture, as well as a bedroom and kitchen. On board was Dershowitz's newest client, one of the richest and nastiest women in America: Leona Helmsley. She was coming to Boston for her first meeting with Dershowitz and his legal team.

Leona was married to billionaire Harry Helmsley, one of the most prominent real estate investors in the country. In addition to owning the Empire State Building, Harry owned a chain of opulent hotels, and after marrying Leona, his bride became the public face of his properties. Starring in a number of ads throughout the 1980s, Leona became famous for posing outside one of the Helmsleys' magnificent hotels in lavish clothing and saying to the camera: "It's the only Palace in the world where the Queen stands guard." She and Harry had opulent properties and lived a life of supreme luxury with servants, employees, and even bodyguards at their beck and call.

But Leona Helmsley's fairytale life soon came crashing down. She was an arrogant and vindictive woman who easily made enemies. A business associate once said, "Don't believe everything you've read about Leona. She's worse than that." Helmsley's temper was so bad that her employees installed an alarm system to warn each other whenever she was coming. Her lawyer, Gerald Feffer, called her "one tough bitch."

In the mid-1980s, authorities in New York claimed Helmsley had evaded sales tax on outrageously expensive jewelry, but she was granted immunity and not charged with any crime. Shortly after, though, some of her own employees leaked information to the *New York Post* that ultimately led to both federal and state charges of income tax evasion. With experienced prosecutor Rudy Giuliani at the helm, the government accused the Helmsleys of listing four million dollars' worth of personal luxuries as business expenses. The media relished the opportunity to attack Leona, dubbing her the "Queen of Mean."

Eighty-year-old Harry Helmsley had mentally deteriorated and was deemed unfit to stand trial, and so, his wife bore the brunt of the legal proceedings. Leona Helmsley's employees gave hostile testimony, and although Helmsley denied saying it, the press seized on an incriminating comment her maid testified Helmsley had once made: "Only the little people pay taxes." When she was convicted and given a four-year prison sentence in the federal case, the *New York Times* declared it was "greeted with uncommon approval by a public who had grown to regard her as a 1980s symbol of arrogance and greed." On top of this, New York State charged Helmsley with 188 counts based on the same transactions highlighted in the federal case.

With an ailing husband, a hostile public, and both the federal and state governments coming after her, Helmsley was in serious trouble. Although she was able to pay the twenty-five-million-dollar bail and stay out of prison for the time being, she needed a superb appellate lawyer to get her out of this mess. Helmsley had apparently heard Dershowitz was the go-to guy for criminal appeals, and on December 13, 1989, the day after her sentencing, she called Dershowitz. Saying the thought of going to prison made her "numb," she asked if Dershowitz would come to New York to meet her. It so happened Carolyn was about to have a baby. Dershowitz told Helmsley he would not be traveling, and so, Helmsley came to his office at Harvard instead.

After hearing her side of the case, Dershowitz explained that appeals are not primarily won on the grounds of a client's guilt or innocence, but rather on a procedural mistake or constitutional violation that took place in the trial. "I do autopsies on trials," he told her. "[My team and I] retry the case from beginning to end." Agreeing to take her case, he quickly assembled a defense team of his most trusted friends, including Harvey Silverglate, lawyer Sandor Frankel, and his brother, Nathan.

Soon after, Dershowitz was by Helmsley's side on the steps of the State Supreme Court in Manhattan as she addressed the press. Her green eyes flashing and veins bulging, she shouted: "We have just begun to fight! I have been vilified!"

In January 1990, she flew to Massachusetts in her private jet for a meeting with Dershowitz and his team at Harvey Silverglate's Boston office, dressed finely and flanked by a bodyguard and employees. Dershowitz went around the table introducing Helmsley to his brother, Silverglate, Frankel, and the rest of the team. Explaining their individual roles, Dershowitz told Helmsley that his brother, Helmsley, Silverglate's partner Andrew Good, and Frankel would be responsible for writing the appellate brief, with Dershowitz supervising and ultimately making the oral argument in the federal case. Arguments in the state case would eventually be divided between Dershowitz, his brother, and Frankel.

As Dershowitz came to know Helmsley, he learned that she had not started her life in the lap of luxury. She was born Leona Rosenthal to Jewish parents and grew up in Brooklyn, where her father worked as a hatmaker. An enterprising woman, she set off on the American dream, eventually landing a career selling luxury apartments, which led her to become the vice president of a real-estate brokerage company in the late 1960s. It was during this time she met and married Harry Helmsley.

"[She was] demanding . . . [and] interrupted a lot," Dershowitz admitted to a reporter, but early on, he actually had something of a soft spot for Helmsley. "I'm this brash kid from Brooklyn, too," he commented to the reporter.

* * *

On January 27, 1990, Carolyn gave birth to a baby girl. "I was thrilled," says Dershowitz. "It was an incredibly wintery day when Carolyn gave birth. I had to carry her to the car and was terrified I would slip because it was so icy." As customary for a Jewish girl, they had a traditional naming ceremony, and in front of family and friends gathered in his home, Alan declared his daughter's name to be Ella, after Carolyn's beloved grandmother whose Yiddish name was Zelda.

Around this time, Helmsley brought a five-foot-tall teddy bear to a meeting with Dershowitz as a present for his daughter. In the spring, Dershowitz posed with Helmsley for the cover of *New York Magazine*.

"The greatest incursions on freedom come when society goes after the S.O.B.'s," the article inside quoted Dershowitz as saying. "If you don't defend the S.O.B.'s, then nobody's there to defend you."

"Today, Dershowitz says that in Leona Helmsley he saw a fellow Jew from Brooklyn—like himself 'a sitting duck' for criticism," continued the article. "'This is not a criminal tax case,' Dershowitz says. 'It's a civil case, a dispute. They targeted her.'" For her own part, Helmsley told *New York* that Dershowitz was "brilliant, brilliant, brilliant."

As Dershowitz was preoccupied with his duties at Harvard and a new baby at home, his team was underway preparing the appellate brief for Helmsley's case. "[We scoured] 'the record'—8,000 pages of trial transcript, all of the exhibits, and all of the pre-trial motions," says Sandor Frankel. What Dershowitz's team learned about Helmsley was vastly different from what the public had been led to believe. "The Helmsleys had paid nearly $58 million in taxes in the years in question, and over one-third of a billion dollars—$342 million—in taxes over the past eight years," says Frankel. "The amount involved in this prosecution [c. $4 million] was minor viewed in that context, and any taxes allegedly due had been paid when the investigation began."

"Years earlier," continued Frankel, "in an unrelated New York State grand jury investigation of sales tax fraud committed by major New York City jewelry stores, Mrs. Helmsley had admitted avoiding New York sales taxes by buying jewelry in New York City and having empty boxes shipped to her Connecticut home. She had testified under a grant of immunity: Nothing she said could be used against her. But the substance of her testimony had been leaked, resulting in a chain of events culminating in the criminal tax investigation that resulted in her tax fraud conviction."

"Leona was stupid and did incredibly stupid things," says Dershowitz. "I think the evidence was pretty clear she tried to avoid paying state taxes on jewelry. Other people who had done similar things, though, had not been sentenced. But she was one of the most prominent people in America, and everyone hated her. Her own people turned her in."

When they appeared in court for the state case, Dershowitz, his brother, and Frankel took turns arguing various elements of Helmsley's defense. Their primary contention was that under New York's law of double jeopardy, all of the 188 counts against Helmsley should be dismissed because they completely overlapped the crimes she was already being charged with on a federal level.

The atmosphere around Dershowitz's courtroom appearances was movie-like. The night before their court appearance, Dershowitz and his team were given rooms at the Helmsleys' palatial Park Lane Hotel, where Helmsley hosted a meeting and dinner inside a large conference room with sweeping views of Central Park stretched out below. The next morning, Dershowitz and his team received room service for breakfast, and Dershowitz rode with Helmsley in the lead car to court, while the other lawyers followed behind. Upon exiting the vehicles, they were instantly swarmed by photographers, and Nathan Dershowitz was whacked in the nose by a camera as a journalist feverishly tried to get a picture of his brother. Claire Dershowitz came to watch her sons in action and sat in the back of the courtroom, chatting in Yiddish with Helmsley.

In the federal case, Dershowitz used his oral argument to convince the judges that the prosecution had improperly used Helmsley's immunized testimony against her. "Alan was extremely knowledgeable about history and specific aspects of the law," says Frankel, who observed Dershowitz's argument.

As with most of Dershowitz's appeals, many months went by as he and his team awaited the decision of the judges.

In the meantime, Dershowitz was growing to detest Helmsley. "She was just the meanest person I'd ever met," he says. "She was gratuitously mean. She lived to hurt people and got pleasure out of causing pain." She privately told Dershowitz that she was trying to get a criminal prosecution against Gerald Feffer, the lawyer who had lost her trial. Apparently one day, Feffer's back had been hurting, and he asked Helmsley for one of her painkiller drugs that had been prescribed to her personally. Helmsley was now claiming that he had used a drug illegally, and she threatened to prosecute Feffer as payback for (unintentionally) losing her trial.

"All she wanted to do was hurt people," says Dershowitz. "She was so annoying. I would be on the phone with her, and Carolyn would see how angry I was getting just holding it in. Carolyn couldn't stand it. Leona wasn't the 'Queen of Mean,' she was the empress of mean."

As much as he detested Helmsley's personality, if there was a certain kind of person Dershowitz fundamentally opposed—whose ideology he fought against—it was an evangelical Christian of the 1980s. Dershowitz's whole upbringing and Jewish worldview made him abhor the idea that America was a "Christian" nation, and Reagan's seemingly obsequious attention to evangelical Christians angered him.

The end of the 1980s saw the downfall of perhaps the most influential evangelical Christian couple in America—Jim and Tammy Faye Bakker. Their talk show, *The PTL Club*, had reached nearly thirteen million households per episode, and it was at one time the highest-rated religious show in America. In the late 1970s, the couple opened a Christian theme park in South Carolina called Heritage USA, which spanned over 2,300 acres and attracted more visitors than any theme park in America after Disney World and Disneyland. Jim and Tammy lived a lavish lifestyle, driving Rolls-Royces, taking exotic vacations, and purchasing posh clothing and jewelry.

But their astounding success unraveled. Tammy was promiscuous, and in an attempt to arouse jealousy and regain her love, Jim had an affair with a young church secretary named Jessica Hahn, whom he paid nearly $300,000 in hush money. He managed to keep the affair quiet for several years. During this time, Jim Bakker's business affairs came under investigation by the FCC and IRS, who alleged he had misappropriated viewer donations and thereby pocketed an outrageous salary. In 1987, after the Jessica Hahn scandal became public, Jim Bakker resigned in disgrace from the board of PTL, and Jerry Falwell of the Moral Majority took over the ministry. The following year, Bakker was charged by a grand jury with twenty-four counts of fraud. The most damning charge was that he had oversold "Lifetime Partnerships" to Heritage USA. Under this scheme, donors could obtain annual stays at the theme park in exchange for a donation of $1,000. Bakker received donations from thousands of viewers—far more than Heritage USA could possibly accommodate in a year.

Despite his personal feelings toward the evangelical Christian world, Dershowitz wrote a syndicated column attacking the government probe of the Bakkers. "The implications of a government probe into whether contributors to Jim and Tammy Bakker were cheated when their money went into expensive homes and cars is frightening," he wrote. "What is the constitutionally correct salary and expense account for a minister, priest or rabbi? The law has generally drawn the line at fraud. If the alleged religious leader really does not believe what he is preaching and is intending to bilk his parishioners, the law is prepared to step in. But the line separating fraud from fanaticism is not a sharp one, and there is a danger that dissident prophets may be seen as falling on the fraud side more often than mainstream preachers are."

The government came down hard on Jim Bakker. The strain became so intense that one day, when he was supposed to be in court, Bakker hid under a couch in his lawyer's office. Marshals physically removed him while cameras captured Bakker crying like a child. In late 1989, he was convicted on all twenty-four counts and sentenced to forty-five years in prison, a virtual death sentence for the forty-nine-year-old Bakker. While delivering the sentence, presiding Judge Robert Potter made a telling remark: "Those of us who do have a religion are sick of being saps for money-grubbing preachers or priests."

"I didn't realize how many enemies I created," says Bakker. "Telecasts of my show were edited by the FBI to support the government's claim that I had committed fraud by diverting partnership funds to other purposes. One author interviewed every juror from my trial, and each of them said a variation of: 'We really don't know exactly what Jim was guilty of. But he has to be guilty of *something* with all these government agencies coming after him.'

"They wanted me so bad. I think one of the reasons they put me in prison was they felt I had power to elect presidents. I campaigned for Reagan and helped elect him in 1984. I worked with Pat Robertson for eight years in the late 1960s and early 1970s, and Pat came to see me one day in the late 1980s when he was considering a run for president. I was eventually told that one of the reasons they put me in prison was they were afraid I would endorse Pat Robertson, and the power of both of our audiences would elect him president. That scared the daylights out of them."

By the time Bakker began to mount an appeal in 1990, he had virtually no money except for what was contributed to a legal defense fund by some of his supporters. Well aware of Dershowitz's representation of Claus von Bülow and Leona Helmsley, he wrote a letter to Dershowitz begging him to join a team of appellate lawyers he had hired from Texas. "When I contacted Alan, I had already been in several prisons by then," says Bakker. "I would say 90 percent of my prison guards were nice to me, but the 10 percent that weren't made life miserable. They made me clean the filthiest things you've ever seen, from showers to toilets. When I heard from Alan that he was interested in my case, I was amazed and overwhelmed."

"There was not enough time before the appellate brief had to be filed for me to take over the entire appeal," says Dershowitz, "but I was particularly appalled by the length of the sentence and the religious basis the judge seemed to give for imposing it." He agreed to argue the sentencing issue.

"Alan came to see me in prison," said Bakker. "Prison is so overwhelming, especially if you go there after literally preaching to the world. I had lost all hope. But then Alan came into the prison and told me, 'Jim, I've observed your case—you didn't get a fair trial.' I knew I hadn't gotten a fair trial. When they ran tapes from my show, the judge put his fingers in his ears and laid his head down on the desk—he demonstrated all the time that he hated me for some reason. But here was one of the great legal minds of all time saying this to me.

"I felt like Alan was a biblical character—an Old Testament prophet almost. That's the way I saw him. When Alan came, he was the only one who said he was going to do something—the only one who said, 'You got a bad deal. You didn't get a fair trial. Your judge was prejudiced.'"

Since the appeal had been filed in the Fourth Circuit Court of Appeals in Virginia, Dershowitz called Morris Rosen, a cousin of Carolyn's who was a Southern lawyer, and picked his brain about how to handle a case in the South. "Morris told me to be down-to-earth and very common-sense," says Dershowitz. "I was set to be arguing before three old Republican judges, and he told me to turn off my professor's side and just act like a regular fella." In October 1990, Dershowitz traveled to Richmond and appeared before a panel of appellate judges alongside Bakker's team of lawyers. When his turn came, Dershowitz forcefully argued that Judge Potter had made an "incredible departure" from typical sentencing procedures by giving Jim Bakker forty-five years. He also argued that Potter had displayed religious bias by declaring, "Those of us who do have a religion are sick of being saps for money-grubbing preachers or priests."

"It was kind of like watching a terrific maestro in front of an orchestra," said one of Bakker's Texan lawyers, referring to Dershowitz's argument before the judges. "[It was] mesmerizing," said another of the lawyers, Brian Wice. "He [looked] like a schlep, wearing suits he could have bought in Filene's Basement, woolen socks, and shoes. . . . But the judges hung on every word he had to say and bought what he was selling." Wice also commented, though, that he had "discovered that the most dangerous place to be in the criminal justice system is not the Federal Penitentiary at Marion or the holding cell at the Tombs, but between Alan Dershowitz and a television camera."

Unfortunately, the Texan lawyers did not hold a candle to Dershowitz in court. "At one point they implied to the judges that I had not intended to defraud the PTL Partners, merely deceive them," reports Bakker. "My lawyer said: 'It is not against the law in this context to deceive.' Of course, I had intended to do no such thing—defraud or deceive the PTL Partners! That was the last day the Texas firm worked as part of our legal team."

Four months later, the Virginia judges reached their decision. While stating that Bakker's conviction was valid, they vacated his sentence. "Our Constitution, of course, does not require a person to surrender his or her religious beliefs upon the assumption of judicial office," they wrote. "Courts, however, cannot sanction sentencing procedures that create the perception of the bench as a pulpit from which judges announce their personal sense of religiosity and simultaneously punish defendants for offending it. . . . Consequently, the sentence is vacated and the case is remanded for resentencing."

"I was in prison, and the inmates told me I had won—I was shocked. It was incredible," says Bakker. "Alan [had done] an outstanding job highlighting the errors in my case and in my sentencing."

The *New York Times* published a cartoon of Jim and Tammy clinging to Dershowitz's legs while he patted them on their heads. The headline next to it stated: "Dershowitz Wows 'Em Again." "Tammy Faye Bakker says Mr. Dershowitz has singlehandedly restored her faith in lawyers. 'Jim and I are really sold on him and think he's the greatest,' she said. . . . 'He's our kind of people, a real down-to-earth, nice man.' . . . Mr. Dershowitz said that insofar as they were victims of the criminal justice system, Jim and Tammy Faye Bakker were 'my kind of people, too.' But he took exception to a statement by Tammy Faye Bakker that the ruling was 'a great victory for Christianity.' Instead, he said: 'I think the fact that a Jewish lawyer helped bring that about must show that it was a great victory for all Americans who believe in religious tolerance and secularism.'"

When Tammy did finally meet Dershowitz at a courthouse in North Carolina during the case proceedings, she kissed and hugged him so vehemently that some of her famous rouge smeared onto Dershowitz's face. Curiously, it took Dershowitz some wrangling to get Tammy to send the money they owed him for travel expenses and hours of work. It was only after two years of sending bills and follow-up letters that Dershowitz finally received payment.

Bakker would spend several depressing years in prison, but because of Dershowitz's persuasive argument before the Virginian judges, he was resentenced and ultimately released in 1994, having served forty years less than his original sentence called for.

"Prison tells you that you're a piece of garbage—that you're worthless," says Bakker. "They did everything they could to take any self-respect from me. Alan gave me back some dignity. He was God's hands extended to me. Two Jewish people rescued me in prison: Jesus and Alan."

* * *

Jim Bakker may have had rosy feelings for Dershowitz, but William "Billy" Bulger most certainly did not. Bulger was the president of the Massachusetts Senate and wielded sizable influence in both state and national Democratic politics. His younger brother happened to be a notorious gangster named Whitey Bulger, who had served time in prison in the late 1950s and early 1960s for a slew of robberies and who, by the early 1990s, was a part of a ring of thugs called the Winter Hill Gang.

Dershowitz had been casually acquainted with the elder Bulger, having debated him once on free speech, and initially had cordial feelings toward him. That all changed when Dershowitz took on representation of a real estate mogul named Harold Brown, who had been arrested for attempted bribery. Brown had been building a high-rise at 75 State Street in Boston and called Billy Bulger to discuss obtaining a final building permit required to begin the project. According to Brown, he was told that to get the permit, he would have to pay a large sum of money to Billy Bulger's law partner for "services rendered." Predictably, $250,000 of this "fee" wound up in Bulger's own pocket. The feds eventually got wind of what had occurred and arrested Harold Brown on bribery charges.

When Dershowitz took on the case and publicized Billy Bulger's alleged extortion, he began receiving death threats. Late one night, he received an anonymous call from a voice which said: "An attack on Billy is an attack on Whitey so watch your back." He had a security guard posted outside the door of his office at Harvard, and Harvey Silverglate, who was working with Dershowitz on Brown's case, made sure his young son was always accompanied when walking to and from school. "You didn't mess around with the Bulgers," says Silverglate.

In the end, Billy Bulger was never indicted.

Not long after the Harold Brown case, Dershowitz and Silverglate learned that Bulger was trying to get a local judgeship approved for a friend of his named Paul Mahoney. Mahoney had allegedly once tried to kill a negative story about Bulger that Silverglate was circulating by asking the reporter—whose last name was O'Neill—"since when does a man with a name like O'Neill believe a man named Silverglate instead of men with names like Bulger and Mahoney?" So when Bulger nominated Mahoney for a judgeship near the beginning of 1991, Dershowitz and Silverglate turned up to oppose him at his public hearing.

Inside a congested chamber filled with Bulger's allies, Dershowitz and Silverglate stood together and watched Bulger as he delivered remarks on behalf of Mahoney. "[While he was my assistant], I knew him to be a splendid individual," said Bulger, while Mahoney sat in silence. "[But] over the years, I have accumulated various foes," he went on. "And when they can do so, they come down very hard on my relatives and my friends."

Pointing to a frowning Dershowitz and Silverglate, Bulger called them manipulative, vindictive, and crafty. "They are reckless, and they are liars," he said. "And they have no moral constraints upon them. Look at them!"—at which point he physically motioned to the two lawyers. "They are beneath contempt in my view." Saying they controlled the media, Bulger mentioned the biblical story of Jacob deceiving Esau in an attempt to create sympathy for himself and Mahoney.

In a quieter tone than was characteristic of his typical style, Dershowitz told the Governor's Council, "This is not Mr. Mahoney's day, this is the people of the state of Massachusetts's day." He then proceeded to quote Mahoney's alleged remark about believing an "O'Neill" rather than a "Silverglate."

Mahoney denied ever making the anti-Jewish remark. In the end, Bulger got his way again, and Mahoney was approved for the judgeship. Prominent newspapers decried Bulger's behavior at the hearing, calling his comments about Dershowitz and Silverglate: "if not anti-Semitic [then] close to it." One person wrote Dershowitz a letter stating, "Thanks for not backing down to Bulger-Mahoney this week. . . . To allow their brand of tribal-politics, which manifests itself in their anti-Semitism, to stand would be wrong."

But along with the support of friends came the vitriol of enemies. In the late 1980s and early 1990s, Dershowitz received a pile of hate mail because of his full-throated demands for Jewish equality and his public support for Israel. One note dated "July 4, 1776," mentioned "the racist 'brew of xenophobia, racial and religious bigotry and the affinity for Zionism' emanating out of the fascist state of Israel. . . . The world Jewish Congress is another disgusting example of the Jewish quest for world domination (behind the scenes). Well, FUCK YOU, slimy hooked-nose kike assholes."

A representative of the "Anti-Communist Confederation" sent Dershowitz a burned Israeli flag with this note: "U.S.A.[,] Jews are your enemies, cockroaches, and parasites. Wake up America." Another letter commented, "If you 'Jews' are such honorable people, '*WHY*' were six million of you fed into the 'ovens'??????? Alan, let me predict a calculated fact. *Much Before* the end of this century, a 'holocaust' will take place in A*M*E*R*I*K*A the like of which will make 'Hitler' appear as innocent as a little 'altar' boy during Mass."

"I had not realized how pervasive hatred against Jews was," says Dershowitz. "I felt very strongly that Jews were not being vocal enough about Israel and about the anti-Jewish situations existing around in the world. I wanted to share my perspective as an outspoken and proud Jew, someone who did not want to be relegated to quiet, second-class citizenship."

The result was a new book titled *Chutzpah: Reflections of a Proud and Assertive Jewish American*, eventually shortened to *Chutzpah*. It was a call to arms to the American Jewish community. "Notwithstanding the stereotype, we are not pushy or assertive enough for our own good and for the good of our more vulnerable brothers and sisters in other parts of the world," Dershowitz wrote in the introduction. "Our cautious leaders obsess about what the 'real' Americans will think of us. We don't appreciate how much we have contributed to the greatness of this country and don't accept that we are entitled to first-class status in this diverse and heterogeneous democracy."

In just shy of four hundred pages, Dershowitz interwove a history of anti-Jewishness over the previous two millennia with personal stories of his own experiences of anti-Jewishness and his struggle for Jewish rights throughout America, Israel, and the Soviet Union. Dershowitz minced no words about people he considered to be anti-Jewish, including Harvard colleagues, Catholic cardinals, US politicians, and Noam Chomsky, whom he labeled a "false prophet of the left." The final paragraph contained a revealing statement about the depths of Dershowitz's love for Israel: "As American Jews, are we prepared to insist on being treated as first-class Jews, rather than as exiles from our only true and normal home, Israel?"

The initial print run was tiny, but against all expectations, *Chutzpah* took off. "One of the most important and controversial books about American Jews since World War II," declared the *Boston Globe*. "[It] ought to be required reading for Jews, and on the suggested list for goyim," wrote the *New York Times*. It was published in May 1991 and by midsummer had sold over 100,000 copies, shooting to the top spot of *The New York Times* best-seller list, where it would remain for several months. It was translated into multiple languages and became a moderate bestseller in Israel and Japan. "[It] shocked everybody when it became a major bestseller," says Dershowitz. "It's hard to believe that a book called *Chutzpah* about Jewish identity in America would become the most widely read book in all of America. It was exactly the right time—the beginning of the 1990s. And it just caught a moment."

Dershowitz received thousands of letters from Jewish people telling him he spoke for them and thanking him for having the courage to write the book. He also got hundreds of letters from Americans of Korean, Irish, and Greek background saying that it was their book, too—that their parents had also taught them to have pride in their heritage. Mario Cuomo, with whom Dershowitz had become acquainted at an event for Israel, read the book and told Dershowitz that he, too, had been blacklisted by Wall Street firms as a young man because of his ethnicity.

"He started life, he makes clear, on the outside: growing up Orthodox in Brooklyn's Borough Park, an enclave of Jewish immigrants where many of his neighbors bore tattooed reminders of Hitler's brutality," read one newspaper that reviewed the book. "He takes pride in an unpromising youth, full of bad grades and rough discipline from administrators at yeshiva. His mother, Claire Dershowitz, confirms his lack of early promise. 'I'm surprised myself at the way he turned out,' she says."

During one television interview, the host asked Dershowitz if, with all the hate mail he received, he was ever worried about the safety of his family. "You can't live in the shadow of fear," answered Dershowitz. "Look, when I was growing up, my grandmother always told me '*Sha Shtil*,' which is the Yiddish word for 'be still, be quiet,' don't be an embarrassment in front of the real Americans—you're here at their sufferance, don't rock the boat. But that didn't work for Jews during the Holocaust. It didn't work for Blacks during the period of segregation in this country. The American way is to stand up for your rights, to show chutzpah, to show a willingness to be assertive. . . . Cowardice is not the American way."

In July 1991, Dershowitz appeared on *Oprah* for a debate about whether there was too much suing going on in America. "So what do you call chutzpah?" Oprah asked Dershowitz, referencing his new book.

"[Chutzpah is] unmitigated gall," he said with a big smile. "A willingness to press for every advantage. I think Americans need more chutzpah. We don't sue enough. When we don't sue, you know who benefits?"

"Who?" Oprah inquired.

"The big corporations, the governments, the power establishment. Suing levels the playing field. Makes everybody equal," said Dershowitz, receiving applause from some of the audience.

While all this publicity was swirling for *Chutzpah*, Dershowitz's brilliance as a lawyer was being witnessed by thousands of moviegoers around the world. Elon had moved out to Los Angeles in the hopes of starting a filmmaking career, and he found work at the production company of Ed Pressman, whose previous films had starred Alec Baldwin and Meryl Streep, among others. Elon gave a copy of *Reversal of Fortune* to Pressman, who liked the book and decided to turn it into a feature film. "No one had ever really made a movie about a criminal appeal," says Elon. "I was living in our house when part of the case was going on, so I knew exactly what happened."

When Claus von Bülow found out about the movie, he and Dershowitz shared a joke over which of them Woody Allen should portray if he was cast. In the end, Glenn Close was enlisted to play Sunny, Jeremy Irons to play Claus, and Ron Silver to play Dershowitz. The film took five years to create. Dershowitz visited the set multiple times and even had a cameo role as—ironically—one of the appellate judges whom his character argues in front of. During the filming, Dershowitz took issue with Ron Silver's intense portrayal of him, particularly a scene where he smashed a phone onto the driveway of Camp Dersh. "I don't throw phones," he said to Elon. "Dad, it isn't you—it's the Dersh character," his son explained.

"A lot of the people that I worked with on the film thought it was not going to turn out well," reports Elon, "but I knew it was going to be pretty good." The film had its world premiere in the fall of 1990 and ended up staying in theaters for nine months. In March 1991, Alan and Elon traveled to Los Angeles for the Academy Awards, where *Reversal* was nominated for Best Director, Best Screenwriter, and Best Actor. Best Actor was ultimately awarded to Jeremy Irons for his portrayal of Bülow. After the ceremony, Alan and Elon snapped a photo with Irons holding the golden statue, and Elon bumped into Martin Scorsese, who told him *Reversal* had a "great script."

"My dad was already quite famous before *Reversal*," says Elon, "but I think it definitely changed his life in terms of a lot more people knowing who he was."

* * *

While Dershowitz was receiving attention from the film, his work on behalf of Leona Helmsley was falling off the rails. Although his team had won the state case on the grounds of double jeopardy and saved Helmsley around five years behind bars, in July 1991, an appeals court affirmed Helmsley's conviction in the federal case. The chief justice accepted Dershowitz's argument that prosecution had improperly used Helmsley's immunized testimony against her, but the other two justices did not. "We had a strong appeal on the grounds of immunity," says Dershowitz. "I was told by a friend of one of the judges that we had the better of the legal argument, but we had Leona Helmsley as our client."

Helmsley was running out of options. Dershowitz and his team submitted a motion for a new trial, which was heard by Judge Thomas Griesa in April 1992. Unfortunately, Griesa had gotten his hands on a letter Harvey Silverglate and a young associate had written to *Newsday* telling the magazine that a "bombshell" was about to drop in Helmsley's case. Dershowitz's team had discovered that several invoices which had reportedly been used by Dershowitz to falsely list personal expenses as business expenses had, in fact, truthfully described the payments as being used for personal expenses.

During the new trial hearing, Griesa informed the lawyers of his discovery of Silverglate's letter to *Newsday* and berated them for trying to involve the press. He began shouting at Silverglate's young associate, who had cowritten the letter, and amid this tension, Dershowitz stood up and fearlessly took the hit. "Your Honor, stop being a bully," he said. "Don't get on this young man. If you want to come after the responsible lawyer, come after me."

In the end, Griesa unsurprisingly denied their motion for a new trial and ordered Helmsley to surrender herself on April 15, Tax Day. Helmsley was hysterical. Nathan Dershowitz tried to help her make the necessary arrangements for herself and her senile husband, but she simply rested her head on his shoulder and wept uncontrollably. Meanwhile, Dershowitz held a press conference, and in a last-ditch effort to drum up support, he declared Helmsley would give all her hotels to house the homeless if it meant she could stay out of jail.

It was to no avail. On April 15, 1992, Helmsley reported to a federal prison in Lexington, Kentucky.

"Almost every year on 'tax day' a prominent American is either indicted or sent to prison to bring home the point that the punishment for tax cheating can be severe," Dershowitz wrote in a syndicated column, bemoaning the outcome of the case. "This year's high-visibility scapegoat was Leona Helmsley. . . . But what kind of message did Leona Helmsley's incarceration really send? To many Americans, it sent the message that if you are an unpopular and highly visible personality . . . then the IRS and the government prosecutors can single you out for special punishment."

While in prison, Helmsley contacted lawyer Milton Gould, who had a corrupt relationship with Judge Griesa and helped put him on the bench. Gould told Griesa that he wanted him to reduce Helmsley's sentence. Griesa replied that he would help only if Dershowitz was removed from the case and Gould became chief counsel instead. Leona approved, and Dershowitz was taken off the case.

During this time, some of the press reported that Helmsley had become fed up with Dershowitz. The *New York Post* commented: "[One] source told *The Post* that Helmsley was jealous of Dershowitz's other clients."

If the report was at all truthful, Helmsley had good reason to be jealous. That spring, Dershowitz had begun representing Mike Tyson, who was in the fight of his life. He had been convicted of raping a Miss Black America contestant in Indiana and was looking for an appellate lawyer. Don King was familiar with Dershowitz's reputation as an appellate lawyer and arranged for Dershowitz to meet Tyson in March 1992, soon before his sentencing.

Tyson was born just a couple miles from Borough Park in a rough neighborhood of Brooklyn called Brownsville. Virtually an orphan, Tyson wafted into gang life, getting arrested thirty-eight times by the age of thirteen. He was saved by an old Italian trainer named Cus D'Amato, who saw Tyson box in prison and instantly predicted he would be the heavyweight champion of the world. Seven years later, after being adopted by Cus and his wife, Camille, and training rigorously, Tyson became the youngest champion in boxing history at the age of twenty. He achieved dozens of stunning victories and became well known for his extreme toughness, earning the nickname "The Baddest Man on the Planet." After the death of Cus D'Amato, though, Tyson's personal life spun out of control. He signed once-murderer Don King to be his promoter and married actress Robin Givens, who together with her mother went behind Tyson's back to steal part of his fortune before their divorce in 1989.

Tyson had access to nearly any woman he wanted and possessed a voracious appetite for sex. This landed him in trouble when he was accused by eighteen-year-old model Desiree Washington of raping her in an Indiana hotel room.

On March 25, 1992, Dershowitz flew to Indiana to meet Tyson, who was accompanied by King and a number of staff. "Before we begin anything, Alan, I need to know two things from you," said Tyson in his high-pitched lisp. "I need to know that you think I'm innocent, and I need to know what kind of a person you think I am."

"Mike, I can't tell you I think you're innocent," said Dershowitz. "All I can do is read the transcript. I can tell you that there are legal issues in the case."

"OK, that's lawyers' talk," replied Tyson. "Now, man-to-man, what do you think of me?"

Looking him straight in the eye, Dershowitz said, "Mike, I think you're a schmuck." Tyson turned to Don King. "He called me a schmuck—you just let him call me a schmuck," he said. "Why am I a schmuck?" he asked, turning back to Dershowitz.

"If you're innocent," started Dershowitz, "then you're a schmuck for going up to a hotel room at two o'clock in the morning with a woman who you didn't know, without any witnesses, thereby putting yourself in a position where she could accuse you of rape." Tyson turned to King once again. "He's 100 percent right," he said. "Why didn't you call me a schmuck? I pay you to call me a schmuck."

That night, Dershowitz stayed up late and began reading the transcript from Tyson's trial. "After reading the material, it quickly became clear to me he had not received a fair trial, and I agreed to take the case," notes Dershowitz.

The following day, he appeared in court with Tyson as Judge Patricia Gifford sentenced him to six years in prison and denied him bail to boot.

Furious at this move, Dershowitz packed up his briefcase and walked out of the courtroom, commenting to Tyson, "I'm off to see that justice is done."

"Alan was really hungry," says Tyson. "He was very confident and determined to win."

Dershowitz immediately gathered a team consisting of his brother, his son Jamin—who by this point had graduated from Yale Law School—and Lee McTurnan, who had clerked with Dershowitz for Arthur Goldberg and was then working as a lawyer in Indiana. Dershowitz reviewed the nearly 2,500 pages of the trial transcript. "I had followed the trial in the media, but I didn't realize what an unfair trial Tyson had had until I reviewed the transcript," says Dershowitz. "Tyson's trial had been a disaster. His trial judge was determined to see him convicted, and his prominent white-collar trial lawyer had little experience in rape cases and didn't seem to like Tyson." Dershowitz went through each page of the transcript, making handwritten notations in the margins: "Ridiculous!" and "Did the state depose all the defense witnesses? Important for excluded witnesses point."

One of the first injustices Dershowitz and his team discovered was that mere days before the jury's conviction, Judge Gifford had not allowed three highly significant witnesses to testify on Tyson's behalf, on the grounds that it would be too late for the prosecution to effectively counter such a revelation.

During the trial, Desiree Washington said that she had jumped back when Tyson tried to kiss her in the limo on the way to the hotel. Tyson testified that when he kissed her, she was also kissing him. These three witnesses were at the hotel when Tyson's limo pulled up. The first two said Desiree was necking with him in the limo, and the third saw Desiree holding Tyson's hand on the way up to the hotel room. They also claimed that when Desiree and Tyson came down together a short time later, Tyson said to Desiree, "That was great. My driver will take you back."

"In all my years of practice and teaching criminal law, I had never heard of a case in which a judge refused to allow a criminal defendant the right to call eyewitnesses who could help establish his innocence," says Dershowitz. "[The] Bill of Rights explicitly guarantees a criminal defendant the right to call 'witnesses in his favor.'"

"It was an outrageous decision," comments Nathan Dershowitz.

Outrageous, but not shocking. Before ascending to the bench, Judge Gifford had been a rape prosecutor who handled over fifty rape cases. Once, while riding to court for Tyson's appeal, Dershowitz and his brother got talking to the taxi driver, who told them, "Don't you know Gifford's daughter was raped? She wanted to handle sex cases—that's why she got the case."

The rumor about her daughter was unconfirmed, but it was obvious Gifford had been specially selected. Under Indiana law, the prosecution was allowed to pick the day of the week on which an indictment was issued, thereby essentially hand-picking the judge they wanted.

As for Desiree herself, whatever her accomplishments or good personal traits may have been, Dershowitz and his team discovered she was not what she had portrayed herself to be in the trial. Because of rape shield laws, Tyson's trial team had been unable to personally attack the anonymous Desiree. She had said she was "a good Christian girl," while the prosecutor claimed she was "innocent, almost naïve." She had hidden her face and name from public disclosure. Devoid of a real person to display to America, the prosecution had created a caricature.

Once her name was publicized, a completely different picture emerged. Several people spoke out and said Desiree frequented nightclubs and was promiscuous. After digging into Desiree's past through old newspaper files and interviews with some of her friends, Dershowitz's team discovered she had had consensual relations with a football player named Wayne Walker in her high school, but had told her father she was raped when he became furious at her for losing her virginity. When Wayne went public with this revelation, he told ESPN that after hearing about Tyson's case, "the first thing that came to my mind was 'she's doing it again.'" Dershowitz's team also tracked down a childhood friend of Desiree's named Marc Colvin, who corroborated Wayne's accusation.

All of this was in addition to the facts which had been revealed at trial, including that she had given her number and a picture of herself in scanty clothes to Tyson at the beauty pageant where they met. Some of the pageant contestants and friends of Desiree also testified she had bragged about her imminent conquest of Tyson: "[This] is Mike Tyson," she reportedly said. "He's got a lot of money. He's dumb. You see what Robin Givens got out of him."

In addition to these damning reports, Desiree found herself in another hole. During the trial, she and her family had hired a private lawyer from Rhode Island, claiming it was to help fend off the press. When asked if she was planning to sue Tyson or if she had signed a contingency fee, Desiree denied both. When Desiree's identity was revealed after the trial, the Rhode Island Supreme Court disclosed the existence of a contingency fee agreement between Desiree's family and their lawyer. Desiree's father then publicly admitted that they had discussed movie rights with the lawyer.

Given the Washington family's perjurious claims in the trial, Dershowitz told *USA Today* that Desiree was "a money-grubbing gold-digger who is a liar to boot." He also attacked her appearance with Barbara Walters in which she said she would have dropped the charges if Tyson had apologized. "Can you imagine anyone saying they'd accept an apology for being raped?" Dershowitz commented to one interviewer.

"On the basis of our investigation and the new evidence we uncovered, I was convinced that Mike Tyson did not intend to rape Desiree Washington, and that he'd gotten a bum rap," says Dershowitz.

While preparing the appeal, Dershowitz flew to Indiana several times to visit Tyson in prison. Prison rules required them to sit side-by-side facing a monitor so the guards could see what they were saying. "People did not believe me when I said that Mike was one of the nicest, sweetest people I've had the privilege of knowing," says Dershowitz. Tyson enjoyed history books, and so Dershowitz sent him dozens of volumes about ancient Egypt, the Roaring Twenties, and other topics that intrigued Tyson.

They spoke often on the phone, and Tyson was forced to wait for hours in long lines for his turn to use the phone. Once when Tyson called Dershowitz, he heard two-year-old Ella crying in the background and told Dershowitz he would call back later. "Take care of your kid," he said.

Sometimes Nathan Dershowitz traveled with his brother to visit Tyson in prison. "I found his deference to Cus D'Amato's wife, Camille, absolutely magnificent," says Nathan, not usually given to effusive praise. "Mike was such a gentleman—so respectful. Immature, yet sympathetic below the surface."

Tyson's prison was filthy. He was brought to visit Dershowitz with irons on his legs and shackles on his arms, and Dershowitz could see him physically struggling against the chains. "He looked like a slave," says Dershowitz. One time, the guard supervising Dershowitz's visit made a subtly racist remark to Tyson, and moments after, Tyson spit—not at the guard, but on the ground. "Now get down on your knees and clean that up!" barked the guard. Worried that Tyson might get upset and cause himself more prison time, Dershowitz stood in between Tyson and the guard, as Tyson got down and cleaned up the spit. "That was scary—it looked like a scene out of *Roots*," says Dershowitz.

Dershowitz received a barrage of letters and calls from friends, acquaintances, and members of the public vilifying his representation of Tyson. "He is an animal and you know it. . . . You are tarnished, baby, you are tarnished," read one letter. "When you choose to represent someone like Mike Tyson, you attach the Jewish community to your action," wrote an angry Jewish correspondent. "I now find it hard to understand how you can mount a passionate defense for a convicted rapist."

Dershowitz faced opposition at Harvard from feminist students, some of whom offered to help the Indiana prosecution pro bono, while others used their student evaluations to attack Dershowitz. One complained Dershowitz "spent two days talking about false reports of rape," and another wrote he did not "deserve to teach at Harvard."

"I was applying the same analysis as I did to other crimes: burden of proof, reasonable doubt, etc.," comments Dershowitz. "They wanted me to teach rape differently, and I would not do that. These evaluations showed me how dangerous it would be for an untenured professor to incur the wrath of the political-correctness patrol."

But not all the feedback was negative. During this time, Dershowitz was invited by a prominent TV executive to an intimate dinner with friends in Massachusetts. Michael Jackson turned out to be one of the guests, and Dershowitz struck up a conversation with him. "Michael told me how outraged he was at the Tyson case," says Dershowitz. Following the dinner, Dershowitz wrote Jackson a letter, saying, "Your support for [Mike] means a great deal to him as well as to me. We are all hoping that justice will be done, though the Indiana legal system leaves much to be desired in terms of doing justice."

During this time Charlie Rose had Dershowitz on to discuss Tyson's case. "I believe that this was a groupie who knows the rules of groupies," said Dershowitz. "And the rules of groupies are very simple: they follow athletes around, they follow rock stars around—they get twenty minutes of not very good sex in exchange for bragging rights."

"Let's assume that he, in fact, had reason to think that, but then at some point she says no," Rose commented. "But he says she didn't say no—ever!" replied Dershowitz. "And she only said no the next day when she found that her father was coming. . . . It's a case of who's telling the truth."

Rose had Dershowitz on several times in the early 1990s, and during one of their interviews, he pulled out a magazine. "This is the new *LIFE* magazine, 'Getting to the Heart of the American Family,'" he said to Dershowitz, rifling through the pages. "Guess who's on page [37]—that's you and your brother, uh?"

"Nathan, Nathan," said Dershowitz, looking at the picture inside the magazine of himself and Nathan playing basketball. "He's complaining because I'm giving him an elbow in the jaw, but look, anything to win at basketball," he explained with a smile. "He's a great lawyer, Nathan. He really has been my secret weapon in a lot of the appeals that I've won."

By the early 1990s, Nathan had started his own appellate firm with two partners, Victoria Eiger and Amy Adelson. Alan often turned to his brother when building a team for a case. "It was a really symbiotic relationship," says Nathan.

"One of my jobs was to read everything that occurred in the trial and to be an issue spotter—figuring out what issues were appropriate to be presented on appeal. Having handled hundreds of appeals when working for Legal Aid appeals and having been responsible for cases sent to large law firms who volunteered to work on appeals, I was well situated to do issue spotting. I also handled both civil and criminal appeals before Alan and I joined forces. I frequently had discussions with Alan, which was an interesting interplay.

"Alan could find a theoretical argument in almost anything, but the trick was not to make a brilliant presentation, but to win. Having isolated several issues, my partners and I would do research in my office—digging up cases and putting together a draft of a brief for Alan's comments. Then we would decide who would argue what. If it was an interesting, theoretical argument, Alan would do that. If it was more of a standard argument, I would do it. If he was going to argue the case, shortly before the argument, we would put together a package consisting of the briefs, the main relevant cases, and the sections of the record he needed to review. Alan would call frequently with questions while he was preparing.

"Arguments with esoteric concepts are the hardest cases to win," Nathan notes. "Alan was very good at that. He was a very, very quick learner. His ability to gather, coordinate, and consolidate information—and his ability to fill in gaps when judges asked questions that were outside the box— was overwhelmingly impressive. Alan really thinks outside the box. He's basically a contrarian. He'll take an adverse position to whatever is the popular position. When that is put to positive ends, it is very significant. Too often, however, esoteric concepts need to be a matter of last resort, and Alan would often get carried away with looking for the esoteric, rather than the straightforward, winnable issue."

"Nat is more the detail person," commented Harvey Silverglate to a newspaper during this time. "Alan's creativity can sometimes go out into hyperspace, and Nat can help bring him down to earth by noting when his ideas fail the giggle test."

At times, Nathan also had to calm Alan down when someone made a statement Alan thought was libelous. "My brother has a thin skin," says Nathan. "Back in the '90s, he wanted to sue everybody. He would call me and say, 'Did you hear what this guy said about me?' I taught libel and privacy, and I would tell him, 'You don't have a shot in hell—you're a public figure.'"

"We had professional disagreements all the time over cases, but we always worked things out," relays Nathan.

If the brothers were arguing a case before a judge who did not like Alan, Nathan would do the oral argument. "Once, Alan had been critical of Judge John Walker on the Second Circuit, who was a cousin of President George H. W. Bush," says Nathan. "Alan had claimed it was a violation of certain nepotism laws for Walker to have obtained his position. Sometime later, Walker happened to be the judge on a case Alan and I were arguing.

We arranged for myself to come in and argue instead of Alan. Judge Walker had prepared extensive notes in order to beat the hell out of Alan during the oral argument. And then *I* got up to talk. It was supposed to be a fifteen-minute argument, and it turned into forty as the judge ranted and raved. While I was standing at the podium, Alan was sitting with a naughty grin on his face because I was getting the abuse and not him."

This was not the situation in Mike Tyson's case. In early 1993, Dershowitz presented his oral argument before three judges on the Indiana Court of Appeals. "The defendant explicitly testified that he believed that Washington expected to have sex with him," he told the judges. "That belief was confirmed during the sex act itself, when according to her testimony he asked her whether, quote, 'she wanted to be on top,' and she responded, 'Yeah'—without explaining the reasons to him. [He then said to her], according to her testimony, 'Do you love me now?'"

He mentioned the three witnesses who were not allowed to testify and also attacked Judge Gifford, saying she was hand-picked by the prosecution. "It's up to the system to make sure that the prosecution doesn't get to pick the judge," he argued. "Can you imagine a system where the defendant got to pick the judge? There'd be an outcry. Judges should pick the judges."

"Mike Tyson had his best day in court Monday," reported *USA Today*. "In spite of a trial record filled with mistakes, omissions and elementary errors by the fighter's ex–defense team, Dershowitz and colleagues argued that Tyson's conviction must be set aside. . . . Reversal of a criminal conviction by a jury is rare, but Tyson's attorneys might have successfully pinpointed the crucial issues that will free him."

"I was feeling pretty confident about my appeals with [Alan] heading the case," comments Tyson.

"It was an open and shut case," says Dershowitz. "Under the Sixth Amendment, you can't prevent witnesses from testifying for a defendant."

Nevertheless, two of the three judges ruled against Dershowitz's argument, and Dershowitz was forced to appeal Tyson's case to the Indiana Supreme Court. "At this point, I didn't think we were going to win the appeal," says Tyson. "But we weren't going to just lay down. We were going to fight them to the end."

"I was fairly confident when we brought the case before the State Supreme Court," says Dershowitz. "We had three out of the five judges in our corner based on their previous decisions, including the chief justice."

Unfortunately, disaster struck. It turned out that the chief justice, Randall Shepard, had attended Yale Law School a few years behind Dershowitz, and they both turned up to a Yale reunion while the case was pending. Dershowitz was catching up with his old friend Stephen Trachtenberg when a woman tapped him repeatedly on his shoulder. "Professor Dershowitz!" she said. "Excuse me, ma'am, I'm sorry, but I'm in the middle of a conversation," replied Dershowitz. "I just wanted to tell you that your New York style of law won't work in Indiana," she stated. "Are you an Indiana lawyer?" asked Dershowitz, confused. "No," answered the woman. Pointing to a man in the corner, she introduced herself as the wife of Chief Justice Randall Shepard. "I can't be talking to you!" said Dershowitz angrily, whereupon he broke off the conversation and took Trachtenberg into a side room. He quickly wrote out an affidavit explaining that this woman had approached him, not vice versa, and he had Trachtenberg sign it as witness.

When it came time for the Supreme Court's vote, the decision was split 2–2, and the chief justice recused himself, causing Tyson's convic-tion to be affirmed. "My own decision not to disclose the reasons for my disqualification was motivated by a desire to protect my wife from the embarrassment she would feel about public disclosure and debate con-cerning her conduct," Shepard announced.

The truth was that Shepard was giving himself cover. Dershowitz later learned that earlier in his career, before his marriage, Shepard had been accused of being sexually improper with a male clerk and carefully covered it up for years. He knew that if he was the one who freed Mike Tyson, an outcry would be raised, and he would be personally scrutinized by Tyson's enemies.

"The incident at the Yale reunion was a whole setup," says Dershowitz. "Shepard sent his wife over to me. He had written opinions previously requiring conviction in similar cases, but didn't want his prior history coming out. His failure to vote cost Mike Tyson his freedom."

"That was a really dark moment," comments Tyson. "They left Alan insignificant after the justice's wife spoke with him. I had never heard of such a thing—it seemed unlike anything that had ever been done in the history of prosecuting."

Throwing a Hail Mary, Dershowitz filed a writ of certiorari before the U.S. Supreme Court, but they declined to hear the case. Mike Tyson would forever be a convicted rapist.

"These guys wanted me in prison," comments Tyson. "Let me tell you something: I shared a cell with a guy who had been sentenced by the same judge as me—he was convicted of rape, and she gave him *forty* years. Now if she really thought I had done it, you think she'd give me six fucking years? Give me a break. She knows I didn't do it. She just wanted to be the judge that sent me away to prison."

"I don't say this about most of my clients, but I think the injustice in Mike's case was overwhelming," says Nathan Dershowitz. "The system was out to get him because of who he was."

"Indiana had a more corrupt legal system than the Soviet Union," says Dershowitz without a hint of exaggeration. "People ask me, 'How do you sleep at night defending guilty people?' But how do you think I feel after losing a case for someone like Mike, who was completely, totally *innocent*?"

* * *

"Tell me, what percentage of your practice as an appellate lawyer is taken up by these celebrity cases?" Charlie Rose asked Dershowitz during an interview in 1992. "10 percent probably," said Dershowitz. "Only 10 percent?" replied Rose, surprised. "What's the other 90 percent?"

"I would say 50 percent are clearly pro bono because I have a rule in my office—half the cases have to be pro bono cases," explained Dershowitz. "I recently saved a woman's children who were taken away from her on the grounds of sexual abuse. We were able to prove that the sexual abuse was committed by her former husband's stepchildren. She now sends me the report cards of the children every semester to show how well they're doing."

"You choose your cases based on what?" inquired Rose. "My feeling that there's been an injustice," replied Dershowitz. "I have to get my passions for justice going."

"And to those who say Alan Dershowitz is a guy who loves the hot focus of media attention—he chooses his cases because of the celebrity involved?"

pressed Rose. "It's interesting, you only know about the famous cases, but most of my cases are for unknown people," responded Dershowitz. "For example, last week I got tremendous joy: I won a case I've been working on for thirteen years. I've been doing it free—it's cost me almost $100,000 out of my own pocket."

It had been five years since Dershowitz argued the Tison brothers' case before the justices on the Supreme Court, who had handed it back down to Arizona. At the time, there was a moratorium on executions throughout Arizona, but in the early 1990s, the moratorium came off and inmates began to be executed, including Randy Greenawalt, who had helped Gary Tison murder the Lyons family.

Together with lawyer Cynthia Hamilton—who had been a student of Dershowitz's—and his brother's law firm, Dershowitz pursued every appeal possible in Arizona to save their lives. After presenting evidence to multiple courts that the brothers were not "recklessly indifferent to human life," the death sentences were finally and irrevocably vacated. "The Tison brothers case was terrible for the anti–death penalty movement," says Dershowitz, "because the end result of the Supreme Court's decision made it easier to execute non-triggerman. But it was going to happen anyway. Sandra Day O'Connor was just waiting for the right case."

Notwithstanding this, when Dershowitz got the news that the Tison brothers' lives were no longer in peril, he felt an enormous high. "The Talmud says, 'he who saves a human life—it's as if they have saved the whole world,'" he comments. "And I felt like I had saved the whole world."

Dershowitz and his team tried to gain parole for the brothers, but to no avail. "There were just too many politics involved in that," says Raymond. "There were still people in Arizona who wanted to see us dead." "We could very easily have ended up dead," admits Ricky.

"I am really thankful for what Alan did for us," comments Raymond, who found it difficult having no relationship with his extended family while in prison. "Prison is mostly dead time—time you lose forever. And you begin to realize that your friends and relatives have moved on. They've started families and careers, and their lives have diverged so significantly from yours."

"Being on death row teaches you not to worry about things you have no control over," Raymond notes. Nevertheless, he laments: "I wish we had known our father for who he was, not who he thought he was. We thought we were rescuing someone, and it turns out we let loose a monster."

* * *

It was around the time of the Tison brothers' victory when Dershowitz got a shocking phone call from Mia Farrow, Woody Allen's girlfriend, early one morning. Farrow rose to fame after starring in the 1968 classic horror film *Rosemary's Baby* and was married to Frank Sinatra before starting a relationship with Woody Allen in 1980. Over the next decade, Allen made thirteen films starring Farrow, and though the couple never married, they had a son named Ronan and adopted two children, Moses and Dylan. Farrow had a heart for orphans and had previously adopted several children.

In the time since Dershowitz had seen Farrow and Woody Allen at his debate about the Rosenbergs, Farrow had periodically called Dershowitz to discuss politics. Dershowitz had also exchanged letters with Allen several times, most recently in early 1992 about revenge in the context of the Holocaust.

When Farrow called early that morning in 1992, Dershowitz greeted Farrow and asked how Allen was doing. "He's abusing my children," Farrow replied concernedly. "Don't even joke about that, it's not funny," said Dershowitz seriously. "No, really," continued Farrow. "He's been sleeping with one of my daughters and acting inappropriately with another one." After Dershowitz asked again whether she was serious, Farrow assured him she was and asked if he could come to her home in Connecticut. Dershowitz told Farrow he would and that he would also bring his wife, who was then working as a psychologist and specialized in helping children who had been traumatized.

When Alan and Carolyn pulled into Farrow's property, Farrow was on the roof of the house fixing a leak. She welcomed Alan and Carolyn and took them inside, where she was caring for her adopted children, including a "crack baby" and a blind girl. "The house was filled with kids and activity," says Carolyn. "I was struck with how hands-on Mia was as a parent."

Farrow told Dershowitz that Allen had begun a relationship with Farrow's adopted daughter Soon-Yi. When Dershowitz asked how old she was, Farrow replied that she was probably between seventeen and nineteen, but no one at the orphanage in South Korea had been sure of her birthdate. Dershowitz asked if there was evidence of the abuse, and Farrow showed him photos that Allen had taken of Soon-Yi naked. She also took him into an attic where she claimed Allen had molested their co-adopted daughter, Dylan.

Dershowitz tried to take everything in and asked Farrow what he could do to help. Farrow said that Allen admired Dershowitz and kept *Chutzpah* on his nightstand. She asked if Dershowitz would help negotiate an agreement with Allen's lawyers. Dershowitz agreed, hoping to keep the matter private for the sake of Farrow and Allen's children.

In August 1992, Dershowitz met with Farrow and Allen's legal representatives in New York, bringing along David Levett, a Connecticut lawyer who had been a classmate of Dershowitz's at Yale.

"[We] offered a series of recommendations, focusing primarily on visitation by Woody," says Dershowitz. "Naturally, there were also discussions of financial issues, payment for therapy, education, broken contracts, etc. It was a conventional settlement discussion, typical in matrimonial cases." Dershowitz and Farrow's lawyers left the meeting content that progress had been made. And then, mere hours after the meeting, they learned that—while the negotiations were taking place—Allen's team had filed a lawsuit seeking sole custody of Ronan, Moses, and Dylan.

Hoping to somehow hold back the tsunami, Dershowitz dashed off a letter to Allen. "Dear Woody: I am writing to you directly—through your lawyers, of course,—because I think there is still some possibility of resolving this incredibly difficult matter without lives being further damaged by publicity and formal legal proceedings," he wrote. "I know that Mia and her lawyers were acting in good faith to avoid litigation and publicity. But while the negotiations were going on, your lawyers were filing a preemptive lawsuit that generated the press interest in the matter. Frankly Woody, it was a stupid and destructive thing to do. . . . As you and Mia both know, I am a great admirer of your work and do not want to see your career and your life destroyed. Right now you are on that road and something must be done to head it off, not only for your sake but for the sake of the children and for Mia."

Unbeknownst to Dershowitz, Allen received the letter, but did not reply. "I refused any idea of a settlement as I had done nothing wrong and much preferred a court hearing, despite the knowledge I would be smeared publicly," says Allen. "Alan was trying to broker a settlement in good faith—unaware his client would never have lived up to any agreement even if I had been willing to settle." The day after Dershowitz's letter was sent, Allen held a press conference, admitting to being in love with Soon-Yi, but denying he had ever molested Dylan in any way—alleging instead that Farrow had put young Dylan up to making the accusation.

And so, despite Dershowitz's efforts, the litigation moved forward, and Farrow and Allen's messy private lives were exposed to the entire country. In October, Charlie Rose had Dershowitz on his show and discussed the whole affair. "Tell me how you feel about this case," said Rose. "I feel awful about it," replied a soft-spoken Dershowitz, "because Woody Allen was one of my real heroes. I quote him extensively in *Chutzpah*. . . . It's been a very big disappointment, but you know you live and you learn and you accept that great artists can be flawed human beings."

"And how is he flawed?" asked Rose. "Oh, I think the decision to have an affair with a twenty-year-old adopted daughter of his lover—his life mate—is just horrible," answered Dershowitz. "It crosses lines within the family. It was a family—a *real family*. And you don't create a competition between daughter and mother. That's just wrong."

Things got spicier in the spring of 1993 when Allen's lawyers called Dershowitz to testify during the trial. They claimed that during the meeting back in August, Dershowitz had told Allen's lawyers that all of this could go away if Allen agreed to pay several million dollars. "[It was a] boneheaded maneuver," notes Dershowitz. "Courtroom observers could not believe that Woody's lawyers would force me to appear as a witness, knowing that I would surely side with Mia in her efforts to maintain custody of her children. But having been falsely accused of trying to blackmail Woody, I had no choice but to testify as to precisely what had transpired."

In April 1993, Dershowitz took the stand in the New York courtroom with Woody Allen seated mere feet away and Claire Dershowitz watching from the spectator section. Referring to the charges of black-mail, Dershowitz declared, "That is not the kind of lawyer I am," and countered that he had simply attempted to be a mediator in the hopes of saving Woody from "career-destroying disclosures."

"He was a hero of mine," said Dershowitz, occasionally looking in Allen's direction. "I thought, maybe naively, that I could prevent this disaster from happening."

One of Allen's lawyers, Elkan Abramowitz, repeated the charge of blackmailing, and Dershowitz lost it. "That's a lie!" he said, voice raised. As Abramowitz continued to make the accusation, Dershowitz started hysterically shouting, "Perjurer! Perjurer!"

When Abramowitz asked if there had been anything nonnegotiable at the August meeting, Dershowitz stared intensely at him. "I'll tell you one thing that was nonnegotiable," he replied, jaw clenched. "What was nonnegotiable was Dylan's welfare. Money wasn't what was at stake here. Dylan's protection was at stake."

In the end, the judge sided totally with Farrow, awarding her full cus-tody of their three children. Following the ugly case, Allen and Soon-Yi started a life together, and Allen was never criminally charged with molest-ing Dylan.

"It was a very difficult case," says Dershowitz. "If Woody had called me first, I probably would have represented him. But once I met with Mia and heard her side of the case, I felt obliged to stay on as her lawyer."

"In hindsight, I think Woody's lawyers only met with Mia's side to see whether they could catch us trying to do something improper," he adds.

"I liked Alan Dershowitz. I believe he tried to find a way to minimize the damage to our reputations, but he didn't know Mia well enough to know she was an extremely troubled woman, a convincing actress, whose word couldn't be counted on," says Allen. "I was the one who recom-mended Alan to Mia long before she found it necessary to consult him. I told her, 'If you ever need a great lawyer, call Alan.' Little did I know she would hire him against me."

* * *

During the Woody Allen–Mia Farrow debacle, America had witnessed an extraordinary presidential election. Incumbent George Bush was defeated by forty-five-year-old Bill Clinton, who had appeared alongside Dershowitz in *Time*'s "Fifty Faces for the Future" back in 1979. Dershowitz voted for the intelligent and suave Clinton, who had promised to be a centrist liberal, but Dershowitz was concerned by Clinton's personal life, which included flirtations with drugs as a young man and extramarital affairs as an adult. Referring in early 1994 to a financial scandal Bill and Hillary were embroiled in, Dershowitz wrote in a column: "As a Democrat and a Clinton supporter, my hope is that a special prosecutor will find nothing improper, unethical, or criminal in the Whitewater mess. As an American, I want the whole truth to emerge so that the voters can judge for themselves. Let there be a full and open investigation and let the chips fall where they may."

Despite his neutral stance on Whitewater, Dershowitz was as liberal as he had ever been. In the past five years, he had donated to the campaigns of John Kerry, Ted Kennedy, Senator Harris Wofford, Attorney General Robert Abrams, and Senator Arlen Specter—all Democrats (in Specter's case, a former Democrat). One of Dershowitz's latest student evaluations at Harvard read, "As far left as you can get [but] he'll be assailed by the politically correct for challenging their knee-jerk reactions."

It was around the time of Clinton's rise to power that Dershowitz taught two students at Harvard who would become extremely influential Republicans.

Mike Pompeo had graduated top of his class at West Point and achieved the rank of captain in the Army by the time he enrolled at HLS in the early '90s. Among the classes he was required to take was Dershowitz's legal ethics course. "Professor Dershowitz was already a legendary lawyer," says Pompeo.

"During classes, he brought in lawyers he had worked with on previous cases, along with some of his former clients, to present some of the most difficult questions that lawyers face. A handful of them were Mafia figures—or at least reportedly real Mafia figures. He brought them in while explaining the ethical issues that arise when a lawyer represents clients engaged in complex business transactions. The class had a touch of realism that I didn't get in many of my other classes at Harvard."

"Professor Dershowitz was a joy to be in the classroom with," Pompeo continues. "He was a known Democrat, and I was a pretty conservative Republican. But he was decent to those of us who had political views that were different from him. He always treated everyone's ideas with respect and decency."

"Although I came to Harvard Law School as an avowed liberal, I have tried hard not to use the classroom to propagandize my captive audience," says Dershowitz. "My goal is not to turn conservatives into liberals, but to make conservatives more thoughtful conservatives, better able to articulate and defend nuanced positions. The same is true of liberals and everyone else.

"I grew up during the McCarthy period, and I never wanted to use the classroom to persuade people of my personal points of view. I was just interested in making them better thinkers. I got a job at Harvard to teach students legal analysis—not change their political opinions."

Ted Cruz was a twentysomething when he arrived at Harvard in the early 1990s. His father, Rafael, had grown up in Cuba and was imprisoned during the reign of Fulgencio Batista before managing to escape to America. His son, Ted, eventually went to Princeton, where he studied public policy and won first place in a national debating competition. By the time he got to Harvard, he was an enthusiastic young conservative.

"Professor Dershowitz was one of the most prominent law professors in the country, and I was thrilled when I arrived on campus and discovered he was my criminal law professor," says Cruz. "I still remember early on in the class, he stood up and told us all, 'I'm Alan Dershowitz, and by any measure, I am among the 1 percent most liberal Americans in our country. And yet here at the Harvard Law School, I'm considered somewhat conservative.' This was because, among other things, he believed in things like free speech—that you have a right to speak even if he hated what you were saying. He believed in due process and civil liberties even for a horrific, violent person.

"Professor Dershowitz thought very little of liberals who couldn't defend their positions," Cruz continues. "He agreed with them usually, but it would drive him crazy when he'd get a law student who would stand up and say, 'Well, I just *feel* this is right.' And he would look at them and say, 'Oh, you *feel*? You're emotive? I'm sorry, I thought we were in law school. I thought you were learning how to present an argument, using reason and facts and the law.'

"Throughout the course, he loved to engage in a vigorous argument. It was his love of engagement and argument that ultimately resulted in he and I becoming friends. As a 1-L, I generally tried not to speak too much in class—I typically spoke no more than once a week in class. But Professor Dershowitz would be teaching a class and bashing an opinion by Justice Scalia or Justice Thomas, and it would tick me off. I couldn't help but raise my hand and say, 'Hold on a second, Professor Dershowitz. What about this . . .' and I'd argue on the other side. He would light up and literally step toward me with a glimmer in his eye.

"If you could argue against him and defend yourself—even if he didn't agree with you—he respected that. Many times after class, I would go back with him to his office and continue our conversation, and we would argue at length."

"[Ted] was one of the best students I ever had because a teacher loves to be challenged," says Dershowitz. "I was against the death penalty—[he was] in favor. I was in favor of the exclusionary rule—[he was] against it. I never had to play the devil's advocate—he was there!"

"I remember a really fun thing that happened during my time at Harvard," recounts Cruz. "When I was a 3-L, I was dating a woman who was a 1-L and who was then taking Professor Dershowitz's Criminal Law class. And he was continuing to bash opinions by Justices Thomas and Scalia. And the students that year got a novel idea. A bunch of them got together and wrote a letter to Justice Scalia which [essentially] said, 'Dear Justice Scalia, We're students in Alan Dershowitz's criminal law class. He regularly criticizes your opinions on the Supreme Court. Why don't you come and defend yourself and argue the other side?'

"And amazingly enough, Justice Scalia did. He came up to Harvard Law School and had a ninety-minute debate with Professor Dershowitz. Both did a masterful job. I actually think there are similarities between Alan Dershowitz and Antonin Scalia: both are (or were) brilliant, passionate, and committed to their interpretation of the Constitution and law. Both reveled in engaging their opponents with humor and good spirits."

Incidentally, around the time he debated Scalia, Dershowitz was working behind the scenes to get Stephen Breyer nominated to the Supreme Court. Breyer had clerked for Arthur Goldberg the year after Dershowitz, and in the time since had served on the faculty at Harvard Law School and on the First Circuit Court of Appeals. Breyer and his wife, Joanna, had visited Alan and Carolyn for dinner on multiple occasions.

Clinton was considering several judges to fill the seat of retiring Justice Harry Blackmun, and when Breyer's name was thrown in the ring, Dershowitz sent a videotape to the White House of Breyer at a judicial conference making humorous remarks. Clinton partially judged people by their sense of humor and was concerned that Breyer did not have one. Dershowitz hoped the tape would demonstrate otherwise. Eventually, Clinton did nominate Breyer, and Alan and Carolyn invited Breyer and his wife over for a celebration dinner, fondly reflecting that Breyer was assuming the seat of Arthur Goldberg, who had passed away of a heart attack a couple years previously.

Breyer invited Dershowitz to attend his swearing-in ceremony in August at the White House, and during the ceremony Dershowitz bumped into the Clintons. Just a few weeks later, he was vacationing on Martha's Vineyard, where the Clintons had a summer home. Dershowitz was making a purchase in the Chilmark Chocolates store when he bumped into a Jewish friend of his. They got talking about the upcoming Rosh Hashanah New Year services and Dershowitz remarked how much he wanted to contact Bill Clinton and invite him to attend. "I can get ahold of him," said the woman, who was a friend of Clinton's. Dershowitz drafted a letter and gave it to her for the president. "Dear Mr. President," he wrote. "It is my honor to invite you on behalf of the Martha's Vineyard Hebrew Center to attend our Rosh Hashanah services. . . . In years gone by, Jews in different countries lived in fear that government officials would enter their religious sanctuaries. . . . In contemporary America, the attitude of the Jewish community is quite different: We welcome our president with open arms."

Shortly after, Dershowitz got a call from the White House saying the president accepted his invitation. On September 5, 1994, the Clintons arrived at the Whaling Church in Edgartown, and before going in, Dershowitz, his wife, and his son Elon exchanged pleasantries with the

First Couple. Dershowitz gave the president a yarmulke to wear, and quickly taught him how to sing a traditional Jewish prayer. When the service began, Dershowitz sat with Clinton in the front row, sharing a *mahzor* (Hebrew prayer book) with him and quietly explaining various words to him, like *mitzvoth* ("good deeds"). It was the first time a sitting US president had attended a Jewish High Holiday service.

After the service, the Clintons invited Dershowitz and his family to dinner at a French restaurant in Edgartown. "It was amazing how friendly they were," says Dershowitz. "It didn't feel like they were the president and first lady." The president was familiar with Dershowitz and his distinguished career and found it easy to get along with him because of Dershowitz's penchant for telling jokes.

Unfortunately, the president had allergies and was sneezing throughout the meal. Elon mentioned that he had learned a trick in China in 1980 that alleviated sneezing. Clinton asked him to demonstrate, whereupon Elon leaned over and squeezed Clinton's nasal bridge, making the nearby Secret Service agents nervous. The maneuver worked, but it was regrettably not enough for Elon to merit dessert. Clinton ordered an enormous Chocolate Bombe, and when it came to the table, Elon grabbed a fork, figuring it was for everyone. But Clinton, who had quite the sweet tooth, looked at Elon with a discouraging expression and ate the whole Bombe himself.

Still the evening ended amicably. A journalist had sent over a bottle of wine, and they all filled their glasses. Clinton raised a toast to the New Year, and as Dershowitz tapped his glass to Clinton's, he uttered the traditional Jewish blessing "L'Chaim!"—"To Life!"

How ironic it was that as Dershowitz celebrated life on that September day, he was about to take on a case that would rock America to its core—a case filled with jealousy, sorrow, and death.

TRAILS OF DECEIT

Over the years, Dershowitz had experienced a recurring nightmare in which Ted Bundy, who had been accused of serially raping and killing many young women, called him seeking representation. A request from such a completely despicable person would have been the ultimate test of Dershowitz's insistence on the constitutional right of every American to a rigorous defense. Would he have accepted Bundy's plea? Fortunately, Bundy never called, and Dershowitz was never faced with the dilemma.

Then in June 1994, former Buffalo Bills star running back O. J. Simpson was accused of killing his former wife, Nicole Brown, and her friend Ron Goldman in cold blood. The circumstances were highly incriminating. The murder had taken place a short distance from Simpson's house in Los Angeles late one evening, mere hours before Simpson boarded a flight for Chicago for a golfing trip. Eyewitness testimony and blood samples taken by police from the crime scene seemed to convincingly point to Simpson's guilt, and the murders were carried out with the savagery and force that a professional athlete could muster. Goldman, a six-foot, one-inch twenty-five-year-old, had been stabbed twenty-five times, and Brown's neck had been slashed so powerfully that her spinal cord was visible from the front. Simpson and Brown's children had been inside the house, sleeping and unaware that their mother was being killed outside.

The week following the murders brought the infamous Bronco chase and the release of a 911 tape from years past in which Simpson was heard swearing loudly at Brown after breaking down the door of her house. Prosecutor Marcia Clark, who had gone into law after being raped as a

teenager, declared Simpson had committed these murders "with deliberation and premeditation." A host of prosecutors joined her crusade to bring
the wrath of the law down on Simpson.

As Dershowitz watched these developments on television, he turned to
his wife at one point and said, "O. J. probably did it. The former husband
is generally the perp in a case like this." He made similar points in articles
and TV appearances and noted in one column, "This promises to be the
most closely watched trial in history, since O. J. Simpson is probably the
most famous American ever charged with murder."

Little did he know that Simpson's lawyer, Robert Shapiro, was putting
together a defense team and wanted Dershowitz's help. With the facts
seemingly on their side and an outraged public behind them, the prosecutors seemed to have an easy path to win both in the courtroom and in the
court of public opinion. On top of this, Simpson was facing the death
penalty if he lost.

Robert Shapiro was a hardworking, methodical lawyer who had represented Linda Lovelace, Johnny Carson, and Christian Brando. Dershowitz
had consulted with him on Brando's case. "I needed a constitutional law
expert for O. J.," says Shapiro, "and the first person I thought of who was
not in my immediate circle of lawyers was Alan."

As the defense and prosecution were lining up their chess pieces,
Dershowitz and his son Elon traveled to a conference in Israel. After checking in to the historic King David Hotel in Jerusalem, Dershowitz got a call
from Shapiro asking if he would join Simpson's team. Dershowitz told
Shapiro that he had spoken about the case on TV and predicted Simpson's
defense would be based on a mental illness excuse. "You've been listening
to Garcetti [the Los Angeles DA]," Shapiro commented. "That's what he's
been saying. It's not going to happen. O. J. swears he didn't do it, and
that's what the defense is going to be—innocence." Shapiro also informed
Dershowitz that Simpson was facing the death penalty.

"We really need you, Alan," Shapiro pressed. "They're going to put
together the biggest and most powerful prosecution team ever assembled.
Garcetti's career depends on winning this case. We need your brief-writing
and constitutional expertise." Dershowitz told Shapiro he would consider
it and get back to him.

That night Dershowitz wrestled with himself mentally. "Because I am a professor with tenure, I believe I have a special responsibility to take on cases and causes that may require me to confront the powers that be—the government, the police, prosecutors, the media, the bar, even the university," he later noted. Since his clerkship with Arthur Goldberg, he had been writing about the unfair way the death penalty was wielded against Black Americans, and he had spent his entire career yammering about the right of the vilest defendants to a rigorous representation. Even with the demands of his teaching schedule, the case was too good to pass up. Dershowitz knew the justice system would be on display to the public like it never had before, and it would be a tremendous opportunity to showcase what he had devoted his life to.

"Dear Bob," he wrote in a letter from Israel. "I very much appreciate your invitation to me to consult with you on the O. J. Simpson case, particularly with reference to the outrageous government misconduct involved in the prosecutor's prediction that Simpson will admit committing the acts. I completely agree with you that this statement—and others made by the in-court prosecutor—has created an atmosphere which makes it virtually impossible for a jury to presume Simpson's innocence. . . . If you have readily available the transcripts of everything the prosecutors said, could you please have your office send a copy to my office so that we can begin working on this immediately."

In the coming weeks, Dershowitz assembled a group of around ten students from Harvard to help on the case and coordinated his efforts with his brother's law firm, who had also joined the case at Shapiro's request. Together, Dershowitz and his coworkers would be creating motions on technical aspects of the law and would also be keeping an eye out for issues in the trial upon which an appeal could be based. Dershowitz became known as the "God-forbid lawyer" since he was to handle Simpson's appeal in the event of a conviction.

In addition to Dershowitz, Shapiro gathered a star-studded team of lawyers, including F. Lee Bailey, Tupac and Michael Jackson's lawyer Johnnie Cochran, Robert Kardashian, and—partly at the advice of Dershowitz and his brother—DNA expert Barry Scheck. All told, thirteen defense attorneys were going up against nearly fifty prosecutors, who had the financial resources of the State of California behind them and the testimony of police officers who had searched the crime scene and Simpson's house in the hours immediately after the murders. The only bright spot for Simpson was that the death penalty was eventually taken off the table. Instead, he was facing life imprisonment without parole.

"From its very beginning to its closing arguments, we regarded this case as essentially forensic in nature," says Dershowitz. "Did the prosecution's physical evidence and the way it was gathered, tested, and testified about prove the defendant's guilt beyond a reasonable doubt?"

The defense scored an early victory when they were unexpectedly granted a preliminary hearing instead of a grand jury, on the grounds that the prosecutors had unfairly biased the public against their client by their press leaks. "A grand jury hearing is conducted in secret," explained Dershowitz. "The defense does not get to cross-examine prosecution witnesses. . . . A preliminary hearing [in contrast], with its opportunity to cross-examine, [allowed] us to lock in the testimony of the prosecution's witnesses before it had the opportunity to coordinate its case."

Two prominent pieces of evidence were brought to the forefront at the hearing. One was a pair of bloodstained socks which police found in Simpson's bedroom and which allegedly contained DNA from both Simpson and Brown's blood. The other was a glove found at Simpson's home which supposedly matched his size and like the socks allegedly contained the blood of Brown, Goldman, and Simpson.

Dershowitz was wary of the policemen involved in the case from the beginning. They had entered Simpson's house without a warrant, and in the case of the socks, blood matching Simpson's had only been found several weeks after the initial investigation—and only after having been carried around by Officer Philip Vannatter for multiple hours.

"The police also theorized that a knife O. J. had bought could have been the murder weapon," says Nathan Dershowitz. "That knife was never found. A search warrant was issued so that the police could look for the knife in O. J.'s house. O. J. then called Bob to let him know that the knife was not in the house. It was—and had been—at a different location. It was in a case and had never been used. When Alan found out about this, he urged the defense not to turn the knife over to the police, since the search was only for the house. He suggested instead that it be turned over to the presiding judge, Lance Ito, who eventually became the trial judge. We decided to do this, and we figured that if the police or prosecutors did their due diligence and properly sought the knife, we'd address the issue at that time. Judge Ito kept the knife in a safe in the courtroom throughout the trial, and it was never again sought or found by the prosecutors.

"Alan made an important strategic decision related to the knife. Since it was sought only through a search warrant of O. J.'s house, the defense was not obligated to give it to the police. Alan was also worried that if we gave the knife to the police, they could find something that wasn't there."

Dershowitz had been familiar with the LA Police Department before Simpson's case, having taught at Harvard about police abuses in California. "The department had previously been under the control of a former Marine, Daryl Gates, who had turned the police force into basically an occupying army," says Dershowitz. "They used Marine tactics and had a terrible reputation among scholars."

Luckily for the defense, the preliminary hearing had brought negative information to light about the officer who claimed to have discovered the incriminating glove on Simpson's property, Mark Fuhrman. By the admission of lawyers in the DA office and fellow cops, Fuhrman was an old-fashioned racist, who particularly hated Black people. One fellow DA informed Marcia Clark, "My police officers are telling me that this guy is an evidence planter, this guy is a racist, this guy is a liar, this is a guy who put a swastika on the locker of a police officer who had recently married a Jewish woman." The defense also received a tip regarding a report Fuhrman had once filed for disability in which he referred to Black people by the n-word.

Dershowitz predicted to the defense that Marcia Clark, Christopher Darden, and the rest of the prosecutors would not be silly enough to call Fuhrman to the stand, since both sides knew of his racism. "Whenever I am on a defense team, I try to put myself in the place of the prosecution and think about how I would decide a particular issue," said Dershowitz. "In doing that with regard to Fuhrman, I came away with the clear sense that I would not call him, for reasons both ethical and tactical." But after the trial of the century officially got underway in January 1995, that is exactly what the prosecution did. In addition to Fuhrman, they also called on Officer Philip Vannatter, who had carried around the sample of Simpson's blood taken from his socks. Vannatter did himself no favors when he testified to the mostly Black jury that when he first went to Simpson's house he did not suspect Simpson as the killer any more than he suspected Robert Shapiro.

The defense brought in a leading expert on blood splatters, Dr. Herbert McDonnell, who examined the socks Vannatter had allegedly discovered with Simpson's blood. McDonnell testified that the mirror-image stains on both sides of the socks appeared to have been caused by someone pouring blood onto them while they laid flat on a surface. On top of this, according to Dershowitz, the defense eventually discovered that the blood on the socks contained a substantial amount of EDTA, a substance which prevents blood from coagulating and is not found in great quantity in the human body.

In another setback to the prosecution, it turned out that Fuhrman's discovery of the glove was suspicious, as well. "At first [the prosecutors] argued that it was accidentally dropped by Simpson as he climbed over the wire fence from a neighbor's adjoining yard," says Dershowitz. "When an analysis of the surrounding vegetation showed that to have been impossible, the prosecutors changed their theory . . . the glove was [also allegedly] still damp from blood when the glove was found. [This] was especially difficult to explain since there was no rain, dew, or moisture on the night in question. Had the glove been dampened by blood at about 10:30 p.m. and dropped behind Simpson's house at 10:45 p.m., it would have been bone dry by about 6:15 a.m., when Fuhrman claimed he found it, since blood dries quickly in the night air."

Dershowitz had first been exposed to police misconduct during his clerkship for David Bazelon, who had told Dershowitz about "dropsie" testimony like the prosecution was putting on in this case. The first case Dershowitz spearheaded as a lawyer, the JDL case, had revolved around a policeman whom Dershowitz caught lying on the stand, a phenomenon referred to as "testilying." As well, in his first book *The Best Defense*, Dershowitz had listed several "Rules" of the justice system, which included the following: "Rule IV: Almost all police lie about whether they violated the Constitution in order to convict guilty defendants. Rule V: All prosecutors, judges, and defense attorneys are aware of Rule IV."

With all the stench around Vannatter and Fuhrman, Dershowitz felt compelled to speak out for the sake of his client. Asked about Fuhrman on *Good Morning America* in March, Dershowitz declared, "Policemen are trained to be cool. They're professional witnesses. The Mollen Commission in New York, after reviewing thousands of hours of police testimony, said police perjury is rampant in the courts, but lawyers can't get at the perjury unless they can confront the witnesses with their own words."

"You're telling me that police departments tell their detectives that it's OK to lie?" asked the host. "Not only do police departments tell their detectives it's OK to lie, they learn it in the Academy," Dershowitz replied. "They have a word for it, it's called 'testilying.'"

All hell broke loose. Dershowitz was flooded with letters and phone calls from furious citizens and police officers, and protesters picketed outside his office. The dean of Harvard received multiple letters from the public and from former alumni asking him to remove Dershowitz from the faculty. Some declared they would no longer help fundraise for the university. A rally was held by the mayor of LA to show support for the police. "It is totally outrageous," Dennis Zine of the LA Police Department told media outlets. "I have never in my entire career of twenty-seven years heard of such a theory; that we're trained to lie."

During all this hullabaloo, Robert Shapiro got a call from Larry King. "You should come over to the studio tonight, Bob," King said. "Alan Dershowitz is in town, and he's gonna be on the show, arguing about police brutality with the head of the Police Protective League." Shapiro immediately contacted Dershowitz and asked him for Simpson's sake to tone it down a bit. "Alan assured me he understood," said Shapiro. "That night, however, I winced as he spoke on Larry's show of police conspiracies, 'testi-lying,' and the way cops are 'trained to lie at the police academy.'"

"Somehow, I get the sense they weren't helpful comments for me," recalled Simpson decades later.

Dershowitz felt no qualms about his actions. "I was convinced that [Mike Tyson] had suffered because his trial was not televised, especially since his trial lawyer never spoke to the media, while the prosecutor talked nonstop to everyone," he explains. "I did not want to see the same mistake made with O. J. Simpson."

Throughout the case, Dershowitz and F. Lee Bailey caused Shapiro the most headaches with their frequent media appearances, in which they occasionally contradicted each other. It got so bad that *The Boston Globe* published a cartoon of Dershowitz and Bailey in barbershop quartet outfits singing, "There's no business like law business!" A friend of Shapiro's sent him a roll of tape with the message "For Lee and Alan." Eventually, Shapiro had to make a rule that all media appearances were to be approved in advance. Bailey did not agree to this condition, but Dershowitz did.

While Dershowitz may have stepped out of line with his media appearances, his instincts about the police in this case turned out to be right on point. Partway through the trial, Dershowitz got a call from a writer telling him of the discovery of tapes in which Mark Fuhrman used the "n" word. Dershowitz alerted Johnnie Cochran, to whom Shapiro had ceded leadership of the team, and Cochran's office tracked down Laura McKinny, a screenwriter who had interviewed Fuhrman as part of her research for a new film. "Anything out of a n*****'s mouth for the first five or six sentences is a fucking lie," Fuhrman had told her. "Did you ever try to find a bruise on a n*****? It is pretty tough, huh?" he also noted.

"You know these people here, we got all this money going to Ethiopia for what," he ranted on another part of the tapes. "To feed a bunch of dumb n*****s that their own government won't even feed." As if it could not have been planned any better by Dershowitz himself, Fuhrman also said the following while referring to a colleague: "He doesn't know how to be a policeman. 'I can't lie.' Oh, you make me [expletive] sick to my guts. You know, you do what you have to do to put these [expletives] in jail. If you don't [expletive] get out of the [expletive] game."

The defense also received a letter from a certain Kathleen Bell, a real estate agent who had bumped into Fuhrman in a bar once. Bell wanted to see Simpson convicted but felt duty-bound to tell the defense something Fuhrman had said. "Officer Ferman [*sic*] went on to say that he would like nothing more than to see all 'n*****s' gathered together and killed," she wrote. "He said something about burning them or bombing them. I was too shaken to remember the exact words he used."

When asked about these embarrassing revelations outside the presence of the jury, Fuhrman invoked the Fifth Amendment.

* * *

Simpson's trial stretched on for eight months and was viewed on television by an average of nearly six million people each day. Dershowitz only appeared in court on a couple of occasions to argue an obscure point of the law which would help the defense if the case ever went to appeal.

"I had mixed feelings about an appeal," says Simpson. "Pretty much everyone I talked to agreed that I would have no trouble getting an appeal—that some of the rulings and things that were done screamed for one. But the idea of it certainly didn't thrill me, because it meant I was going to be locked up a lot longer. I was also well aware that some on my team had to get back to their jobs at university. Johnnie had other cases that he was looking at. I knew I wouldn't get all the guys back together for a second go-around."

Dershowitz met with Simpson in jail several times, where they would sit opposite a thick glass and touch their hands to the glass in a gesture of greeting before discussing points of the case. "O. J. was very thankful I agreed to take the case," says Dershowitz. "I lost a lot of money because O. J. couldn't pay my fees, and I lost a number of other cases because people were upset at me for taking O. J.'s case.

"O. J. was charming, but when I knew him, he was very angry. He was totally committed to his innocence. Like Claus von Bülow, O. J. encouraged me to pore through documents and expose relevant facts. I require all my clients to be like that—to not keep anything from me because I don't want to be caught sandbagged.

"O. J. really, honestly felt he was being framed, which means there were three possibilities in this case," recounts Dershowitz. "1. He really was being framed; 2. He was not being framed, but he honestly believed it and had amnesia about the murders; or 3. He was lying about everything."

Dershowitz was closely involved in strategy meetings for the defense team and at times had to step in the middle of ego-clashing between the high-profile attorneys. "This was not the dream team—this was the nightmare team," he says. "There were some clearly who were not happy with the hierarchical arrangement." Once, F. Lee Bailey accused Shapiro of going to Simpson in jail behind the team's back in order to convince

Simpson of his point of view about one matter. "Lee, you weren't even there. I was," retorted Dershowitz, who had accompanied Shapiro to the jail. "Bob wasn't undermining anybody."

On another occasion, the team was having a discussion with Simpson about whether he should take the stand. Bailey, who believed Simpson was innocent, argued he should, while Dershowitz took the opposite view. At this Simpson got upset, thinking that Dershowitz was implying his guilt. But Dershowitz explained that his main worry was how Simpson would appear in front of a jury. "Right now, we're winning based on scientific evidence, and the jury may hold your personal history against you," Dershowitz told Simpson.

"I had known who Dershowitz was before my case," says Simpson. "He was pretty famous by that point, and I had seen *Reversal of Fortune*, in which his students helped him turn a case around. Bringing him on certainly helped me feel more emotionally comfortable about my case. He was a very bright guy—you sensed that almost immediately when you started talking to him. I liked the fact that he came to the point quickly. I never felt, at any time, that he was feeding me baloney to make me feel good. I always felt that what he said is what was really going on. Sometimes, he explained to me the game plan of both sides: what the prosecution was trying to do—whether they were being successful or what they were missing—and what our game plan was going to be. I guess that's the teacher's side of his personality coming out.

"Once, I remember we talked in the interview room of my jail, and he basically told me that Johnnie, F. Lee, Shapiro, and the other core group of my lawyers were doing a great job and that I shouldn't worry because, based on rulings Judge Ito had given in previous cases, I was pretty much guaranteed a retrial if I were to lose. He was the first person to mention that to me, and shortly after, I think it became pretty apparent by some of Ito's rulings that I would, at the very least, get a retrial."

Dershowitz got on well with Johnnie Cochran, who was pro-Israel and had even visited the Holocaust museum Yad Vashem in Jerusalem. At one point, though, Dershowitz confronted Cochran about his use of bodyguards from Louis Farrakhan's Nation of Islam, an organization Dershowitz viewed as rabidly anti-Jewish. When the bodyguards escorted the defense team into the LA courthouse, Dershowitz refused to walk with his fellow lawyers and instead followed behind as a protest. When Dershowitz explained his reasoning, Cochran changed his mind and stopped using the bodyguards.

"Cochran knew what he didn't know," says Dershowitz. "He never tried to take over areas like legal issues, where I was better. He encouraged me to be imaginative. I tried to second-guess him on one thing, but he put me in my place. The first time I went into the courtroom, the defense team was commenting on how expensive his suit was. Usually in a court you wear dark, solid suits, but Cochran wore suits whose color popped a little. During the lunch period, I reminded him that he was arguing in front of jurors who couldn't afford expensive suits. 'You've got to dress down,' I said. 'I know my jury,' retorted Cochran. 'I'm going to wear my suits. When my jurors go to church, they want to see the minister well dressed, and when they come to court, they want to see their lawyer well dressed.'"

"Cochran brought in the Nation of Islam and did some things with Bailey that I didn't appreciate, but he was not as difficult as Bailey," says Robert Shapiro. "Bailey was somebody I had to put on a smiling face to even walk in the courtroom with. I never had any disagreements with Alan that I can recall. I liked Alan not only for his intellectual ability, but as a person. He's highly intelligent. I remember we would discuss things outside of the law, like Israel and the two-state solution."

"When it came to the trial, we had instant communication with Alan, both on computer and phone messages," continues Shapiro. "An issue would come up about admissibility, and we would take a recess and send a note over to Alan. We'd get a brief back right away during the trial. His role was to protect each and every issue that would come up that had any constitutional significance in the event there was an adverse verdict."

Nathan Dershowitz and his law firm played a significant role in this part of the case, writing numerous memos about various legal issues along the way. "F. Lee Bailey had a silent fax machine in the courtroom," says Nathan. "We watched the trial on TV and did research on issues when they came up. Once, Judge Ito asked for support on an issue, and we could see everyone on TV waiting for our memo to come out. Then they'd say, 'Judge Ito, here is the support.'"

Once during the trial, in the summer of 1995, Dershowitz was on his way to Australia to deliver a series of lectures to the Sydney Jewish community, and he planned a stop in Los Angeles to visit the trial and argue a motion before Ito. His son Elon was living out in LA at the time and sat in the courtroom's spectator section, while Dershowitz took a seat with Cochran, Bailey, and Shapiro, and Simpson at the defense table. Within minutes of Dershowitz's arrival, prosecutor Christopher Darden rose and asked Simpson to try on a pair of bloody gloves found on his property. "Pandemonium ensued," says Elon. "The reporters rushed outside to let everyone know what was about to happen."

Shortly after, Simpson rose from his seat to try on the gloves, passing right by Dershowitz. In a moment that would become iconic, he struggled to fit on the gloves, as the jury and millions of television viewers watched. "It was about the dumbest ploy any prosecutor could have attempted," says Dershowitz, "since under California law, he could have insisted that Simpson try on the glove outside the presence of the jury, before he decided to conduct this experiment in front of the jury."

During one of Dershowitz's appearances in court, the family of Ron Goldman approached him and said they could not believe someone like Dershowitz with his reputation for helping Jewish causes could be defending someone like Simpson who had killed a fellow Jew. "I told them if you had called me first, I probably would have helped you," says Dershowitz. "This was a case where there were arguments to be made on all sides. I was tremendously sympathetic to the victims. I was on a TV show with one of Ron's family. I had the greatest respect for them. I told them, 'If I were, God forbid, in your position, I'd be doing exactly what you're doing.' I cared deeply about the victims as a human being, but as a lawyer, I put blinders on. I had a job to do."

* * *

By the fall of 1995, the jury was ready to decide the outcome of perhaps the most-watched trial in American history. Cochran stole the show with his closing argument. "Stop this cover-up," he told the jurors. "Both prosecutors have now agreed that . . . there's a lying, perjuring, genocidal racist and he's testified willfully false in this case on a number of scores. . . . You are empowered to say we're not going to take that anymore."

"I thought there was going to be a hung jury," says Dershowitz, who began outlining the issues that would be brought up on appeal.

Robert Shapiro asked Dershowitz if he would fly out to LA to be in the courtroom on the day of the verdict and be ready to hold a press conference to announce the start of an appeal. "But it was the night of Yom Kippur, and I didn't want to come," says Dershowitz, who instead opted to watch the verdict with the students who had helped him on the case. Early in the afternoon on October 3, 1995, a cluster of journalists and friends gathered outside Dershowitz's office as he turned the television on. He asked his eight students to write down a piece of paper what they believed the verdict would be.

Over 150 million other people—one out of two Americans—were also glued to their television sets, including President Clinton, who had been briefed on security responses in the event of riots. After deliberating, the twelve jurors—two of whom were white, nine black, and one Hispanic—entered the courtroom. The court attendees rose, and the verdict "not guilty" was announced. Simpson heaved a sigh of relief. Cochran clasped Simpson's shoulder. The prosecutors were expressionless. Ron Goldman's sister wept.

Inside Dershowitz's office in Cambridge, it was totally quiet. As Dershowitz sat surprised, processing this news, he leaned forward silently and touched the glass of the TV screen near Simpson's hand—just like he had when visiting Simpson in jail. None of his eight students had written "not guilty" on their pieces of paper.

"It was not a moment for celebration," says Dershowitz. "There were two victims, brutally murdered. I don't get joy out of celebrating victories when people are lying dead."

* * *

"My job is not to prove whether or not my client did or didn't do anything," Robert Shapiro notes. "I am here to put the prosecution to their constitutional test—as to whether or not they can prove each and every element of a crime that's been charged, beyond a reasonable doubt. It's as simple as that. And it goes back to the old saying that 'I'd rather see one hundred guilty men go free, than one innocent man be convicted.'"

"The jurors in the Simpson case were not asked to vote on whether they believed 'he did it,'" says Dershowitz. "They were asked whether the prosecution's evidence proved beyond a reasonable doubt that he did it. Juror number three, a sixty-one-year-old white woman named Anise Aschenbach, indicated that she believed that Simpson was probably guilty 'but the law wouldn't allow a guilty verdict. . . . If we made a mistake, I would rather it be a mistake on the side of a person's innocence than the other way.'" Aschenbach also said that Fuhrman's sordid history had been a "big issue for me."

Dershowitz quoted another juror, Brenda Moran, who told the press that "the jury found Vannatter's decision to carry Simpson's blood sample around with him for several hours 'suspicious because it gave him the opportunity to plant evidence.'" Another juror interviewed, Sheila Woods, admitted to a journalist she believed it was possible Fuhrman had planted the glove.

"I think the jury's decision was a combination of the race of the jurors and their doubting of police testimony," reflects Dershowitz.

Whatever the motivation of the jurors, nearly 70 percent of whites thought Simpson was guilty and that the verdict was abhorrent, while only 16 percent of Blacks agreed. Another telling statistic was that nearly 80 percent of Blacks reported police lying to be common in their communities.

"Although I didn't lose any close friends because of the case, a lot of people were angered by my participation," says Dershowitz. His childhood friend, Barry Zimmerman, sent him a one-word fax when the verdict was announced: *Feh*"—Yiddish for "crap."

"There was a class reunion at Harvard, and one of the programs was Alan talking about the trial," says Nadine Strossen, a former student of Dershowitz's who was by then serving as the first female president of the ACLU. "Alan was fielding people's questions about the trial, along with hostile comments. People were extremely upset. The overwhelming majority of the people attending that reunion were white, and they were very, very upset. It took place in the Ames courtroom, which is the largest room and auditorium at Harvard Law School. It was absolutely packed, standing room only, and it was just Alan all by himself. You could have cut the air with a knife. You could just feel the anger, frustration, and fury—and the sense of injustice."

With Simpson's blessing, Dershowitz would go on to write a book about the case titled *Reasonable Doubts*. "This book is lovingly dedicated to my brother, Nathan," he began, "who was my secret legal weapon in the Simpson case as he has been in many other cases—and to Marilyn, Adam, and Rana, who are his secret weapons."

"If the only goal of the adversary system were to find 'the truth' in every case, then it would be relatively simple to achieve," he wrote. "Suspects could be tortured, their families threatened, homes randomly searched, and lie detector tests routinely administered. Indeed, in order to facilitate this search for truth, we could all be subjected to a regimen of random blood and urine tests, and every public building and workplace could be outfitted with surveillance cameras. If these methods—common in totalitarian countries—are objected to on the ground that torture and threats sometimes produce false accusations, that objection could be overcome by requiring that all confessions induced by torture or threats must be independently corroborated. We would still never tolerate such a single-minded search for truth, nor would our Constitution, because we believe that the ends—even an end as noble as truth—do not justify every possible means."

In the coming months, passions remained high. Geraldo Rivera, who had covered the trial extensively on his CNBC show *Rivera Live!*, had Dershowitz and prosecutor Chris Darden on together, and a bitter tirade ensued. "The fact of the matter is that this blood [was] not planted," declared Darden. "It [was] blood that O. J. Simpson tracked into his home and got onto his socks as he murdered Ron and Nicole."

"Well, you don't know that," countered Dershowitz. "You don't know that any more than I do."

"Oh I absolutely do know that," stated Darden, voice raised. "You are so biased!"

"Are you willing to admit finally, Alan, that the evidence in this case is more than enough to establish O. J. Simpson as the murderer?" Darden interjected at one point. "If you had read my book, you'd see that months after the trial I wrote in the book that *of course* there was more than enough evidence to convict—*if it was truthful evidence!*" replied Dershowitz. "You failed because of your lack of credibility to convince the jury because you put on false witnesses."

"*My* lack of credibility?" scoffed Darden. "You have no credibility! You will sell your soul for a buck, and you will release a double murderer to the public for a couple of bucks."

"Hey, you've made a lot more *bucks* on this case than anybody else did, so don't start talking about who's making the bucks," retorted Dershowitz.

In addition to Darden, Dershowitz also took on Mark Fuhrman. Fuhrman was making the media rounds to promote a new book, and CNN hosted him and Dershowitz on their debate program *Crossfire*. At one point, Dershowitz started to read from the notorious tapes, in which Fuhrman made racist comments, but was cut off by one of the hosts. "I want to throw CNN a challenge," Dershowitz then stated, "[to host] a one-hour show in which the tapes are played from beginning to end in context. Let the public judge for itself whether these are the words of a racist or these are the words of an actor trying to persuade a screenwriter and this is the way other policemen act. Do you accept that challenge, Mark Fuhrman?"

"No I don't," replied Fuhrman emphatically, "and I'll tell you why. Because all you're doing is fueling a problem in this country and you're trying to exacerbate it and make it worse."

Toward the end of the debate, Dershowitz pointed out, "What happened in this case—and it was very important—is that the public got an inside view at police *testi-lying* of the kind attested to in the Mollen Commission and other places that they had never seen before."

"You know, you have gone on several shows for almost two years talking about police learning to lie," retorted Fuhrman. "Where do attorneys learn it? Law school?" "Well, attorneys are so regulated," replied Dershowitz. "I've been in practice thirty-two years. If anybody ever even suggested that I had gone close to violating a rule, I would have been disciplined. . . . There are rules that, Mark Fuhrman, you may not understand or may not want to understand—but we have an obligation to defend our clients."

Dershowitz's claims about police "testi-lying" did not leave a bad taste in everyone's mouth. "I had no doubt about what he was saying," says

O. J. Simpson. "A whole lot happened in LA after my trial. During the subsequent Rampart scandal—where they found so many cops were lying and had to release many people from jail because of it—the LA chief of police got on TV and said that the 'blue wall' had to come down. This was something my lawyers had stressed during my trial—that these cops were all protecting each other, and there was a phrase they used: a 'blue wall' of silence, or something similar.

"So, Dershowitz's comments certainly didn't make me mad because I believe cops 'testi-lie'! I respected Dershowitz before my trial, and I'll always respect the man."

Many Americans did not share Simpson's sentiments. "I hope I can still be alive when I hear someday that you have terminal cancer or even better, that you are a victim of a vicious crime which would be so appropriate for dreck like you," read one letter Dershowitz received. Another said he would do to Dershowitz's mother "what your client did to Ron Goldman."

"Whose side are you on?" demanded one exasperated writer.

Dershowitz had numerous paid speaking events at Jewish venues canceled. He had multiple credible death threats issued against him, which he had his secretary report to the FBI. Dershowitz and his wife, Carolyn, would also not allow Ella to stand outside with her friends waiting to be picked up from school, instructing her teachers to keep her inside the building until her ride had pulled up.

Due to the TV cameras in the LA courtroom, Dershowitz's face and name became nationally recognizable. "There may not have been an applause meter at the Celtics-Rockets game at the FleetCenter Wednesday Night, but there were some there who got more cheers than jeers," noted one *Boston Globe* article. "As . . . Joe Public emceed a half-time shooting contest, he noted a few celebrities in the crowd: Drew Bledsoe and Steve DeOssie of the Patriots both got loud cheers. . . . But when Public mentioned legal Dream Team member Alan Dershowitz, the crowd erupted—in boos."

"My job as a lawyer is not to see that justice is done," Dershowitz once declared. "That's the job of the system. My role is to defend the most unpopular and even the most guilty of defendants." When one interviewer asked if that would apply to Adolf Hitler, Dershowitz responded, "Oh sure, I'd tell him I'd take the case. Then when I went to meet him, I'd strangle him with my bare hands. Yes, I certainly hope I'd have the courage to do that."

* * *

O. J. Simpson's case launched Dershowitz into immortality as one of the "Dream Team" lawyers who pulled off the impossible case. He became the subject of Trivial Pursuit questions, a crossword puzzle in the *New York Times*, and was even parodied on *The Simpsons*. In an episode titled "Round Springfield," a character hires a lawyer with curly hair, a mustache, and large round glasses, who is introduced mockingly as "Albert Dershman, who can hold three billiard balls in his mouth."

His frequent media appearances raised eyebrows among some of his fellow Harvard faculty, causing one colleague to contemptuously dub him the "Phil Donahue of law."

"Look, I could sit in my office all day and write a long, long article for *Podunk Law Review*, which would have 400 footnotes and 12 people would read it," responded Dershowitz in one interview. "Or I can say what I would say in that article in 60 or 90 seconds (on television) and have 10 million or 20 million people hear it, and have a real impact on civil liberties."

"I had Alan on even before he became the lawyer for O. J. He would come on as a legal expert," says Geraldo Rivera. "I definitely felt O. J. was guilty beyond any doubt, not just any reasonable doubt—any doubt. And Alan, of course, when he appeared on my program, vigorously advocated for his client. A lot of people found that awkward. I thought it was terrific. He always made great TV. The issues he raised were real. He was a perpetual motion machine. He bubbled with energy and intellectual curiosity. He was a piercing analyst with a grasp of the law—not merely the specifics, but the concepts behind it."

"Lawyers . . . were not included in the guest list of the various programs, nor were legal cases, complicated cases, much discussed until the era of Dershowitz," Geraldo explains. "He reduced these concepts to precepts that were [understandable]. . . . He was the first, he was the best, of all the TV lawyers. . . . Man, that guy [could] deliver a sound bite."

* * *

As Dershowitz's fame grew, so grew his connections in the world of the elite. Lynn Forester was a wealthy businesswoman who eventually married into the prominent Rothschild family, and she and Dershowitz became acquainted through mutual friends in New York. In the summer of 1996, Forester asked Dershowitz to meet a rich friend of hers who was flying into the Vineyard. Forester said he was a "wonderful, brilliant" man and a "good person" who donated to Harvard and was fascinated by law and science. His name was Jeffrey Epstein. As a favor to Forester, Dershowitz invited Epstein to his place on the Vineyard and introduced him to his family.

"We started talking to each other, and I just remember thinking, 'This guy is so fucked up,'" says Carolyn. "I didn't like Jeffrey at all. He exhibited an attitude towards people in general that came across as totally uncaring. He just seemed totally unconnected to people."

Dershowitz and Epstein hit it off. Epstein was born to Jewish immigrants and grew up in Brooklyn in the 1950s and 1960s. As a young man he showed an aptitude for math and skipped two grades. In the 1970s, he became a math and physics teacher at a prestigious private school called Dalton Academy, where he was noticed by a wealthy father of one of the students and recommended to the Wall Street investment firm Bear Stearns. After working at Stearns for a few years, Epstein left the company and eventually formed his own money-management firm, J. Epstein & Company. His most notable client was billionaire Leslie Wexner, owner of Bath & Body Works and Victoria's Secret. Epstein racked up a fortune, enough to purchase luxurious properties in Manhattan, Palm Beach, Paris, and New Mexico, along with his own private Caribbean island.

"Jeffrey was a real intellectual groupie," says Dershowitz. "He loved to be associated with smart people." Shortly after their meeting on the Vineyard, Epstein was scheduled to attend a birthday party for Leslie Wexner, who asked Epstein to bring the most interesting person he had met the previous year. Epstein invited Dershowitz, who accepted. Epstein had his private jet fly Dershowitz to Wexner's mansion in New Albany,

Ohio, where Dershowitz met Wexner and schmoozed with his guests, including John Glenn and Shimon Peres.

Around this time, Lynn Forester invited Dershowitz to a birthday party on the Vineyard for her boyfriend Evelyn Rothschild. Dershowitz bumped into Epstein and met Mortimer Zuckerman, Ron Perlman, and Donald Trump. He also struck up a conversation with Prince Andrew, and the two went to lunch the next day. Prince Andrew was eager to attend one of Dershowitz's criminal law classes, which he eventually did in the fall of 1999. "The opportunity to be a student for just one lecture was an expanding experience and I cannot begin to thank you enough for your kindness," the prince wrote to Dershowitz afterward. "Look forward to continuing my intellectual challenge with you and Jeffrey E in the coming months."

Epstein had rented an office in Brattle Square right next to Harvard and financed an entire evolutionary department. "He came to my classes from time to time," says Dershowitz, who also asked Epstein for comments on his book manuscripts. "I would have loved to have my friends Steven Pinker or Stephen Jay Gould look over my manuscripts, but they were too busy. Jeffrey was more accessible. He never seemed to be doing anything. He was almost never at work. I visited his office on Madison Avenue in New York a few times, and he was seldom there. He was mostly at home, had plenty of time, and liked to read. He had street smarts and I enjoyed discussing my work with him. He would always say, 'Alan, you're being too pedantic—that's not the way people think.'

"Jeffrey didn't like to go out for meals, and we rarely spent social time together," continues Dershowitz. "Occasionally, though, when I was in New York, we would take a walk through Central Park, and I went to a couple parties at his Manhattan home. We never talked about our families, and I only learned a little of his personal history. He was not as enamored of Brooklyn as I was. He wasn't a member of any political party, but he was pro-Israel. He was chock full of ideas, which were always interesting but at times weird. He had some strange views of evolutionary biology—he believed very strongly in genetic differences between people and wanted to improve humanity through genetic manipulation, which was very common at Harvard in the 1920s, a period we discussed."

"Jeffrey organized wonderful educational conferences and dinners," Dershowitz notes. "He introduced me to some Harvard professors whom I had never met, despite being on the same faculty for many years. Jeffrey liked showing me off to his friends."

* * *

Once while Dershowitz was vacationing in the Caribbean with his wife and daughter, Epstein invited them to his breathtaking island. "While Epstein was working in his office, my wife had a massage from a professional massage therapist and my daughter and I explored the island," says Dershowitz. "[We dined] with Professor Michael Porter of the Harvard Business School, his then-wife and their relatives. The island was empty, except for some staff and Epstein's erstwhile girlfriend Ghislaine Maxwell. She ran his properties—when you came to one of his houses, she would be there paying bills, making reservations for you to fly, etc. She was always very nice, and Carolyn liked her a lot.

"On another occasion, Jeffrey invited us to stay at his house in Palm Beach. It was a large, roomy house on the intercoastal waterway. There were essentially two houses under one roof. If you turned right, there were a series of steps that were his private area. Straight ahead, you walked downstairs through a living room and the kitchen, and you went a long way to the other side of the house where there were more steps. Up those steps were four bedrooms, and that's where his guests stayed. And his guests were never, ever allowed to go into the area of the house that was his. His housekeeper instructed us to not go up the stairs to the right. Jeffrey was a germaphobe and a clean freak, so we just assumed that was the reason."

"Jeffrey never shared financial details with me," Dershowitz comments. "At one point, he was thinking of retiring from his business and devoting himself full-time to things he was interested in. I commented, 'Well, you can afford it,' and he replied, 'Yeah, I can afford it.' He did mention at one point that he had never been a billionaire, but he was worth more than $500 million. Leslie Wexner had given him power of attorney, and he invested all of Wexner's money. He said that he had other clients, and he would take a percentage of what he advised on. He did get people tax benefits. I know he got tremendous tax benefits for Leon Black, who paid him millions of dollars for that.

"I wouldn't myself have invested with him, but he did give me some financial advice at one point. He told me to invest with a particular guy, and I did—about $100,000. It backfired. The money just disappeared. When I told Jeffrey about it, he persuaded his friend to give it back to me."

"Carolyn suspected Jeffrey might be financially sleazy, but I had contact with so many people on a range of sleaziness that I wasn't sure," Dershowitz says. "I don't judge people by their outside reputation. I judge people based on my own experiences with them."

Though Epstein maintained a low public profile, he made the news for his donations to Harvard. "Jeffrey E. Epstein's recent $30 million gift to Harvard was one in a series of donations that the elusive magnate has given anonymously to the University over the past decade," reported one article in *The Harvard Crimson*. "Epstein counts a number of professors—including Dershowitz, Lindsley Professor of Psychology Stephen M. Kosslyn and former Dean of the Faculty Henry A. Rosovsky—among his bevy of eminent friends . . . 'Jeffrey is totally irreverent,' Dershowitz says. 'To him, it doesn't matter if it's a prince, a pope, or the president; if Jeffrey has a good joke or a good idea, he'll share it.'"

Vanity Fair took notice of Epstein's donation and ran a piece titled "The Talented Mr. Epstein," mentioning his friendship with Dershowitz in the article. "Harvard law professor Alan Dershowitz says, 'The only person outside of my immediate family that I send drafts [of my books] to is Jeffrey.'"

"Many people comment there is something innocent, almost child-like about Jeffrey Epstein," the article noted at the end. "They see this as refreshing, given the sophistication of his surroundings. Alan Dershowitz says that, as he was getting to know Epstein, his wife asked him if he would still be close to him if Epstein suddenly filed for bankruptcy. Dershowitz says he replied, 'Absolutely. I would be as interested in him as a friend if we had hamburgers on the boardwalk in Coney Island and talked about his ideas.'"

* * *

Amid all the excitement and busyness of Dershowitz's life, Carolyn provided him a partnership of love and stability. "In the decade after I met
Carolyn, I became more self-confident—writing books, litigating more
cases, and generally achieving a better balance among the different aspects
of my life and career," says Dershowitz.

"Alan was very loving and very loyal," says Carolyn. "He was very supportive to me when my parents died and when I was not happy in an earlier job. I eventually landed a job as a psychologist at the Manville School,
which was part of Boston Children's Hospital and Harvard Medical
School—I worked as a therapist for high-risk kids with special needs."

Remarking on her husband's unique personality and lifestyle, Carolyn
says, "I think Alan has an unusual way of looking at things. He's attracted
to the exceptions about things, so he often argued the unusual point of
view. He liked being provocative. In some ways, what brought him the
most joy was fighting for what he believed in. In private, though, he was
averse to fighting. He did not like having stressful personal conversations."

Carolyn never opposed any of Alan's clients. "I've known many lawyers and understand they have a job to do," she notes, "but at times, I've
certainly been concerned for the safety of our family, like during the
O. J. case."

When Alan's ego flared up, Carolyn kept his feet on the ground. Once
they were perusing a shop after dropping off Ella at a summer camp in
Maine. The shop owner said to Alan, "It's a pleasure having you in our
shop, Mr. Dershowitz."

"They even know me in Maine," whispered Alan to Carolyn gleefully.
"That's because you didn't take off the name tag they gave you in camp,"
she instantly replied, referring to the sticker on his lapel which read:
HELLO, I'M ALAN DERSHOWITZ.

Carolyn was shy about being in the limelight. She and Alan once gave
a rare joint interview to a *Boston Globe* reporter who visited them in their
artsy home on Reservoir Street near HLS. "Married 17 years, they grin
like new lovers as they sit close together on the roomy black leather couch
where Dershowitz writes most of his books and prepares for cases," wrote
the journalist. "According to Cohen, people don't know the family side of
Alan Dershowitz. . . . 'He's such a good father, a wonderful son, a loving

and supportive husband, and an incredible friend,' Cohen says. 'Anyone who knows him sees what a genuinely caring and good person he is.' As she pours on the compliments, her husband cuts in: 'You see why I love her?'"

Together they raised their daughter with joy. "Ella's birth kept me home more," Dershowitz says. "I turned down cases and speaking engagements that required extensive travel."

"He was always there for Ella when she was growing up," says Carolyn. "When she was in elementary school, they'd go to basketball games together, which was cute. As she grew up and became interested in acting, he was very supportive of her passions."

A proud moment in Alan's life occurred when he and Carolyn took Ella to Israel for the first time in 1996. She was six years old, and her father had been invited along with other prominent pro-Israel figures on an all-expenses-paid trip in honor of their dedication to Israel.

As part of the trip package, Dershowitz met with Shimon Peres—who had nicknamed Dershowitz "Professor Chutzpah"—Jerusalem mayor Ehud Olmert, and recently elected prime minister Benjamin Netanyahu. Since meeting Netanyahu at the twenty-fifth anniversary celebration of Israel's founding at MIT back in 1973, Dershowitz had bumped into him occasionally while Netanyahu served as Israel's ambassador to the UN. In the late 1980s, Netanyahu was elected to the Knesset and quickly rose through the ranks of the right-wing Likud Party, ultimately being elected Israel's youngest prime minister in 1996.

While in Israel, Dershowitz took the opportunity to show his daughter the Western Wall in Jerusalem, a site near to his heart and the hearts of their ancestors. He also caught up with childhood friends and relatives and visited Aharon Barak, the president of the Israeli Supreme Court, whom Dershowitz had met back in the 1960s while Barak was on a visit to Harvard.

Aharon Barak was born in Lithuania in 1936, and following the Nazi occupation of their country, his family was placed into a ghetto into the city of Kovno. Jeopardizing his own life, a courageous farmer hid little Aharon beneath a pile of potatoes and smuggled him out of the ghetto. Miraculously, Barak's family survived the war and immigrated to Palestine in 1947, a year before the founding of Israel. Barak received a law degree from the Hebrew University of Jerusalem and worked in the attorney general's office before being appointed to the Israeli Supreme Court.

At the time of Dershowitz's 1996 visit to Israel, Barak was in the process of granting the Supreme Court greater power over the Knesset in order to protect a series of Basic Laws the Court had enacted. Among them was Barak's Basic Law of Human Dignity.

"One of the major lessons I learned from the Holocaust was the importance of equal rights for everyone—not just for Jews and our supporters, but also for our enemies," says Barak. "If we are not dignifying our enemies, we are not dignifying ourselves."

"If Israel's enemies commit crimes against humanity or against Israel, they will, of course, be judged by an independent, objective judge. But they are human beings, and they should be treated as human beings. During the Holocaust, the Germans murdered us Jews. They tried to take away our human dignity while we were in the ghettos and the camps. But we held onto the idea which is central to Judaism and Christianity: that man is created in the image of God. Equality should be a basic principle of law for everyone, regardless of nationality. Alan and I both shared this ideal."

During the trip, Netanyahu invited Dershowitz to his office in Jerusalem, where they schmoozed and discussed the state of the world. Near the end of their conversation, Netanyahu asked what else was on Dershowitz's agenda for the trip. Dershowitz mentioned he would be taking his family to a Reform synagogue called Kol HaNeshamah and invited Netanyahu to join them. "Alan, you're such a troublemaker," responded Netanyahu with a smile. "Do you know what would happen to my government if I were seen in a Reform synagogue in Jerusalem? Maybe I could get away with it in America, but not here."

"Bibi was the best educated leader I've ever known," reflects Dershowitz. "He just had an incredible amount of knowledge about the world. He and Bill Clinton had that in common. They both read voraciously. They both had an ability to sense a room, predict the future, and analyze situations—in a manner unlike any other politicians. They both had big egos, but inside they both cared deeply about people."

Dershowitz had gotten to know Clinton on a personal level since their meeting in 1994. Because of his increasing wealth from high-profile clients, Dershowitz was eventually able to purchase apartments in New York and Miami and a home in his beloved community of Chilmark on Martha's Vineyard. During the summers, Dershowitz and Carolyn often bumped into the Clintons at social functions, and the president invited them to his birthday parties and various events at the White House. (Once, Dershowitz was at a party with Clinton when he got the news Princess Diana had died in a car crash, following which the president left the party ashen-faced.) Dershowitz also attended dinners with Clinton and their mutual acquaintance Caroline Kennedy, JFK's daughter.

"Bill and I talked about Israel often," says Dershowitz. "I gave him advice about the internal workings of Israeli politics and told him that he should not assume Bibi personally agreed with every decision his right-wing government made. I assured him Bibi was much more centrist and pragmatic than he appeared to be."

Once, things got tense between Dershowitz and Clinton when Dershowitz repeatedly urged the president to commute the sentence of Jonathan Pollard, a Jewish American who had been sentenced to life imprisonment in 1987 for secretly providing American intelligence information to Israel. Although many Jewish people and organizations—including Arthur Goldberg while he was still alive and the Anti-Defamation League—supported Pollard's sentence, Dershowitz was convinced it was disproportionate to his actual crime and that some of the American Jews who berated Pollard did so out of fear they would be smeared with the charge of "dual loyalty" to Israel. "If one American of English descent were to provide classified information to Great Britain, there would be no call for loyalty checks on all American government officials of English descent," he argued in *Chutzpah*.

Clinton understood Dershowitz's position, but said he could not commute Pollard's sentence because of opposition from his CIA director and several Jewish senators. This did not stop Dershowitz, who continued to press Clinton about it. Once, Dershowitz bumped into Clinton at an event on Martha's Vineyard and said, "Hey Mr. President, how are you?"

"Alan, if you're going to talk to me about the Pollard case, don't even bother," replied Clinton shortly. "I'm sorry, Mr. President," said Dershowitz brazenly, "but my job is to talk to you about it, and your job is to either listen or not listen."

"Look, don't tell me what my job is, and I won't tell you what your job is," replied Clinton, voice raised slightly.

Despite this interaction, Dershowitz and Clinton remained friends. Clinton sought Dershowitz's advice about legal and Middle East matters, and Dershowitz occasionally recommended people for appointments, including his colleague Larry Tribe for the position of solicitor general. Once, Clinton sent Dershowitz an inscribed copy of the 1979 *Time* magazine in which they had both appeared on page 38 in an article titled "Fifty Faces for the Future." "To Alan: Even back then, we are on the same page!" wrote Clinton.

Dershowitz's connection to Clinton thrust him into the midst of a fierce political battle, as Clinton's scandal-ridden personal life brought his presidency to the brink of collapse.

During Clinton's first term, an independent counsel had been appointed to investigate white-collar scandals Whitewater and Filegate, along with a sexual harassment lawsuit that had been filed against Clinton by Arkansas state employee Paula Jones. Although he liked Clinton, Dershowitz was supportive of these investigations in the interests of equal accountability for all Americans. He became worried about the motives behind the investigation when Kenneth Starr was selected to lead it. Starr was the son of a Southern pastor and sold Bibles to help pay his way through college. A Republican, he clerked for Chief Justice Warren Burger and served as the solicitor general for George Bush. After taking over as independent counsel, Starr managed to charge eleven Clinton associates and ultimately made the president the focus of his investigation, at times leaking salacious reports of the president's sex life.

"Starr replaced a truly non-partisan counsel, Robert Fiske, who had earned a well-deserved reputation as an independent and nonpartisan prosecutor," Dershowitz wrote in a syndicated column in December 1996. "That is precisely why he was fired: because the Republican hatchet men feared that he was too independent of them. Instead they wanted one of their own. And they certainly got one—an active Republican, who was thought to be seeking either political office or a Republican appointment to the Supreme Court."

In another column, Dershowitz blasted the whole concept of an independent counsel. "[It] is an anomaly made necessary by a structural defect in our system of government," he wrote. "Our system of investigation and prosecution is unique in the world. We have politicized the role of prosecutor, not only at the federal level but in all of our states and counties as well. Nowhere else are prosecutors (or judges) elected. Indeed, it is unthinkable in most parts of the world to have prosecutors run for office, make campaign promises and solicit contributions."

"Alan was very opposed to what was happening to his friend Bill," says Mark Levin, who at that time was a noted legal commentator on conservative news outlets. "During this time, John Gibson moderated a debate between Alan and I on MSNBC over the use of the independent counsel statute, which Alan was vehemently against. Alan got very angry with me during the debate—in fact, he walked off."

As Clinton's second term got underway in 1997, he could not shake the scandals. Geraldo Rivera had Dershowitz on several times to discuss the president's woes. "This case never should have gotten this far," he told Geraldo's viewers in May 1997 when there was talk of the president giving a deposition in the Paula Jones lawsuit. "It should have been settled early when he could have settled it easily. . . . Remember, depositions are very broad in latitude. He could be asked questions about adultery. He could be asked questions about his prior sexual life. . . . What I would do if I were his lawyer is to say, 'Look, the dignity of the office precludes the president from answering any of these questions.'"

Shortly after, Clinton's lawyer, Robert Bennett, made a decision that Dershowitz would later characterize as the greatest legal blunder of the twentieth century. He advised Clinton to submit himself to a deposition in the Paula Jones case. On January 17, 1998, Clinton appeared for his deposition and was asked by Bennett about a sexual encounter he allegedly had in the Oval Office with a young intern named Monica Lewinsky. Bennett specifically asked Clinton about an affidavit Lewinsky had made: "In paragraph eight of her affidavit, [Monica Lewinsky] says this, 'I have never had a sexual relationship with the president, he did not propose that we have a sexual relationship, he did not offer employment or other benefits in exchange for a sexual relationship, he did not deny me employment or other benefits for rejecting a sexual relationship,'" Bennett quoted. "Is that a true and accurate statement?" he asked Clinton. "That is absolutely true," replied Clinton.

Not long after Clinton's private deposition, his affair with Lewinsky became public knowledge, and Kenneth Starr immediately brought it to the forefront of his investigation. Rumors spread that Lewinsky had saved a dress with a semen stain which apparently had come from Clinton.

"Bill Clinton is clearly being targeted by the Independent Counsel, who is using means more typically associated with attempts to prosecute mafia dons, rather than political figures," Dershowitz wrote in a column. When asked about a specific example, he replied, "The investigators put an enormous amount of pressure on Monica Lewinsky personally. They threatened to prosecute her mother at one point. I was contacted by a friend of Lewinsky who gave me the phone number of where she was then staying and pleaded with me to help represent her. Because of my relationship with Bill, though, I thought it would be a conflict of interest and so never called."

On January 23, Dershowitz appeared on MSNBC and attacked Bennett's decision to have Clinton testify and thereby fall into a potential perjury trap. In his columns, Dershowitz argued Bennett should have advised Clinton to default the Paula Jones case rather than allow himself to be deposed. "Every litigant in a civil case has the right to default—which means, essentially, to settle the case unilaterally by simply refusing to contest the allegations in the complaint," he wrote. By doing so, Dershowitz argued, Clinton would have paid the money Jones demanded, received a few days of bad press, and then moved on with his presidency.

Unfortunately, Clinton dug his grave deeper on January 26 when he held a televised press conference and told reporters with a shake of his finger, "I did not have sexual relations with that woman, Miss Lewinsky. I never told anybody to lie, not a single time never. These allegations are false." In the coming months, he continued to deny the affair, but eventually changed course. On August 17, he testified before a grand jury and admitted the relationship with Lewinsky. That evening he publicly acknowledged the affair to the nation. There were calls for his resignation, and Starr soon released a report filled with titillating details of Clinton's sex life that charged him with perjury, obstruction of justice, and abuse of power. Impeachment was in the air.

"Were President Clinton to accede to these demands, or were Congress to impeach him, a terrible precedent would be established, under which voters who were dissatisfied with the outcome of a presidential election would look to Congress for relief," proclaimed Dershowitz in an article. "For Clinton to resign in the face of these charges would be for him to legitimate the kind of sexual McCarthyism that has driven this entire episode."

The day after he announced the affair to the nation, Clinton flew to Martha's Vineyard, where Dershowitz was spending the summer. Dershowitz and a small group of supporters greeted Clinton at the small airport, and that evening, Clinton had Dershowitz sit next to him at a small dinner attended by Clinton's friends Steven Rattner and Harvey Weinstein. At the time Dershowitz was working on a book about the Old Testament called *The Genesis of Justice*, and he and Clinton chatted about Abraham, Jacob, and Joseph, and other characters from the Bible, a book Clinton knew well.

Dershowitz also mentioned his wish that Clinton had defaulted the Jones case rather than undergo a deposition. "Nobody ever told me I could have had the case dismissed if I had paid the money," said a surprised Clinton. "[My lawyer] told me I had to be deposed."

Over the next several weeks, as the threat of impeachment loomed, Clinton sought Dershowitz's advice about impeachment. Dershowitz asked his brother to prepare memos about what Clinton's defense should be, and Dershowitz left the documents in the Chilmark Chocolates store for the Clintons to pick up.

Beyond private conversations with Clinton, Dershowitz continued bashing a proposed impeachment in the court of public opinion. "For Our System's Sake: Don't Impeach," he pleaded in a column. "Our Constitution provides for presidential impeachment as an extraordinary measure of last resort against an incumbent who has engaged in the most serious kind of official misfeasance or malfeasance. Unlike parliamentary systems, which can remove a prime minister by a legitimate vote of no confidence, our constitutional system does not permit removal on the basis of general dissatisfaction with the policies, preferences or lifestyle of a President."

At the suggestion of author Philip Roth, an acquaintance from the Vineyard, Dershowitz published a book titled *Sexual McCarthyism*, which compiled his columns about the Starr investigation and included a lengthy section overviewing his involvement in the legal proceedings and making the case against Clinton's impeachment. "Those in Congress who are now pushing for a full-fledged impeachment proceeding against President Clinton are playing with constitutional fire," he wrote. "They see short-term, partisan advantage in exposing the President's mistakes. Like the President, they are guided in their actions by tonight's sound bites, tomorrow's polls and the next election. Perhaps that is in the nature of politicians. But who is looking after the long-term interests of our nation?"

Mentioning the case of Richard Nixon, Dershowitz wrote, "Richard Nixon's offenses fit within the core definition of high crimes and misdemeanors. They involved a criminal cover-up of matters of state, such as a burglary and break-in directed against political enemies. . . . I believe that the criminal conduct must also relate to matters of the state and not to private conduct, unless it is an extremely serious crime like murder. Consensual sex does not qualify. Nor, in my view, does a sex lie told during a deposition in a civil case that was dismissed."

Charlie Rose invited Dershowitz on his show to discuss his new book. "I didn't write *Sexual McCarthyism* to defend Clinton or to attack Starr," Dershowitz told Rose and his half a million viewers. "It's to defend the Constitution because these two men brought us to the brink of a constitutional crisis which the electorate pulled us back from."

Around this time, Larry King invited Dershowitz on his show to debate young conservative attorney Ann Coulter. "Everyone keeps saying, 'Oh, the sex alone, the sex alone,' as if it's an outrage to expect the president to have a minimally decent personal life," said Coulter. "[It's] one thing to have scoundrels in the Congress or scoundrels as governors, but the president—because he would have vast powers, he is the man with his finger on the nuclear button, he's the man who [is] going to have to look the American people in the eye and say, 'We're sending your boys to war, they're going to fight and may die for this'—his word has to be believed."

King asked Dershowitz for his thoughts. "Well, she's right in some respects," he said. "It certainly doesn't have to be a crime. If you have somebody who completely corrupts the office of president and who abuses trust, and who poses great danger to our liberty, you don't need a technical crime. . . . [But you] don't use this grave impeachment power against the president—never used in our history, successfully at least, to remove a president—unless there is such a threat to our liberty."

"Remember," Dershowitz cautioned at another point, "we have one president, and to impeach a president is like a nonviolent revolution. It is the most dramatic act of undoing democracy. . . . That's why the framers use the terms treason, bribery, high crimes, and misdemeanors—to suggest the English analogy to great offenses of state."

Shortly after this debate, Republicans in the House moved forward with Clinton's impeachment. They charged him with abuse of power and obstruction of justice and argued he had committed perjury during his grand jury appearance in August by making allegedly misleading statements about the extent of his relationship with Lewinsky. "I think Bill misled the grand jury, but it was not impeachable—it was not a high crime or misdemeanor," says Dershowitz. "I think a lot of people didn't like Bill's personal life because he was supposed to be this born-again Baptist. I think the Republicans believed they would get political advantage by bringing the impeachment. They wanted to destroy the last part of Bill's presidency."

At the request of Democrats serving on the House Judiciary Committee, in December, Dershowitz traveled to Washington, DC, to testify before the Committee in the Capitol.

"For nearly a quarter of a century I have been teaching, lecturing, and writing about the corrosive influences of perjury on our legal system, especially when committed by those whose job it is to enforce the law, and ignored, or even legitimized, by those whose responsibility it is to check those who enforce the law," he began in his opening statements, as the Republican committee members stared down at him from a mahogany dais. "If [we] continue deliberately to blind ourselves to pervasive police perjury and other equally dangerous forms of lying under oath and focus on a politically charged, tangential lie in the lowest category of possible perjury—hiding embarrassing facts by evasive answers to poorly framed questions which were marginally relevant to a dismissed civil case—we will be reaffirming the dangerous and hypocritical message that perjury will continue to be selectively prosecuted as a crime reserved for political or other agenda-driven purposes!"

At one point, Dershowitz engaged Republican Henry Hyde of Illinois, chairman of the committee, in a heated back-and-forth. "Nothing can trivialize the rule of law more than to selectively isolate this case and act as if it is the only case [of perjury that's] important," said Dershowitz vehemently in response to a committee member's question, with hints of his Brooklyn accent popping up.

"And Mr. Chairman, you contributed to that in the beginning," he continued, fearlessly turning his gaze up to the white-haired, bespectacled Hyde as the other representatives looked on. "[You] said that this was going to be a broad hearing about the pervasive influence of perjury on the American system. That is *Hamlet* without the prince! To talk about the pervasive influence of perjury on the American legal system and ignore a hundred years of police perjury and documented reports about police perjury and pretend—and close your eyes and make believe—that the only perjury worth considering is perjury about a sex lie committed by a president of the opposite party trivializes the rule of law and trivializes the oath of office."

"I thank you, Professor Dershowitz," Hyde began stiffly. "I don't thank you for criticizing the motives, saying that we're out to get the president," he protested, glaring down and pointing his finger at Dershowitz. "You haven't the slightest idea of the agony that many of us go through over this question. . . . We are concerned about the double standard. That may mean nothing to you . . ."

"It means a great deal to me," interrupted Dershowitz. "When is the last time this committee has expressed concern about the rights of criminal defendants?" he declared, as calls for "regular order" rose from the other committee members. "It's a sham," Dershowitz added with frustration.

It was to no avail. Two weeks later, the House voted to convict on counts of perjury and obstruction of justice, and Clinton became one of only two US presidents ever to be impeached. When a trial was held in the Senate soon afterward, five Republicans joined the Democrats in opposing the count of obstruction of justice, and ten sided with the Democrats on the charge of perjury.

"Our system of checks and balances requires that each branch be independent and serve the people in its own way," Dershowitz told the *Washington Post* during Clinton's Senate trial. "The impeachment power is like the ax behind the glass that says 'Do Not Break Except in Case of Emergency.' Removal of a president was intended as a last-resort safeguard against constitutional tyranny. We are trivializing it by applying it to conduct which does not threaten the liberty of Americans."

* * *

Clinton managed to hold on to his presidency, and the following year, George W. Bush took on Clinton's vice president, Al Gore, in the presidential election of 2000. Following the Supreme Court's controversial intervention in the extremely close race, Dershowitz wrote a book titled *Supreme Injustice* which excoriated the five conservative justices—including his friend Scalia—for "[peeking] beneath the blindfold of justice" by voting in favor of Bush, rather than Gore.

While working on *Supreme Injustice*, Dershowitz sent the manuscript over to Jeffrey Epstein for his comments. Epstein went through the typed pages, checking spelling and fixing punctuation mistakes with a black pen. He also added carets with minor details like "also Davis—3rd Cir," referring Dershowitz's attention to a certain judicial decision, and he occasionally added short, substantive passages like: "The overwhelming consensus of professional opinion is that the majority opinion in stopping the recount on equal protection grounds was wrong and improper. Within that broad consensus lies deep division regarding the [nature of] this judicial impropriety. It is to this issue that I now turn."

Around this time, Dershowitz was caught in the middle of a personal spat between Epstein and Lynn Forester. "They had a big fight over real estate," says Dershowitz. "It was a dispute over some apartment in New

York that Jeffrey had helped Lynn purchase, and he wanted it back to give to his girlfriend Ghislaine Maxwell. They turned viciously against each other. Lynn was a vengeful person, and so was Jeffrey in a way. He spitefully told me Lynn had an affair with Evelyn Rothschild while Evelyn was still married and even told me the name of the hotel where it happened. He and Lynn grew to hate each other."

While this was going on, Dershowitz received a letter from Prince Andrew. "Dear Alan. It has been sometime since I was in touch but I have a slight problem that I would like to ask your advice," wrote the Prince in May 2001. "Very briefly, I was in New York the other day and [Lynn] and Sir Evelyn held a dinner for me. As far as I can tell she made no secret of the dinner in the media and a convenient, friendly journalist, had an article in the UK tabloid paper The Mail on Sunday under the headline 'Can Lynn rescue Andrew's image' . . .

"I would like to express my displeasure and also to clearly show my loyalty to JE and GM [Ghislaine Maxwell] is undiminished by her behaviour. Would you be very kind and have a look at it for me to see that I have got the essence right but not overdone it?"

"Dear Prince Andrew," Dershowitz replied, "I would be happy to see your proposed letter and offer you my assessment, since I think I know all of the people fairly well."

"Dear Alan, Now I have a slightly different problem," the prince wrote in a second letter. "I ran into Lynn at the weekend and had a face to face grown-up discussion covering everything in my letter. . . . She profusely apologised and admitted her transgression. . . .

"I have spoken to GM and told her that I have given Lynn a piece of my mind already. I have yet to speak to JE. By the way Lynn has sent me an email as a result accepting her mistake but also expressing her concerns over JE. 'I want you to know that I will never trust him, or like him again. It would be impossible for me. I believe he is a truly evil person. I only want you to be careful. Character is destiny and he will be trouble, but you have to decide for yourself.'"

"I think that Lynn's e-mail to you does suggest the need for a brief written response reiterating your face-to-face message," responded Dershowitz. "Because so many people know of your associations with

Jewish residents of Przemyśl, 1924; Dershowitz's relative Zelig Dershowitz is marked "12".

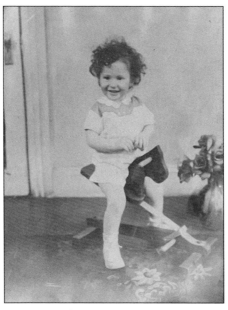

Dershowitz baby photo.

Dershowitz (bottom left) with his father, mother, and brother, c. 1942.

מחנה מסד א' תשי"ח

Camp Massad, 1948; Dershowitz (aged nine) is in the second row from the front; Noam Chomsky (aged nineteen) is believed to be in the far back row.

Dershowitz (at the podium) as captain of his high school's varsity debate team; (Talmudical Academy Brooklyn is also known as Yeshiva University High School).

Dershowitz with friends at Brooklyn College, c. 1955; the young woman with her hand on her head is Leah Trenk, who was Dershowitz's girlfriend at the time.

Dershowitz outside the U.S. Capitol, during his 1956 trip to Washington, D.C., with Alan Zwiebel.

Chief Judge David Bazelon (seated, center) and the D.C. Court of Appeals, 1962 (note Judge Warren Burger in the top row, second from left); credit: U.S. Court of Appeals for the D.C. Circuit.

Dershowitz (right) with Arthur Goldberg, c. 1967.

Dershowitz with Black students taking part in the "Special Summer
Program for Negroes," 1965.

Dershowitz (right) with Harvey Silverglate (left) and Jeanne Baker (center) during the Sheldon Seigel case.

Dershowitz (third from right) and members of the Soviet Jewry Legal Defense Project, 1974; from left to right: Eugene Gold, Melvin Stein, George Fletcher, Telford Taylor, Dershowitz, Leon Lipson, Nicholas Scoppetta; credit: Wagner International Photos.

Dershowitz speaking at a rally for Natan Sharansky and Soviet Jewry, c. 1978.

Dershowitz (fourth row, fourth from left, with poofy hair) with the 1978-1979 faculty and staff of Harvard Law School (note Professor Laurence "Larry" Tribe in the second row, fifth from right).

Elie Wiesel in a light-hearted moment during his remarks at the
ADL's presentation of the First Amendment Freedom Award to Dershowitz
(seated), 1982.

Dershowitz (far right) with Jim Cramer (far left), Eliot Spitzer (second from left), and Cliff Sloan
(second from right), c. 1982.

Dershowitz lecturing at Harvard, 1982; note the copy of *The Best Defense* on the podium.

Claus von Bülow celebrating with Dershowitz after being acquitted in the second trial, 1985; at left is Bülow's girlfriend Andrea Reynolds; credit: AP Images.

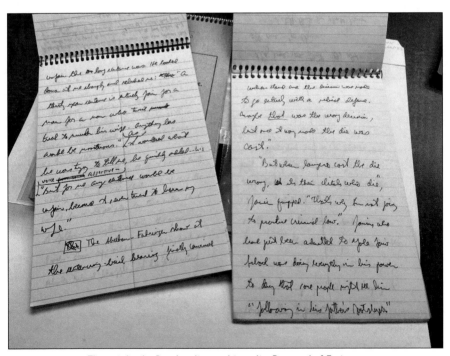

The notebooks Dershowitz used to write *Reversal of Fortune.*

Dershowitz with Carolyn, Elon (left), and Jamin (standing), c. 1985.

Dershowitz in front of crematoria at Auschwitz, c. 1987.

Dershowitz's office door at Harvard covered with anti-Jewish hate mail.

Dershowitz (center) with Carolyn (right) and Natan Sharansky at a
Cambridge restaurant, 1988.

Dershowitz (far right) with Aharon Barak (raising arm) and Carolyn in Israel, c. 1988.

Dershowitz (far left) at an event with John Kerry (pointing), c.1990.

William "Billy" Bulger criticizing Dershowitz during the hearing of Paul Mahoney, 1991; credit: Getty Images.

Dershowitz (left) with Jeremy Irons (center) and Elon (right) at the 1991 Academy Awards; Irons is holding his Oscar statuette for Best Actor.

Dershowitz (right) with Tammy Faye Bakker and Bakker's friend Roe Messner, 1991; credit: AP Images.

O.J. Simpson conferring with Dershowitz in court, 1995 (note F. Lee Bailey to Dershowitz's left); credit: Getty Images.

Dershowitz (at podium) in the Supreme Court, c. 1995; he is speaking at an event honoring Justice Stephen Breyer (seated).

Dershowitz with Don King at an event at Harvard, 1996; credit: AP Images.

Dershowitz with his wife, Carolyn, in San Francisco, c. 1997.

Dershowitz arguing with Rep. Henry Hyde during the impeachment of Bill Clinton, 1998; credit: Getty Images.

Dershowitz sharing a laugh with David Boies at a conference, 2001; credit: Getty Images.

Dershowitz with Jeffrey Epstein at an event at Harvard, 2004; credit: Getty Images.

Dershowitz (left) and Larry David (right) with Congressman Gary Ackerman (center) at a bakery during John Kerry's 2004 presidential campaign.

Dershowitz with President Bill Clinton, who is holding a copy of Dershowitz's book *The Case for Peace*, c. 2005.

Dershowitz (right) with Sen. Ted Kennedy (left) and author Richard North Patterson (center) on Martha's Vineyard, c. 2005.

Dershowitz (right) with Justice Antonin Scalia, c. 2009.

Dershowitz being led away by Swiss security after trying to challenge Mahmoud Ahmadinejad to a debate, 2009.

Dershowitz with Julian Assange in London, 2011.

Dershowitz discussing Iran with President Barack Obama in the Oval Office, 2012.

President Donald Trump handing a pen to Jared Kushner after signing an executive order against anti-Semitism on college campuses, 2019; note Dershowitz (in blue shirt and red tie) standing next to Robert Kraft (in blue suit) with Vice President Mike Pence behind Kraft.

Dershowitz with Trump at Mar-a-Lago, December 24, 2019; the President is asking Dershowitz if he will represent him in the Senate trial.

Dershowitz delivering his speech during the Senate trial of President Trump, January 27, 2020; note Jay Sekulow (red tie, glasses) at the defense table to Dershowitz's left, Rep. Adam Schiff (dark blue tie, circular lapel pin on his suit) at the House Managers' table to Dershowitz's right, and Chief Justice John Roberts in a black robe seated at the dais behind Dershowitz.

Dershowitz (right) discussing U.S.-Israeli relations and strategic issues with Prime Minister Benjamin Netanyahu (center) and Lt. Col. (Ret.) Danny Grossman (left), c. 2021; Grossman arranges Dershowitz's high-level meetings during his frequent trips to Israel.

These yard signs were placed on Martha's Vineyard in June 2023 when Dershowitz had a public spat with the Chilmark Public Library.

both Lynn/Evelyn and Jeffrey/Ghislaine, any criticism Lynn makes of Jeffrey or Ghislaine will implicitly involve you, even if you are not explicitly mentioned."

"I note everything and will write to Lynn this weekend," said the prince in a final letter. "Thank you very much and I look forward to seeing you sometime soon if I am in your part of the States."

Though he was unaware of it at the time, Dershowitz was soon to learn what Lynn Forester was evidently referring to when she warned that Epstein was a "truly evil person."

* * *

The new millennium had gotten off to a difficult start for people like Dershowitz who supported both America and Israel. 9/11 had rocked the world, and toward the end of Clinton's presidency, he had failed to negotiate a two-state solution between Israel and Palestine as he had always hoped to do. In 2000, he had brought Yasser Arafat and left-leaning Israeli Prime Minister Ehud Barak to Camp David for a new round of talks. Dershowitz spoke to Clinton in the lead-up to the summit and warned the president to expect a "no" from Arafat, a man Dershowitz despised for his decades of violence perpetrated against Israel. Dershowitz advised Clinton that Arafat would never agree to a two-state solution for fear that he would be killed by the PLO.

At Camp David in 2000, Clinton managed to get a commitment from Ehud Barak to allow the Palestinians control of a substantial portion of the West Bank and Gaza Strip, along with permission to declare Arab East Jerusalem the capital of their state. Dershowitz was lecturing at the University of Haifa in Israel while the negotiations were underway. He was enthusiastically in favor of Barak's offer, and along with many Israelis he encountered, he was cautiously optimistic this summit would result in a lasting peace between Israel and Palestine. He was horrified when he learned Arafat had flatly rejected Israel's offer of statehood and walked away from the summit with hardly a word of explanation.

Dershowitz, along with many in the international community, watched in sadness and frustration as the deal tanked, Clinton left office, and Ehud Barak was voted out as prime minister in 2001 by the Israelis in favor of the right-leaning Ariel Sharon. After being elected, Sharon visited the Al-Aqsa Mosque in Jerusalem, one of the holiest Islamic sites, and Arafat initiated an *intifada*—Arabic for "uprising." In the coming months, violent clashes erupted between Israeli troops and Palestinians throughout the West Bank and Gaza Strip, resulting in the deaths of thousands. Nearly three times as many Palestinians were killed as Israelis.

"For many, the bare arithmetic was enough," says Dershowitz. "Ignored was the fact that although 'only' 810 Israelis were killed. . . . Palestinian terrorists had attempted to kill thousands more and had failed only because Israeli authorities had thwarted 'about 80 percent of the attempted' terrorist attacks."

While the *intifada* raged, Paul Hanson, master of Harvard's Winthrop House, circulated a petition throughout Harvard and MIT calling for divestment from Israel and from companies that sold weapons to Israel. Almost six hundred students and faculty from both schools signed.

"Dershowitz [said] Israel should not be singled out as a violator of human rights," reported *The Harvard Crimson* during the divestment controversy. "'By any criteria, Israel's record on human rights is better than any country in the Middle East,' he said. He cited examples of human rights violations in countries that the U.S. supports, such as the execution of homosexuals in Egypt and the repression of women in Saudi Arabia."

During an interview with the *Financial Times* around this time, Dershowitz unloaded on Arafat. "[Dershowitz] accuses [Arafat] of instigating terrorist attacks for decades," reported the *Times* journalist. "'Arafat could have had a state a hundred times over,' says Dershowitz. 'Israeli leaders come and go, but the constant is Arafat. Peace will come when Arafat leaves.' I ask Dershowitz if he's not afraid of something more than verbal retribution for his views . . . 'I'm not going to let them shut me up,' he says. 'I'd rather die telling the truth than live a life of silence.'"

In the aftermath of the 2000 Camp David Summit, Dershowitz was convinced he needed to write a book geared toward college students which debunked the historical and moral accusations swirling against Israel. Drawing on his vast knowledge of the Israel-Palestine conflict from decades of study and dozens of research trips to the Middle East, Dershowitz laid out thirty-two prominent accusations against Israel and attacked each accusation individually in a concise, readable chapter. He had a team of students help with the research involved in rebutting each accusation.

One particularly sharp student was twenty-year-old Natalie Hershlag, who was born in Jerusalem to Jewish parents and raised in Long Island. She was studying psychology at Harvard and took a course from Dershowitz called "Neuropsychology and the Law." "She was a terrific student," says Dershowitz. "I can't overstate the quality of her academic work." It was only a few weeks into the course that Dershowitz learned she was a famous actress who went by the name Natalie Portman.

"I picked her as one of my research assistants because she got the highest grade in the entire class—and it was blind grading," says Dershowitz. "She was a sweet, generous person and didn't want a lot of people at Harvard to know who she was. She was pro-Israel and her politics seemed to be center-left, like most people at Harvard then."

As part of her work for Dershowitz, Portman traveled to Israel and inspected how Palestinians were cared for in Israeli hospitals, and she also investigated how terrorists were devising bombs with rat poison in order to prevent the blood from coagulating.

Dershowitz decided to call his book *The Case for Israel*. In the introduction, he explained his frustration at the public portrayal of Israel during the *intifada*. "Israel is a tiny nation, with few natural resources and little natural wealth, that has had to devote an enormous percentage of its gross national product to defending itself against external and internal enemies," he wrote in the conclusion, going on to praise Israel's healthcare system, biotechnology and medical advances, and Supreme Court. "The Palestinians have the widespread support of a billion Muslims. Add to that the United Nations, the European community, the third world, the Vatican, many influential academics, the international left, the far right, and many Protestant churches. The Palestinians have far more support than the Tibetans, the Kurds, the Armenians, the Chechens, and other real underdogs."

Dershowitz asked his publisher to make copies of *The Case for Israel* available at a lower cost for college students. Against Dershowitz's expectations, after publication in 2003, it took off in sales among the general public, becoming a *New York Times* bestseller and being translated into dozens of languages. A spin-off documentary was produced, and the book went on to sell around 200,000 copies.

Inevitably, as the book's influence grew and Dershowitz was flooded with invitations to speak on campuses, he faced backlash from numerous anti-Israel figures in academia and the media. Once again he had placed himself on the front lines of an international controversy, and the stage was set for some dramatic confrontations.

DAVID *AND* GOLIATH

Nearly two and a half centuries after American colonists gathered inside Boston's Faneuil Hall to protest the tyrannical overreach of the British government, Dershowitz stood inside the same hall in 2004 arguing passionately about the importance of protecting civil liberties in the aftermath of 9/11. After finishing his speech, Dershowitz was presented with a justice award and given a round of applause from his admirers.

But not everyone was pleased with the proceedings. A dozen Boston police officers were following Dershowitz that day, and as he left the hall carrying his award, he was confronted by a small crowd of young people. They were holding signs calling for Dershowitz to be tortured and killed and began chanting in chorus: "Dershowitz and Hitler, just the same, the only difference is the name." Thinking of his family members who were killed by Hitler's government, Dershowitz turned to say something to the protesters, when an officer grabbed him and urged him to head to the car.

"It was not only their words; it was the hatred in their eyes," reflects Dershowitz. "The protestors' eyes were ablaze with fanatical zeal."

* * *

Following Dershowitz's publication of *The Case for Israel*—and the book's remarkable sales figures—Dershowitz was invited to debate prominent Palestinian American academic Edward Said on the left-wing show *Democracy Now!*. Dershowitz accepted, but was surprised when Said's place was taken by one Norman Finkelstein. The son of Holocaust survivors and a professor at DePaul University, Finkelstein had made waves in the American Jewish community with his ferocious attacks on Israel's treatment of the Palestinians and with his book, *The Holocaust Industry*, which claimed prominent Zionists exploited the memory of the Holocaust following the Six-Day War in order to stir up support and sympathy for Israel.

When Finkelstein appeared with Dershowitz on *Democracy Now!*, he systematically picked apart *The Case for Israel*, alleging that Dershowitz had made an improper citation to Mark Twain, inaccurately stated that two to three thousand Palestinians had been displaced during one period of Israel's history when in fact the number had been 200,000 to 300,000, and plagiarized a substantial portion of *The Case for Israel* from a book by journalist Joan Peters called *From Time Immemorial*.

Dershowitz defended himself against each of these charges and vehemently declared his innocence of any scholarly wrongdoing. "I don't purport to be an independent historian who goes back to the Middle East and reads original documents," stated Dershowitz. "I'm making a case. I'm doing what a lawyer would do, and what lawyers do is—they find sources [and] they check the sources. I had a research staff that obviously checked the sources."

The debate turned nasty, with both participants raising their voices and Dershowitz repeatedly interrupting Finkelstein. At one point, the host had to mute both mics as the men continually talked over each other. As they exchanged barbs, Finkelstein said in irritation, "Mr. Dershowitz, I read your book—or the book you purport to have written."

"Now you're claiming somebody else wrote it?" replied an exasperated Dershowitz. "I hope so!" said Finkelstein. "For your sake, I truly hope . . . I think the honorable thing for you to do would be to say, 'I didn't write the book, I had no time to read it.'"

"I proudly wrote it," said Dershowitz with a smile. "I wrote every word of it. I have the handwritten drafts."

"Alan writes everything by hand," says his typist, Maura Kelley. "Nobody writes anything for him." "A plagiarism charge is very serious in the academic world," says Dershowitz. "I'm the most original person anyone could ever meet. Everything I write is original. I don't go back to sources—my research staff does that. The idea I would plagiarize is absurd. Everything I write comes from my heart and my brain. I write a first draft on yellow legal pad, which Maura Kelley types up for me to review and edit."

Dershowitz asked Elena Kagan, his former student who had by this point become the dean of Harvard Law School, to investigate Finkelstein's plagiarism charge. Kagan appointed former Harvard president Derek Bok to the task, and after viewing Dershowitz's original handwritten manuscripts, Bok found no substance to the charge.

After this, things turned increasingly nasty between Dershowitz and Finkelstein. When Finkelstein published a book called *Beyond Chutzpah*, which outlined his criticisms of Dershowitz's scholarship on Israel and the libelous plagiarism charge, Dershowitz wrote to Governor Arnold Schwarzenegger asking him to block Finkelstein's California publisher from printing the book. Dershowitz failed to prevent the book's release, but, partly through a threatening letter from his lawyer Rory Millson, he managed to get the editors to remove the evidently false section which alleged he had plagiarized. Not long after, Finkelstein wrote an article for *CounterPunch* titled, "Should Alan Dershowitz Target Himself for Assassination?" which mocked Dershowitz as a "born-again Zionist" and argued that Dershowitz's recent book *Preemption* supported Nazi-like tactics of the Israeli government, including targeted assassination and purposeful attacks on civilians. According to Dershowitz, Finkelstein also arranged for a political cartoonist to create an image of Dershowitz sitting on a chair labeled "Israel Peep Show" and masturbating gleefully in front of a TV screen which showed dead civilians in Beirut.

Dershowitz turned the tables on Finkelstein by attacking his scholarship. Dershowitz created a list of what he believed were Finkelstein's most outrageous comments about Israel and the international Jewish community and made them available to colleges throughout the country. Incidentally, Finkelstein was being considered for tenure at his home university, DePaul, and Dershowitz was asked by one of Finkelstein's colleagues to submit a formal document outlining Finkelstein's scholarly malpractice. "Finkelstein's entire literary catalogue is one preposterous and discredited ad hominem attack after another," Dershowitz wrote in the introduction to the document he provided DePaul. "By his own admission, he has conducted no original research, has never been published in a reputable scientific journal, and has made no contributions to our collective historical knowledge."

Dershowitz's battle with Finkelstein gained the attention of the *New York Times*. "In the latest round, first reported in The Chronicle of Higher Education, Dershowitz, a law professor at Harvard and a prominent defender of Israel, is trying to derail Finkelstein's bid for tenure at DePaul University in Chicago," it reported. "He has sent a blast of e-mail messages to faculty and administrators there accusing Finkelstein of shoddy scholarship, lying and anti-Semitism. Finkelstein, who last week was involved in the third and final step of the tenure process, said that so far two committees—one from the political science department and one from the college as a whole—voted in favor of tenure. But the college dean rejected an advisory committee's vote and recommended against an appointment. 'I am personally confident that had the process been without outside interferences, I would have gotten tenure,' Finkelstein said . . .

"Dershowitz said he found it paradoxical that Finkelstein was complaining about outside interference when Finkelstein tried to discredit the historian Daniel Goldhagen by publishing a book that excoriated his scholarship on Germany and the Holocaust, and tried to disbar Burt Neuborne, a law professor at New York University, saying he lied and blackmailed Swiss banks when he was representing Holocaust survivors."

Finkelstein had fought Dershowitz and lost. Many on the far left became outraged at what they perceived to be Dershowitz's undermining of Finkelstein's free speech rights.

"We went through a lot when Finkelstein made his plagiarism charge," says Elon Dershowitz. "As far as I can remember, it was the first time my father had to defend himself against a personal attack on his scholarship. He is a really nice person until you decide to raise the red flag against him. And I think that's what happened with Finkelstein. Usually my father just has intellectual conversations with people he disagrees with, but he hates when guys like Finkelstein go after Israel in a manner that seems to be anti-Jewish."

"I was asked for input by DePaul University," says Dershowitz. "I didn't volunteer letters, and I disclosed my bias. I'm very proud of any role I may have played in getting Finkelstein denied tenure. As an academic, I have to make decisions about who deserves tenure and who doesn't. This case was not about defending Finkelstein's First Amendment rights, but about attacking his scholarship.

"I would have supported tenure for Noam Chomsky and opposed efforts to silence him because he was a man of stature. The same is not true of Finkelstein—he wouldn't have deserved tenure even if he was pro-Israel."

Shortly after, Jeffrey Toobin hosted an event with Dershowitz about free speech at the 92nd Street Y in New York, a Jewish events center where Dershowitz was a much-sought-after speaker. "Do you think people in your classes—students in your classes, less outspoken, less-established faculty members than you—worry about expressing certain sentiments on campus?" Toobin asked Dershowitz. "Absolutely," said Dershowitz. "What's considered unacceptable speech?" inquired Toobin. "On 50 percent of American college campuses today—fully 50 percent—there is not a single faculty member, dean, administrator, junior faculty, [or] senior faculty who will speak out on behalf of Israel . . .

"When I wrote my book *The Case for Israel*, Norman Finkelstein, Noam Chomsky, and [Alexander] Cockburn got together—literally got together—and decided they had to trash my book [because] it was becoming a bestseller. And so they decided—this was a calculated plot—to do what they had done to six or seven other pro-Israel writers: to accuse me of not having written the book and to accuse me of having plagiarized it. Now, I fought back, and as a result, Norman Finkelstein didn't get tenure at DePaul University"—at which point the audience applauded—"and I hope we sent out a very powerful message to fight back," concluded Dershowitz.

Although Dershowitz maintained that Alexander Cockburn had personally told him of Chomsky's conspiring with Finkelstein, Chomsky vehemently denied the accusation. "I don't know who else could be so depraved as to have claimed this," he says. "Unless Dershowitz gave a source that can be checked, it's fair to assume—from the record—that he was simply lying.

"I can guess why he might have made up this particular ludicrous tale. I have mentioned something about that book, not in print, in fact to him (he smirked). It contains one of my favorite Dershowitz fabrications. One of the chapters is about how everyone hates the Jews. It has an epigraph, a quote from me: Jews don't need Israel, they already have New York. All that's missing is the rest of the sentence and the context. The sentence reads: 'It is as if someone were to say that Jews don't need Israel. . . .' The context is my response to an article in the *New York Times* saying that Palestinians don't need a state because there are lots of Arab states. This is not just carelessness. It is carefully contrived deceit."

"I first met Norman Finkelstein in the mid-80s," Chomsky notes. "He was a graduate student in Middle East studies at Princeton, studying Zionist history. Joan Peters's fraud had just appeared, to great acclaim. He was surprised by what she claimed, checked her sources carefully, and found that it was incredible fraud—as now acknowledged. He wrote a paper on it and sent it to some thirty people who wrote about these issues, asking whether they thought it was worthwhile for him to pursue it. He got one response—from me. I said I thought it was worthwhile. . . . We soon became close friends."

"I followed Dershowitz's incredible campaign to get university authorities to overturn the department's decision to grant Finkelstein tenure—I wasn't surprised that they caved in," continues Chomsky. "Considering the scale of Dershowitz's lies and his grotesque record as an apologist for terrible crimes, plagiarism is a minor concern."

"When has Dershowitz defended the free speech rights of critics of Israel?" asks Chomsky. "For example, the fact that until a few years ago I had to have police protection, even on my own campus, if I was talking about Israel-Palestine? Or when [Israel Shahak], Israel's leading civil rights activist and a Holocaust survivor, spoke at MIT at my invitation and the meeting was virtually broken up by young supporters of Israel? Incidentally, he had been viciously attacked by Dershowitz in the *Boston Globe*, which permitted me to write a response refuting Dershowitz's disgraceful lies, another example of his bitter hatred for freedom of speech and elementary civil rights."

Chomsky's view on Dershowitz's commitment to freedom of speech did not seem to square with all the facts. When Yasser Arafat died in 2004, a group of Palestinian students at Harvard were denied permission to raise the Palestinian flag in Harvard Yard on the ground that only the flag of an officially recognized country could be raised. Attempting to reverse this decision, the Palestinian students went to Dershowitz and asked him to lobby the university to allow the raising of the Palestinian flag on free speech grounds. Dershowitz had written an article after Arafat's passing in which he slammed him as a Jew-killer and an "uncontrite terrorist," but he agreed to help the students in the interests of the First Amendment and was successful in his lobbying of the university's legal counsel. On the day the students raised the Palestinian flag, Dershowitz stood by the flagpole handing flyers to passers-by which argued Arafat's death had been "untimely—because if he had just died five years earlier, the Palestinians might have a state."

The following year, Chomsky traveled to Harvard for a debate with Dershowitz hosted by the John F. Kennedy Jr. School of Government. Since their debate in 1973, Dershowitz and Chomsky had sparred several times: debating at Harvard in 1983 over issues related to the West Bank, exchanging scathing letters in 1989 over an alleged Holocaust denier named Robert Faurisson, and attacking each other in their books (*Chutzpah* in Dershowitz's case and *Chronicles of Dissent* in Chomsky's).

By 2005, Chomsky had risen to extreme prominence. He had taught at MIT for decades and achieved international attention for his studies in linguistics and his struggle against what he perceived to be repressive governments, including the United States and Israel. *The Times* in London had called him one of the "makers of the 20th century," and he had achieved the rank of eighth-most-cited scholar of all time, just behind Freud and one spot ahead of Hegel.

"Chomsky was the only person in my adult life who told me the opposite of what Yitz Greenberg told me as a teenager," says Dershowitz. "In one of his books, he said I was 'not very bright.'" Despite these insults— or perhaps because of them—Dershowitz relished his interactions with Chomsky. "I've always picked my enemies carefully and I have a lot of them," he told an interviewer around this time. "And you know one of the reasons I want to live a long time is I don't want to give my enemies the pleasure of dancing on my grave. . . . It's such a perverse infantile attitude, but [I] have to admit it's there."

In their 2005 debate, Dershowitz and Chomsky were once again representing opposing sides of the Israel-Palestine conflict. The stated topic of the debate was "Where do we go from here?" In recent years, following the 2000 Camp David summit and Ariel Sharon's withdrawal from the Gaza Strip, Dershowitz had become fervently interested in the two-state solution and wrote a book titled *The Case for Peace*, in which he outlined a blueprint for a viable Palestinian state and fervently urged both sides to make compromises for the interests of long-term peace.

Both Dershowitz and Chomsky came prepared to address the topic at hand, but the debate soon descended into acrimony.

"I was invited to a debate at the JFK School of Government by a group of Harvard Law students, and I told them that though I was happy to debate anyone freely, in the case of Dershowitz there would have to be formal ground rules agreed on by both of us and by the moderator," says Chomsky. "The reason, as I explained to them, is that I was by then familiar enough with his antics to know that he would not participate in an honest discussion. He is well aware that he cannot defend his positions, so his style is that of a defense attorney with a guilty client who tries to change the subject. What's sometimes called the 'thief, thief' technique: if you're caught with your hand in someone's pocket, shout 'thief, thief,' pointing elsewhere.

"For that reason, I informed the students that I would not agree to a debate without a formal agreement, with the moderator, that both debaters would keep to the issue and not try to evade it by accusations against the other. There were several months of discussions about this. Finally a formal agreement was reached. It was reiterated when we met privately with the moderator right before the debate."

During a meeting before the debate, as the audience took their seats, Dershowitz tried to exchange pleasantries with Chomsky. "You know we go back a long time—I recently found out we were at Camp Massad the same year back in 1948," said Dershowitz, who went to shake Chomsky's hand. But Chomsky simply ignored Dershowitz and walked onstage.

Carolyn came to show support for her husband, and after winning a coin toss by the moderator, Dershowitz made his opening statement first. "The debate today occurs at a time of real potential for peace," he said. "Shimon Peres, Israel's elder statesman in the peace camp, today quit the Labour Party and announced his support for Ariel Sharon in the upcoming election. 'In my eyes it is not a problem of parties, but a problem of peace—how to create a strong coalition for peace.' The elements are now in place for a real peace. As I wrote in *The Case for Peace*, when the Palestinian leadership wants a Palestinian state more than it wants to see the destruction of Israel there will finally be a two-state solution."

"I believe that peace is a realistic possibility," continued Dershowitz, "whereas Professor Chomsky apparently believes there is no chance for peace, at least as reflected by the German title of his new book *Chance für Frieden*, which translates as 'No Chance for Peace: Why a Palestinian state is not possible to be established with Israel and the United States.' I hope you're wrong," said Dershowitz, turning left and looking at Chomsky.

"I travel around college campuses in the United States, I notice a stark difference," said Dershowitz at another point. "Many of those who support the Palestinian cause tend to be virulently opposed to Israel, comparing the Jewish state to Nazism and apartheid; *comparing Shimon Peres to Hitler and Idi Amin*"—at which Dershowitz glanced at his opponent with a look of rebuke for this quote from Chomsky—"calling Israel the world's worst human rights violators and suggesting that Israel should be flattered by a comparison with the Gestapo."

Chomsky was fuming. "During his tirade I got up from my seat and walked over to the moderator," he says. "What [no one could hear] was that I reminded him of the ground rules we had just agreed on. He pretended that he didn't notice that I was there. . . . At that point I should have just walked off, but as a courtesy to the audience, I decided to continue."

When Dershowitz concluded his opening statement, Chomsky rose to his podium. "Mr. Mandel will confirm there was an explicit condition for this debate," he said in a monotone voice. "That is, that neither participant tried to evade the issue by deceitful allegations about the other. . . . I'll keep to the topic—*and the rules*."

Chomsky went on to cite a meeting between America, Israel, and the Palestinians in Taba, Egypt, following the 2000 Camp David summit. "[This meeting] made considerable progress and might have led to a settlement, but Israel called them off," he declared. "That one week at Taba is the only break in thirty years of US-Israeli rejectionism."

For much of the debate Dershowitz and Chomsky rehashed the past, casting blame and defending their side. Barbs were thrown out. Dershowitz accused Chomsky of living on another planet, and Chomsky mocked Dershowitz at one point for finally making "a true statement."

During the Q&A period, Dershowitz got a chance to lay out part of his proposal for a viable Palestinian state. He said that Palestine should have control over East Jerusalem, and holding up a map from *The Case for Peace*, stated, "Now there are all kinds of creative proposals for functional contiguity between the West Bank and Gaza, including a high-tech rail line recently designed by the Rand Foundation. . . . Under this proposal no point in Palestine would be more than ninety minutes away from any other point in Palestine, including Gaza—it would take thirty-four minutes to get from Hebron to Gaza City on the rail line."

"If that's a valid approach to contiguity for the Palestinian state in 22 percent of the former Palestine, let's propose it for the Israeli state in 78 percent of the former Palestine," countered Chomsky.

"When thousands of people have been killed by terrorism, you don't expect a country to go back to a proposal that was offered and rejected many, many years earlier," replied Dershowitz. "Options change when rejectionism sets in."

Intriguingly, although they disagreed over who was to blame for the failure of Camp David and Taba, Dershowitz and Chomsky both separately voiced their support for the Taba proposals mentioned by Chomsky, with Dershowitz stating in his closing statement: "I think the prospects for peace based on the Taba proposals are quite realistic." Unfortunately, this point of agreement was swallowed up in the intense exchanges between the two debaters.

Glenn Greenwald was a budding political journalist who observed Dershowitz and Chomsky's clashing from a distance. "It is interesting how much animus this issue of Israel can produce, even among people who otherwise share a similar worldview when it comes to the steadfast nature of civil libertarianism and a defense of free speech—which isn't a particularly common worldview," says Greenwald, who was on Chomsky's side of the aisle and would later gain notoriety for breaking the Edward Snowden story in 2013.

Greenwald had read some of Dershowitz's books on Israel and constitutional law while he was in law school and went into private practice as a civil liberties lawyer before turning to journalism. "Alan and I both shared a liberal framework of how rights are understood," says Greenwald, "but it is not an uncommon dynamic that people who go through life espousing a certain set of political values adopt a completely different framework when it comes to Israel. American Jews have been indoctrinated from the earliest parts of our childhood to believe that Israel is this noble country that we're duty bound to love and defend and protect. It's very ingrained within us on the deepest kind of psychological and cultural levels."

"I think if I were a black Protestant woman, I would still support Israel," counters Dershowitz. "I attribute zero percent of my support for Israel to the fact that I am ethnically Jewish. I attribute it to my morality and ideology. I always support the underdog, and Israel is the only democracy in the Middle East. I also support Israel on its merits. I don't believe Israel is so much more special than every other nation, but I do believe that it has done more for the world scientifically, technologically, and medically in the first decades of its existence than any other country—certainly far more than any of its Arab neighbors who oppose it."

"If Israel became an evil country, I'd turn against it," says Dershowitz. "But unless that happens, I don't think there are two sides to this issue. I think Israel is in the right and anti-Israel people are in the wrong."

* * *

In early 2006 Dershowitz was going about his business one day at Harvard when he got a call from Jeffrey Epstein. Dershowitz had seen Epstein periodically at educational conferences and seminars over the past few years, and he had stayed at Epstein's Palm Beach estate in 2005 along with Jamin, his wife Barbara, and their two children, Lori and Lyle. Dershowitz's granddaughter, Lori, was participating in a soccer tournament, and when Dershowitz mentioned in a conversation with Epstein that they were coming down to Palm Beach, Epstein asked where they were staying. Dershowitz mentioned which hotel, and Epstein replied, "No, don't stay there—stay at my house. I have a full-time cook and maid, and no one's going to be there that week." And so they did, and apart from being instructed by Epstein's housekeeper to please keep away from his private section, they had free rein of the house.

Then one day in 2006, Epstein called Dershowitz and said he needed some legal help. He told Dershowitz that he was being investigated by the police for engaging in sexual acts with a seventeen-year-old woman. "I was completely surprised," says Dershowitz. "Jeffrey had girlfriends who were in their late twenties, including one woman who was a business school student and whose father was the head of a bank in Germany. But I never saw him hanging around with teenagers."

Without a hint of hesitation or embarrassment, Epstein told Dershowitz he had done nothing wrong and asked Dershowitz to join his legal team. "This may not be a good idea, Jeffrey," said Dershowitz. "I know you. We have an acquaintanceship." But Epstein persisted, and in the end, Dershowitz agreed. "I didn't get a lot of requests for legal help from people I knew," says Dershowitz. "This case was right within my wheelhouse. I had done cases about sexual accusations and taught about the subject at Harvard. It would've been surprising if I hadn't agreed."

Many young women claimed to the authorities that Epstein had paid them in cash to perform sexual acts in the private bedroom of his Palm Beach house. Police had entered Epstein's house and searched the nooks and crannies, discovering nude photos of young women and even finding a girl's high school report card hidden inside a clock.

To oppose the prosecution, Dershowitz brought in Boston attorney Martin Weinberg, a former student of Dershowitz's, and the prominent lawyer Roy Black. Epstein had also separately hired Kenneth Starr.

"At that time, the allegations were minimal," says Dershowitz. "Jeffrey admitted to having massages with three girls, one of whom turned out to be underage. She had been a month shy of eighteen when she came to Jeffrey's house, and she had presented him with a driver's license which showed she was over eighteen. The license was eventually found to be a fake. Jeffrey maintained he had not engaged with anyone very young, and there was no compelling evidence he had encounters with girls aged fourteen, fifteen, or sixteen."

The defense's goal was to strike a deal with prosecutors whereby Epstein would not serve any jail time and would not be listed as a sex offender in New York. Epstein had hired private investigators who discovered through the site MySpace.com that some of his accusers admitted to being addicted to drugs. Dershowitz flew down to a meeting with the state attorney's office in Palm Beach, where he showed the prosecutors the damaging information about Epstein's accusers. This tactic did not sit well with the members of the public, but Dershowitz was not ashamed. "It's obligatory," he says matter-of-factly. "A failure to learn all one can about complaining witnesses is a cardinal sin among lawyers. If you don't do this, you can be disbarred."

Dershowitz would later be mocked for referring to Epstein as an "underdog" in the case, but he stood by the label. "The authorities in Florida, the police, and the media were after him, and when the government comes after a defendant, the defendant will always be an underdog even if he's powerful and strong like Jeffrey," he says. "The government has enormous resources, including most importantly that they can get anyone to cooperate and be a witness by threatening them with prosecution. Most judges are former prosecutors. And jurors love the government—the first thing the prosecutor says in a federal case is 'I represent the U.S. government,' which immediately creates an implication that the U.S. government as a whole is going against the defendant. That's why more than 90 percent of indictments result in convictions, 95 percent of convictions are affirmed on appeal, and 90 percent result in plea bargains. There was no possibility Jeffrey could have gotten a fair trial, which is why we were inclined to plead."

Eventually, in 2008, a deal was struck whereby Epstein would plead guilty to a state charge of soliciting a minor for prostitution, be placed on the national sex offender registry, and serve eighteen months in the local Palm Beach jail. "It was a mediocre deal for all sides," says Dershowitz. "It was based on the weakness of the federal case. There was no proof of a federal crime—no proof Jeffrey had brought prostitutes across state boundaries. The prosecution knew that and were prepared to do what prosecutors do all the time—make a deal. They said they were doing it to protect the young women from having to testify."

Even though he had gotten what some in the media labeled a "sweetheart deal"—due to his significant exit privileges while in jail—Epstein was furious with Dershowitz for not keeping him out of jail altogether. He vengefully withheld some of Dershowitz's legal fees.

Although Epstein was capable of friendliness, he could be nasty and demanding. "Jeffrey was cold," says Sarah Neely, one of Dershowitz's assistants at Harvard. "When he would call the office and I would answer the phone, he would simply say, 'Jeffrey.' Not 'Hi, this is Jeffrey. Can I speak with Alan?' or even 'Can I speak with Alan.' Just 'Jeffrey.' And we were supposed to just transfer the call."

"My partners and I did some procedural work on the Florida case, and I met Jeffrey a number of times in New York," says Nathan Dershowitz. "He invited me over to his place to socialize, and I wouldn't go. There are some people that just seem to be slimy. He had a very good ability to turn people he had contact with into friends, and what he told me about himself had inconsistencies and gaps. I felt uncomfortable around Jeffrey and never accepted social invitations.

"Jeffrey gave my brother gifts and invited Alan to events that got him pulled further into Jeffrey's orbit. I commented to my partners about my feelings of sleaziness around Jeffrey and told Alan on at least one occasion that I didn't think he should be socializing with Jeffrey. But Jeffrey liked to collect noteworthy people, and Alan liked to associate with prominent people."

* * *

Amid his many duties as a professor and lawyer, Dershowitz devoted as much attention as possible to fighting for Israel in the international arena. In 2009, he and Carolyn traveled with Elie Wiesel and Irwin Cotler to a summit of the UN Human Rights Council in Geneva, Switzerland, at which the president of Iran, Mahmoud Ahmadinejad, was the featured speaker. Ahmadinejad had publicly called for the destruction of Israel, had questioned the historical validity of the Holocaust, and was then seeking to develop nuclear weapons. Following one of his speeches in Iran, his listeners had raised cries of "Death to America!" and "Death to Israel!"

Before the UN summit, Alan and Carolyn were having a drink in the lobby of their hotel when Ahmadinejad walked in, surrounded by an entourage. Carolyn hissed at him and shouted a comment about the Holocaust having actually occurred. "I was so proud of her," says Dershowitz. Ahmadinejad gave Carolyn a dirty look and walked on.

Ten minutes later, he passed back through the lobby, and this time Dershowitz got up and walked over to his entourage. With Ahmadinejad less than twenty feet away, he introduced himself to a handler and said he was challenging Ahmadinejad to a debate about Israel and the Holocaust. "Where, at Harvard?" replied the handler. "No, the debate should be at Auschwitz, that's where the evidence is," shot back Dershowitz. When the handler would not give Dershowitz a commitment from the president, Dershowitz tried approaching Ahmadinejad directly. As he did, two of the Swiss security guards at the hotel grabbed him by both arms and led him to the front entrance. "He's entitled to be physically safe, but he's not entitled to be protected from hard questions," protested Dershowitz as they walked him out of the hotel.

Dershowitz immediately got on the phone with a friend who worked in the Obama White House, who called the embassy in Switzerland and arranged for Dershowitz to be allowed back into the hotel. "The other conference attendees in the hotel were as angry at Ahmadinejad as Alan was, but he was the only one brave enough to get up and say anything to him," says Carolyn.

Later on, during the summit, when Ahmadinejad took the podium and began slamming Israel, delegates from dozens of countries stood up and walked out past the podium, provoking cheers throughout the chamber. Dershowitz and other supporters of Israel left with the protesting delegates, and before exiting the chamber, Dershowitz pointed at Ahmadinejad and shouted "Shame!" when he made a Holocaust-denying remark.

By this point in his life Dershowitz was perhaps the most recognizable defender of Israel on the world stage. His books and media appearances garnered him many speaking invitations, and hatred followed him virtually wherever he went. He was heckled in London when he participated in a symposium about Israel with noted British lawyer Anthony Julius at the University of London. While advocating the two-state solution in a speech at the University of Toronto, he was flanked by guards onstage and spoke behind bulletproof glass as a result of credible death threats he received before coming.

During a visit to France, the streets of Paris were filled with protests over the Israel-Palestine conflict, and anti-Jewish attacks had been occurring in the city. Dershowitz wore a yarmulke during a speech in the French Assembly to show solidarity with the Jews of the city who were being specifically targeted by protesters. "It's easy for you to wear one when you're flying out tomorrow," said the disgruntled chief rabbi of France who came to listen to Dershowitz. "If my congregants do that, they'll get the crap beat out of them."

In Norway, Dershowitz was dissed by the Universities of Trondheim, Bergen, and Oslo, who refused an offer from a Norwegian pro-Israel organization to host events with Dershowitz at no cost to the universities. Despite Dershowitz's international prestige as a lawyer, the three schools declined the offer. Dershowitz learned that prominent academics from the schools had signed a petition which called for divestment from Israel and began with the words: "Since 1948 the state of Israel has occupied Palestinian land." He ended up being invited by Jewish student groups and spoke to packed halls at the three universities, where he was greeted by applause and escorted by police.

"Whenever I go to hear him talk, I always scan the room," says Carolyn. "The events in Norway were very scary. At one point, this large man came up to the stage. He just glared at Alan for a minute and then made a hateful comment. He looked like he had murder in his heart."

Closer to home, Dershowitz was interrupted during a 2009 speech about the two-state solution at the University of Massachusetts. When a large group of students and faculty members began loudly shouting and booing, it became so deafening that the moderator ended the event before Dershowitz finished his speech.

"I told Ariel Sharon in 2003 that the most important battlefield against anti-Semitism was American campuses," says Natan Sharansky, who had gone onto a successful career in Israeli politics after his liberation from Soviet prison. "The most useful book in those days was *The Case for Israel*. Alan and I appeared together in several speaking engagements to fight for the souls of Jewish students and teach them to defend Israel. Once, I was listening to Alan talk with a group of students, and I was amazed at how he was able to speak on their level. He was understanding of the nuances of their questions and gave hard answers which were difficult for a younger generation to accept."

At Harvard, Dershowitz was the only professor who had an office with bulletproof windows. In addition to his personal barrage of vicious hate mail, Dershowitz's assistant Sarah Neely periodically had threatening messages in her voicemail, including death threats and one warning from a man who said he would make sure Neely was never able to bear children. Once Neely opened a package labeled for Dershowitz and a bunch of white powder spilled out onto her. Harvard fire officers were called in, and Neely had to be taken to the hospital for fear she had been contaminated by anthrax powder.

"I think Alan's passion for Israel comes from the amount of hate people have for Israel," admits Neely. "That, and he loves the underdog, which Israel can be in many international situations."

The responses to Dershowitz were not always hateful. After one trip to Israel with his father, Elon tweeted, "He's Elvis over there."

"Once we were going for a walk on the beach in Tel Aviv," says Elon, "and a small group of kids in their late teens or early twenties saw my dad and did a double take. 'Are you Alan Dershowitz?' they asked. And my dad stood there for ten minutes just shooting the breeze with these kids. I mean, we were in the middle of fucking Israel! It was amazing to see."

"When I meet people on the street and introduce myself with the last name Dershowitz, they invariably respond 'Are you related to Alan?'" said Zecharia Dor-Shav, Dershowitz's uncle who lived in Israel. "To Alan, Israel is family, and just like with your family, there may be things you don't like about them, but they're your family. So his predisposition is not 'Israel's right.' His predisposition is 'Israel is family.'"

In 2008, Israel had come under international condemnation for a twenty-two-day offensive in the Gaza Strip in response to rocket attacks from Hamas. The 2008 Gaza War, also known as Operation Cast Lead, resulted in the deaths of over one thousand Palestinians and thirteen Israelis.

"Six thousand missiles have hit in Israel," declared Dershowitz in a debate with pro-Palestinian scholar James Zogby hosted by Larry King on CNN. "They've hit kindergartens, they've hit schools. . . . Proportionality doesn't require a nation to sit back and accept these kinds of missiles. The fact that civilians are being killed is completely the fault of Hamas for hiding behind civilians." Dershowitz slammed Hamas's brutality and defended Israel's response in a book called *The Case for Moral Clarity*, which bore a cover illustration of an Israeli soldier firing in front of a baby carriage and a Hamas fighter firing from behind one.

"I had zero tolerance for attacks on innocent civilians," says Israeli prime minister Ehud Olmert, who gave the go-ahead for Cast Lead. "The ultimate responsibility of any prime minister is to provide security for the people he is responsible for. In this respect, I had no patience towards anyone who killed an Israeli civilian."

Olmert and Dershowitz had been friends since the mid-1990s when Olmert was the mayor of Jerusalem, and they appeared together at various media events. Left-leaning politically, Olmert served as prime minister from 2006 to 2009 and led Israel through some of its tensest moments, including Cast Lead, the bombing of a Syrian nuclear reactor, and a war in Lebanon in 2006.

"For me, to have the chance to check with Alan and to discuss with him the different issues I was facing was always something I valued very much," says Olmert. Among other things, Olmert sought Dershowitz's advice on an offer he presented to the Palestinians to form a state with 93 percent of the West Bank, which the Palestinians ultimately rejected. "I am absolutely confident that Alan was in favor of a two-state solution," Olmert notes. "He never agreed with a policy that did not recognize the right of Palestinians to self-determination. He may not be the most extreme liberal, but he's liberal enough and decent enough as a human being and as a believer in human rights to support this position.

"Many can speak up for Israel during good times. But in bad times, like when Israel was criticized for bombing Gaza while I was prime minister—when many people, including Jews, said Israel was committing war crimes and its leaders were violent—it required courage to stand against the tide and speak the opposite. Alan had that courage.

"I think one thing Alan feared," continues Olmert, "was that if he said something not necessarily identical to the Israeli government, it would be used by the opponents of Israel against Israel. And he didn't want to be used against Israel under any circumstances."

Dershowitz demonstrated this in a profound way one year after Olmert left office. Dershowitz's old friend Bibi Netanyahu had once again been elected prime minister after being voted out in 1999. Dershowitz visited Netanyahu during his frequent trips to Israel, and Netanyahu read Dershowitz's books and articles related to Israel and periodically sought his counsel. In 2010, a representative of Netanyahu flew to Miami for the sole purpose of visiting Dershowitz, who was spending the winter with Carolyn at their Florida apartment. He arranged a lunch meeting with Dershowitz and told him that Netanyahu's Security Cabinet had unanimously voted to nominate Dershowitz to become Israel's ambassador to the United Nations. Netanyahu's representative asked Dershowitz if he would take up the post. Dershowitz was completely surprised and enthused by the offer, but told Netanyahu's representative he would have to decline because it could create a conflict of interest for him as an American citizen if Israel and the United States ever clashed at the UN. The representative urged Dershowitz not to make a quick decision and to talk it over with his wife.

After leaving the restaurant, Dershowitz immediately went home and discussed it with Carolyn, who understood his excitement at the offer but agreed with his response. When Dershowitz relayed his answer to Netanyahu, Netanyahu replied, "Please, don't decide until you give us a chance to convince you." Netanyahu asked Dershowitz to fly to Israel and meet with him for a private dinner in the prime minister's home in Jerusalem.

Over the course of several hours, Netanyahu pulled out all the stops to persuade Dershowitz. He told Dershowitz he was the only person his security cabinet had agreed on. "You are the strongest advocate for Israel in the world," said Netanyahu. "I know you will fight back hard against the UN's bigotry." Dershowitz's role would be primarily as a vocal advocate for Israel during debates at UN meetings but would also involve Dershowitz working behind the scenes as a negotiator to try to change votes.

"It would have been the best fun of my life to play the role Bibi wanted," says Dershowitz. "Although I identify strongly with Israel, I am 100 percent American and my allegiance is to America. For me to switch sides—even to a nation that is so close an ally to my own nation—would raise the specter of dual loyalty that has been directed at Jews since biblical times, when they lived as minorities in the lands of Egypt and Persia."

Dershowitz told this to Netanyahu, who responded that haters of Israel would "think and say [that] even if you don't take the job." Dershowitz argued he could best serve the Jewish people by remaining an independent advocate for Israel.

When Netanyahu saw Dershowitz's mind was made up, he backed down. At the end of the dinner, though, he looked Dershowitz straight in the eye and said, "I need you to be Israel's unofficial ambassador to the Jews of America, especially the young ones. America's political support for Israel is every bit as important as its military support, and the two are, of course, related. Please help keep American Jews supportive of our small country."

Dershowitz assured Netanyahu he would continue to do so, following which the prime minister smiled and wrapped his arms around Dershowitz in a hug. As Dershowitz walked back to his hotel in the dark, his stomach was tight with regret at the incredible offer he had turned down, but he knew in his mind that, despite his feelings, he had made the right decision.

A couple years later, Dershowitz was in Israel again to accept the prestigious Begin Prize, and Netanyahu took time to meet with him. The two discussed the ever-growing threat of Iran. Ahmadinejad had made friendly overtures to Barack Obama, who had been elected US president in 2008, and Netanyahu was concerned Ahmadinejad was trying to sway Obama from preventing the Iranian nuclear program. Both Dershowitz and Netanyahu believed Ahmadinejad would drop an atomic bomb on Israel if he was able to develop one and discussed tactics for convincing the international community of Iran's threat to world peace.

During Dershowitz's 2012 trip to Israel, both he and Netanyahu spoke at an economic conference. "First off, I would like to congratulate the Globes Conference for its foresight in inviting Alan Dershowitz," said Netanyahu to the large crowd, "and I would like to say to Alan: Israel has no greater champion and the truth has no greater defender than Alan Dershowitz." Netanyahu's words were played on news networks, and that night, Dershowitz got a call from the White House, saying the president would like to speak with him.

Shortly after, Obama called Dershowitz's cell phone. "Hey Alan, I hear you're in Israel," started Obama, who had met Dershowitz as a law student at Harvard in the late 1980s. Obama's mentor at Harvard was Dershowitz's colleague Charles Ogletree, whose office was right next to

Dershowitz's. Ogletree often ran late to meetings with Obama, and so the young man, dressed in a leather jacket and with a cigarette hanging from his mouth, would pop into Dershowitz's office and chat. Obama tried to enroll in Dershowitz's legal ethics class, but the computer selection system prevented him from being registered.

By the time the 2012 election rolled around, Dershowitz was on the fence about Obama's level of resolve to keep Israel safe. When Obama called Dershowitz in Israel, he asked about Dershowitz's meeting with Netanyahu and what the prime minister's most pressing concerns were. "Number one is Iran," replied Dershowitz. "What's number two?" asked Obama. "Iran," shot back Dershowitz. "If you want to know what number three is, it's Iran. So is number four, five, six . . ."

"I get the point," interrupted Obama with a forced chuckle. "Can you come see me in the Oval Office, when you get back, to discuss Iran? I want to tell you what we're doing." Dershowitz immediately answered yes, and a couple weeks later found himself with Obama in the Oval Office. Dershowitz gifted the president a commemorative hat from Boston's Fenway Park, where Dershowitz often attended Red Sox games, and then the two men got down to brass tacks.

"Alan, you've known me for a long time, and you know I don't bluff," Obama told Dershowitz as they sat in chairs beneath a portrait of Washington. "You can count on what I'm telling you. I will never allow Iran to develop a nuclear arsenal, no matter what it takes. My policy is not containment of a nuclear Iran, it's prevention."

Dershowitz replied that his concern was not that Iran would create a nuclear bomb during Obama's presidency, but that they would use centrifuges to create nuclear power for *civilian* purposes and then convert it to military purposes once Obama was gone. Obama told Dershowitz that America and Israel had enough intelligence to prevent this and that sanctions his government had placed on Iran would deter its leadership from doing anything out of line. Dershowitz replied with skepticism and reiterated Netanyahu's nervousness.

"There is no perfect solution," said Obama. "But we won't allow Iran to become North Korea. I will not take the military options off the table as a last resort, but I will try not to have to use it."

"Mr. President," said Dershowitz, "George Washington said a long time ago that 'To be prepared for war is one of the most effectual means of preserving peace.'"

"We are prepared," replied Obama. "But we are also prepared to negotiate, to sanction and to take other actions." Obama then locked eyes with Dershowitz and firmly said, "I want you to know, and I want your friend Bibi to know, I have Israel's back and I will always have Israel's back."

Following his meeting with Obama, Dershowitz traveled to the battleground state of Florida and made several speeches to help convince the state's large Jewish population to vote for Obama over Mitt Romney, who had been a student of Dershowitz's in the 1970s. "Professor, any Jew who voted for Obama is asking for a second holocaust & the destruction of Israel and Jews," read one piece of hate mail Dershowitz received. "You, sir, are a Judas."

* * *

Though he supported Obama, during the president's first term Dershowitz took on a forty-year-old client who was one of the Obama administration's worst enemies.

Julian Assange had founded a website in 2006 called WikiLeaks where whistleblowers and others could upload classified material from governments around the world. As head of the site, Assange vetted the uploaded material and forwarded bombshell reports to the media. Among the pieces Assange made available were reports about the Guantanamo Bay detention camp, internal communications from a prominent government-funded British university, a list of members of a far-right British political party, and military intelligence about the wars in Afghanistan and Iraq.

Although he became a hero to dissidents like Noam Chomsky, Assange became hated by Western governments. A charge of sexual assault was brought against him in Sweden, and based on this charge, an extradition case was brought against Assange in the United Kingdom, where Assange was then living. Simultaneously, in 2011, Obama's attorney general Eric Holder began creating an indictment against Assange in the United States.

It was at this point that Geoffrey Robertson, noted Australian human rights lawyer then working as Assange's chief counsel in the UK, asked Dershowitz to join Assange's legal team due to the looming US indictment.

"I grew up with Alan's books," says Robertson. "I was a law student in Sydney, Australia, and he had an 'Advise and Dissent' column in *Penthouse* magazine. When I became the advocate for Julian Assange, a fellow Australian, I had to prepare Assange for the impending prosecution in the United States. There were some who wanted to frame Assange's case into a 'U.S. versus the rest' issue. They wanted to play up the anti-American side of it. I had no doubt that the case would be better for Julian as a civil-liberties case, based on First Amendment traditions in America. And that was my reason for inviting Alan into the case. I told Julian he was a brilliant, maverick, American lawyer, who had the requisite independence of mind to go up against the Pentagon."

Dershowitz agreed to join Assange's team. "If Assange were convicted, the [US] government would be able to control information online, which would violate the First and the Fourth Amendments," he told a reporter from the Italian newspaper *La Stampa*.

"Secretary of State Hillary Clinton has said the Wikileaks incident 'began with a theft, just as if it had been executed by smuggling papers in a briefcase,' and that 'Wikileaks does not challenge our commitment to Internet freedom.' How do you respond?" asked the Italian reporter.

"My friend Hillary is wrong on this," replied Dershowitz. "It was not a theft. Julian Assange and Wikileaks did not steal anything. They obtained private documents, and they published them. The [US] Constitution guarantees this as a right."

Geoffrey Robertson got Dershowitz on the phone with Assange, who wanted to discuss the legal implications of a US indictment. "We had a number of conferences talking about issues that were cropping up, like the grand jury in the U.S. which was about to unload indictments," says Robertson. "Alan provided input based on the 1917 Espionage Act, which we understood was being deployed against Julian, but also on matters that were rather difficult for British lawyers to understand about grand jury proceedings, since they haven't used the grand jury in Britain since 1860."

After some time, Dershowitz and Assange decided they needed to meet in person in order to have a fuller discussion. In March 2011, Dershowitz flew to London and was driven to Assange's solicitor's office, where he met the white-haired forty-year-old considered by some politicians to have committed crimes as serious as terrorism. "Assange was aloof and distant," says Dershowitz, "but he seemed to be very principled. He believed he was doing the right thing for the world and thought he had taken proper vetting precautions."

Among other things, Dershowitz told Assange that he believed Assange was the equivalent of *The New York Times* in the Pentagon Papers case of the 1970s. Dershowitz told Assange he would be standby in case Assange needed US representation.

"Reasonable people could disagree about the wisdom and morality of Assange's actions, but he did nothing criminal," Dershowitz states. "And my job is to prevent criminal prosecution."

Dershowitz used his influence in the court of public opinion to stick up for Assange, as he had time and time again. "WikiLeaks is different [from the case of someone like Bob Woodward] precisely because Assange is not publishing selectively in order to tell a story favorable to one group or another," Dershowitz wrote in a book about his legal career, *Taking the Stand*, written shortly after he joined Assange's legal team. "Assange allowed the chips to fall where they may, and they often fall on the heads of the current officeholders around the world. . . . Prosecuting WikiLeaks or its founder for 'the crime' of publishing classified information, while at the same time rewarding with prizes, access, interviews, and status— 'reputable' journalists and newspapers for doing essentially the same thing, would constitute selective prosecution."

In a sold-out event in New York hosted by Intelligence Squared U.S., Dershowitz debated with George W. Bush's secretary of homeland security Michael Chertoff, who argued for the motion "Freedom of the press does not extend to state secrets."

"There obviously are occasions when the press should be prosecuted for publication . . . of state secrets," said Chertoff. "The government doesn't overreach on [these prosecutions]. It is possible to have a workable system where people who are responsible journalists know where they can't go . . . and the irresponsible ones—dare I say Assange—may find themselves in different circumstances."

"And who decides who's responsible and irresponsible on the basis of what criteria?" Dershowitz immediately responded. "The issue is whether or not somebody should be punished for publishing state secrets. The answer to that is clearly no. . . . If you want to have a list of things that can't be published, that's a very different criteria. . . . But [you shouldn't] punish people for violating 'state secrets.' That sounds like other countries which have prior censorship."

Obama's administration ultimately never brought an indictment, but Assange remained in legal peril in the UK, despite his lawyers' best efforts.

"Assange was demonized from a lot of angles," reflects Geoffrey Robertson, "but particularly from an alleged association with a Holocaust denier. Alan put out a statement saying there was no substance to this charge against Assange, and given Alan's reputation—even his notoriety—as a pro-Israeli advocate, he shut up the accusers. Unfortunately, in the long term, hostility to Alan from a number of groups on the left was part of the move that turned Assange's cause into an anti-American case, rather than a civil liberties case. So Assange, in due course, went to lawyers who were more associated with the American left than the American civil liberties division."

* * *

Amid all of Dershowitz's advocacy work and increasing fame, he once told a close friend what mattered more to him than anything in the world was "the health and safety of my family. I don't have a lot of personal fear, but I am always afraid people will attack those close to me."

Alan remained as close to Carolyn as ever. Over the decades, they had retained a newlywed kind of love. "I think part of my role is to support him," says Carolyn. "Alan doesn't need a shoulder to cry on because he's not a crier. When he gets mad, he fights. I try to have his back and share my opinion about things."

"Alan goes after life with a vengeance," she continues. "But he also finds time to relax. He likes walking on the beach, and he enjoys sitting in our hot tub on the Vineyard. He and I also like to sit and watch a movie at night and have a glass of wine."

"My dad is incredibly kind and talks to my siblings and I all the time," says Elon. "Sometimes when he's on television facing a disingenuous person, my dad can be very aggressive, but he's very different in private. I could give names of kids of friends of ours on Martha's Vineyard who were pulled over for drunk driving, and my dad would get calls at two in the morning asking for legal advice. He would always try to help out in any way he could."

Dershowitz was the toast of the elite on Martha's Vineyard. His assistant, Sarah Neely, described the Vineyard as his "sanctuary." During the summer, the picturesque community of Chilmark was filled with sunshine, a breeze from the ocean, and relaxed locals. "Martha's Vineyard had a special place in my heart," says Dershowitz.

"Every time I [saw Alan] and we were with a group of people, [he was] telling jokes and making everybody laugh," says Larry David, another Vineyard neighbor. Dershowitz had been introduced to the star of HBO's *Curb Your Enthusiasm* by Peter Simon, a resident of Chilmark and brother of Carly Simon. Dershowitz and David hit it off. Besides kibitzing, David also wrote reviews for Dershowitz's books and spoke at a dinner honoring Dershowitz's human rights work, and in turn, Dershowitz made a phone call to help one of David's children get into college. Back during the 2004 presidential elections, they had even traveled through parts of Florida together making speeches for John Kerry.

"I see Alan often on the Vineyard," says Robert F. Kennedy Jr., environmental lawyer and oldest son of Robert Kennedy, whom Dershowitz had known back in the 1960s. "I have a house on the Cape and drive my boat over to Menemsha Pond in Chilmark to have lunch with him and play volleyball.

"Whenever I had a constitutional issue during one of my cases, I'd always call Alan," continues Kennedy. "He would also play the part of a judge in a mock trial for cases I was arguing. Alan has a brilliant, analytical mind, and he also has essentially total recall. He helped me prepare for my argument before the Court of Appeals in the Ninth Circuit in a suit against Facebook, which was a First Amendment case. He also prepped me for a case against the FEC over an issue with 5G. A lot of the things I asked him to do were laborious. It was not just that he had to sit for two hours and grill me. He had to do homework, read complaints, and spend time thinking about the case. It's an example of his generous spirit towards his friends."

"Alan and I have had a lot of boating misadventures—we've often gone for rides on my sailboat *Voyager* and *Bell*, my motorboat," says Geraldo Rivera, who periodically visits the Vineyard. "Before the days of 'cancel culture,' Alan really shined at the General Store in Chilmark, where he presided over a kind of intellectual soiree. Larry David and prominent people in the entertainment and legal world would gather there on weekend mornings. Alan would bring up a topic, and we would all start opining. We did that many times, and the exchange was invigorating and challenging.

"Alan is a true friend," continues Geraldo. "He helped my daughter Sol learn her haftorah verses when she was preparing for her bat mitzvah. In 2013, there was a big party celebrating Alan's thirty books, fifty years at Harvard, and his seventy-fifth birthday. Alan had invited President Obama, who was renting a house on the Vineyard at the time, but the president told Alan he would not come unless I was disinvited, because I was a Fox News guy. Alan respectfully refused. The president's rental house was next door to Alan's, and during the party, we could literally see him through the shrubbery. I just so admired Alan's loyalty as a friend."

* * *

In 2013, Dershowitz's career at Harvard finally came to an end. After teaching approximately ten thousand students and twenty different courses over fifty years, Dershowitz was retiring from Harvard Law School. His dramatic career was coming to an end for rather undramatic reasons. "Carolyn and I had grown tired of the Cambridge winter weather and wanted to spend our time in Florida," says Dershowitz. "I also wanted to do many things in my life—I wanted to write more books and travel more frequently. I thought fifty years was a good number to end on."

Dershowitz was retiring with the honorary title of Felix Frankfurter Professor of Law, Emeritus. His final salary was $300,000, as compared to the $8,000 he had started with in 1964.

When Dershowitz's retirement news broke, tributes poured in. He received gushing letters from Barack Obama and Bill Clinton, the latter of whom included this handwritten comment at the bottom of the letter: "You're not the retiring type!" Ted Cruz, who had recently been elected a

senator from Texas, read an effusive tribute to Dershowitz on the floor of
the Senate.

Vice President Joe Biden filmed a short video that was sent to a team
of editors at Harvard who were creating a special tribute montage for
Dershowitz. Since campaigning with Biden for Ted Kennedy back in
1980, Dershowitz had bumped into Biden several times, including at
White House Chanukah celebrations which Obama invited Dershowitz
to. Biden, who has Jewish in-laws, once invited Dershowitz to the vice
president's official residence to deliver a talk and the blessing during a celebration of the holiday Sukkoth, which commemorates the Hebrew slaves'
escape from Pharaoh into the wilderness. During one visit together, Biden
took Dershowitz aside and filmed a short tribute video with Dershowitz.
"I know Harvard's been around for a long, long time, but I'm not at all
sure it's going to survive as well after Alan leaves," he said to the camera.
Turning to Dershowitz, Biden commented, "Alan, you're the best. I'm
proud of you. I've known you for a long, long time. You have a great
conscience."

In late 2013, Martha Minow, dean of HLS, organized a large event
at Harvard to honor Dershowitz. Many of his family, friends, and colleagues turned out. Video of the tributes were uploaded to YouTube and
included heartfelt messages from Harvey Silverglate, Bibi Netanyahu,
Guido Calabresi, Yitz Greenberg, Geraldo Rivera, Steven Pinker, Antonin
Scalia, Stephen Breyer, and Elena Kagan, among others.

Jeffrey Toobin, who had interviewed Dershowitz for some of his
bestselling legal books and periodically had dinner with him, said how
"delighted" he was to be participating and described Dershowitz as having
"all-around terrific-ness." Larry David humorously praised Dershowitz's
brilliance and devotion to his family.

A particularly warm tribute came from Massachusetts lawyer Kenneth
Sweder, whom Dershowitz had first met in the early 1980s and who had
since become a close friend of Dershowitz's family. "I was approached some
years ago to see if I could get Alan to make a call to a family Thanksgiving
dinner, in which the patriarch of the family—a very successful athletic
guy—had become a quadriplegic as a result of a bicycle accident," Sweder
said. "Alan did it. He did it for an hour. It was reported to me that he was

brilliant—completely engaged, as was the entire family. It was the high-light of that year for that family. . . . Alan is, as a friend and a family man, a real *mensch*."

As Dershowitz basked in the praise of his friends and the love of his family who were with him on that day, he could never have predicted how much his life was about to change.

PART THREE

INTO THE WILDERNESS

TO THE "DARK SIDE"

"Hello gorgeous, I hope this message comes to you on a bright, sunny day!!!" It was May 2011, and a mysterious woman named Virginia Roberts Giuffre was writing an email to British tabloid journalist Sharon Churcher, asking for help with the manuscript of her new—and highly confidential—project *The Billionaire's Playboy Club*. "Just wondering if you have any information on you from when you and I were doing interviews about the J.E. story," Giuffre wrote. "I wanted to put the names of some of these assholes, oops, I meant to say, pedo's that J.E. sent me to."

As part of her reply, Churcher added this note: "Don't forget Alan Dershowitz," she wrote. "J.E's buddy and lawyer . . . good name for your pitch as he repped Claus von Bülow and a movie was made about that case . . . title was *Reversal of Fortune*. We all suspect Alan is a pedo and tho no proof of that, you probably met him when he was hanging out w JE."

"Thanks again," acknowledged Giuffre. "I'm bringing down the house with this book!!!"

* * *

Three years after this email exchange, Dershowitz found himself retired from Harvard and busier than ever writing books and articles, traveling to Israel, litigating cases, and enjoying life with his family and friends. In late 2014, while in Miami, he had a cardiovascular health scare and visited two doctors to get their opinions about whether he should go in for heart surgery. Both gave different answers. After thinking it over, in December, Dershowitz decided to forgo surgery.

By New Year's Eve, he was feeling good about his choice and looking forward to 2015 when on that day, out of the blue, a reporter from

Politico called and told Dershowitz a major story had just hit. "You've been accused of having sex with an underage girl," said the reporter. "What do you have to say?" Flabbergasted, Dershowitz asked, "Who, when, where?" The reporter said it was thirty-two-year-old Virginia Roberts Giuffre, who was claiming Jeffrey Epstein trafficked her to high-profile friends of his, including to Dershowitz when she was sixteen.

Dershowitz firmly told the reporter the charges were totally false. After hanging up and sharing the news with Carolyn, the two of them almost laughed together with shock. The name "Giuffre" was totally unfamiliar to Dershowitz, who had reviewed allegations from several young women during the 2006 case against Epstein. After seeing a picture of teenage Giuffre which was publicly released, he and Carolyn were completely certain they had never seen her during their visits to Epstein's properties. Besides, the thought of Dershowitz engaging in such an illegal and disgusting act was absurd.

They were tempted to not take the accusation seriously. But the day after the phone call from the reporter, they—and the rest of the world—learned from the media that Giuffre's legal team had included Dershowitz's name in a court document as part of a bombshell lawsuit brought by several women. These women claimed to have been trafficked by Epstein and his associates and were seeking to reverse the 2008 plea deal and bring Epstein to justice.

Dershowitz was bombarded with emails and calls from family, friends, and the press. Dershowitz vehemently denied the accusation at every turn. He communicated with Prince Andrew's lawyers and discussed Giuffre's lack of credibility.

Thankfully for Dershowitz, no one in his family or close circle of friends—or even more casual acquaintances on Martha's Vineyard—believed the charge. In addition to teaching for half a century at Harvard without any complaints of sexual impropriety from students or faculty, it was simply not his personality, according to many of his relatives and friends.

"Avi and I talked about the accusation," said his childhood friend Norman Sohn. "Avi said, 'You knew me when I was a kid—I wasn't able to seduce underage girls even as an underage male!'"

"I was mad," says Dershowitz's assistant Sarah Neely, who started working for Dershowitz in her mid-thirties. "I've seen how he is around young students, and how he is around his wife and children. He's not that kind of guy. I once went to give him a hug, and he stopped me, saying, 'Oh, no, no, no—I have clients who get in trouble for things like that.'"

"Alan's not the kind of guy who elbows you and says, 'Look at that girl. Look how pretty she is.' He's not into checking out women," says defense attorney Arthur Aidala, a rising star in the legal world who became a close friend of Dershowitz's in the late 2000s and volunteered to help in any way when the Giuffre accusation was announced. "Look, anything can happen once. But when these accusations came up, and Giuffre claimed things happened multiple times in multiple locations, I realized it was obviously BS."

When the accusation was proclaimed to the world on January 1, 2015, Dershowitz's old friend Mario Cuomo was on his deathbed and heard the news. Cuomo's daughter Maria told Dershowitz that her father had furiously declared, "Alan would never do anything like that!"—mere hours before passing away.

"One of the things that made the fallout from the accusation bearable was that I didn't have to worry about whether the accusation was true," says Carolyn. "The least powerful reason is that I know he loves me. But I also think Alan would never trust someone, especially Jeffrey, with that kind of secret hanging over his head. Also, morally, he doesn't believe in having affairs or paying someone for sex."

According to Giuffre, this was untrue. "Professor Dershowitz was around a lot and there were always young girls around a lot," she claimed in a deposition. "Dershowitz was so comfortable with the sex that was going on that on one occasion he observed me in sexual activity with Epstein." She claimed she and Dershowitz had engaged in sexual intercourse several times at Epstein's properties in Florida and New Mexico, on his Caribbean island, and on his private jet.

With the help of Carolyn and Sarah Neely, Dershowitz quickly gathered all his travel, phone, and credit card records from the previous two decades and waited for Giuffre to give dates so that he could easily disprove her.

Up to this point, Giuffre's life had been a sad story. Born in 1983, she spent part of her childhood in California and ran away from home at age thirteen. She was put into a foster care facility, but eventually left there, too, and lived on the streets for a time. According to her employment records, it was in 2000, when she was around seventeen years old, that she was discovered by Jeffrey Epstein while working as a spa attendant at Donald Trump's estate, Mar-a-Lago. Epstein invited her to his home to give him sexual massages in exchange for hundreds of dollars. Over the next two years, Giuffre became close to Epstein, performing sexual favors for him and traveling with him around the United States, the Caribbean, and other places. In 2002, Epstein sent Giuffre to Thailand for a massage course, and while there, Giuffre fell in love with a young man and told Epstein she was not coming back. She married the young man, and together they moved to Australia, disappearing from public view for a time. Eventually, Giuffre resurfaced and burst onto the international scene in 2015 with her trafficking accusations against Epstein and his powerful friends.

When Dershowitz was accused by Giuffre, his hands were tied as to how he could respond. If he publicly called the charges false, her lawyers could sue for defamation, while Dershowitz, on the other hand, could not sue them for defamation since Giuffre's accusation had been made in a court filing, which made them exempt from a defamation suit under the litigation privilege. Dershowitz decided to go after Giuffre in the media anyway.

"Do you know her? Have you seen her? Have you ever met her?" asked Savannah Guthrie on *The Today Show*. "I've never seen her. I've never met her," fired back Dershowitz. "And I can prove categorically by documentary and other evidence that I couldn't have been in the places she said I was at the time. For example, she said she had sex with me in Jeffrey Epstein's ranch in New Mexico. I was there for one hour with my wife, my daughter—who are here with me today in the studio—never out of their sight. Two other people were with me. *Nobody was on the ranch at the time.* Only time I've ever been there. Said I had sex with her on the private island. I was there once with my wife, my daughter, [a] prominent professor at Harvard Business School, his whole family—she is categorically lying and making the whole thing up."

"A court motion filed last month by attorneys Paul Cassell and Bradley Edwards says quote 'in addition to being a participant in the abuse of Jane Doe #3 and other minors, Dershowitz was an eyewitness to sexual abuse of many other minors by Epstein and several of Epstein's co-conspirators,'" reported Lawrence O'Donnell on MSNBC in January 2015. "Alan Dershowitz has denied the allegations and has called on attorneys for Jane Doe #3 to be disbarred. But on Tuesday, Bradley Edwards and Paul Cassell, those attorneys, filed a defamation lawsuit against Alan Dershowitz."

Friends of Dershowitz rallied around him to help raise the funds necessary to fight Cassell and Edwards' defamation suit in court, including his childhood mentor Yitz Greenberg. Many former colleagues and students volunteered to help in any way they could, and even casual acquaintances like Senator Orrin Hatch and former U.S. attorney general Michael Mukasey called to tell Dershowitz how outraged they were and to offer their support.

Dershowitz's friend Kenneth Sweder led the litigation efforts against Cassell and Edwards, drafting and editing court pleadings and overseeing mediation in the coming months.

Meanwhile, Dershowitz said he would waive any privileges against self-incrimination, and he also filed an affidavit to the court, thus exposing himself to a perjury prosecution if he was lying. He also contacted his acquaintance Louis Freeh, the former FBI director, who agreed to conduct an independent investigation of all documents, records, and testimony related to Giuffre's accusation and whether it was possible for Dershowitz to be guilty of what she claimed. Dershowitz gave Freeh all his travel, credit card, and phone records, along with any other document Freeh requested—nothing was off-limits.

At the same time, Dershowitz also approached his old friend David Boies, who was working as one of Giuffre's lawyers, in an attempt to persuade Boies that the allegations against him were false. Dershowitz and Boies had both worked for Al Gore's legal team in 2000 and had occasionally appeared in the media and at speaking events together.

"To an ordinary member of the public, Boies has a stellar reputation," says Dershowitz's close friend, Harvey Silverglate. "But Boies has a brass-knuckled way of dealing with his critics. He also ran a very unconventional law firm, Boies, Schiller & Flexner. A student I knew got a job there despite my suggesting that he avoid the place. A few months later, he quit and told me that he was horrified and disgusted by the firm's misogyny, as well as by Boies's almost pathological animosity toward Dershowitz. I've always thought that this hatred stemmed from Boies's jealousy. Alan is smarter, more accomplished, and more famous than Boies."

Dershowitz was aware of Boies's somewhat sordid reputation, but he nevertheless contacted Boies, who suggested they meet to discuss the Giuffre situation. When they met in early 2015 in Boies's apartment in New York, Boies told Dershowitz he was not aware Giuffre was going to be accusing Dershowitz when he became one of her lawyers and that he never would have agreed to help her if he had known this. Over the coming months, Dershowitz met with Boies in New York and had several phone calls in which they reviewed all the relevant evidence, which pointed to Dershowitz's innocence. Boies told Dershowitz multiple times he would try to convince Giuffre she was mistaken about Dershowitz, but as time went by, he never did. Finally, Dershowitz decided to record a conversation without Boies's knowledge, which was legal in New York.

"I felt uncomfortable doing it, but I believed I had no choice," says Dershowitz. "I'd given him every opportunity to follow through on his promise—that he would get Giuffre to withdraw her charges."

"You're as persuaded as we are that it was not possible for me to be on the island[,] to have sex with her in New Mexico[,] on the airplane[,] and Palm Beach," said Dershowitz in one of their recorded conversations. "But New York, as you say, is a little bit up in the air. What is the next step at this point?"

"I think the next step would be for me and Sigrid [McCawley], both of us together, to sit down with our client and say explicitly: 1) 'We know you believe that you had relations with Professor Dershowitz,'" replied Boies. "'However, we have now reviewed the documentary evidence and we are convinced that your belief is wrong and we would like to explore with you how you could have come to this conclusion. . . .'"

Armed with this astonishing admission, in October 2015, Dershowitz gave a deposition in which he relayed Boies's self-incriminating statements. "The only explanation I have is that he is so emotional about this that he starts saying things without being careful," Boies told the press. "He has been someone whose approach in litigation is to attack the other side."

"There were so many lies," says Dershowitz's assistant Sarah Neely. "And Alan is a truth seeker to his core. He doesn't get stressed out easily, but the whole ordeal took a toll on him. I think he became obsessed with declaring his innocence from the rooftops—writing op-eds, doing media appearances, and fighting in court.

"What made it so difficult for him was the timing of the accusation. He had just closed an amazing career at Harvard. For decades, he had been fighting for people's rights and protecting the rule of law in the United States. He had done so much good, and this accusation was going to overshadow everything he had ever accomplished.

"I was pretty heavily involved with the response to the accusation," continues Neely. "I gave Alan my perspective as a female. I'd also treat him like a father. I'd tell him things like: 'Get some sleep, Alan,' or 'Alan, take a break from this.' I was a trainer, and when I was down Miami with him and Carolyn, I would talk to him while we walked along the beach, just to make sure he got his exercise in and could detach a little from this.

"One of the things we reviewed together were his calendars. Every year I worked for him, I would purchase these tiny, Harvard Law School calendar books. His notes inside looked like chicken scratch. He would keep track of where he had been and for how many hours—all his time with clients, his teaching hours, etc. When the Giuffre accusation broke, he didn't have to contemporaneously create these notes. He had been keeping track of his schedule since he started working at Harvard in the 1960s. He always had that little book in his pocket. I think it's a weird, OCD-kind-of thing. Alan also never used a calculator. He had a watch that had a little calculator inside it. He loved that watch. It went with him everywhere. Alan is just a very quirky and careful person."

Incredibly, Giuffre refused to provide any specific dates to go along with her accusation. "She remained quite unclear about that," says Kenneth Sweder.

Luckily for Dershowitz, near the end of 2015, three people close to Giuffre and Epstein decided to offer eyewitness testimony to help his case. Jeffrey Epstein's Palm Beach house manager Juan Alessi and Giuffre's former boyfriend Anthony Figueroa provided affidavits which thoroughly debunked Giuffre's claims about having known Dershowitz and having seen him participate in illicit activities at Epstein's Palm Beach residence. As well, Giuffre's close friend Rebecca Boylan made the agonizing decision to record a conversation with Dershowitz in which she admitted, through tears, that her friend's accusations were simply made-up. "I think these people saw that Alan was being unfairly charged and simply wanted to tell the truth," comments Sweder.

In April 2016, Louis Freeh concluded his months-long investigation. He and a team of law enforcement officials had interviewed several witnesses and thousands of relevant documents. "Our investigation found no evidence to support the accusations of sexual misconduct against Professor Dershowitz," they publicly declared.

That same month, Giuffre's attorneys Paul Cassell and Bradley Edwards dropped their defamation suits against Dershowitz. During the proceedings, Dershowitz had tried to get all of Giuffre's emails that mentioned him released, but her lawyers refused to provide them. Sitting next to her lawyer, Giuffre herself told the court under oath there were no emails in which she mentioned Dershowitz.

In a victory for Dershowitz, the judge ordered Giuffre's accusation against Dershowitz to be struck from the record in the case which had been made public in January 2015. Although the accusation had been spread around the world by the media, Dershowitz seemed to have survived the storm.

* * *

While Dershowitz was fighting to clear his name against Giuffre's heinous charge, frightening developments were taking place for Israel on the international stage. Obama was advocating a deal with Iran wherein economic sanctions by the United States would be lessened in exchange for certain concessions. "We're now in a position where Iran has agreed to unprecedented inspections and verifications of its program, providing assurances that it is peaceful in nature," Obama told NPR in April 2015. "You have them rolling back a number of pathways that they currently have available to break out and get a nuclear weapon. You have assurances that their stockpile of highly enriched uranium remains in a place where they cannot create a nuclear weapon."

Dershowitz was furious. "Most people today are not aware that British Prime Minister Neville Chamberlain helped restore Great Britain's financial stability during the Great Depression and also passed legislation to extend unemployment benefits, pay pensions to retired workers, and otherwise help those hit hard by the slumping economy," he wrote in one of his widely read articles. "But history does remember his failure to confront Hitler. That is Chamberlain's enduring legacy. So too will Iran's construction of nuclear weapons, if it manages to do so in the next few years, become President Barack Obama's enduring legacy."

In the coming months, Dershowitz called several members of Congress to lobby against the deal, including his former student Mike Pompeo. "After law school, I didn't run into Professor Dershowitz frequently, but we talked on occasion—I also regularly saw him on TV and read his articles," says Pompeo. "The Alan Dershowitz I came to know as a member of Congress was the same one I knew in law school: he was incredibly pragmatic in the way he thought about bringing America forward. During the Iran Deal debate, I was a fairly junior member of Congress, but I was one of the most vocal voices pushing back against the Obama administration from the summer of 2015 on. And I spoke to Professor Dershowitz on the phone about how we could protect American interests—and Israeli interests when they were in line with American interests—as this deal moved forward."

In the end, Obama failed to drum up the necessary support in Congress to get the deal ratified as a treaty, but he nevertheless implemented it through an executive order. In September, Dershowitz spoke to hundreds of Iranian Americans at a rally in New York City's Dag Hammarskjöld Plaza, where he had spoken on behalf of Natan Sharansky forty years earlier. "Many times in this Plaza, I've spoken on behalf of the oppressed of the former Soviet Union, I've spoken on behalf of human rights in China—I have spoken on behalf of human rights all over the world!" began Dershowitz. "And today it is my great honor to speak out on behalf of human rights for the wonderful people of Iran, who are now oppressed by the terrible leaders of Iran," prompting whistling and clapping from his listeners.

"What does this deal do? It provides tens of billions—perhaps hundreds of billions—of dollars of material support for *terrorism*," Dershowitz said loudly, mic in hand and standing on a podium decorated with Iranian flags. "Of every dollar that the Iranians will get, much of it will go to repressing dissent within Iran. The rest of it will go to encouraging terrorism around the Middle East and ultimately around the world . . .

"I wish we could have here today the wonderful Iranian people who have a different sexual orientation, who are hanged because of their sexual orientation. I wish we could have here today, as witnesses, the Bahá'ís who were murdered, the other Muslims who were murdered, the Christians who were murdered, the Jews who were murdered. They would be great witnesses. But the one thing that the Ahmadinejad-Rohani-Khamenei-Khomeini regime specializes in is killing witnesses. They are obstructing justice because if you are a witness to injustice you will be imprisoned and you will be executed and you will be silenced. Because the last thing this regime wants is truth. Truth is the enemy of repression."

"I'm not partisan here," he continued. "I am a Democrat. I am a liberal. But I am a pragmatist. I understand evil! And I understand there is evil in this world. And I understand that the current Iranian regime *is evil.*"—whereupon his listeners cheered and waved Iranian flags. "And you don't make deals with evil people that give them the financial ability and the material ability to increase the evil they're doing. That becomes complicity with evil!"

After his advocacy against the deal, Dershowitz no longer received an invitation to Obama's yearly White House Chanukah party.

Despite his estrangement from Obama, Dershowitz supported the liberal front-runner Hillary Clinton in the 2016 presidential election. In addition to being friendly with the Clintons, Dershowitz supported nearly all of her domestic and foreign policy initiatives and believed she would be wise when it came to Iran. Dershowitz could not say the same thing when it came to Hillary's unexpected challenger, the iconoclastic Donald Trump.

"On the issue of tone, there is little doubt that Trump has been extraordinarily negative, mocking the disabled, referring to a woman's menstrual cycle and a man's penis size, using racist, sexist, and scatological

0

language—and in general being crass and bombastic," Dershowitz wrote in a 2016 book titled *Electile Dysfunction*. "For those of us who seek a president from whom our children and grandchildren can learn good manners and basic decency, and who is more presidential in tone, the choice of Clinton should seem obvious." At the end of the book, Dershowitz presented a list of ten essential questions for all voters to ask themselves, such as: "Who will best protect our civil and constitutional rights?" "Whose policies will best benefit the middle class and the economically disadvantaged?" and "Whose policies will better help reduce gun violence?" In all ten categories, he argued in favor of Hillary.

Dershowitz made the media rounds drumming up support for Hillary. Some on the right were threatening to impeach her on the day she entered the Oval Office, and Dershowitz began outlining a book titled *The Case Against Impeaching Clinton* in the event this threat was carried out. Based on new research he had done using *The Federalist Papers* and the debates at the Constitutional Convention, Dershowitz determined that the Constitution's Framers had intended impeachment to be based on criminal-type behavior, not behavior that one political party deemed "corrupt" because of suspicious circumstances (like, in his view, the alleged destruction of a private email server).

Dershowitz donated nearly $6,000 to Hillary's campaign and also supported his former student Jamie Raskin, who was the Democratic candidate for Maryland's Eighth Congressional District that year. "He reached out to me during that race and sent me a campaign contribution, which was nice," says Raskin.

Although Raskin would go on to win his election, the outcome of the presidential election stunned the world. Dershowitz had grown increasingly leery of Hillary's election prospects after a trip to Europe with his wife and daughter, where they observed the increasing popularity of right-wing politicians in several countries, including Austria, Hungary, and Poland. In August 2016, just a couple months before Election Day, Dershowitz bumped into Hillary at an event on Martha's Vineyard. After her speech, she and Bill came up to Dershowitz to say hello, and he bluntly issued a warning. "My wife and daughter and I just came back from all over Europe," he said. "There is a wave of nationalism in Europe. People are looking for different kinds of leaders—leaders who are more populist. I think Trump has caught this wave, and you haven't." He then offered to organize campaign events among the heavily Jewish communities in southern Florida, and he told Hillary that his friend, who was a high-ranking Democratic official in Florida, was also willing to help with any such effort.

Hillary brushed aside Dershowitz's concerns and declined the campaign offer. "She was so arrogant," comments Dershowitz, "and so convinced of her victory."

On Election Day, Dershowitz cast his vote for Hillary and wrote an article in which he looked ahead to the problems the United States might face, no matter who became the next president. "Following the election President Obama may try to tie the hands of his successor," he predicted. "During the lame-duck period, when presidents can act without political accountability, he may foolishly send the Israel-Palestine conflict to the United Nations."

When Trump was elected, that is exactly what Obama did. "In a stunning diplomatic rebuke of Israel, the United States on Friday abstained on a controversial United Nations Security Council resolution demanding an end to Israeli settlements on Palestinian territory, allowing it to pass easily," reported *Vox* in December. "The measure demands that Israel 'immediately and completely cease all settlement activities in the occupied Palestinian territory, including East Jerusalem,' and declares that the establishment of settlements by Israel has 'no legal validity and constitutes a flagrant violation under international law.'"

The resolution included this controversial line: "*Underlines* that it will not recognize any changes to the 4 June 1967 lines, including with regard to Jerusalem, other than those agreed by the parties through negotiations." In Dershowitz's view, this implied all of Jerusalem, including the sacred Western Wall, was now declared to be illegally occupied by Israel.

Dershowitz came to regret he had ever supported Obama. "It was clear he wanted me to endorse him for reelection in 2012, and he put on a full-court press," says Dershowitz. "Obama was like a robot—cold and calculating. You did not get the sense that he was someone who looked deeply into his own soul to determine the right course of action. With Democrats like Joe Biden, Israel has a place in their heart. With Obama, it clearly had no place in his heart. It was purely a political calculation."

* * *

Dershowitz had bumped into Donald Trump at various social functions over the years, including a party at the Rothschilds' on Martha's Vineyard and most recently at a Patriots playoff game in the box of owner Robert Kraft, a mutual friend of both Alan and Trump.

Trump had vowed to shake up the liberal establishment if he was elected, and following the stunning turn of events in November 2016, a bitter war ensued between Trump and virtually the entire Democratic voting base, along with some on the right. Trump's bombastic personality combined with his highly controversial policies on matters like immigration and the climate turned him into "the closest thing we have to the Devil Incarnate," as described in 2017 by Dershowitz's former Harvard colleague Larry Tribe. In the eyes of Trump's critics, he was a megalomaniac who would do anything to increase his power, including flagrantly violate the Constitution.

From the beginning of Trump's presidency, Dershowitz saw the battle lines being drawn. "From his early days in office—whether justified or not—Trump was politically and constitutionally targeted," says Dershowitz. "I saw what was happening to him as part of what was going on throughout America—the weaponization of the criminal justice system against political enemies. And Trump was the most visible target of that weaponization." He deliberately set about defending the president's civil liberties.

Trump was beset early on by allegations he had colluded with the Russians to boost his chances in the 2016 election. A special counsel was eventually appointed to investigate the matter under the supervision of former FBI director Robert Mueller. The investigation took on a life of its own, and Trump found himself surrounded by a host of enemies in academia, the media, the government, and even his own political party. His critics readily pounced on any action he took which they perceived to be unconstitutional.

"I come not to praise President Trump nor to defend his policies, but to defend the Constitution," Dershowitz told Chris Cuomo on CNN in

June 2017, following Trump's firing of FBI director James Comey, who had recently told the Senate that Russian interference in future elections was a significant threat. "The president has the right to fire the director of the FBI and the president has the power to tell the director of the F.B.I. who to investigate, who not to investigate."

"The president himself said, both on television and in a meeting with the Russians, that he was motivated at least in part to end the Russian probe," Dershowitz relayed in another interview on NBC with Chuck Todd. "I'm sure he was also motivated in part by what Comey refused to tell him. . . . We don't want to turn motives and analysis of the president's mind into criminal statutes. We have to look at what the president did, not what his motives are because motives are always complex[.]"

As he had done during Kenneth Starr's investigation of Bill Clinton, Dershowitz railed against the appointment of a special counsel. "The appointment of a special counsel to investigate Russian meddling in the 2016 presidential election was misguided and, instead, Congress should have created a nonpartisan commission of objective experts to conduct the investigation," he wrote in an article.

No such commission was appointed. In early 2018, things heated up when the FBI conducted a raid on the home and office of Trump's personal attorney Michael Cohen after receiving a tip from Mueller's team. The agents nabbed recordings of Cohen's phone calls with his clients, including Trump, along with some of Cohen's business records. An investigation was opened into whether Cohen had violated finance laws in 2016 by authorizing the payment of hush money to porn star Stormy Daniels, with whom Trump purportedly had an affair in the mid-2000s.

Following the raid, George Stephanopoulos invited Dershowitz onto his ABC show *This Week*. "The president is clearly agitated by all of this pressure on Michael Cohen," said Stephanopoulos. "He also called the raid on Cohen an attack on our country. After those raids, how serious is the threat to Cohen and Trump?"

"Oh, it's a very serious threat," replied Dershowitz. "This is an epic battle for the soul and cooperation of Michael Cohen. And prosecutors have enormous weapons at their disposal. They can threaten [him] essentially with life imprisonment. They can threaten his parents. They can threaten his spouse. They have these enormous abilities to really put pressure and coerce a witness. . . . Michael Milken, they told him they were going to indict his brother unless he pleaded guilty. Jonathan Pollard, they told him they were going to indict his wife. I can go down case after case after case."

Dershowitz's appearances on shows like *Sean Hannity* and *Tucker Carlson* were noticed by the president, a regular viewer of Fox News. "A must watch: Legal Scholar Alan Dershowitz was just on @foxandfriends talking of what is going on with respect to the greatest Witch Hunt in U.S. political history. Enjoy!" tweeted Trump in late 2017.

"I met Alan watching television actually," says Trump. "Alan's very much been a legal media star. I often saw him and was always impressed with him. He seemed to have a lot of the same ideas as me. I mean, the only thing I didn't like about Alan is that he always prided himself on saying, 'I didn't vote for Trump, but Trump is innocent.' In a way, that's a mixed bag. Because in one way, he says that Trump is innocent—that's the good news. But then he says, 'I didn't vote for Trump' because he's a Democrat or something. I don't like that. But the bottom line is, he'll almost always say I'm innocent, because I am. This is just what they do. They throw out disinformation and persecute their enemies. These are bad people. These are very sick people we were dealing with."

"I've got to admit," says O. J. Simpson, "I was surprised when Dershowitz got involved with Trump. I think that surprised a lot of people. I felt in general that he leaned to the Democratic side and was somewhat liberal. I'm not saying I liked it or didn't like it, but it surprised me."

Dershowitz walked a fine line between standing up for Trump's civil liberties rights and becoming perceived as one of the president's cronies. He was still at heart a Democrat.

When recently fired FBI director James Comey was appearing before a Senate Intelligence Committee hearing, a high-level figure in the Republican National Committee emailed Dershowitz the following note: "We are starting to prepare for the response to the Comey hearing on Thursday and wanted to see if you are interested in doing any media. We are happy to facilitate interviews and will provide talking points."

"I'm a liberal Democrat and have no interest in mouthing Republican 'talking points,'" emailed back Dershowitz. "The way the RNC went after

Hillary Clinton makes it clear you have no interest in civil liberties except as a tactic to defend your party and attack your opponents. Perhaps if you were to defend the civil liberties of people you disagree with—as I do—you could provide me some relevant talking points."

In mid-2018, Dershowitz attacked Trump's immigration policies. Trump had instituted a "zero-tolerance" policy at the border, whereby any adult who was caught crossing the border illegally would be prosecuted. Inevitably, parents were separated from children in the process. "President Trump, you know I've been defending your civil liberties and will continue to do so on this show, but you have to end this policy of separating parents from children," Dershowitz said on *Fox & Friends*, using the platform to speak to Trump, who was likely watching. "Not because of the parents, but because of the children. It imposes a trauma on the children. . . . There are better ways of doing this. You're better than this, the American people are better than this. The American government is better than this."

"I don't dislike Trump personally," says Dershowitz, "but I dislike his political style. I don't like his personal attacks on people, nor the fact that he can put himself in front of the needs of the country. I also don't like many of his policies—the fact that he wants to get out of NATO, his efforts to keep the border too closed, his stance on gun control and transgender rights, etc."

* * *

From watching Dershowitz's many news appearances, Trump was aware that Dershowitz was a friend of Bibi Netanyahu and a passionate Zionist. "He was very much into peace in the Middle East," says Trump. "Unlike many Jewish people that live in the United States who really don't care for Israel, Alan did."

In late 2017, Dershowitz was having dinner in a large banquet hall at Mar-a-Lago with Newsmax journalist Chris Ruddy when Trump and his entourage walked in. Trump started to head for his table, but when he saw Dershowitz, he immediately made a beeline for him. "You I have to talk to!" he bellowed. While hundreds of people in the hall looked on, Trump spoke with Dershowitz for nearly ten minutes about Dershowitz's friendship with Netanyahu and asked him to convey a message.

"Basically, I let Bibi know that Trump had been told it was Bibi who was a barrier to peace and the two-state solution," explains Dershowitz. "It was important for Bibi to disabuse Trump of that notion, which Bibi did."

Soon after their Mar-a-Lago meeting, Trump invited Dershowitz to spend a couple days at the White House in the spring of 2018 to provide counsel to his Middle East team, which included Trump's son-in-law Jared Kushner.

"The first time I met Alan was probably at the opening of the Chabad at Harvard when I was a student there," says Kushner. "He was one of the best known faculty members. I found him to be warm and engaging. I read *The Case for Israel* when I was young, and among many other books, it helped shape my perspective on Israel."

"When I came to work in the White House, I knew he'd written several books about the Middle East. He had a lot of technical knowledge and passion for the subject, and he was very close to Bibi. At the time, we were working on the 'Peace to Prosperity' plan. Back then, it was very controversial and had a lot of risk. Our plan was a big mystery to a lot of people, and it didn't leak out. We wanted a couple outside perspectives to examine and were trying to think of who we could trust. Alan understood PR, as well as Israeli politics. He had a lot of qualifications as an expert on the subject matter and was a wordsmith. He's also not shy about giving his opinion. We felt that if there were things he didn't like, he wouldn't be intimidated. I trusted Alan would keep discretion, and so, we asked him to get involved and provide his perspective. He told me he thought the plan was really, really impressive."

"It gave both sides what they needed," says Dershowitz. "It gave Israel some degree of peace and recognition, and it gave the Palestinians a road to economic and political independence."

"When you're working through a plan like that, you have an argument you need to adjudicate," continues Kushner. "You need to understand human psychology and see something from the other side's perspective to create a win-win situation. We thought Alan would help us make sure we weren't inadvertently stepping on any landmines by trying to push things forward, which he did."

"Alan was very much opposed to the Iran nuclear deal," adds Trump, who pulled the United States out of the deal in the spring of 2018. "That probably was the most important thing we got done for Israel," notes Trump.

Dershowitz also advised the president to make a failure to denounce anti-Semitism one of the reasons a public university could be sanctioned, which Trump eventually implemented by executive order. "Alan's counsel on the Middle East was important," says Trump. "He is a brilliant guy who understood life. He is a man of common sense. A lot of times brilliance doesn't go with common sense, but it does with Alan."

At the end of Dershowitz's first day at the White House with Trump's Middle East team, Trump asked to see Dershowitz privately. Trump led Dershowitz into Abraham Lincoln's former bedroom, where the sixteenth president had drafted the Emancipation Proclamation. Trump showed Dershowitz an original copy of the Gettysburg Address framed on the wall.

"This was a holy room to me!" says Dershowitz. As he looked at a picture of Lincoln on the wall, he thought back to his junior year of high school when he researched in a library in Brooklyn for an oration on Lincoln. Trump sat down on Lincoln's bed, which had a large redwood bed frame, and he motioned to Dershowitz to sit down next to him. They chatted briefly about their mutual acquaintance Jeffrey Epstein and the accusation brought against Dershowitz by Virginia Giuffre.

"I would say knowing Alan, it was a false accusation," comments Trump. "But what are you going to do when somebody makes a false accusation? All you can do is fight it, right?"

During subsequent discussions on the Middle East, Dershowitz called Trump's attention to the Golan Heights, which had been captured by Israel from Syria during the Six-Day War and had been a disputed zone between the two countries since. Having been to the area nearly ten times, Dershowitz described how it would put Israel at a significant military disadvantage if Syria were ever to gain control of that high ground. Referring to the international calls for Israel to give up the Heights, Dershowitz asked the president rhetorically if a nation had ever returned a battleship it had captured during a war.

"Alan understood the Golan Heights very well," remarks Trump. Several months later, the president declared the United States' formal recognition of Israel's sovereignty over the Heights.

Dershowitz also encouraged Trump to undo the damage done by Barack Obama near the end of his presidency and recognize the entire city of Jerusalem as the capital of Israel, in place of Tel Aviv. In Dershowitz's mind, this move would not merely be retaliation against the Obama-backed UN resolution, but more importantly, it would be a political, cultural, and symbolic gesture to affirm Jerusalem as the capital of the Jewish nation. "Jerusalem *is* the capital of Israel," notes Dershowitz. "I thought the U.S. should lead the way in recognizing that." Trump had decided back in December 2017 to move the embassy, and he remained steadfast in that decision.

"Alan was very strong on Jerusalem being the capital of Israel," comments Trump, "and he was very strong on having the embassy in Jerusalem, which essentially made it the capital. This was a very easy thing to do, and I did it."

The Palestinian leadership was upset at the move, but their frustration was not as vehement as Dershowitz had expected. "We discussed this issue extensively before the move," Dershowitz says. "The main question to us was whether it would anger Saudi Arabia or other prominent Arab countries, which it didn't thankfully."

One month after his meetings in the White House, in May 2018, Dershowitz flew to Israel for the ceremonial opening of the new embassy in Jerusalem. Traveling with him was his grandson, Lyle, who was soon to enter Columbia Medical School. Dershowitz wanted his grandson to see the land that had meant so much to their ancestors. During their weeklong trip, he and Lyle traveled to the top of Masada, visited the Western Wall, and toured Yad Vashem, where Dershowitz told Lyle the story of Louis Dershowitz saving members of their family from Germany.

Before the embassy opening in Jerusalem, they had a conversation about the significance of the capital move. "I explained to Lyle that every other country is able to determine their own capital city, so why shouldn't Israel?" says Dershowitz. "Especially in the case of Jerusalem, which goes back in history as a city of the Jewish people. 'Jerusalem' is a Hebrew word which comes from the Scriptures, and Jews prayed to return to the city for 2,000 years."

Looking back on their work in the Middle East together, Trump comments: "Alan's an exceptional guy. He's only got one problem. It seems like he doesn't vote for Republicans. He should certainly vote for me. I think he's being dishonest with himself. He's very big into Israel and what I've done for Israel—almost no one else has ever even come close to doing. Among presidents, it's not even close. And what I've done for peace—I've kept this country out of war. I'm the only one in seventy years, I guess they say. I've kept the country out of wars by holding to the concept 'peace through strength.' But Alan likes saying that he never voted for me because he's a Democrat or something."

Trump raised this issue with Dershowitz in person at Trump's New Jersey property of Bedminster, where he had invited Dershowitz to a dinner with the Emir of Qatar. "Why don't your people vote for me?" asked Trump, referring to the Jewish community. Dershowitz acknowledged that Trump had done a lot for Jews, but added, "Mr. President, Jewish people in general are very diverse. They want a lot of good for a lot of people. They care about abortion, gun rights, the climate, gay rights. They care about a range of issues—not just what's good for the Jews."

Despite this disagreement, Trump liked Dershowitz, remarking once that he had a "a great way about him—a great personality." "We had some interesting talks," remarks Trump. "One of the things we spoke about was Alan's involvement with a group we call the settlement people. Prosecutors will tell defendants, 'We go to trial, and you're convicted—you're going to jail for fifty years. But if you take the plea right now, we'll give you ninety days.' Guys that aren't guilty can't take a chance of something happening at trial, and so they plead guilty. Alan is very much opposed to that whole thing, and so am I. I think it's really unfair. We had a lot of talks about that."

Dershowitz worked behind the scenes on behalf of the Aleph Institute, a Jewish human rights organization, to convince Trump to reduce the sentences of some of these so-called "settlement people." One prominent example was Sholom Rubashkin, owner of a kosher meat-processing facility in Iowa, who was arrested on charges of employing several hundred undocumented immigrants, as well as diverting company funds to pay personal expenses. Rubashkin went to trial and was given a twenty-seven-year prison term in 2010. At the urging of Jared Kushner, Dershowitz, and others, Trump commuted his sentence.

"It was a very sad case," comments Rabbi Zvi Boyarsky, director of national policy at the Aleph Institute. "Sholom had ten children, including an autistic child. Alan put in hundreds of hours of advocacy, working together along with lawyer Gary Apfel. Alan firmly advocated inside the White House and was instrumental in securing Sholom's release.

"Alan had an incredible willingness to help Aleph in our work. We've called him at all hours of the day with emergencies—sometimes six in the morning or late at night. He's always there to help. Once there was an Israeli man named Menashe Levy, who found himself in prison in Ethiopia for essentially tax evasion. The case had no legs whatsoever, and Menashe was placed in the same cell with a Sunni terrorist, who had tried to knock out a Jew on a plane from Ethiopia. And Menashe clearly looked Israeli. We were trying very hard to get him released immediately, and Alan was able to get Bibi Netanyahu to call the Ethiopian prime minister, which was a catalyst towards Menashe's release a few days later. Alan literally saved his life."

"Everything Alan does for us is pro bono," continues Boyarsky. "The amazing thing is that Alan doesn't want recognition for his work. He's always appreciative of the opportunity and excited to help. This is what makes him tick: fighting for these people and saving their lives. One of his cherished verses is from Deuteronomy: '*Tzedek, tzedek, tirdoff*—'justice, justice shall you pursue.' He quotes that all the time."

Dershowitz's noble work with Aleph remained largely unknown to the public. His ties with Trump on the Middle East and his ardent advocacy for Trump's civil liberties, however, gained plenty of notice and prompted disgust in many quarters. In the summer of 2018, Dershowitz made national headlines when he claimed some people were shunning him on Martha's Vineyard. A poll taken by the *Martha's Vineyard Times* found that only 37 percent of residents would choose to invite Dershowitz over for dinner. Once, a Hollywood producer, whom Dershowitz had dinner with a few times a year, saw Dershowitz approaching the porch of the Chilmark

General Store and walked away. When Dershowitz saw him again soon after, he stopped him and said, "You know, we're still friends. You should talk to me." "Well, I'm not an asshole," snapped the man. "I think maybe you are," fired back Dershowitz.

After Dershowitz had a coffee with a centrist Republican friend, the friend told him they had been spotted and that he had received calls from several people demanding he stop associating with Dershowitz. A couple of people threatened to stop donating to event centers on the Vineyard that hosted talks by Dershowitz. Another time, Dershowitz was at a party when Caroline Kennedy, JFK's daughter, walked in and was seated next to Dershowitz by the host. "I wouldn't have agreed to come if I had known you were invited," sneered Caroline.

"Once Alan and I were at a party on the Vineyard," related Carolyn, Dershowitz's wife, "and we were standing on the outside balcony of the house where the party was being hosted. We saw some acquaintances pull up and park, but when they glanced over and saw us standing on the porch, they took off and drove away."

But Dershowitz continued exposing what he saw as a microcosm of McCarthyism on the Vineyard. "So, just as a reference point, you were involved in the defense for a little while anyway of O. J. Simpson, who I think was credibly accused of murdering two people with a knife," said Tucker Carlson during one of Dershowitz's appearances on his show. "When you went to Martha's Vineyard during those years, 1995–1996, did people attack you at dinner parties for that?"

"A little bit," replied Dershowitz. "But not as much as this. It's never been like this."

It was different because this time, people close to Dershowitz were putting pressure on him to stop speaking out for an unpopular person. "My retired former colleague seems proud of playing devil's advocate here," tweeted Larry Tribe in late 2017, nearly forty years after serving on the committee formed by Arthur Goldberg to honor Dershowitz's commitment to the Constitution. "But this is no game. I think he should be deeply ashamed of helping legitimate [Trump]."

"How has this come about?" asked a frustrated Jeffrey Toobin in early 2018 while debating Dershowitz on *Anderson Cooper*. "That in every situation over the past year, you have been carrying water for Donald Trump. This is not who you used to be. . . . What's happened to you?"

"I attacked Pres. Trump for his banning of Muslims," replied Dershowitz. "I attacked President Trump for leaking material [to] Russia. . . . I'm not carrying his water! I'm saying exactly the same thing I said for fifty years. And Jeffrey, you ought to know that—you were my student. . . . Don't you understand that principle requires bipartisanship and nonpartisanship?"

"It never surprised me that Alan, as a defense lawyer, criticized Robert Mueller and other prosecutors in connection with the Trump investigation," reflects Jeffrey Toobin. "What surprised me was his 100 percent, wall-to-wall defense of Trump on every issue—at least, that's how it appeared to me.

"I think Alan's behavior in the Trump years was a departure from the Alan I once knew. Of course, Alan believes he has been completely consistent, and I just disagree about that. I think the Epstein accusation was not only painful, but very embittering to Alan. Although I can't say for sure, I also think Alan's hawkish views on Israel shaped his view of the modern Democratic Party."

Although they never descended into personal attacks, several members of the Big 8 confronted Dershowitz by email and in person at their New Year's Eve gatherings. "Why are you doing this?" asked one. "He's such a terrible man who will continue doing terrible things. You're better than this."

Friends of Dershowitz's son Jamin criticized Dershowitz in front of Jamin, and some refused to spend time with Jamin's family anymore. Both Jamin and Elon asked their father to stop going on TV to talk about Trump.

But Dershowitz would not be silent. "I grew up as an underdog," says Dershowitz. "For most of my professional life, I was not an underdog personally, but I still fought for underdogs philosophically. By this point, though, I had become an underdog. I was much more empathetic to those hated by society as a result of the accusation from Giuffre.

"I also like to stand up to authority. I like to buck trends. I like to confront people. I think that partly comes from being Jewish—an Eastern

European Jew in particular—and partly from being raised in a humble background. It's also part of my personality. I've never been one who went along with the crowd. I've always asked myself, 'If everyone agrees with something, there must be room for argument or disagreement on the other side.'"

Some accused him of standing up for Trump's civil liberties as thanks for the president's generous policies toward Israel. "I don't think that was a factor," says Dershowitz. "If he had been virulently anti-Israel, I may not have been as vocal, but I was very, very concerned about the rule of law in America."

As the Mueller investigation continued through 2018, Dershowitz repeatedly attacked it. "There's no such crime as collusion in the federal statute—you can't just make up crimes!" he declared on *Sean Hannity* in mid-2018. "If collusion had occurred—and there's no evidence it did—if collusion had occurred, it would be a political sin. But neither [Deputy Attorney General Rod] Rosenstein nor Mueller can simply magically make up a crime and say, 'Now collusion is a crime.' You want to make collusion a crime in the future? *Pass a statute*. It's not on the books."

In criticizing Mueller's investigation, Dershowitz drew on his extensive knowledge of criminal law. "The ancient principle of *nulla poena sine lege* stands for the proposition that no one can be punished for doing an act that is not prohibited by law," he wrote during this time, turning on his professor's side. "This principle has been characterized as 'one of the most widely held value judgements in the history of human thought.' Under that rule, prosecutors don't get to charge people with crimes based only on their state of mind—thought crimes. There must first be proof of an illegal act."

"It would damage our system of checks and balances and separation of powers if prosecutors or Congress could turn a president's improper motives into a crime," he concluded. "Presidents are motivated by a range of factors: reelection, financial gain after leaving office, potential book contracts, paid speaking engagements, a desire to do favors for friends, a wish to hurt enemies. . . . Going back to President George H. W. Bush, his pardoning of Casper Weinberger and others was clearly improperly motivated. The special prosecutor so concluded. And yet, nobody tried to turn the 'improper motive' into a crime because the act of pardoning itself was constitutionally protected."

Dershowitz laid out these and other arguments in a book published in 2018 titled *The Case Against Impeaching Trump*. Although no formal charges had been brought by Congress at this point, talk of impeachment was always in the air. Dershowitz had formed the thesis of the book—that criminal-like behavior committed while holding office was requisite for impeachment—while Hillary was running back in 2016 and it looked like Republicans would try to impeach her if she won.

The book made the *New York Times* bestseller list, and the ladies on *The View* invited Dershowitz for an interview. "I think so many people get confused," said host Sarah Haines. "When your argument happens to fall in line with someone legally, which happens to be Trump, people assume so much because the emotion of the time doesn't allow them to see that your love is of the law."

"But it's so dangerous," answered Dershowitz, sitting in between the ladies at a glass table, "because that means you can't represent unpopular people because you get tagged with their unpopularity. You must have lawyers able to represent the most despised people in the world."

"You need to find a legal argument to impeach him, and then we'll all like you more," said the fiery Joy Behar, prompting laughter from Dershowitz. "But if that same legal argument were then used to impeach the next Democratic president, you wouldn't like me so much," Dershowitz answered with a smile.

"I was saying in 'Hot Topics,'" remarked Behar at another point, "that the guy is under investigation by the F.B.I. for collusion, for obstruction, for violating the emoluments clause—I mean, there's a list of things. And as you just mentioned, Mitch McConnell stole the last Supreme Court justice—which I think should be illegal, but it probably isn't. So then why should we give this president, who is under investigation, a chance to affect the lives of millions of people with this next Supreme Court justice?"

"Because if you don't," replied Dershowitz, "then every president will be investigated by the opposing party in order to prevent them from making Supreme Court nominations. And remember, too, that when Clinton was in trouble and being investigated, [he] took his case to the Supreme

Court, [and] the two justices he appointed voted against him. . . . We have to have faith in our system of justice."

* * *

By 2018, Dershowitz found himself increasingly alienated from the liberal establishment. As if Trump bursting on the scene were not enough, a new movement called #MeToo was taking a grip on America's consciousness and threatening to unhinge the lives and reputations of some of the country's elite. Interestingly enough, the movement had been launched by journalist Ronan Farrow, son of Dershowitz's former client Mia Farrow, who published an exposé in *The New Yorker* about film mogul Harvey Weinstein. Over the previous forty years, Weinstein had built a massive production company in Hollywood. By 2017, his numerous films had garnered 341 nominations and 81 wins at the Academy Awards. His empire came crashing down when Farrow at *The New Yorker* and two reporters at *The New York Times* published exposés based on reports that Weinstein had engaged in sexual abuse of his employees for decades. After an investigation, Weinstein was charged with rape, forcible oral sex, and other nonconsensual sex crimes—all of which he pled not guilty to.

Dershowitz had known Weinstein since the 1990s, having represented him in several cases where Dershowitz believed Weinstein's First Amendment rights were violated by overly restrictive ratings on his movies from the Motion Picture Association. Since then, Dershowitz had seen Weinstein at several functions, including at a party with Bill Clinton on Martha's Vineyard and at a dinner for the Blavatnik Scholars organization in September 2017 mere weeks before the exposés were published.

"I was surprised by the allegations," says Dershowitz. "Harvey had a reputation for transactional sex: he'd tell female employees that if they had sex with him, he'd help along their careers. But he certainly never had a reputation for being violent or a rapist. I didn't believe those allegations against him."

Although Weinstein did not retain him as a lawyer, Dershowitz was contacted by Weinstein's attorney Ben Brafman to consult on the issue of Weinstein obtaining access to personal emails between himself and his accusers, which Weinstein claimed would help exonerate him. His accusers wanted the court to block Weinstein from obtaining the emails, and Dershowitz helped his legal team draft motions arguing for their release. Dershowitz had sought to unseal emails in the Giuffre case and shared tips with Weinstein's lawyers for how to go about this.

"He should be getting all the tapes, all the information," Dershowitz told *The Harvard Crimson*, "and then let the judge, the jury, the public decide."

In August 2018, the judge granted Weinstein permission to view around forty email exchanges between himself and one of his accusers, but he ordered Weinstein and Brafman not to name the woman in any court filings based on the emails.

Ultimately, Weinstein was convicted and sentenced to a lengthy prison term. Under this sentence, he would not even be eligible for parole until 2039 (at which point he would be eighty-seven).

Born out of Weinstein's downfall, the #MeToo movement ignited the passions of young people throughout America. According to the *Pew Research Center*, nearly 70 percent of Americans aged 18–29 supported the movement.

Amid these volatile times, Jeffrey Epstein's name was brought front and center to the headlines in November 2018 when *Miami Herald* journalist Julie Brown published a bombshell article titled "Perversion of Justice." Brown interviewed over sixty women who claimed they were sexually abused by Epstein and also dug into the circumstances which led to the 2008 plea deal between prosecutors and Epstein's attorneys.

Until Brown's article, the plea deal Dershowitz and Epstein's other lawyers arranged with prosecutors had received little publicity, but in light of this barrage of new accusations, the public assumed that the deal had been an underhanded maneuver on the part of Epstein's lawyers to keep the ring of accusers quiet. The deal became vilified as a "sweetheart" arrangement on the part of Epstein's sleazy lawyers.

Following the *Miami Herald* exposé, Epstein earned a worldwide reputation as a pedophile and sex trafficker, and he became the face of everything the #MeToo movement stood against.

Around this time, Dershowitz ran into a litany of legal troubles. Dershowitz had infuriated David Boies by filing a bar charge against Boies and branding him a "villain." In late 2017, Dershowitz attended a legal conference at the Loews Hotel in Miami Beach, and as he was leaving the conference, a stranger stopped as he was headed down the hotel escalator. "Look, I'm close with David Boies, and I don't want to give you my name in case Boies finds out," said the man. "I have to let you know that Boies told me unless you withdraw the bar charge, he's going to find another woman. He said, 'Two are better than one.'" Unsure of what to make of this, Dershowitz thanked the man and later tried to figure out his identity, but was unable to.

Dershowitz did not withdraw the bar charge, and a short time after this escalator encounter, another client of Boies launched an accusation against Dershowitz. As part of a lawsuit against Epstein's girlfriend Ghislaine Maxwell, Sarah Ransome said in a deposition that she had been forced into a threesome with Dershowitz when she was twenty-two years old. Ransome described Dershowitz: "white, pasty skin; not very attractive. Wears glasses. Bit of an ugly man, really." She said that Dershowitz had engaged in oral sex with her and another woman at Epstein's New York property.

"Let me be very clear," Dershowitz declared to the press. "I have had sex with one woman since the day I met my wife. . . . And during the entire relevant period of time, I never had any contact with Ransome."

Dershowitz told the press that this accusation had been orchestrated by David Boies out of revenge. "Why is he going after me?" Dershowitz angrily said on Fox's *The Ingraham Angle*. "I have to tell you, I have a theory: I think he's projecting. David Boies has a terrible reputation for sexual activities. And I've issued a challenge to him. Look, I've had sex with one woman since the day I met Jeffrey Epstein. I challenge David Boies to say under oath that he's only had sex with one woman during that same period of time."

As for Boies, he denied Dershowitz's accusation that he put Ransome up to the accusation, saying: "Mr. Dershowitz should be ashamed of himself. . . . I am ashamed he is a member of my profession."

Eventually, Dershowitz's bar charge against Boies was dismissed on jurisdictional grounds. "I still believe he engaged in ethical misconduct," Dershowitz says. "Bar associations tend to protect the wealthy and powerful."

As for Ransome, she was eventually shown to be something of a kook. "Her claims to have had sex tapes of two of our most famous politicians [Hillary Clinton and Trump] turned out to be false," says Kenneth Sweder. "Therefore, her claims about Alan have to be very, very carefully examined before being believed."

Dershowitz had unwittingly run into the buzz saw of the #MeToo movement. In the aftermath of the *Miami Herald* publication, Virginia Giuffre emerged as one of Epstein's prominent accusers. Dershowitz vociferously attacked her, and in March 2019, she brought a defamation lawsuit against him.

Even still, Dershowitz did not back down. "I can tell you she is still a prostitute," he told a Miami TV station in April. "She is selling false stories now for money about me."

"Do you have any concern calling her a prostitute when she was victimized at such a young age by this wealthy man?" asked the reporter. "She was not victimized," replied Dershowitz. "She made her own decisions in life."

Luckily for Dershowitz, bombshell revelations about Giuffre appeared while she was suing him for defamation. Giuffre was simultaneously involved in a lawsuit against Ghislaine Maxwell. Maxwell's lawyers won the unsealing of the manuscript of Giuffre's book *The Billionaire Playboy's Club*, along with the 2011 email exchange between Giuffre and journalist Sharon Churcher, in which Churcher had brought Dershowitz to Giuffre's attention. Giuffre's lawyers Bradley Edwards and Paul Cassell had managed to keep these emails sealed during their defamation case against Dershowitz, but now they were out.

Giuffre responded to them in an interview with *The New Yorker*: "I can't say what she was thinking, but I think she threw Alan into it forgetting that I had already mentioned him, even informed her of the experiences I had with him," she commented.

"The emails speak for themselves," says Kenneth Sweder. "They show very clearly that prior to 2011, Alan was not a factor. They are a smoking gun."

Giuffre's unsealed book manuscript glaringly contained no account of Giuffre having sex with Dershowitz. One salacious paragraph described him as Epstein's "colleague in finances and personal solicitor, a bird of the same feather I had seen hanging around the island and Jeffrey's Manhattan mansion, more and more these days. Alan's taste for the young and beautiful was a bias [sic] for a blooming business relationship between him and Jeffrey."

In addition to this manuscript revelation, Dershowitz also learned that Giuffre had neglected to mention him during a 2013 interview with federal agents in which she named the people Epstein allegedly directed her to have sex with. It turned out that the lawsuit brought in 2015 was the first time Giuffre had mentioned Dershowitz in connection with the scandal.

"The totality of the evidence should have exonerated Alan," says Sweder.

But Giuffre did not back down. While her defamation suit moved forward, Dershowitz published a book titled *Guilt by Accusation*, which outlined the case for his innocence. "Some friends and relatives have urged me not to write this book, because it will only continue the focus on the false accusation against me," he wrote in the introduction. "They argue, quite persuasively, that the less attention paid to the accusation, the more likely the story will 'go away.' But it is not my goal to make the story 'go away.' My goal is to disprove it, categorically and definitively, until there is no lingering doubt in the minds of all fair and open-minded people."

Although his evidence was overwhelming, Giuffre's accusation lived on, and the #MeToo-enthused public gobbled it up.

"Whose side should Alan Dershowitz be on?" asked a BBC reporter in a tense interview with Dershowitz during this time. "Should you be on the side of high-profile, rich clients who are accused of perhaps rape or murder, or should you be on the side of alleged victims, often poor young women who do not have, as it were, the firepower behind them?"

"I represent 50 percent of my cases *pro bono*," replied a seemingly annoyed Dershowitz. "I have represented numerous women. I represented a woman who killed her husband because she was a battered woman. I represented another woman who was accused of killing her husband. I represented a woman who was locked up by her husband in a mental hospital. I represented a young girl who was taken away from her mother because her mother was having a relationship with another woman."

Unfortunately for Dershowitz, he was now indelibly associated with Giuffre's accusation and his widely abhorred friend Jeffrey Epstein.

Epstein himself was in a world of trouble. Over a decade after his plea deal, a sex trafficking case was opened against him, and he was arrested while traveling through Teterboro Airport in New Jersey. He was placed in Manhattan's abysmal Metropolitan Correctional Center without the option of bail.

Since he was unhappy Dershowitz had not kept him out of jail in the 2008 plea deal, Epstein turned to other lawyers to help him this time around. Despite Epstein's frustration with Dershowitz in 2008, the two remained on speaking terms after Epstein got out of jail in 2009. "He'd call me from time to time to ask a legal question," says Dershowitz. Around 2013, Dershowitz went to Epstein's New York apartment for a fifteen-minute legal meeting, but Dershowitz refrained from spending any more time at Epstein's other properties, as he had done in the past.

"Jeffrey told me that he knew Giuffre's accusation was totally false," says Dershowitz, "as did Ghislaine Maxwell. Although I, of course, never sought for them to provide testimony, if they had been subpoenaed, they would have told the whole truth."

Before the 2006 case, Dershowitz had always gotten on well with Epstein, and although their post-2006 relationship was essentially lawyer-client, Dershowitz treated Epstein more as a friend than a client. "Where are you for summer?" Epstein emailed Dershowitz in mid-2013. Dershowitz replied that he was spending the summer on Martha's Vineyard and then wrote: "Where are you. I called you a couple of times when I was in NYC. Miss you."

"I have said 'miss you' to other clients," explains Dershowitz. "I've said it to Phil Shawe, who I advised during several cases related to his translation company TransPerfect. I don't regard 'miss you' as anything particularly personal. It's just a greeting. I didn't mean it as anything but a salutation. I would have written the same thing to my other clients like Claus von Bülow."

"I think that Alan spoke to people warmly in texts and emails," says his assistant Sarah Neely. "I think that he probably tried to distance himself from Jeffrey when everything became so public. But you can have a friendship that's more private than public because it's the right thing to do for your client.

"I can say that at times when I've reached out to Alan, he's said, 'How are you these days? Miss you.' I was his assistant—is that weird? Not necessarily, because we've had a long relationship. I think no matter what the relationship is, when you spend a lot of time with somebody and go through a difficult circumstance, it's natural to develop some sort of a bond.

"This email exchange with Jeffrey hints at the Pandora's box of Alan Dershowitz," continues Neely. "He always fought for the underdog. I think he was quoted somewhere saying that he only took the guiltiest clients. He really loves fighting 'the good fight'—and I think he uses that term quite a bit. Alan is probably one of the most loyal lawyers you could ever hope for. He is ride-or-die. He flourishes amidst the chaotic blend of debating his way through restrictions imposed by others. This doesn't necessarily imply a moral judgment of right or wrong, but he is determined to contend."

Some wondered how Dershowitz could be friendly with people he knew committed disgusting acts. "If you're a criminal lawyer, you have to overlook faults," explains Dershowitz.

"I've never seen somebody be able to do it the way Alan does," comments Neely. "People would say to him, 'Alan, you have a daughter around these victims' age. How do you put your head on your pillow at night?' I don't believe he thinks about that. I don't mean he's mentally ill or doesn't have a moral compass, but I think he's absolutely one of a kind in that he can really put aside what's going on in someone's life in order to fight for the law. He looks at someone like Jeffrey as a human being—someone who's a business owner, an entrepreneur—and he wouldn't judge Jeffrey by the stories out there about him."

"Jeffrey surrounded himself with many interesting people, and I think that was a big draw for Alan," says Carolyn. "I don't think it was so much Jeffrey's riches. He would provide entrées and introductions for Alan to very interesting people. Many of the people who criticized Alan for spending time with Jeffrey would have had a hard time turning away from the interesting, elite circles Jeffrey moved in."

"I love that I get a Christmas card and present from Matt Menschel [*sic*], the guy that put me in jail," Epstein emailed Dershowitz in late 2012. "Appropriate," Dershowitz replied. "Christmas celebrates the birth of another innocent Jewish guy who was crucified."

"I think he was innocent of the extreme accusations against him," a close friend once heard Dershowitz say. "What he did was: he had improper sexual contact with quite a few women, some of whom were below the age of consent. Almost all of them worked in the sex industry before he met them. Some had worked at so-called 'whack shacks,' where they were paid around $25 dollars to masturbate people. He would pay them $200 to do the same thing. And these were not children—many were in their late teens and in some cases early twenties. As far as I knew, Jeffrey didn't introduce any young woman to sexuality."

This was an extremely unpopular viewpoint, to say the least. Epstein's accusers did not see it Dershowitz's way, of course, and neither did the government when they launched a criminal case in 2019 and locked Epstein in jail. Although Dershowitz did not visit Epstein during his time at the Metropolitan Correctional Center, he had been there previously to visit other clients. "It was a maximum-security jail with no open-air spaces where criminals from across the spectrum were detained," he says. "One had to go through several security doors to enter the jail, and the cells were jammed close together. The facility was dimly lit, rat-infested, and had a constant odor."

In late July, Epstein was discovered in his cell with signs on his body that he had tried to hang himself. Two weeks later, on August 10, 2019, he was dead. State officials reported it as suicide, but some in the public suspected he was murdered by one of his elite associates in an effort to silence him before trial. His cellmate was removed shortly before he was supposed to have killed himself, and cameras in the facility had been off at the time—which the officials said was due to technical malfunctioning.

"I don't think Hillary Clinton or Donald Trump or anyone else murdered him," says Dershowitz. "Jeffrey was a hedonist. He liked his pleasures. At the time, his lawyer Marty Weinberg had a decent shot of getting him off on federal crimes, but I believe the thought that he might potentially end up getting life in prison was something he could not bear. My suspicion is that he paid the guards to turn off the camera and not witness him doing it."

Dershowitz once said his greatest regret was ever meeting Jeffrey Epstein. "I really hate Lynn Forester for introducing us," he says. "I suspect she had an affair with Jeffrey and knew what she was potentially roping me into."

On the matter of how Epstein kept his nefarious activities secret, Dershowitz comments, "I suspect he divided his friends in two: those who knew and those who didn't. Leslie Wexner obviously knew. Lynn Forester obviously did, too. I'm not sure about Prince Andrew.

"I never saw young women in Jeffrey's homes. He had some younger girlfriends, but they were in their late twenties—they were certainly not teenagers. The only time I ever saw Jeffrey in the presence of a young woman was at a lunch at Harvard with Jeffrey, President Larry Summer, Steven Pinker, and Stephen Jay Gould, where there were a couple young waitresses who looked to be around eighteen or nineteen.

"There were no indications in any of Jeffrey's homes that hanky-panky was going on. He had his private areas that were off-limits to guests, but my family and I attributed that to the fact that he was a germaphobe and a clean freak. I would never have let my grandchildren stay in his Florida home if there had been lewd pictures."

"The public has an image of Epstein's Florida property as a place where all these young females were hanging around," says Kenneth Sweder. "From what I have reviewed in court documents, that is simply inaccurate."

"I think Jeffrey had two—if not more—lives," comments Carolyn. "There was no indication in any of the properties I was at—New York, Florida, or the island—of anything nefarious. He didn't have pictures of naked women and stuff like that—at least in the areas we were in. That's just total BS.

"Jeffrey name-dropped everybody to everybody, so that everyone thought that he was good friends with somebody else that was important. He didn't make a huge impression on me. I thought he was just a sleazy guy who had tons of money and hung out with rich people. I'm totally stunned that Jeffrey's brought down the world."

Theories have abounded as to how Epstein became rich. "I think he made his money through getting a percentage of Leslie Wexner's fortune, which Jeffrey had power of attorney over," comments Dershowitz. "One of the theories I've heard is that he and Wexner had a homosexual affair, and Jeffrey extorted Wexner in exchange for remaining quiet about it."

Epstein was gone forever, but his image as the personification of evil endured. "He was the most unpopular person I ever defended," says Dershowitz. "More than O. J. and more than Trump—he was the most hated. In 2006, we thought there was no possibility he could've gotten a fair trial, which is why we were inclined to plead. As far as the government and media were concerned, he was the devil incarnate. John Kerry once told me he thought Jeffrey was the worst person ever."

Dershowitz, in turn, received vilification for his ties to Epstein, as well as for Giuffre's accusation. In 2019, journalist Connie Bruck at *The New Yorker* penned a lengthy article overviewing Dershowitz's life and career. The piece was largely a hack job. Certain cases from his career and various anecdotes were taken out of context and jammed together, painting a picture of Dershowitz as essentially a bully and a misogynist. Bruck only contacted Dershowitz once the piece was completed, would not agree to a face-to-face interview with him, and even pulled a bait-and-switch on Elon to get him to divulge juicy details about his deceased mother, whom Elon had cared a great deal about. "Bruck was a brutal woman," says Elon.

One of the aftereffects of Giuffre's accusation which shocked Dershowitz was watching certain Jewish institutions disassociate from him. In 2019, Dershowitz published a memoir titled *Defending Israel*, and his agent reached out to the 92nd Street Y, a famous Jewish events center in New York where elite people speak. Since the release of *Chutzpah* in the early 1990s, Dershowitz had regularly received invitations to speak, and his talks or debates were almost always sold out. But in 2019, the 92Y told Dershowitz they were not interested in having him speak, saying they did not "want trouble" as a result of Giuffre's accusation.

"I was disappointed and shocked by their decision," says Yitz Greenberg, who by this point had become a well-known Jewish scholar and rabbi. "They were afraid of being boycotted and criticized rather than sticking with someone who they thought was telling the truth. They simply dodged, and it was very sad."

On another occasion, the Ramaz School, a Jewish high school in New York, extended an invitation for Dershowitz to address the students about how to face anti-Semitism when they went off to college. Shortly before his scheduled visit, though, the headmaster of the school called Dershowitz and said that they would have to cancel his visit, explaining that they could not have him associating with young female students.

"Alan was hurt by how some in the Jewish community canceled him and didn't believe him," reflects Carolyn. "They loved him when it was convenient, and he gave his all to the Jewish community. Then, certain synagogues and organizations—places where had previously been very active and welcome—disinvited him. There were honors and awards he did not receive."

"This whole 'guilt by association' mindset and the canceling of Alan by various institutions was not only unfair to an individual I greatly respect, but was also dangerous to the rule of law, civil liberties, and democratic self-government," notes Nadine Strossen, Dershowitz's former student and the first female president of the ACLU. "I'm not exaggerating when I say these kinds of acts are shades of McCarthyism. They lead to a corrosion of the fabric which holds our pluralistic democratic society together. The so-called 'cancel culture' is beginning to distort the legal profession in the United States."

Once, while Dershowitz was giving a lecture on civil liberties at Colgate University in central New York, several young people lined the aisles of the auditorium with their backs turned toward Dershowitz and holding signs with messages like: "Our Voices Matter" and "Believe Survivors." In advance of Dershowitz's talk, signs had been put up around the campus which warned students this incoming speaker was an "accused child rapist."

"I invite the students who are protesting to listen to what I have to say," said Dershowitz, as the protesters stood silently in the aisles. "I admire your protest and I accept your protest as a form of disagreement." Citing the "child rapist" posters, he declared, "Every time a radical feminist issues a false accusation as those who produced this pamphlet did, it puts an arrow through the heart of the important [#MeToo] movement."

On Martha's Vineyard, no one that Dershowitz was personally familiar with said they believed Giuffre's accusation. After observing Dershowitz's close relationship with his wife over many summers, such a claim would have been hard to conceive. But on a bright, sunny day in the fall of 2019, Dershowitz pulled into the local library in the village of West Tisbury for a talk on his book *Defending Israel*, only to find a group of middle-aged women (and one man) lined together near the entrance. Their signs included a mock cover of Dershowitz's new book with messages like: "Brilliant lawyers defend the victims, not the rapists" and "We stand for Jane Doe." As a smiling Dershowitz entered the library, he told the protesters, "If the police tried to remove you I would defend your right to free speech, unlike you not defending my right to free speech"—whereupon one woman shouted, "We don't need you!" and the entire group commenced chanting "Shame! Shame! Shame!"

On Twitter, where Dershowitz has a highly followed account, he was regularly labeled by users as a "baby fucker" and "pervert."

"Alan Dershowitz is a certified perennial pedophile, but he won't be arrested, charged, prosecuted and punished because he is a Zionist," wrote one user with nearly three million followers.

"It bothered me greatly that this lovely, great civil libertarian, the savior of public relations of the state of Israel, was suffering from the lies that famous people often are victims of," said Dershowitz's uncle Zecharia. "He suffered greatly from it."

The extraordinary stress brought on by Giuffre's accusation caused Dershowitz to have four strokes, one causing numbness on the left side of his face.

"The fallout from the accusation was very hard on Alan's family and of course on Alan personally," says an anonymous close friend of Dershowitz. "For a time, his daughter kind of turned on him and didn't want to be associated with him in some ways, which I think was difficult on their relationship."

"I'm not surprised by the disdain people had for Alan, but disappointed—he doesn't deserve this," says Megyn Kelly. Kelly started her career as a corporate lawyer before turning to journalism and becoming a popular host on Fox News and NBC. "I would invite Alan on my show at

Fox," says Kelly, "and I was completely bowled over that I had the chance to talk to him because I had watched him as a young law student on TV and followed his career. He was a hero of mine."

In 2016, Kelly had become a forerunner of the #MeToo movement when she reported being sexually harassed by Fox News owner Roger Ailes. Her accusation ultimately contributed to Ailes's downfall.

"I didn't know what to believe in the case of Virginia Giuffre," says Kelly. "I knew I was going to interview Alan, and I said to my team, 'This is going to require a deep dive, because if I do think he did something, we're going to be spending some time on this.' So my team, which is excellent, went and did a very deep dive into all the Epstein stuff. I read Alan's book *Guilt by Accusation* and had been following Epstein pretty closely. I knew the story better than most. And I knew there were questions about Giuffre and her credibility prior to reading anything about Alan. So, the deeper I dove, the more it was very clear she was not credible, and in my view, was making up everything about Alan. And I wasn't surprised to hear him very capably defending himself in our interview.

"Something I thought was unfortunate," continues Kelly, "was that it seemed to bother Alan that the left turned on him. I wanted him to be able to let that go. And I wanted him to be able to let go of the Giuffre allegations. I wanted him to lean into the legacy he created and the legal giant that he is and walk with the same swagger he always had. I hoped he wouldn't stay mired in any of the negativity that people with a political agenda tried to foist on him, because he's always been a force for good— and just for what's right."

TAKING THE STAND

Giuffre's accusation lived on. As 2019 drew to a close, Dershowitz found himself eighty-one years old and fighting for his legacy. Meanwhile, a storm was brewing in Washington. Trump's presidency appeared to be on the brink of collapse.

The previous year, Democrats had retaken control of the House and now had a comfortable majority. Dershowitz had made media appearances and donations on behalf of various candidates in an effort to help the Democrats have a successful midterm showing. "A divided Congress is an important check and balance against one-party rule," he wrote in an updated edition of his book *The Case Against Impeaching Trump*. "But the Democrats risk weakening their power if they foolishly prioritize impeachment, investigations, and revenge over legislative priorities that could help the American public."

As the country neared the 2020 presidential election, Dershowitz told the press his ideal presidential ticket would be Amy Klobuchar with Julián Castro as a running mate, and he made it clear he would not support Bernie Sanders. "I don't think under any circumstances I could vote for a man who went to England and campaigned for a bigot and anti-Semite like Jeremy Corbyn," he told one outlet.

Although Klobuchar was his first choice, he also endorsed his friend Joe Biden. "I'm a strong supporter of Joe Biden," he said to one reporter. "I like Joe Biden. I've liked him for a long time, and I could enthusiastically support Joe Biden."

"Over Donald Trump?" asked the apparently surprised reporter. "Over Donald Trump, yeah," answered Dershowitz.

"People just don't understand how you can be liberal Democrat politically and support a Republican constitutionally," comments Dershowitz. "They either don't understand, or they pretend not to. But this has been the key to my whole life: not making constitutional decisions based on political preferences."

Shortly after the Democrats obtained control of the House, the Mueller investigation released its findings after a nearly three-year probe. In the end, the investigation found no evidence Trump had personally colluded with the Russians to help his election in 2016. Trump had dodged a bullet, but in July 2019, he jumped out of the frying pan and into the fire during a phone call with Ukrainian president Volodymyr Zelenskyy. Following the call, reports began to circulate that Trump had conditioned aid to Ukraine on Zelenskyy assisting with two matters: (1) finding a computer server which was—according to some reports—hidden in Ukraine and would show that Democrats had conspired with the firm CrowdStrike to invent the story of Russian collusion in the 2016 election; and (2) investigating Joe Biden for ordering the firing of a Ukrainian prosecutor who wanted to go after Biden's son, Hunter, who was on the board of Ukrainian energy company Burisma.

Led by Nancy Pelosi, Adam Schiff, and others, Democrats in Congress began drafting impeachment articles on the ground that Trump had violated his oath of office by extorting a foreign government to benefit himself politically.

"They never even saw the transcript of the call," tweeted Trump on September 24. "A total Witch Hunt!" After releasing the transcript the next day, Trump maintained he had done nothing wrong, but the Democrats pressed forward with impeachment proceedings. Since the Democrats had a comfortable majority, the president stood no chance in the House, and his legal team began looking toward the inevitable trial in the Senate.

"I was putting together an A-team of legal experts and I needed someone who would handle the constitutional issues involved in the impeachment proceedings without political bias," says Trump's lawyer Jay Sekulow. "I first heard about Alan when I was in law school in 1977. Alan was already well known as a defender of the First Amendment and was a recognized national expert in constitutional law. We met in the late 1980s at an ACLU conference and immediately became friends, even though we disagreed on the relationship between church and state, abortion, and other major issues. I turned to him in 2019 when we needed someone to defend the Constitution."

At first, Dershowitz was noncommittal, knowing his entire family and most of his friends would be totally opposed to it. Then, on December 18, 229 Democratic representatives, including Dershowitz's former student Jamie Raskin, voted to impeach Trump on the grounds of "abuse of power" and "obstruction of Congress." Dershowitz was upset that the Democrats had taken this history-altering step based on charges he believed were insufficient grounds to remove a democratically elected president. When he had written his book *The Case Against Impeaching Trump* in 2018, he had pointed partly to the Framers' rejection of "maladministration" as an impeachable offense to demonstrate that impeachment should be based on clearly criminal behavior, which "abuse of power" and "obstruction of Congress" were not, in Dershowitz's view.

As preparations for Trump's trial in the Senate got underway, Dershowitz mulled the weighty invitation from Sekulow. It was a historic opportunity for Dershowitz, but for the first time in his life, nearly all the people he had ever loved and cared about were imploring him to remain silent.

"I thought this was different—this was more of a political case, not a criminal case," says Dershowitz's former student Stuart Eizenstat, with whom Dershowitz had remained on close personal terms. "Everybody's entitled to a defense, but a lawyer doesn't have to take on every potential client. Alan would be associating himself with someone who was quite cavalier about the Constitution and about all the things I would have thought Alan cared about: the rule of law, respect for minorities, and deference towards courts and judges."

"It was extremely misguided for Alan to use his talents to defend Trump," said Dershowitz's close friend Kenneth Sweder. "His appearances on Fox and other right-wing stations to defend Trump had done way more harm than good, even if what he was saying had some degree of validity to it. President Trump was actively seeking to do harm to our democracy and to various people within it, and Alan was going to help enable Trump to carry on doing that."

Bernie Beck, one of the Big 8, reached out to Dershowitz and said he would be crazy if he took the case. "I know he always prided himself as a defender of lost causes and constitutional rights, but I thought Alan would have the common sense to think through what the implications of this decision would be," says Beck. "Unfortunately, he seemed to now be defending only right-wing causes, and I think that forced him into a corner."

"I was shocked when Alan considered it," says Carl Meshenberg, whom Dershowitz had known since they were toddlers. "I recognized his strong commitment to the First Amendment and to following the letter of the law. He is very honest. However, I think that he didn't always have to be the one to defend people who are indefensible. My wife and I were disappointed about the direction he was heading."

Hal Jacobs, a particularly hard-core liberal among the Big 8, urged Dershowitz through emails and calls to reject the offer. "In my view, the most flagrant violator of the constitutional process in our democracy was none other than Donald Trump," says Jacobs. "I didn't see how Alan could defend the Constitution by defending the person who has violated that document more than anybody else in our country. But Alan likes to be in the limelight, and he always wants to defend the underdog and take on the unpopular viewpoint."

Elon, Jamin, and Ella begged their father not to do it. "Trump was the kind of person who would turn against someone even if they go out on a limb for him," says Elon. "That's just what he does. I didn't think Trump deserved my dad because what my dad was going to do was strictly on principle." Jamin repeatedly pleaded with his father in person and by phone and email.

"My brother was desperate to be high-visibility," says Nathan Dershowitz. According to one of the partners at Nathan's law firm, in recent years, Alan had gotten in a habit of leaving them to do the menial, difficult background work on a case and then taking the credit for the cases they won together. For his part, Nathan had—in the opinion of some family members and friends—grown jealous of his uniquely successful brother.

"I knew he would destroy his reputation by taking the case," continues Nathan. "He was also messing up my social life—a number of women wouldn't go out with me because of him.

"I thought his whole involvement with Trump was despicable. I abhorred Donald Trump. I thought he was dangerous for our society. I sent Alan a number of notes telling him he was being used by Trump. I said to him, 'Would you have supported Hitler's election in the 1930s because it was legitimate and take that to its extreme, which is what you're doing now? You're dealing with a very dangerous man and giving him credence. And you're doing it for your own ego.' And I laid into him on that.

"I just could not understand why he would do it, except by attributing it to his narcissism, his contrarian views, and his need to be in the middle of everything. That's the only reason he was going to do it—to show he was smarter than everyone else."

"I asked Alan explicitly not to do it," comments Carolyn. "I asked him repeatedly not to do it. I wrote a long list of reasons why he shouldn't.

"I think Trump encouraged the worst in people. I think he played to the lowest common denominator. He got people riled up and encouraged hate. The way he derides people is just like a child having a tantrum. I think his narcissism affects his judgment and that he puts himself before America, which is very dangerous, I think. Those are just personal critiques—that's to say nothing of his policies! He may have achieved some good things, but at a huge cost to America in terms of the civil discord he's encouraged."

"I didn't think Alan needed to do it," Carolyn continues. "I knew it would be very controversial. He had always been asked to advise presidents on both sides of the aisle, and I knew if he participated in Trump's trial, future Democratic presidents wouldn't touch him. I mostly agree with everything else Alan's fought for, and I've always supported the clients he's wanted to take on—except for Trump."

Despite all these voices, Dershowitz wanted to say yes.

"What he wanted to do for Trump didn't surprise me at all," says Dershowitz's longtime colleague and friend Susan Estrich, who helped him win the Claus von Bülow case. "It was, in some respects, disappointing because I didn't like Donald Trump. I don't think he deserved Alan's advocacy. But it was totally textbook Alan to put himself all the way out there for an unpopular client—even knowing that in the circles in which he traveled, he would be reviled for doing so. Alan will say what he thinks, and that gets him in trouble. He doesn't think along the lines of: 'if I support Trump, these people are going to think such-and-such.' He doesn't make decisions like that. He speaks up and lets the chips fall where they may."

By the end of December, the Senate trial was looming, and Dershowitz was still on the fence. As usual, he and Carolyn were in Miami for the winter, and they were invited to have Christmas Eve dinner with Dershowitz's client Philip Shawe at Mar-a-Lago. Just before dinner, Dershowitz saw the president and his family enter from the far end of the banquet hall. He had known it was possible for Trump to be at Mar-a-Lago that night, but did not know for certain whether Trump would turn up. Dershowitz made no attempt to approach the president, but when he went up to the buffet line, he suddenly noticed Trump standing right behind him in line. They exchanged pleasantries, and Dershowitz offered Trump the empty plate he had just picked up. Trump declined with thanks and then popped the question. "So are you going to be my lawyer in the Senate?" he said. "Everyone wants the job, but you're my first choice." Dershowitz said his wife was opposed to it, and Trump asked if he could speak to her.

Dershowitz walked across the banquet hall back to his table and told Carolyn the president wanted to talk with her. "About that?" she asked in an annoyed tone. "Yes, about that," said Dershowitz. The two walked over to the president's table, and as soon as they came up to his seat, Trump rose and spoke to Carolyn.

"Alan was trying to get Trump to convince me, but I wasn't going to be convinced by Trump," says Carolyn. "I was very clear to Trump that I thought Alan would be more helpful on constitutional issues—and have more credibility—as a neutral spokesperson."

Trump tried to persuade Carolyn this was a historic opportunity which Dershowitz should take up, but when he saw Carolyn's mind was made up, the president said, "I know how much Alan loves you and how much you love him, and he ought to listen to what you have to say, so you should discuss it and do what's best for you."

"But," he added, "I really would like Alan to do it, and I think it would really be good for the country if you and Alan decide he should do it."

Carolyn and her husband respectfully told the president they would discuss it and provide him with an answer speedily.

After dinner, the couple was picked up by an Uber outside Mar-a-Lago. It was nighttime by now, and as they rode back to their condo through the darkened streets, Carolyn commented, "I know how much you want to do this."

Over the next few days, they decided Dershowitz would accept Trump's offer on the conditions that the president would not see his speech to the Senate ahead of time and that Dershowitz would discuss the unconstitutionality of the Democrats' charges, not the political circumstances surrounding Trump's impeachment. Trump agreed.

"Alan is a man of principle," says Trump. "And I think he felt I was being screwed."

"I was very, very concerned about the abuse of the Constitution," says Dershowitz. "I didn't need any more attention—I'd gotten enough of that after Epstein. When Trump told me it was important for the country and that I'd be representing the presidency, I think that pushed me over the edge."

The media got wind of Dershowitz's decision, and the country soon learned Dershowitz had joined Trump's team. "From my knowledge, Alan was the only Democrat on our team," says Jay Sekulow. "He knew there'd be consequences to his decision, and he made it clear he was going to stay strictly focused on the constitutional issues."

In January 2020, the Senate trial got underway. Working feverishly inside the office of his Miami apartment, Dershowitz prepared for his hour-long speech before the Senate. He read every word of the *Federalist Papers* and also pored over the debates at the Constitutional Convention, Blackstone's *Commentaries On the Laws of England*, the debates during Andrew Johnson's impeachment, and the debates during the ratification of some of the state constitutions.

After gathering the quotes he needed, Dershowitz wrote out the speech on his beloved yellow legal pad and sent it over to Maura Kelley, who quickly typed it and then read it over with Dershowitz.

Dershowitz's speech was scheduled for Monday, January 27, and as he publicly voiced his criticism of the president's impeachment, the liberal media took him to task. "He's perfectly entitled to defend the president," said Larry Tribe on CNN, "although I don't like that he pretends he's defending the Constitution instead of the president. . . . The stakes here are enormous. We've got a president who was shaking down a foreign government for his own benefit—for his own reelection. He was using taxpayer money to do it. He's engaged in the kind of abuse that Alexander Hamilton, James Madison, any of our Framers would have said requires that we end the presidency, especially when the abuse goes to meddling in the next election. And when Alan Dershowitz or anybody—although I don't know anybody else who really does it—comes up and says 'Well, [it's] an abuse, but it's not a crime or crime-like, and therefore we can't remove him for it,' that really, that's disgusting." Acknowledging that Dershowitz was a "great teacher" at Harvard and that he "used to be a good colleague," Tribe concluded: "right now he's selling out."

"You say you're not a formal part of the legal team—how so?" asked Anderson Cooper in an interview with Dershowitz. "Well, I've been asked to prepare and deliver the case—the constitutional case—against impeachment. *That* benefits the president. It's the same argument I would have made if Hillary Clinton had gotten elected and she were being impeached. It's similar to the arguments I made when I testified as a witness against the impeachment of Bill Clinton and when I consulted with the Bill Clinton legal team."

"Why are you playing these semantic games?" chimed in Jeffrey Toobin, who regularly appeared on Cooper's show as a legal analyst. "Whose side are you on? I mean, you're part of the defense team. What, are you embarrassed?"

"You sound like my mother," replied Dershowitz, "when . . . I was defending the right of Nazis to march through Skokie, and she said to me, 'Son, are you for the Jews or are you for the Nazis?' I said, 'Ma, I'm for the Constitution.' She said, 'I'm your mother! Don't tell me that. You have to pick sides: the Jews [or the Nazis]. . . . I picked the side of the Constitution."

Dershowitz came under fire during an appearance on *The View* when host Whoopi Goldberg referenced Dershowitz's 1998 interview on Larry King during Clinton's impeachment when he said, "If you have somebody who completely corrupts the office of president and who abuses trust and who poses great danger to our liberty, you don't need a technical crime."

"Now some would say you've rethought some of your thinking about what is impeachable," said Goldberg in an annoyed tone. "May I point out that the only difference between then and now is that your side is flipping out for the same reasons the Democrats were flipping out?"

"I'm a scholar. I have written forty books. I have changed my mind many times," replied Dershowitz quickly. "About three years ago when I started looking into the *Hillary Clinton* possibility of impeachment, I decided you needed a crime. I wrote a book about it several years ago. I didn't change my mind on partisan grounds."

On the weekend before Dershowitz's Senate appearance, *Saturday Night Live* aired a cold open themed around Dershowitz's upcoming argument. "It's I! Alan Dershowitz!" said comedian Jon Lovitz, portraying Dershowitz in a mockingly arrogant way. "Ah, it's wonderful to be here, 'cause I'm not welcome anywhere else," he continued, prompting laughter from the audience. "A lot of haters out there for no good reason. But like I said to my client and my dear friend *Jeffrey Epstein*—haters gonna hate!"

"Yeah Alan, I think you're gonna wanna stay away from Epstein," said Beck Bennett, portraying Mitch McConnell.

Later in the skit, Lovitz traveled to Hell, where he met an awestruck Devil played by Kate McKinnon. "Well, good luck, Mr. Dershowitz," said McKinnon at the end. "We're gonna be watching the trial this week—so make us proud."

Many years previously, Arthur Goldberg had written a job recommendation for his young law clerk, which noted that Dershowitz had "demonstrated great capacity and profound dedication to the fundamental rights and liberties of Americans enshrined in our Constitution and Bill of Rights." Six decades later, on January 27, 2020, Dershowitz found himself in Washington, DC, on his way to the magnificent domed Capitol Building, just across the road from where he had gone to work each day for Goldberg at the Supreme Court.

Carolyn and Elon had traveled with him, and after passing through security, they made their way to the Senate chamber. Along the way, Dershowitz bumped into Kamala Harris. A reporter caught Harris smiling and shaking Dershowitz's hand, and though a vehement opponent of the president, Harris told Dershowitz that she understood what lawyers do.

Amy Klobuchar also greeted Dershowitz warmly, and Dershowitz mentioned how much he wanted her to be president someday.

As Dershowitz's time approached, his wife and son took their seats in the gallery, and Dershowitz sat down next to Jay Sekulow and others at the defense table near the front of the chamber. Directly across from their table were the House managers, led by Representative Adam Schiff, who were arguing for Trump's removal. Seated on a dais overlooking the entire chamber was Chief Justice John Roberts, who was mandated by the Constitution to preside over the trial. Dershowitz had met Roberts when he was a young student at Harvard and had once taken his granddaughter, Lori, to visit Roberts at his office in the Supreme Court.

The chamber was packed. Virtually all of the senators had turned out, and the galleries were filled with murmuring guests and reporters. Dershowitz had been told by a Senate official that, at eighty-one, he was the oldest lawyer to ever address the Senate in a presidential impeachment trial.

As Dershowitz listened to the opening remarks of Schiff, he quickly became annoyed. "They made the Senate sound like a political rally," he says. "Though I personally [shared] many of their political views, I thought it inappropriate to have to listen to them in an impeachment trial of the president of the United States."

Dershowitz tried to keep his mind on the task at hand, but found himself thinking about his family. "I knew my family didn't want me to be there, and I was considering the impact this would have on their lives."

Dershowitz was roused from his thoughts when he was called to the podium by the Chief Justice. Picking up his printed-out speech and a first edition of the *Federalist Papers* and a volume of Blackstone's commentaries, he walked slowly to the podium. As he looked out to the sea of senators, he could see his former students Mitt Romney and Ted Cruz, along with his former colleague Elizabeth Warren. Carolyn and Elon were looking down from the gallery above.

"Mr. Chief Justice," he opened with a glance behind him at Roberts. "Distinguished senators, our friends"—turning to Schiff's table—"and fellow lawyers"—turning to the defense table.

"It is a great honor for me to stand before you to present a constitutional argument against the impeachment and removal not only of
this president, but of all and any future presidents, who may be charged
with the unconstitutional grounds of 'abuse of power' and 'obstruction of
Congress,'" he read off calmly from his prepared notes. "I stand before you
today as I stood in 1973 and 1974 for the protection of the constitutional
and procedural rights of Richard Nixon—who I personally abhorred and
whose impeachment I personally favored—and as I stood for the rights of
Bill Clinton, who I admired and whose impeachment I strongly opposed.
I stand against the application and misapplication of the constitutional
criteria in every case and against any president, without regard to whether
I support his or her parties or policies."

Glancing up from his notes and scanning the room, Dershowitz added
an unprepared comment: "I am here today because I *love my country* and
our Constitution. Everyone in this room shares that love."

"I will argue that our Constitution and its terms 'high crimes and misdemeanors' do not encompass the two articles charging 'abuse of power'
and 'obstruction of Congress,'" he said, turning back to his notes. "The
conclusion I will offer for your consideration is similar, though not identical, to that advocated by the highly respected Justice Benjamin Curtis,
who as you know dissented from the Supreme Court's notorious decision
in *Dred Scott*, and who, after resigning in protest from the high court,
served as counsel to President Andrew Johnson in the Senate impeachment trial. He argued, and I quote, that 'There can be no crime, there
can be no misdemeanor without a law, written or unwritten, express or
implied.' In so arguing, he was echoing the conclusion reached by Dean
Theodore Dwight of the Columbia Law School, who wrote in 1867 just
before the impeachment: 'Unless the crime is specifically named in the
Constitution—treason and bribery—impeachments, like indictments,
can only be instituted for crimes committed against the statutory law of
the United States.'"

At one point, Dershowitz noticed Senator Mike Lee, whose father had
clerked on the Supreme Court the same time as Dershowitz, and occasionally, he attempted to look directly at Lee, believing Lee would appreciate
the argument he was making. Dershowitz also noticed Bernie Sanders,

whom he had publicly condemned for his friendship with the anti-Israel British politician Jeremy Corbyn. Bernie glowered at Dershowitz throughout the speech, and occasionally, Dershowitz locked him in an eagle-eye gaze.

Throughout the speech, Dershowitz remained measured in his tone. At times, his law professor side came out as he made impassioned, off-the-cuff remarks and threw out hypotheticals with vivid hand motions.

"Congresswoman Maxine Waters recently put it more succinctly in the context of a presidential impeachment," Dershowitz read from his notes partway through the speech. "Here's what she said: 'Impeachment is whatever Congress says it is. There is no law.'" Turning away from his notes and looking to his right at Schiff and the House managers, Dershowitz declared, "For Congress to ignore the specific words of the Constitution itself and substitute its own judgments would be for Congress to do what it is accusing the president of doing.

"And no one is above the law," he concluded with great emphasis in his voice.

"During the broad debate about whether a president should be subject to impeachment, proponents of impeachment used vague and open-ended terms such as 'unfit,' 'obnoxious,' 'corrupt,' 'misconduct,' 'misbehavior,' 'negligence,' 'malpractice,' 'perfidy,' 'treachery,' 'incapacity,' 'peculation,' and 'maladministration,'" he stated at another point. "They worried that a president might quote 'pervert his administration into a scheme of speculation or oppression,' that he might be 'corrupted by foreign influence' and yes—this is important—that he might have 'great opportunities of abusing his power.' . . . But not a single one of the Framers suggested that these general fears, justifying the need for an impeachment-and-removal mechanism, should automatically be accepted as specific criterion for impeachment. Far from it, as Gouverneur Morris aptly put it: 'Corruption and some other offenses . . . ought to be impeachable, but . . . the cases ought to be enumerated and defined.'

"In our long history, many presidents have been accused of abusing their powers," he continued, citing over a dozen examples from Washington to Obama. "By their very nature, words like 'abuse of power' and 'obstruction of Congress' are standardless. It's impossible to put standards into words like that. Both are subjective matters of degree and amenable to varying partisan interpretations. It's impossible to know in advance whether a given action will subsequently be deemed to be on one side or the other of the line. Indeed, the same action, with the same state of mind, can be deemed abusive or obstructive when done by one person but not when done by another."

Once again adding a remark from his notes, Dershowitz scanned his head around the room and senators and forcefully stated: "That is the essence of what the rule of law *is not*: when you have a criteria that could be applied to one person in one way and another person in another way, and they both fit within the terms abuse of power."

After detailing the Anglo-American scholarship on impeachment and shredding modern left-leaning academics, Dershowitz concluded, "I end this presentation with a nonpartisan plea for fair consideration of my arguments and those made by counsel and managers on *both* sides. I willingly acknowledge that the academic consensus is that criminal conduct is not required for impeachment, and that 'abuse of power' and 'obstruction of Congress' are sufficient: I have read and respectfully considered the academic work of my many colleagues who disagree with my view and the few who accept it. I do my own research and I do my own thinking and have never bowed to the majority on intellectual or scholarly matters.

"I am here today because I love my country," he reiterated. Without looking down at his notes, he added, "I love the country that welcomed my grandparents and made them into great patriots and supporters of the freest, most wonderful country in the history of the world.

"I love our Constitution—the greatest and most enduring document in the history of humankind," he passionately declared. "I respectfully urge you not to let your feelings about one man—*strong as they may be*—to establish a precedent that would undo the work of our founders, injure the constitutional future of our children, and cause irreparable damage to the delicate balance of our system of separation of powers and checks and balances. As Justice Curtis said during the trial of Andrew Johnson: 'A greater principle' is at stake 'than the fate of any particular president.' The fate of future presidents—of different parties and policies—is also at stake, as is the fate of our constitutional system. The passions and fears of the moment must not blind us to our past and to our future."

After thanking his distinguished listeners, Dershowitz gathered his notes and books and walked back to the defense table.

"Although they've been few and far between, there have been times I've listened to Alan when he didn't do such a great job," says Carolyn. "But I thought he did an incredible job in the Senate. He was amazing. He was substantive, very articulate, and he built the constitutional case carefully and persuasively. I thought, 'Well, maybe people will see how serious he was about the constitutional issues, and there won't be repercussions after all.'"

"I thought Alan did a masterful job," says Jay Sekulow. "He helped set a substantive tone for the rest of the proceedings. And it was so impressive to watch senators, both Republicans and Democrats, coming up to him saying, 'Professor Dershowitz!' and saying that they were glad to see him."

After the speech, Ted Cruz walked up to greet his old law professor, along with Mitt Romney, who warmly reminded Dershowitz that he had given Romney an A+ in Criminal Law. Romney took issue with Dershowitz's argument, though, citing a hypothetical case of a president only pardoning members of his or her own political party. "Wouldn't that be an impeachable crime?" asked Romney. "No, it wouldn't be," Dershowitz replied. "It would be a terrible thing—it would be something that would cause me to vote against him. But the pardon power is vested in the president, and many presidents have used friendship—maybe even political contributions and partisanship—in granting pardons. Wrong! But not impeachable."

Norm Eisen, one of the lawyers for the Democrats, told Dershowitz he disagreed with his argument but said he had made a brilliant presentation. Elizabeth Warren was not so gracious. When Warren was on the faculty of Harvard Law School in the 1990s, she and Dershowitz and their colleagues had a weekly lunch in the cafeteria, and when Warren ran for a Senate seat in Massachusetts, she reached out to Dershowitz to help educate her on the complexities related to Israel and the Middle East. "While at Harvard, her political views were similar to mine," says Dershowitz. "She was not then a radical leftist. She changed when she got into the Senate. I tried to give her helpful advice on the Middle East, but failed. She turned into a completely one-sided zealot against Israel."

When Dershowitz bumped into Warren in the Senate hallway, she nastily remarked that she had not understood a word Dershowitz said. "Well, that's more a reflection on you than me," Dershowitz shot back.

Dershowitz's speech was filmed by several news outlets and gained nearly two million views on YouTube. Dershowitz's inbox quickly filled up with notes from both admirers and critics.

On Tuesday, Dershowitz got a call from Trump expressing appreciation for the speech. "You know, Alan, you should thank me," commented Trump, "for making you famous."

"Alan worked with our people, but I did not consult with him before the speech," says Trump. "When he stood before the Senate, he gave an extremely complex version of everything. He had a very complex subject. But he did a good job. A lot of people understood what he was saying, but others did not—it was over their heads."

That day, Dershowitz was invited by both Trump and Netanyahu to attend the unveiling of the "Peace to Prosperity" plan which Jared Kushner had sent to Dershowitz for review some time back. In exchange for Israel retaining its West Bank settlements and Jerusalem as its capital, the plan called for the creation of a Palestinian state with limited sovereignty. The United States would open an embassy in the new country and also arrange $50 billion of investments in the West Bank, Gaza, Egypt, and Jordan.

Unfortunately for Trump's Middle East team, the Palestinians quickly rejected the proposal.

After the ceremony, Dershowitz got a call from Mitchell Webber, one of Trump's lawyers, asking him to come back to the Senate on Wednesday to help answer senators' questions during a scheduled Q&A period. Carolyn advised her husband against it, saying he had done a great job on Monday and could potentially walk into a minefield by returning. But after Webber urged Dershowitz that he had an obligation to return since the senators might ask questions about his speech on Monday, Dershowitz decided to go back to the Capitol.

"There are three possible motives that a political figure can have," answered Dershowitz in reply to a question from Ted Cruz. "One, a motive in the public interest . . . the second is in his own political interest; and the third, which hasn't been mentioned, would be in his own financial interest, his own pure financial interest, just putting money in the bank. I want to focus on the second one for just one moment. Every public official whom I know believes that his election is in the public interest. Mostly, you are right. Your election is in the public interest. If a president does something which he believes will help him get elected in the public interest—that cannot be the kind of quid pro quo that results in impeachment. . . . [It] cannot be a corrupt motive if you have a mixed motive that partially involves the national interest, partially involves electoral, and does not involve personal pecuniary interest."

That week, several Senators privately thanked Dershowitz for his work and publicly acknowledged his contribution to the trial. "All I can tell you—as we've gone on with the trial, the talk [Democrats] dislike the most is what comes from Professor Dershowitz," Republican Mike Braun of Indiana told the hosts of *Fox & Friends*. "The whole dynamic changed where it got more defensive on the prosecution side."

Amid this adulation, Carolyn's worst fear was realized. CNN took the following segment from one of Dershowitz's answers and played it as a stand-alone clip: "Every public official whom I know believes that his election is in the public interest. Mostly, you are right. Your election is in the public interest. And if a president does something which he believes will help him get elected in the public interest—that cannot be the kind of quid pro quo that results in impeachment."

It was a damning clip. Although the *Wall Street Journal* and the *New York Times* corrected CNN and did not follow the network's lead, many outlets did, and Dershowitz was hit by a tsunami of condemnation.

"[He's giving Trump a] license to commit crimes," said CNN's Joe Lockhart, who added that such an argument came from the likes of Stalin, Mussolini, and Hitler. "[He's saying a president is] immune from every criminal act, so long as they could plausibly claim they did it to boost their reelection effort," said commentator Paul Begala.

With his glasses on the bridge of his nose, Chuck Schumer commented to reporters: "On Monday night, Mr. Dershowitz advanced a scarcely believable argument of impeachment. Yesterday he went even further, suggesting that because presidents believe their reelection is in the public interest—when they do things to benefit their reelection, it is in the public interest, and they can basically do whatever they want. I hear he's correcting it on TV today. That seems to be Mr. Dershowitz's pattern—he gives a statement on the floor and then spends the next day correcting it. What a load of nonsense! By Dershowitz logic, President Nixon did nothing wrong in Watergate. . . . The Dershowitz argument frankly would unleash a monster—more aptly, it would unleash a monarch."

"Imagine that you would say—ever, of any president, no matter who he or she is or whatever part—if the president thinks that his or her presidency . . . is good for the country, then any action is justified—including encouraging a foreign government to have an impact on our elections," said Nancy Pelosi angrily to the press corps. "I think [the President's lawyers] disgraced themselves terribly in terms of their violation of what our Constitution is about and what a president's behavior should be. . . . I don't know how they can retain their lawyer status."

"Richard Nixon once made this argument: 'When the president does it, that means that it is not illegal,'" tweeted Dershowitz's former friend Hillary Clinton. "He was forced to resign in disgrace. In America, no one is above the law."

"He's basically saying Trump could just do whatever he wants, by saying that his reelection is in our best interest," remarked late-night host Jimmy Kimmel, who had portrayed Dershowitz in a SNL skit during the Clinton impeachment. "By that logic, he could start eating bald eagles for breakfast and he'd say, 'I have to. I need my strength for the campaign trail!'"

"You saw Alan Dershowitz, the president's chief lawyer there at the trial, say that any action taken by this president to help his reelection is, by definition, in the public interest. When did we decide that?" mocked Bill Maher on his show. "Alan Dershowitz, I tell ya. What happens to these people? Alan Dershowitz used to be normal! . . . He [must have come] up with this idea when he was on Jeffrey Epstein's plane."

"You say uh, Professor, you've been misinterpreted," commented CNN host Wolf Blitzer during an interview with Dershowitz. "Briefly explain why you say that."

"I haven't been misinterpreted," replied Dershowitz angrily. "*Deliberately*, efforts have been made to put that quote on television completely out of context. Let me explain. First, unequivocally, I do not believe—I have never said—that a president can do anything if he believes that his election is in the public interest, to get reelected. That's simply false. I started my speech in the Senate by saying I completely support[ed] the impeachment of Nixon, who everything he did, he did because he wanted to get reelected and clearly he thought his reelection was in the public interest."

Dershowitz was excoriated not only by politicians and the media, but by his fellow academics. "[His argument was] absurd and outrageous," Dean Erwin Chemerinsky of the UC Berkeley School of Law told NBC. "[It was] on its face, preposterous," added Sanford Levinson, professor at the University of Texas.

"A republic—if you can keep it," tweeted Larry Tribe to his nearly two million followers. "With charlatans like @AlanDersh at the gates, I fear we would soon lose it. Happily, no real student of our Constitution would take seriously the made-for-TV views @AlanDersh is bellowing to defend @realDonaldTrump."

"Dershowitz May Have Argued Himself Out of Relevance," summed up the *Washington Post*.

Nearly two hundred legal scholars from universities across the country signed an open letter to the Senate which, in part, argued that Dershowitz had contradicted the Constitution. Among the signatories was Martha Minow, Dershowitz's former dean at Harvard Law School who had overseen the heartwarming day of tributes at Harvard when Dershowitz retired in 2013.

"According to what I'm reading, you're the only constitutional scholar who goes with [this] line," Joy Behar said to Dershowitz during an appearance on *The View*. "There is not one other who agrees with you."

"Shortly after the Constitution was enacted, the dean of the Columbia Law School said that the weight of authority was in favor of it being a crime," replied Dershowitz. "Now the academics all say it isn't. Why? Because Donald Trump is being impeached. If Hillary Clinton were being impeached, they'd all be on my side."

"That's just baloney!" fired back an angry Behar.

During this torrent of criticism, one headline—though hyperbolic—seemed to sum up where Dershowitz found himself: "'The Dersh' Stands Alone."

EPILOGUE

As the 2020s kicked into gear, Dershowitz found himself in the midst of controversy after controversy.

Less than two weeks after Dershowitz's appearance in the impeachment trial, Trump was acquitted by the Senate. Dershowitz's former student Mitt Romney was the only Republican to vote against Trump on either of the counts. "Impeachment hoax number one was pretty easy because we had a tape of my phone call," says Trump. "If it hadn't been taped, with all the sleaze we were dealing with in the form of Adam Schiff and all of those dishonest people, it might have been a different story. What they were saying was pretty far out, but I let them talk—and they talked themselves out. They made up all sorts of BS. And then I released the tape, which was a transcribed version of the phone call by two very professional stenographers. I think they died when we released that because it showed the whole thing was a fake deal. It really was a pretty good phone call."

Following Dershowitz's Senate speech, when CNN played the infamous out-of-context clip, Dershowitz brought a $300 million defamation suit against the network. "I urged Alan not to bring the case—in order to protect freedom of the press—but he brought it anyway," said a close friend of Dershowitz's who remained on good terms with him through the Trump era. "He's not necessarily a First Amendment absolutist when it comes to his reputation." Dershowitz's case was eventually dismissed by a Florida federal judge on the ground that he had proved negligence, but not malice.

In March 2020, Dershowitz and his wife were visiting Bibi Netanyahu at his home in Jerusalem when COVID-19 first broke out in Israel. The couple made it out of the country and traveled to Martha's Vineyard, where they stayed put during the lockdown-ridden months of 2020. Dershowitz remained in the headlines with the publication of his book *The Case for Vaccine Mandates*, which led to a debate on the Valuetainment YouTube channel with his friend Robert F. Kennedy Jr., sworn enemy of Big Pharma.

That tumultuous year brought a square-off between Donald Trump and Joe Biden, for whom Dershowitz voted. Toward the end of Trump's presidency, Dershowitz lobbied the president to commute the sentences of several people, including Brandon Bernard, a reformed middle-aged man who was being executed for his complicity in the murder of two missionaries decades before as a teenager. Reports also circulated in the media that Dershowitz had asked Trump to pardon Jeffrey Epstein's girlfriend Ghislaine Maxwell, but these rumors were false.

Trump left office with a bang when his supporters entered the US Capitol on January 6, 2021, disrupting a counting of Electoral College votes by the Senate. The events of January 6 were seen as an insurrection by the Democrats and some on the right, and Trump was impeached a second time by the House. Dershowitz was not part of Trump's team this time around. "We thought that impeachment hoax number two was very much under control," says Trump. "We had a very smart jury."

Trump was once again acquitted in the Senate along largely party lines, but the public outcry against the events of January 6 was fierce.

"I think what Trump did on January 6 was a danger to democracy because of his effort to undo a legitimate election," says Dershowitz, "which was one of the reasons I ultimately decided not to have anything to do with him during the second trial. The other reason was that I didn't want to be associated with his claims that the 2020 election was stolen."

"Although he was not directly involved in the second impeachment trial, I know that Professor Dershowitz very much second-guessed the mediocre lawyering of Trump's team—and rightfully so," says Jamie Raskin, who was named the lead Democratic impeachment manager in the House.

During an interview with Court TV, Dershowitz commented on Trump's controversial speech to his supporters before they entered the Capitol. "[I] disapprove of [it] thoroughly," said Dershowitz. "I think he was wrong to give it." Nevertheless, he argued that it was "constitutionally protected" because it was not an "immediate incitement—a direct incitement—to violence."

In the aftermath of January 6, Dershowitz agreed to represent a young law student who attended Trump's speech on that fateful day and then walked over the Capitol with the crowd of supporters, intending to stand outside and protest. A Capitol security video Dershowitz obtained showed that the police inexplicably began waving some of the crowd inside. The young man followed everyone else in and perused the hallways and Senate chamber for a few minutes. He did not destroy any property and left the Capitol shortly after when the police directed him to. Despite not engaging in any form of violence, he was charged with a felony, and his law degree was withheld. As of 2024, Dershowitz was still working on the case and hopeful it would be resolved positively.

"January 6 was a protest gone bad," says Dershowitz. "No one was trying to take over the government by force. It was akin to the 2020 BLM protests and the Chicago Seven protests decades earlier. It was not an 'insurrection.' Incidentally, the term 'insurrection' has to be defined by Congress, and they have never done so."

Commenting on Trump's divisiveness, Dershowitz notes: "Trump brought a lot of people together with the Abraham Accords and other initiatives, but he often created tension among Americans with his destabilizing rhetoric and attacks on people. Thankfully democracy is stronger than any one person. Our system of checks and balances made it impossible for him to overthrow the 2020 election results. He was a danger to democracy, but so were people like Larry Tribe, who wanted to keep Trump off the ballot."

As the stigma of being perceived as Trump's lawyer clung to Dershowitz, so Virginia Giuffre's accusation remained latched onto his public persona. In 2020, Netflix premiered a show called *Jeffrey Epstein: Filthy Rich*, and both Dershowitz and Giuffre were invited to give interviews. One episode showed a clip of Dershowitz angrily saying, "I challenge Virginia [Giuffre] to come on your show, look in the camera and say the following words, 'I accuse Alan Dershowitz of having had sex with me on six, or, seven occasions.' She has never been willing to accuse me in public, so please, accuse me on this show. I challenge you." Immediately after, Giuffre appeared on the screen telling viewers, "I was with Alan Dershowitz multiple times—at least six that I can remember. . . . I was trafficked to, to Alan Dershowitz from Epstein. Epstein made me, essentially forced me, to have sex with him."

Until that time, Giuffre had refrained from making specific allegations to the media, keeping them to court filings, but following her appearance on this Netflix show, Dershowitz brought a countersuit to her defamation lawsuit against him in New York. "I think David Boies put her up to the interview," says Dershowitz. "He wanted a lawsuit."

Dershowitz found himself intertwined in the Giuffre lawsuits and two defamation lawsuits brought by himself and Boies against each other. As months of court proceedings dragged on, the press speculated about when Dershowitz and Giuffre's case might finally go to trial. Meanwhile, no evidence was produced to establish the truth of Giuffre's accusation.

Then, in November 2022, both sides agreed to finally put the case to rest. Headlines flashed in newspapers across the world with the report: "Epstein Victim Says She May Have 'Made a Mistake' in Accusing Dershowitz."

"I have long believed that I was trafficked by Jeffrey Epstein to Alan Dershowitz," read the prepared statement from Giuffre. "However, I was very young at the time, it was a very stressful and traumatic environment, and Mr. Dershowitz has from the beginning consistently denied these allegations. I now recognize I may have made a mistake in identifying Mr. Dershowitz." Simultaneous to the settlement of the Giuffre case, both Dershowitz and Boies agreed to drop their respective defamation suits.

"As I have said from the beginning, I never had sex with Ms. Giuffre," read a public statement from Dershowitz. "I have nevertheless come to believe that at the time she accused me she believed what she said. Ms. Giuffre is to be commended for her courage in now stating publicly that she may have been mistaken about me. She has suffered much at the hands of Jeffrey Epstein, and I commend her work combatting the evil of sex trafficking. I also now believe that my allegations that David Boies engaged in an extortion plot and in suborning perjury were mistaken."

After eight years of fighting in media interviews and court appearances, experiencing four strokes, and losing ten million dollars (a significant percentage of his net worth) in legal fees, personal expenses, and canceled speaking engagements, Dershowitz's war with Giuffre was over.

* * *

As Dershowitz approached his mid-eighties, even his summers on Martha's Vineyard continued to be filled with controversy.

During his time on the Vineyard, Dershowitz spent part of each day writing in his office that overlooked the Atlantic, and he also commented weekly on the political and legal news of the day on his podcast and YouTube channel, *The Dershow*, which is produced by his son Elon. Summer after summer, Dershowitz pumped out books and articles, and for years, he would be invited to deliver talks at local libraries and the Hebrew Center about his latest projects. "I've seen him sit down while we're at the beach and take out a pad and write an article for the *New York Times* or some other paper," says Carl Meshenberg. "And he doesn't have to rewrite it. He's just got this incredibly sharp mind. Once, I was going to listen to Alan speak at some event and I asked him if he had any notes with him. He showed me a napkin with four words on it, and then he proceeded to speak for forty minutes very coherently."

According to the librarian at the Chilmark Public Library, Dershowitz brought in more people to his annual talks than the small library could reasonably handle. Citing public safety concerns due to crowds, the library declined to invite Dershowitz in the summer of 2022. Dershowitz cried foul, saying it was simply a cover for canceling him because of his ties to Trump.

For whatever reason, the Hebrew Center and Chilmark Community Center followed the library's example, and Dershowitz grew agitated at finding himself shut out from these places that had once welcomed him. In June 2023, the Chilmark library decided to reinvite Dershowitz after he threatened to sue them. The library limited the event to around twenty-five attendees. When Dershowitz arrived, he showed one of the attendees a yard sign he had nabbed from a street corner. "Impeach Alan Dershowitz—He must go! It is the right thing to do," the sign read. Dershowitz told the attendee that the signs had been spotted all around the Vineyard, and he said he was going to display this one in his home.

During the talk, which was monitored by security guards, he managed to keep to topics like the death penalty, abortion, and organ donation. At one point, he mentioned Trump in passing, but after glancing over at the watchful librarians sitting near the entrance, he quickly changed the subject.

Beyond a decline in speaking engagements, Dershowitz also found himself excluded from social circles he had once cherished. "I knew Alan's Trump defense would have an impact on us," says Carolyn, "but I had no idea how unsophisticated and petty some people would be—that they would literally turn their backs on us."

Far worse than that, people Dershowitz had once counted as close friends distanced themselves.

"I think that incident where he was yelled at by Larry David in the Chilmark General Store really changed Alan," says Sarah Neely. "I think his circle of who he thought he could trust got much smaller. The Vineyard was his sanctuary. His times on the Chilmark porch were very important to him, and he was excommunicated from there."

The person who hurt the most, however, was Kenneth Sweder. Since meeting in a Massachusetts courtroom in 1980, Dershowitz and Sweder had spent endless hours together, working on cases, organizing pro-Israel events, going to dinner with their wives, watching baseball games, and celebrating birthdays and Jewish holidays. Both had summer places in Chilmark, and when Sweder's extended family visited, Dershowitz would join them at the local flea markets and buy presents for Sweder and his family. "Alan was always buying sports cards and memorabilia for my children in the early days, and later on, my grandchildren," says Sweder. "He was the kind of friend who would see something in an antique mart and say, 'Oh, this is great for you or so-and-so,' and he would buy a book or a sign or another item for me and other members of my family.

"My grandchildren and I used to frequent a baseball card seller in Chilmark. One summer, Alan insisted we buy some cards and ask the seller to apply the 'Dershowitz discount.' Of course, I knew the seller as well as Alan and wondered why he was getting such a good deal! So, my grandchildren and I visited the seller, and he told us the 'Dershowitz discount' was that Alan would pick up the cost of whatever we were buying.

And Alan was very attentive like that to many of the children of our friends on the Vineyard."

During the Giuffre ordeal, Sweder had worked *pro bono* to help Dershowitz be rid of what Sweder saw as a totally false accusation. When it came to Trump, however, Sweder—a decent and kind man—drew a line. He no longer invited Alan and Carolyn over for dinner and stayed away from social functions where he knew they would be in attendance. "He was not particularly loyal to me during my Martha's Vineyard cancellation—he didn't want to commit social suicide," says Dershowitz, who in turn became bitter toward Sweder. "Maybe I have a different standard from others, but I expect people to have courage," he explains. "I expect my friends to stand up to people for me, because I would do it for them."

"I didn't lose any friends on the Vineyard over the O. J. Simpson case or the Giuffre accusation," continues Dershowitz. "Trump was the only case this happened. The people who shunned me thought I was aiding Trump in doing significant harm to the country, even though I was trying to get him out of office by my vote."

"President Trump was actively seeking to do harm to our democracy and to various peoples within it," says Sweder. "Previous cases involved clients who had done an act for which they were being charged criminally. Alan defended them without the prospect of enabling them to continue to do harm, which is what happened in the Trump case."

Many in the public mocked Dershowitz when these stories of his "shunning" were reported in the media. To these people, Martha's Vineyard was an exclusive abode of the elite, but to Dershowitz, it was a second home. Amid the endless Giuffre court proceedings and the hustle and bustle of New York life, it had been a place where his body could soak in the ocean breeze and his heart could enjoy the calm of the flea markets and quiet villages.

"When I think of the Vineyard now," comments Dershowitz's friend Geraldo Rivera, "and those really spirited exchanges Alan used to preside over on the porch of the Chilmark General Store, I lament cancel culture and how Alan has been savaged by a woke crowd."

"I watched everybody turn against him on the Vineyard—many were his friends who had always loved him," says another of Dershowitz's

Vineyard friends, Robert F. Kennedy Jr. "Alan became a pariah on the Vineyard. People were absolutely appalled when he started defending Trump. But I think Alan believed the principles he was defending were more important than his friendships or personal comfort. I know he treasured those relationships on the Vineyard, and he lost some of them— probably permanently."

"That's the way the left fights," says Donald Trump. "They try to punish you. The right doesn't fight that way, perhaps incorrectly or wrongly. But that's the way the left fights. They'll go to a store and say, 'Don't buy from that store.' But a lot of people, when they see that, they do just the opposite. I've heard some people who got canceled actually got great deals because of it and ended up doing much better. I think Alan was one of them."

Dershowitz certainly obtained book deals with Skyhorse Publishing and many appearances on Fox News, but he had become blacklisted by left-wing media.

In 2023, Trump found himself in hot water when he became the first US president ever to be criminally indicted. With the 2024 election around the corner and Trump an early favorite to be the Republican nominee, four criminal cases were brought against him in New York, Florida, Georgia, and Washington, DC, for alleged financial fraud, mishandling of classified documents, thwarting vote counts, and attempting to overturn the results of the 2020 election.

Dershowitz denounced the indictments as politically motivated and extremely dangerous to America's rule of law. "As everybody knows, it's the first time that a man who is the leading candidate against the incumbent president has been indicted by the incumbent administration in an effort to prevent him from running," he said on Maria Bartiromo, referencing the fact that Jack Smith, a member of Biden's Justice Department, had opened the Florida indictment against Trump.

"I have to tell you, in sixty years of practicing criminal law, I have never seen a worse abuse of prosecutorial discretion," said a now–white haired Dershowitz on Fox News after prosecutor Alvin Bragg's New York indictment against Trump. "And the left—including today's *New York Times*, including CNN—they're all cheering this on as if it won't establish a terrible precedent, which today is used against Trump, tomorrow is used against a Democrat, and the day after tomorrow used against your uncle Charlie or your nephew. . . . It's like what the Soviet Union used to do, when Lavrentiy Beria, the head of the KGB, said to Stalin: 'Show me the man, and I'll find you the crime.' Or South American dictators, who said: 'For my friends, everything! For my enemies, the law!' That's just not the way American law is supposed to operate. American law is supposed to have a crime, and *then* you look for who committed it. Not: first decide who you want to prosecute and then rummage through the statute books to try to find some technical violation."

Trump called Dershowitz to discuss the indictments. On April 3, Trump was sitting in his plane in Florida about to take off for New York, where he would appear in court, and he fired off a text to Dershowitz. "Alan, getting ready to leave for New York and can't really believe it," he wrote. "These maniacs want to destroy our country. So sad . . . Anyway, your words are very important. Save America!"

Some in the public wondered whether Dershowitz was considering representing Trump in any of the four cases. Although the president had asked for his participation, as of the writing of this book, Dershowitz had declined. According to Dershowitz, this was partly due to opposition from his family and partly because of a policy he has to never defend any client a second time, in order to prevent himself from becoming directly associated with the client's actions or ideology.

As if the year had not brought enough division, Dershowitz watched with frustration as protests raged across Israel against what thousands of Israelis perceived to be an attempt by Bibi Netanyahu to curtail the jurisdiction of the Israeli Supreme Court. In September 2023, Netanyahu traveled to New York to address the UN, and two warring rallies formed nearby. One was hosted by Americans for a Safe Israel (AFSI) and attended by people wearing Netanyahu paraphernalia, while on the other side of the street was a crowd protesting Netanyahu and his stance on the Supreme Court. Eighty-five-year-old Dershowitz took the podium at the AFSI rally. Mic in hand and half-shouting, Dershowitz praised Israel, declaring, "What other nation allows citizens of its country to come to America and to protest . . . the country that they are citizens of?"

As Dershowitz spoke, the anti-Netanyahu crowd across the road continually shouted through megaphones toward the AFSI group, and Dershowitz stopped mid sentence and turned around to face them. "Shame on you for trying to prevent us from speaking!" he proclaimed, as the megaphones blared and the AFSI supporters cheered. "It is *you* who doesn't believe in democracy! If you believed in democracy, you would listen to my talk. You would disagree with me, but you would not try to shut me down, which is what you are doing in the most undemocratic way possible!"

Following Netanyahu's speech, Netanyahu invited Dershowitz to dinner with his wife Sara and a small group of friends. "I urged Bibi to compromise on the Supreme Court issue," says Dershowitz. "He seemed open to doing that."

Israel's concerns over the Supreme Court quickly dissipated in the aftermath of Hamas's invasion and massacres on October 7. The attack had caught Dershowitz completely by surprise, and he watched the news channels in horror and sorrow as the country he loved so much plunged into chaos, heartache, and war.

"Professor, we've been friends a long time—I know this is deeply personal for you," said Sean Hannity on his show, just days after October 7. "I know, I just spoke to my cousin in Sderot," replied an ashen-faced Dershowitz. "Several of his congregants were killed. Massacres occurred— literally right in front of him."

He then immediately launched into an attack on a group of Harvard students who had issued a statement blaming Israel for the October 7 attacks. "The president of Harvard [and] the Board of Overseers ought to treat these clubs as if they were the Ku Klux Klan club advocating the lynching of Jews," he declared. "That's what Black Lives Matter was doing in Chicago—advocating the lynching of Jews. That's what Amnesty International at Harvard is doing—advocating the lynching of Jews. *These are lynchings.* These are comparable to what happened in the 1920s and 1930s in the South. And we shouldn't mince words about that. I want the name of every student who has ever signed a petition supporting these rapists and murderers. . . . They have free speech rights, just like the Nazis and the Ku Klux Klan had free speech rights, but universities have an obligation to condemn these groups as forcefully as they would condemn the Ku Klux Klan. They are not doing it!"

On the day of the massacre, Dershowitz called his publisher Tony Lyons and told him he was pausing work on a new book called *War on Woke* and was going to immediately start working around the clock to pump out a book responding to October 7. Over the next several weeks, Dershowitz wrote over one hundred pages, added a few appendixes, and then sent the manuscript over to Lyons, who worked the presses as quickly as possible to get it published on December 12 as *War Against the Jews.*

"I think my dad was always ahead of the curve when it came to anti-Semitism," says Dershowitz's son Elon. "There was a story he told from his childhood of how he came home one day from a baseball game and excitedly told his Grandma Ringel that the Brooklyn Dodgers had won. 'Is that good or bad for the Jews?' she asked. She was right! She was 100 percent fucking right.

"The reason my dad got *War Against the Jews* out in a month is because he already had written it in his head long before the event had occurred."

"Hamas's attack on October 7 did not surprise me," said Dershowitz in early 2024. "I knew they would kill, rape, and kidnap at large if they got the chance. What shocked me was the failure of the IDF to respond. I have no idea how it happened and am anxiously awaiting the report. It was simply the perfect storm of failure, and blame goes all around: the Mossad, Shin Bet, Southern Command, and every other aspect of the military. Ultimately, though, the blame starts at the top. Anybody in a position of authority on October 7 will resign or be booted out of office. Bibi's career will come to an end."

Controversy refused to stop clinging to Dershowitz. One month after he published *War Against the Jews*, numerous documents from a 2015 court case brought against Ghislaine Maxwell were unredacted and made public. Even though the old Giuffre accusation was the only material about Dershowitz which these documents contained, the media used the document dump to revive speculation into whether Dershowitz had known of Epstein's second life. Dershowitz was once again smeared in some quarters, and as of early 2024, he was being protested on one college campus as a "pedophile."

Try as he might to disassociate himself from such labels, Dershowitz will perhaps forever be intertwined with Jeffrey Epstein's crimes in the minds of some. To those who understand his significance as a professor, author, speaker, Zionist, and lawyer, though, this is a perversion of the true legacy he has built.

"Alan doesn't deserve the stigma he gets," notes Megyn Kelly. "He's had a storied career. He should be revered universally for the service he's done for America as an attorney and for the gifts he passed down to countless generations of lawyers through his writings, cases, and interviews—and his *Dershow* podcast, where he's created a record of his beliefs on so many issues. He's a very clear voice on very complex legal matters, and that's rare.

"Freedom of speech is the bedrock of who we are as America, and Alan is so much better equipped than others to stand up for the First Amendment. There are some of us who would like to fight for free speech, but maybe don't have the time or don't have the ability. Alan finds a way. He is a very important force for good and for holding on to the things that make America special in this world. If we give up free speech and freedom of the press so easily, do we really deserve him?"

"The clarity with which Alan speaks about anti-Semitism, about the Holocaust, and about the arc of Jewish history is so unique," says Geraldo Rivera. "He really has a grasp on how to communicate the trials and tribulations and triumphs of the Jewish people. He is a wonderful representative of the tribe. And he does it in a way that's not pushy or obnoxious. He's not what his critics are—he's not closed minded. If you make a good argument he'll listen, and he'll rebut it. Alan's a classic intellectual. The fact that he's Jewish and perky and all the rest—that's just the spice, the flavor. But I would put him up with Aristotle, Socrates, Plato, or any of the great thinkers throughout history. I really think he is one of those very special characters."

"Alan Dershowitz is a man that is not afraid to speak his mind or to take chances," comments Patriots owner and philanthropist Robert Kraft. "While most people play between the forty-yard lines, Alan has never been known to do so. I have known him for decades and there are few people that behave with the courage and conviction he does—something we need more of in today's society."

"The State of Israel and Jews everywhere owe Alan Dershowitz an eternal debt of gratitude for being one of the earliest defenders of Israel to emerge, as the tsunami of hatred began to engulf the Jewish state in the media and academia," says "America's Rabbi" Shmuley Boteach. "When you stand up for Israel, you get hatred. I get death threats every day. The animosity is indescribable. People need to remember how brave Alan has been. He helped to pioneer the methods of advocating for Israel and wasn't afraid of a defamation suit or any of the punitive measures that are taken against Israel's defenders. You're blackmailed. You're called a racist, a colonialist, or an Islamophobe—there's no labels they won't find to character assassinate you. Alan doesn't care. He stands up for his people. He lives by his creed—that you have to show chutzpah. You can't take it on the chin."

"As a defender of Israel, Alan's significance lay in the fact that he was not considered a political person," says Ehud Olmert. "He was a distinguished professor associated with civil rights and human rights. There were so many occasions in which he stood up for Israel in a powerful and persuasive manner—from his speeches to his books, which I read. He became the most powerful advocate of the State of Israel and the Jewish people in the most important country in the world, America."

"I have almost reverent respect for Alan's legal mind—I don't know that he has an equal," notes Mike Huckabee, who has regularly invited Dershowitz on his various TV shows. "While governor of Arkansas, I faced over one thousand criminal cases every year—people wanting some level of clemency action. I realized that I had a duty and responsibility not to look at those cases politically. Quite frankly, there's never a political upside to extending any type of clemency, but constitutionally, it is part of the job of the executive branch to review the judicial branch. In my mind, to not take those clemency cases seriously would have been a dereliction of duty. What I have always seen in Alan is that, within the judicial sphere, he recognizes that every single person—no matter how repulsive they may be—has a right to due process and the presumption of innocence. If the justice system doesn't work for the worst among us, then it won't work for the best among us either."

"Professor Dershowitz is most famous in my mind for the idea that everybody deserves the best defense no matter how monstrous their deeds or how corrupt their character, which is certainly a good rationale for someone helping out Donald Trump," echoes Jamie Raskin. "Although he and I have sharply disagreed over political matters, I think that principle is critical to a system of freedom and due process. He is rightfully known for purporting that concept—and for following through on it."

"The Alan Dershowitz I continue to observe and interact with," says Mike Pompeo, "is the same Alan I came to know in law school: a man with a brilliant mind and a clever, decent disposition. Someone who isn't deeply ideological, but incredibly pragmatic in the way he thinks about bringing America forward."

"Alan never strays from his belief of what the law says," notes reporter John Solomon, who worked with Dershowitz on the representation of a hotel maid who accused prominent French politician Dominique Strauss-Kahn of sexual assault. "He'll never look at a prominent person in trouble and try to say something in their favor so that they will notice him and hire him to be their lawyer. He argues whatever point he thinks is right, even if it means he won't be chosen as someone's lawyer and make a lot of money. It's very interesting to see him apply the law that way.

"He has certainly been a counterweight against this new era of McCarthyism. Though I hate to use a Disney characterization, in many ways, Alan is Jiminy Cricket on the shoulder of the American conscience, still trying to remind people of what our ethos used to be."

"Alan stands out as somebody for whom the principle of defending the unpopular is as integral to the law as any other principle," says Eliot Spitzer. "That is what differentiates American society from others at the end of the day: it is not the majority that wins the day, but rather the protection of the minority. That is something for which Alan should be remembered.

"As well, I point out to many people who are not favorably inclined towards him these days, that it was he who wrote the memo as a law clerk to Justice Goldberg that began the process of deeming the death penalty unconstitutional. This is somebody whose constant compass has been limiting the role of government and ensuring there's due process attached to the exercise of government authority. For that, I have enormous respect for him."

"Alan's a real lawyer," says news commentator Greta Van Susteren, who conducted numerous interviews with Dershowitz on her shows on Fox, MSNBC, and Newsmax. "He believes in effective assistance of counsel. I'm 100 percent sure Alan is not in favor of murder. But a real lawyer will defend the constitutional rights of someone accused of murder. You never want a lawyer who is afraid of what the bar, the judge, or people at the country club are going to say. Alan actually understands what it means to be a lawyer, and he is fearless. The rest of them are mostly just a bunch of cowards."

"Alan is unique for this reason: he's a distinguished American lawyer who, in fact, adopts a very British ethic which we Commonwealth lawyers call the 'taxi rank principle,'" says renowned human rights lawyer Geoffrey Robertson. "We English lawyers see ourselves as taxis on the rank, available for hire by anyone who chooses to retain us. This means that any person, however demonized by the government or the media, can at least have a barrister to defend him or her. This becomes important when matters of principle are at stake in a prosecution. Alan is a rare example of this ethic in the American legal world, where trial lawyers are free to refuse difficult briefs or difficult clients."

"One of the reasons I like Alan is because of a certain quality he has, which was also shared by my uncle Leo," says Justice Stephen Breyer. "Uncle Leo tried to teach philosophy at different schools. And he'd always lose his job because he always said exactly what he thought. Once he took a position, that was it. It didn't matter if the earth was coming to an end, if he lost his job, if he ruined himself—he was going to argue that position because he thought it was right. There you have Alan! He believes everyone is entitled to a good lawyer, and he *is* a very good lawyer. He knows the criminal law, and he knows how the courts work. Once he takes up a position for a client, he's not going to change his mind because of the political winds. And it's a good thing we have people like that."

"As a professor, Alan left an intellectual legacy as a vigorous advocate of making policies and laws explicit—that is to try to remove human subjectivity and judgment calls and to lay out precise guidelines for how the law may be applied," says Dr. Steven Pinker, a colleague of Dershowitz's at Harvard. "During the War on Terror, Alan advocated for torture warrants, and this was widely misunderstood as advocating torture. It earned him a lot of enemies. But it missed the point of his argument, which was: torture was going to occur anyway in ticking-bomb scenarios and so, it was better if there were legal guidelines for when torture may or may not be applied. And Alan was willing to push that even at the risk of courting a lot of criticism.

"Alan was precocious on the issue of free speech in America," continues Pinker, "and I think he was one of a small number of prominent Jewish faculty who did not try to hide their Jewish background, despite Harvard's rather WASPy atmosphere. And beyond all the controversies he was embroiled in, he was a serious legal theorist. His books and articles on the insanity defense, First Amendment law, and several other issues contributed to the scholarly literature of those fields."

"It is very rare that a law professor of Alan's caliber was also a practicing lawyer of Alan's caliber," says Jay Sekulow. "Alan is an American icon. In his approach to criminal law, he has mandated putting the government to the test, and that serves everyone in this country. If that principle is no longer followed, we'll no longer have a constitutional republic. The Fifth Amendment right against self-incrimination and the Fourth Amendment guarantee of due process are what has made our legal system unique."

"I think what Alan has done more than any other human being is to make clear to the public that the job of the criminal defense lawyer is to provide the best defense possible, and that it doesn't mean that he (or she) approves of murder, theft, bank robbery, etc.," comments Harvey Silverglate. "It's simply the lawyer's ethical duty. Period. And because of his extensive experience, clients, and legal cases, he, through his writings, has left a vast historical record of some of the most important, consequential cases of the era."

When asked what the greatest service Dershowitz has done for America is, Donald Trump replied, "I think giving an example of courage. Alan calls it like it is. A lot of people know what the answer is, but they're afraid to say it. Alan is not afraid to say it. He does what's right."

* * *

During the controversy over Dershowitz's representation of Trump, an article in *Politico* exhaustedly asked, "What happened to Alan Dershowitz?"—seeming to sum up the feeling of many.

The truth was nothing had happened to Alan Dershowitz. Whether his actions were motivated by principles or ego—or perhaps both—no one will ever truly know but him. But some things are clear. From his childhood in Borough Park to his career as a renowned professor and lawyer, Dershowitz constantly fought against the cries and attacks of those who tried to silence him. Throughout his life—whether it was an alleged murderer or rapist, a dissident in the Soviet Union, his beloved Israel, or a sitting president of the United States—Dershowitz struggled with all his being to provide the best defense for his client and to ensure that right prevailed over might, even if it meant he had to stand alone.

Alan Dershowitz is a legal gladiator, and the world may never see another person quite like him.

APPENDIX

HUMAN ALAN

At various points of Dershowitz's career, the media has commented on how there appear to be two Dershowitzes: the firebrand Dershowitz who appears in public and the private Dershowitz who is described by some in his family as kind and even a pushover. For nearly three years between 2022 and 2024, I interacted closely with Dershowitz during in-person and virtual interviews, speaking events and social functions, and visits with him and his wife Carolyn at their properties. I saw him when he was happy, angry, sad, annoyed, tense, and relaxed. Here's a look behind the curtain at human Alan.

* * *

Watching him interact with people of all different races and religions, I can say that Alan doesn't seem to have a prejudiced bone in his body. He doesn't care if someone is straight, gay, black, white, Muslim, Christian, rich, poor, etc., he will be friendly with anyone. Once, I was having dinner with Alan, along with my father, Mike, and my adopted brother, Judah, who is black. Upon arriving at the table and being introduced to Judah, Alan immediately launched into an intellectual conversation with Judah, engaging with him the whole meal. During one of my visits to his apartment in New York, Alan and I somehow got to talking about the Biblical character Joshua, and we both spontaneously began singing a song we both learned at religious school (his being Jewish, mine being

Christian)—"Joshua fought the Battle of Jericho, Jericho, Jericho! . . . And the walls came tumbling down." Typically when we spoke on the phone, Alan was all business, but once when I had just gotten out of church, he paused at the end of the call and said warmly, "I hope you had a meaningful church experience."

Alan is not Jewish in a religious sense, though he is profoundly Jewish in a cultural sense. Although he does not keep the Sabbath or keep kosher, he identifies deeply with his Jewish heritage, attending an Orthodox synagogue a few times a year and observing the High Holidays. Once, I tried reaching him near the end of September and could not get a response by phone or email, and since he was normally quick to respond, I became nervous that he might be experiencing a health crisis. I nervously dialed one of his friends, who proceeded to inform me that it was Rosh Hashanah, the Jewish New Year. Though I did not know it at the time, Alan was in synagogue with his phone turned off.

Although identifying strongly as a Jewish person, Alan never distanced himself from me or made me feel uncomfortable, even though I am German by ethnicity and some of my distant relatives fought in the German army during World War II.

As far as politics are concerned, it was clear to me that Alan is an old-school liberal Democrat at heart. A couple stories he told me off the record showed his disgust at certain stances of Donald Trump, though he pointed out that he does not dislike Trump as a person. For two years, Alan would not spend the winters in Florida due to DeSantis's COVID-19 policies, and as of the writing of this book, he was still wearing a mask at public events. During one of my visits to New York, Alan had CNN running in his apartment, but he clarified that he got his news from a variety of outlets. Once, I was at a meal with Alan when someone mentioned that a close relative of Alan's was thinking of having an abortion, and the matter was discussed in the most normal way possible—there was no hint he was disturbed by the idea of it. Alan also told me the only Republican he ever voted for was Massachusetts Governor Bill Weld, who was Alan's next-door neighbor.

Despite his wholehearted identification with liberal principles, he is capable of meaningful dialogue with people on the right. Alan told me that he exchanges emails every week with a Republican judge on the Ninth Circuit, in which they debate a range of philosophic and political points. Alex Kozinski, a conservative appellate judge on the Ninth Circuit whose parents survived the Holocaust in Romania, told me that Alan had called Ted Kennedy to convince the senator to support Kozinski's nomination in the 1980s under Ronald Reagan. In the summer of 2023, I learned that Alan and Carolyn were going on a cruise in Italy with Mike Pompeo and Mike Huckabee and their wives, whom Alan and Carolyn consider friends.

During the entire process of writing this book, Alan was (as far as I could tell) totally transparent. Virtually no document was out of bounds—among other things, I examined bills he sent to clients, book manuscripts, decades' worth of calendars, and heated correspondence between himself and people he was engaged in lawsuits with (of course, some information was confidential, and therefore, I was not able to include it in this book). He encouraged me to talk with people who dislike him, including Noam Chomsky and certain family members—his one condition was that I give him a chance to respond to their attacks. During our interviews, we covered some dicey topics, including Alan's divorce and Jeffrey Epstein, and he told me numerous times that no question was off-limits.

Fortunately, I was able to verify minor details throughout this book as a result of Alan's extraordinary memory, which he says he got from his mother. He could recall names of people he went to grade school with, non-famous students he had taught half a century ago, and colleagues he had last worked with decades previously. While Alan may not have always recalled specific details accurately, if he said that a meeting, event, debate, etc., occurred, it *did* occur. Early on during our correspondence, Dr. Noam Chomsky told me it was "unlikely" that he and Alan had debated in the 1970s and 1980s as Alan had claimed. Alan was adamant that both debates had occurred, but for months I couldn't find proof beyond Alan's word. And then, one day, I discovered a recording of their 1973 debate on the American Archive of Public Broadcasting, and not long after, I found a newspaper article in Brooklyn College about a debate they had in 1983 over the West Bank.

Alan is a very careful person. When my dad and I were having dinner with him in Miami, he leaned in and said to my dad, "I hope you don't think I'm cheap because I'm not picking up the bill. I don't want critics to have a single reason to accuse me of trying to influence Solomon to write favorably about me." He was never obsequious toward me. When I asked him to sign a paper granting me permission to write his "authorized biography," he struck the word "authorized" for fear people would think he directed me what to write. (Incidentally, he did not read—and never asked to read—a single word of this book before it was published.)

For being in his mid-eighties, Alan has enormous energy. Once, while we were in the car driving back to his New York apartment, I saw him feverishly typing on his phone, and I asked him what was the matter. "I'm trying to get this article off to the *Wall Street Journal*," he exclaimed. On another occasion, I was sitting in the second row for a speech he gave at a conference in Tel Aviv addressing US-Israel relations. Slightly hunched, Alan shuffled over to the podium after being introduced, and as soon as he got in front of the podium, he launched into a fiery speech—arms waving, voice raised—warning the gathered audience that Israel needed to be ready for the United States to no longer support it as a nation, which he predicted would happen "not tomorrow, but the day after tomorrow."

Alan is slightly mischievous. Early on in my research, he and I spent some time walking the streets of Borough Park, where he grew up and where many Orthodox Jewish people still live. At one point, as my father followed behind Alan, taping him, an older woman passing by looked angrily at my dad and declared, "You have no right! *No right* to film me without my permission!" "Uh, yes he does!" called out Alan as the woman began crossing the street.

Once I asked Alan: "For someone who—with all due respect—was a rebellious kid, why does the rule of law matter so much to you?" "Because the alternative is so unthinkable," he replied without hesitation. "The alternative is bullies and the rule of the jungle. The alternative is power rather than some degree of justice. I was influenced in this thinking by my studying of the Bible when I was young. 'Justice, justice must you pursue,' says the Torah. The Torah has many stories and narratives, but it's largely a law book with 613 commandments, half of them positive and half of them negative. In some respects, Jews invented the rule of law. The rule of law was an important part of my heritage, and I will add that after growing up in the shadow of the Holocaust, I wish the rule of law had prevailed in Germany, Poland, and other places."

Alan told me that the key to being a good lawyer is to be able to think on your feet. Once, we were walking through the Brooklyn Botanical Gardens and trying to find our way to the exit. Alan noticed a woman standing attentively next to the path we were walking on and asked her if she worked at the Gardens. "Do I look like I work here?" sneered the lady, who was black and clearly offended that Alan had assumed she was an employee rather than a visitor. "No, you just looked so comfortable standing there that I only assumed that you must work here," replied Alan tactfully with a smile. On another occasion, during his talk at the Chilmark Library in June 2023, he got into a mini debate with an attendee who said she had refused to be an organ donor—a position which greatly annoys Alan. When someone objected to organ donation based on the Christian belief of the resurrection of the body, Alan brushed the point aside and remarked without missing a beat: "I doubt Christians believe that disabled people are going to be resurrected with all of their dysfunctions unfixed."

Though he is known for representing the elite, Alan also does an enormous amount of work for clients no one has ever heard of. Once in the fall of 2022, my father, Mike, and I offered to drive him out to a meeting with a female client who was in a prison in Connecticut. The woman's father had been friends with Alan. Unfortunately, she had become psychologically disturbed, eventually landing herself in prison and calling Alan for help. Alan took half a day to travel to the prison to see her face-to-face and help her understand what legal recourses she had.

Alan told me that for his wealthy clients, he charges $2,000 an hour. For being a rich and famous lawyer, though, he does not parade his wealth. He wears T-shirts and baseball caps. He does have condos in New York and Miami, along with a house in Martha's Vineyard, but none of his properties are lavish. Alan does not own a car in New York or Miami, preferring to walk wherever he needs to go, and the car he drives on Martha's Vineyard is a dumpy old Volvo with rust on the outside and tattered cushions on the inside.

I do not mean to gush when I say that Alan is compassionate. His assistant Maura Kelley told me that Alan once loaned her $17,000 without interest to bury her father and also attended the wake. He donates to the American Cancer Society and many Jewish philanthropies, and he also has a policy of carrying around ten one-dollar bills in his pocket for when he sees a homeless person. When we were at lunch together at an outdoor restaurant in Tel Aviv, a clearly drug-addicted woman walked by our table and begged for money. Without asking questions, Alan pulled some bills out of his pocket and handed them to the troubled lady. "The few dollars I give mean little to me, but it could mean a sandwich to the person I give it to," he remarked once.

Even though he kept our relationship professional, when the occasion called for it, he treated me like he would any of his other friends: buying me salted chocolate and lemonade during a relaxed visit to a Martha's Vineyard food market and signing books to my family and friends who requested his autograph. Once, I invited him to attend an event where my friend Dr. Jane Goodall was speaking at the 92nd Street Y in New York. Alan's wife, Carolyn, was a big fan of Dr. Goodall, and I hoped to make the event a surprise for her. At first, Alan adamantly refused, since the 92Y had been one of the venues that disinvited him after Giuffre released her accusation. But when I pressed him and also added that it was going to be a surprise for Carolyn, he said, "Well, if it's important to you and to Carolyn, I'll swallow my pride and go." And he did.

On the flip side of compassion, Alan can be vengeful and bitter. He once said that the most important book "cathartically" for him to write was *Just Revenge*, a novel about a Jewish family that struggles with the decision to murder a former Nazi who helped kill their relatives. He told me he "loathes" Noam Chomsky, and he referred to Glenn Greenwald—whom I found to be an extremely reasonable person—with contempt, saying Greenwald was "fanatically anti-Israel." He expressed no remorse for any part he may have played in the denial of tenure to Norman Finkelstein and told me he would gladly have opposed tenure for former Harvard President Claudine Gay if he had known her at that point in her career. During a conversation about Epstein, he said that he "really hates" Lynn Forester, who introduced him to Epstein. As well, I know of two instances where friends who had distanced themselves from him during his Trump representation tried reaching out to Alan to make amends, and he gave them curt replies. When I respectfully suggested he was being a bit harsh,

"I expect people to have courage. I expect people to stand up to people—I judge people by that."

Though Alan can be extremely intense, he also possesses a surprisingly gentle side. When we discussed opportunities he turned down that he wishes he hadn't, he said he had once been invited by NBC to host a TV show called *The Law Firm*, which would be the legal equivalent of Donald Trump's *The Apprentice*. Alan turned down the offer, and it was ultimately hosted by Roy Black and ran only one year. When I asked Alan why he turned it down, he said: "Because they wanted me to fire people on the show. In all my career, I've never fired anybody. I didn't want to insult people on television by doing that." On another occasion, I mentioned to Alan that his enemy Noam Chomsky (whom I formed a friendly acquaintanceship with) was dealing with a health crisis, and he replied with a look of genuine sadness, "Oh that's too bad." After pausing, he continued, "You know, in a way, I admire Chomsky—he's ninety-four years old and still doing advocacy work. He's firm in what he believes."

There were several times I observed Alan frustrated, but only a couple occasions when I heard him become angry. Once, we were having lunch in Tel Aviv, and somehow the conversation turned to a segment of society Alan referred to as "ethicists"—people, for example, who complain about a couple that allows a nonessential organ to be taken off one of their children in order to save the life of another child. "I hate those people," said Alan. "Mind your fucking business!"

When I spent time with Alan in Israel in November 2022, a couple things stood out. One was how relaxed Alan was—at lunch, walking through Tel Aviv, schmoozing at a private venue at a beachfront penthouse, etc. He seems to be proud of Israel like he would be proud of one of his children or relatives—which brings to mind a comment his uncle Zecharia made: "To Alan, Israel is family." I can understand why someone who cares deeply about their Jewish identity would love being in Israel. What the Jewish people (with, of course, help from others) have created there—from the gorgeous beachfront of Tel Aviv to the incredible medical and scientific start-up companies housed in gleaming skyscrapers to the charming tourist town of Eilat and beyond—is stunning. Far more importantly than architecture, a Jewish friend of mine reminded me that "seeing your people flourish in your religious and cultural homeland" is deeply meaningful. While in Israel, it was also fascinating to see how many Israelis were familiar with Alan from famous athletes to military commanders to street vendors and taxi drivers alike!

When I asked Alan why he loves Israel, he replied, "I love Israel because it is a place where the Jewish people can finally determine their own destiny. I am a big fan of Theodor Herzl. I have one of only two hundred original copies of his pamphlet 'The Jewish State.' I think he was as close to being a prophet as one could be—he predicted the Holocaust and that the Jews of Europe, like my ancestors, would always be regarded as second-class citizens."

Martha's Vineyard, where Alan has spent many summers, is serene and picturesque, with its country lanes overhung with lush green birches, white beaches splashed by royal blue waters, and quiet villages filled with rustic brown houses and restaurants, which glow soft yellow in the light of streetlamps when evening sets in. The night sky in the summer is beautiful. "I *do* believe in God when I look up at the stars," Alan remarked once during my time on the Vineyard.

My first visit to the Vineyard was relatively uneventful because almost no one would talk to me! I tried to interview the staff of the Hebrew Center, Chilmark Library, and the Chilmark Community Center about why Alan was no longer receiving invitations to speak, but everyone declined interviews, presumably for fear of being sued by Alan.

One of Alan's great delights is perusing the Chilmark Flea Market, where over the years he has purchased many gifts for relatives and friends. (He used to cross paths at the Market with the late David McCullough, who also had a place in Chilmark.) When I visited the Market with him on a gorgeous summer day, I purchased a Chilmark T-shirt at one of the tents, and after saying goodbye to the seller, I noticed Alan buying a wooden sign at a nearby table. "I'm sending this to Donald Trump," he said to the seller. The sign showed a hooked fish next to the words: IF I HAD ONLY KEPT MY MOUTH SHUT, I'D STILL BE SWIMMING.

My second visit to the Vineyard came about in June 2023 after Alan threatened to sue the director of the Chilmark Library, Ebba Huerta, for not inviting him to speak since the year he represented Trump. Alan had called it an act reminiscent of McCarthyism. After this threat, in June 2023, the library invited Alan to return for the first time in several years and deliver a nonpolitical talk to a small audience. I had spoken to Ebba on the phone back in 2022 when I was trying to set up an interview during my first visit to the Vineyard, and I will never forget how nervous she sounded. She told me that as a result of an appearance by Alan on Steve Bannon's show, in which Alan complained that the Library was "canceling" him, some of the Proud Boys had called Ebba and issued her death threats. Obviously, Alan did not put them up to this, but I could understand why Ebba feared Alan all the same.

"People used to tell me 'Oh my goodness, I sat near Alan Dershowitz!'" said a waiter at the Chilmark Tavern, a restaurant Alan frequents. "Now people say, 'Ugh, I can't believe I had to sit near Alan Dershowitz.' Despite this, I must say Alan's being a bit of a crybaby. He should have known that the Vineyard is a left-wing place."

Indeed, it was a left-wing place. Outside the Chilmark Tavern, I noticed a sign posted by the local Black Lives Matter chapter: KNEELING EVERY SUNDAY AT 10 A.M. it read.

Many people online mock Alan's alleged "cancellation," but it is a real thing. I was at an event once where Alan told the audience that his daughter Ella (who is an actress) had recently been advised by her agent to change her last name. (Alan said this would have made him "very sad" because of the honor his grandfather Louis had bestowed on the Dershowitz name by saving relatives during the Holocaust). While Alan and I were driving through Martha's Vineyard together in June 2023, I popped him a question that had been on my mind for many months. "Alan, why hasn't anyone else written a biography about you?" "Someone started working on one several years back," he replied, his hands on ten and two on the wheel. "Someone here on the Vineyard actually. But he stopped after I represented Trump."

In addition to Martha's Vineyard, I was fortunate to visit Alan's apartment in New York, which is made up of a living area, kitchen, office, and a couple bedrooms. The door opens onto a narrow hallway with an early copy of the Declaration of Independence on one of the walls, which Alan proudly showed me. He also allowed me to peep into his office. Several *pushkas* were displayed in a glass case (See Chapter 1: "A World of Struggles"). Among the interesting items Alan had framed were a portrait of Theodor Herzl; a false German newspaper report declaring Hitler had died heroically in action; a 1948 original copy of the *Palestine Post* which announced the U.N. vote to partition Palestine into two states; a picture of Joseph Goebbels looking angrily at a Jewish photographer; a flier created by students at Colgate University labeling Alan a "child rapist" in advance of a talk he gave; a picture of a bearded Alan with Netanyahu in the 1990s; two pictures of Alan and his family with Bill Clinton; and a picture of Bill Clinton with Yitzhak Rabin with a handwritten note from Clinton thanking Alan for his counsel on the Middle East.

During one of my visits to his New York apartment, Alan went out of his way to show me a framed document right next to his office door. It contained the words "Shutz-Pass" and a small picture of an elderly lady. It was a passport issued by the Swedish government in the early 1940s to a Jewish woman in Germany, enabling her to escape the country before the Holocaust was unleashed. Alan had no idea who the woman was—she was not a family relation—but he nevertheless called the framed document his "most prized possession." When I inquired why, he said matter-of-factly, "This piece of paper saved a human life."

When it comes to sexual matters, Alan is old-fashioned. "I got married as a virgin—my first sexual appearance was with Sue Barlach," he told me. "I'm just a very traditional person sexually." I never once heard him tell anything close to a crude joke, and when he and I were at meals or events where young women were present, he treated them no differently than any of the other people there.

Alan and his wife, Carolyn, have a strong relationship. Though I once observed a minor scuffle, I saw them interact many times like newlyweds. They kissed each other in public before Alan started speeches. Once, when I was driving with Alan on Martha's Vineyard, he answered a call from Carolyn and started bantering with her in front of me. "I've got a surprise for youuu!" he said playfully, referring to a birthday present he'd bought. "Oh, what is it?" I heard Carolyn ask happily on the other end. "Ah, ha ha! I'm not telling youuu!" Alan replied with a smile.

When I asked Alan what matters more to him than anything in the world, he answered, "The welfare of my family and the happiness of children and grandchildren. The second thing would be—and it's going to sound like a cliché—my principles. Sometimes these two things clash, like during my representation of Trump. In that situation, I didn't do what was best for my family."

Alan cares deeply about his family. He told me that if he had a genie in a lamp and could make three wishes, the first would be that his son Elon had never gotten cancer (the second was that Jeffrey Epstein had never existed, and the third was that the international community would leave Israel alone and let it "thrive as a democracy"). Alan speaks of his grandchildren with pride. I remember how upset he got (which happened rarely) when he heard that some person had suggested his granddaughter, Lori, only got into Harvard through his influence. "That is ridiculous—that is so insulting!" he said angrily. "I don't give money to Harvard, and a professor emeritus doesn't get benefits at the University. Lori was in a master's program in neuroscience at Oxford and also went to Harvard, where she was first in her class and graduated *summa cum laude*. And there are very few *summa cum laudes* at Harvard. As for my grandson, Lyle, he was the only person at Columbia to finish first in his class and receive three honors at graduation. They would have been as successful as they are even if their last name had been 'Smith.'"

* * *

As of the writing of this book, Alan is eighty-five years old. Although he is mentally and physically vibrant (he walks five miles a day and writes three thousand words a day), he is in the last phase of his life. Once, our conversation turned to the subject of death. He told me that he had brought his three children to his New York apartment in 2022 and divvied up his vast art and antique collection, to ensure there would be no fighting over the objects after he was gone. He said he did not want to be cremated because the Nazis cremated Jews during the Holocaust and it gives him a "bad feeling." He also told me that the Israeli government offered to have him buried in a cemetery honoring the greatest Zionists, but Carolyn wants him to be buried in a small cemetery on Martha's Vineyard instead. When

I visited him on the Vineyard in June 2023, he said he drives by the cemetery every day and thinks about his passing a lot.

Whatever years Alan has left, he does not plan to go out quietly. As recently as February 2024, I attended an event at the University of Miami where Alan faced students screaming anti-Israel statements in the middle of his speech. He handled the situation calmly and then continued to make his points vigorously, talking out to the large audience without a mic at one point.

Once, I asked Alan if there was anything he wished he had accomplished that he had not. "I wish I had won Mike Tyson's appeal," he answered, "and I wish I could participate in some way in bringing lasting peace between Israel and the Palestinians—that would be the culmination of my life."

"You know, Alan, some of these things are—or were—outside of your control," I commented, trying to uplift him.

"Most of life is," he replied. "All you can do is do what you can do— and that is: to fight."

ACKNOWLEDGMENTS

This book would not exist without the encouragement and assistance of many, many kind people. First and foremost is Professor Dershowitz himself. During all our correspondences and interviews, he was unfailingly helpful, understanding, and transparent. I am grateful he opened up his life to me, as well as his voluminous archives at Brooklyn College.

The same was true of his lovely and intelligent wife, Carolyn, who welcomed me into her homes and made herself available whenever I had questions. Professor Dershowitz's son, Elon, shared much wisdom and was generous with his time. Nathan Dershowitz provided helpful background to the historic cases he was involved in with his brother and even welcomed me to his home in New York.

My everlasting thanks to Harvey Silverglate, legendary lawyer and cofounder of the Foundation for Individual Rights and Expression, for taking an interest in a young author and believing in me. Without Harvey's influence, this book would not have come to be.

Lt. Col. Danny Grossman (Ret.), a veteran of both the U.S. and Israeli Air Forces, arranged many meetings and interviews and helped me to see the human side of the extremely divisive Israeli-Palestinian conflict, which was helpful in making this book as balanced and objective as possible. Thanks also to Shira Allen, Simmy Allen and his family, Molly and Joel Felderman, Muhammad Hussien Get, Ilan Greenfield, Kivi Grossman and his family, Lisa Grossman, Nili Grossman, Dvir Hollander, Rabbi Ari

Katz, Yogi Levi, and Ruth Oren for making my Israel trip enjoyable and educational.

For their gracious willingness to be interviewed and their helpful perspectives on Prof. Dershowitz, my great thanks to Arthur Aidala, Woody Allen, Gary Apfel, Jeanne Baker, Pastor Jim Bakker, Judges Aharon and Elika Barak, Bernie and Judy Beck, Patrick Bet-David, Rabbi Shmuley Boteach, Rabbi Zvi Boyarsky, Justice Stephen Breyer, Tal Brody, Judge Guido Calabresi, Dana Cernea, Dr. Phyllis Chesler, Dr. Noam Chomsky, Prof. I. Glenn Cohen, Mark Cohen, Stanley L. Cohen, Sen. Ted Cruz, Lyle Dershowitz, the late Rabbi Zvi Dershowitz, the late Rabbi Zecharia Dor-Shav, Artie Edelman, Ambassador Stuart Eizenstat, Susan Estrich, Sandor Frankel, H. Bruce Franklin, Lord Daniel Finkelstein, Glenn Greenwald, Jamie Gorelick, Rabbi Yitz Greenberg, Gov. Mike Huckabee, Maura Kelley, Megyn Kelly, Robert F. Kennedy Jr., Joel Klein, Judge Alex Kozinski, Robert Kraft, Jared Kushner, Alyza Lewin, Nathan Lewin, Mark Levin, Tony Lyons, Mike Materni, Carl and Joan Meshenberg, Hal Miller-Jacobs, Lee McTurnan, Sarah Neely, Eli Noam, Prime Minister Ehud Olmert, Dr. Steven Pinker, Joel Pollak, Sec. Mike Pompeo, Itamar Rabinovich, Rep. Jamie Raskin, Drs. Kobi and Judith Richter, Israel Ringel, Itamar Ringel, Norman Ringel, Shirley Ringel, Geraldo Rivera, Geoffrey Robertson, Judge Elyakim Rubinstein, Jeffrey Toobin, Stephen Joel Trachtenberg, Richard Sandler, Jay Sekulow, Robert Shapiro, Natan Sharansky, Gen. Eliezer Shkedi, Barry Shrage, Harvey Silverglate, the late O. J. Simpson, Dr. Norman Sohn, John Solomon, Alex Spiro, Gov. Eliot Spitzer, Nadine Strossen, Kenneth Sweder, Raymond and Ricky Tison, Pres. Donald Trump, Mike Tyson, Greta van Susteren, Prof. Michael Walzer, Martin G. Weinberg, Josh Weisberger, Judge Itzhak Zamir, Barry Zimmerman, and Alan Zwiebel.

I regret that, due to word count limits, I was not able to include all the content each interviewee provided. I would also like to note that any mistakes in this book are entirely my own fault, and not the result of any errors on the part of interviewees or any other person connected with this book.

For their assistance in arranging interviews and providing helpful information, my thanks to Caleb Baca, Mary Booth, Sam Carvajal,

Steven Cheung, John Curtin (producer of *The Trials of Alan Dershowitz*), Sara Dadon, Ronald Daniels, Mondo De La Vega, Elon Dershowitz, Jude Ellen, Brittani Evans, Abigail Finan, Wyatt Godbold, Karina Green, Lt. Col. Danny Grossman (Ret.), Steve Guest, Stacey James, Nicole Kachikian, Linda Kubassek, Mike Ladge, Marcos Levy, Cassidy Luna, Marcella "Cookie" Magerer, Rachel Marble, Margo Martin, Elizabeth Moore, Darin Miller, Emily Nayyer, Sarah Neely, Caroline Reger, Emma Reilly, Jim Richardson, Craig Rivera, Deborah Shorter, Harvey Silverglate, Armig Smorey, Pamela Steigmeyer, Sarah Stillman, Eliza Thurston, Lakiha Tyson, Kimberley Warrick, Dave Vasquez, and Valeria Wasserman.

My thanks to Professor Colleen Bradley-Sanders, as well as Marianne LaBatto and Izabella Nudellis at Brooklyn College, who were extremely helpful during my frequent visits to the college. My thanks also to the welcoming staff at Goodrich Coffee & Tea and Tim Hortons, where I wrote much of this book.

My friend Mike Ladge, one of America's top financial advisers, graciously set up several significant interviews and allowed me to tap into his reservoir of wisdom about the world. His caring wife, Ripa, and their beautiful baby, Arthur, made me feel welcome during my visits to the West Coast.

Thanks to my dear friend and mentor Prof. Verlyn Flieger for her Galadriel-like counsel and encouragement, without which this book might never have seen the light of day. Thanks to another dear friend and mentor, Bill Potter, a real-life mix of Dumbledore and Gandalf, who has their wisdom and kindness to boot.

Michael Levine, a hard worker and a kind man, has been like a second father to me. His warmth, common sense, and easygoing, loving personality make him the perfect traveling companion and a great friend.

For their encouragement and kindness, I thank my friends Jonathan Andrews, Sarah Arnold-Hall, Stephen Barnett, Bill Belichick, Stephen Bianchi, Chuck and Andrea Black, Rich and Rachel Budde, Dinny Bullard, Ron Burgio, Philip Casilio (author of the forthcoming *Little Billy Kipperbody*), James and Alexandra Como, John Curtin, Brian DeCicco, Brian Dugan, Colin Edmunds, the Ente family, Marcus and Adi Fugate, Sec. Jennifer Granholm, Saroz Gurung, Lindsey Lalka, Vincent

LoTempio, Jojo Mendiola, Rachel Mazur, the Katyal family, Ron Kiener, Jerry Kelly, Khalfan Kikwale, Mark and Wendy Kiczewski, Elliott Lewis, Mary and Mike Lewis, the Ludecke family, Bridget Migas, Cody Mitchell, Dan Oehman, Tim Prise, David Nunnery, Al and Ellen Marks, Philip Panzera, Andrew Pudewa, Mike and Billie Jo Radecke, Ethan Robinson, Paul Ryberg, Randy Sanderson, Dr. Tom Shippey, Kevin Turley, Mike and Kiki Tyson, Paul Stephens, Dr. Tibor and Noemi Spitz, Joey Varney, Lou and Donna Visone, Joshua Williams, Brian Wright, and Tom Zackey.

My extended family showed me constant love. My thanks particularly to Frances Aderman (my wonderful Nana), Michele Björkman, Greg Borden, Lisa Hardtke, Martha Nikoulusi, Sam Oleyede, Jay Schmidt, John Schmidt, Tim and Andrea Schmidt and their wonderful girls, Charlene Skingley, Craig and Jill Sprague, and Valerie Wadams.

My church family often provided love, encouragement, and prayers. My thanks especially to Mary Alberts, Kevin and Sharon Backus, Allen Bingham, Larry Boone, Paul Brown, Pastor David Chi, Barb Hunt, Eric and Natty Lasch, Jim and Lisa Logel, Eric Miller, Patrick Mullen, Sue Rice, Jim and Nancy Walker, Russ Whitley, Frank and Ann Williams, and Joe and Erin Zilbauer.

This book literally would not exist without Tony Lyons, president of Skyhorse. I am so grateful to him for taking a chance on a young author. Tony is courageous and one of a kind, both as a man and as a publisher.

Thanks to my literary agent Karen Gantz, along with Michael Campbell, Hector Carosso, Rachel Marble, and Stephan Zguta at Skyhorse. Isaac Morris made himself available whenever I needed help, and he and Mark Gompertz provided insightful comments and very helpful edits to the manuscript.

Over the many months it took to complete this book, my parents and siblings have been endlessly loving, patient, and encouraging to me from the very beginning to the very end of this project. From the late nights to the early mornings to my frequent trips, my work on this book often took me away from spending time with them, and I am so thankful for their understanding and support. My dad, Mike, is my rock and constant companion and did everything he could to make sure this book came to completion. My mom, Lisa, is my biggest fan and advocate and often encouraged and prayed for me. My older sister, Cecelia, has been my dear friend since we were little, and together, we've made countless happy memories. My brother, Judah, has been by my side during the many days I wrote this book and has been a great traveling companion to boot. My little sister and friend, Sofia, provided much joy during the time I wrote this book.

Through it all, at every single step of the way, my Creator, my King, and my friend Jesus was there for me, drawing me to Himself. He has earned all glory and praise and love.

NOTES

Please note: Although Wikipedia is cited at various points, I only used Wikipedia articles to provide myself with general background on a historical figure or event when no other suitable alternative was available. Never, at any point, was Wikipedia my source for disputed facts related to controversial subjects.

Please also note that, throughout the book, some minor editorial changes have been made to quotes from interviews or online videos to correct typographical errors and grammar and to avoid repetition—in all instances, though, no change has been made to the substance of what the person was saying. Also, when conflicting accounts of the same event were presented to me, I made the best judgment call I could on what information and quotes to include, based on my interviews with the participants and, in various instances, my access to primary sources in Brooklyn College. Finally, quotes that appear from Dershowitz are a mesh of content from our interviews and content from one of his books or media appearances, but in no instance has this ever resulted in altering the substance of what he was saying.

Epigraph & Prologue
Interviews
Alan Dershowitz, Carolyn Cohen, Elon Dershowitz, Nathan Dershowitz, Geraldo Rivera, Megyn Kelly, Harvey Silverglate, Justice Steven Breyer, Glenn Greenwald, Eliot Spitzer, Sarah Neely, Robert Shapiro, Robert F. Kennedy Jr., Susan Estrich, Nadine Strossen

Books
Dershowitz, Alan:
Just Revenge. Warner Books, 1999.
The Price of Principle. Hot Books, 2022.

Articles
Chtatou, Mohamed. "Understanding the Endless Conflict Between Israel and Palestine." *Morocco World News*, October 17, 2023. https://www
.moroccoworldnews.com/2023/10/358366/understanding-the-endless
-conflict-between-israel-and-palestine.

Coleman, Oli. "Larry David 'screamed' at Alan Dershowitz at grocery store over Trump ties." *Page Six*, August 18, 2021. https://pagesix.com
/2021/08/18/larry-david-screamed-at-alan-dershowitz-at-grocery-store
-over-trump-ties/.

A World of Struggles

Interviews
Alan Dershowitz, Israel Ringel, Itamar Ringel, Shirley Ringel, Josh Weisberger, Bernie Beck, Hal Miller-Jacobs, Barry Zimmerman, Nathan Dershowitz, Carl & Joan Meshenberg, Zecharia Dor-Shav, Norman Ringel, Zvi Dershowitz, Norman Sohn, Yitz Greenberg, Dr. Noam Chomsky, Arthur Edelman

Books
Barsky, Robert. *Noam Chomsky: A Life of Dissent*. MIT Press, 1998, 1–13, 170–71, 180–82, 186.

Campanella, Thomas J. *Brooklyn: The Once and Future City*. Princeton, 2019, 2–3, 6, 8–9, 12–13, 30, 109, 284, 330, 413, 436–38, 444–48, 454.

Dershowitz, Alan:
Chutzpah. Touchstone, 1992, acknowledgments, 3–53, 56–65, 69–70, 73–74, 79–97, 101, 125–26, 134–35, 137, 139–42, 144–46, 149–50, 170, 172–78, 184–86, 192–95, 197, 199, 201–5, 213–14, 217, 219, 221–22, 227, 233–34, 236–37, 241–44, 250–63, 267–76, 289, 296, 304–6, 310–17, 324, 327–28, 342–54, 362.

Defending Israel. All Points Books, 2019, 6, 8–18, 20–21, 24, 26, 29–40, 42–50.

Taking the Stand. Crown Publishers, 2013, chapter 1.

Just Revenge. Warner Books, 1999, dedication.

The Case for Liberalism in an Age of Extremism. Hot Books, 2020, 4–7, 28–31, 41, 110–11, 114–17.

The Best Defense. Vintage Books, 1983, Chapter 1.

The Genesis of Justice. Grand Central Publishing, 2001.

The Vanishing American Jew. Little, Brown, 1997, acknowledgments, 7, 181, 187, 194, 215, 254, 266, 268–71, 280–81, 294–95, 302, 308, 310, 334.

Abraham: The World's First (But Certainly Not Last) Jewish Lawyer. Nextbook, 2015, 23, 44, 57, 89, 106, 114, 130–32.

Devine, Michael J. *Harry S. Truman, the State of Israel, and the Quest for Peace in the Middle East.* Truman State University Press, 2009, 93.

Dor-Shav, Zecharia. *Dershowitz Family Saga.* Skyhorse Publishing, 2022.

Dosick, Rabbi Wayne D. *Living Judaism.* HarperOne, 1995, 10, 41, 47, 49, 52–53, 59, 61–62, 66–68, 74, 78, 80, 95–99, 101, 106, 116–19, 121, 123–25, 128–34, 137–38, 147–58, 160–70, 172–73, 177, 179, 181, 183, 185–87, 192, 195, 198, 205–6, 208, 210–18, 220–22, 224–25, 228, 230, 232, 247, 249–60, 262–63, 265–68, 271, 275–80, 282, 284–88, 290, 293–94, 296, 298–300, 305, 308, 312–13, 323–32, 335–37, 339–40, 352, 354, 357.

Gilbert, Martin. *Israel: A History.* Harper Perennial, 2008, 6–7, 9–15, 19, 22, 34, 40, 42–43, 47–48, 50, 53, 61–63, 80, 90–92, 94–95, 99, 102, 110, 112, 115–17, 120, 123, 127, 129, 132, 134–135, 138–42, 144, 146, 149–52, 154–56, 158–59, 162–63, 168–69, 173, 177, 181–82, 184–86, 188–89, 191–93, 200–2, 211, 226, 228, 230, 233–34, 251, 255, 257, 261, 263–64, 266, 270, 280, 284, 287, 292, 296–97.

Sarna, Jonathan D. *American Judaism.* Yale, 2019, 60, 89, 152–54, 202, 216–17, 219–21, 225, 228, 259–63, 265–68, 276–77, 296, 334–36, 338.

Shapira, Anita. *Israel: A History.* Brandeis, 2012.

Taylor, A. J. P. *Origins of the Second World War.* Simon & Schuster, 1996.

Articles

Baseball Databank. "Jackie Robinson baseball statistics." Stats Crew. https://www.statscrew.com/baseball/stats/p-robinja02.

"Claire Dershowitz." Geni, April 26, 2022. https://www.geni.com/people/Claire-Dershowitz/4406087306210052245.

Quarles, Philip. "David Ben-Gurion comes to New York." WNYC, May 10, 2017. https://www.wnyc.org/story/david-ben-gurion-comes-new-york/.

Raskin, Rabbi Levi. "A Practical Application of Techum Shabbat." Chabad. org. https://www.chabad.org/library/article_cdo/aid/4494176/jewish/A-Practical-Application-of-Techum-Shabbat.htm.

Saffir, Milton Dr. "Choice of School Depends on Child's Loyalty to Judaism." *Jewish Post*, Indianapolis, Marion County, May 14, 1954. https://newspapers.library.in.gov/?a=d&d=JPOST19540514-01.1.8&e=-------en-20--1--txt-txIN-------.

United States Holocaust Memorial Museum, Washington, DC. "ANTI-SEMITIC LEGISLATION 1933–1939." United States Holocaust Memorial Museum. https://encyclopedia.ushmm.org/content/en/article/antisemitic-legislation-1933–1939.

Wikipedia. "Punchball." Wikipedia, April 1, 2024. https://en.wikipedia.org/wiki/Punchball.

Videos

Dershowitz, Alan. "Alan Dershowitz." Leadelnet, YouTube video. https://www.youtube.com/watch?v=cZyZ1Io4vEg.

Brooklyn College/other

Dershowitz Archives—Series 2.1; Alan Dershowitz's oral history with Philip Napoli

Coming into His Own

Interviews

Alan Dershowitz, Nathan Dershowitz, Barry Zimmerman, Hal Miller-Jacobs, Norman Ringel, Norman Sohn, Alan Zwiebel, Stephen Joel Trachtenberg, Guido Calabresi

Books

Albany Law Review 71, 2008.

Dershowitz, Alan:

Taking the Stand. Crown Publishers, 2013, chapter 2.

Chutzpah. Touchstone, 1992, acknowledgments, 3–53, 56–65, 69–70, 73–74, 79–97, 101, 125–26, 134–35, 137, 139–42, 144–46, 149–50, 170, 172–78, 184–86, 192–95, 197, 199, 201–5, 213–14, 217, 219, 221–22, 227, 233–34, 236–37, 241–44, 250–63, 267–76, 289, 296, 304–6, 310–17, 324, 327–28, 342–54, 362.

Letters to a Young Lawyer. Basic Books, 2001.

The Vanishing American Jew. Little, Brown, 1997, acknowledgments, 7, 181, 187, 194, 215, 254, 266, 268–271, 280–281, 294–295, 302, 308, 310, 334.

Dosick, Rabbi Wayne D. *Living Judaism.* HarperOne, 1995, 10, 41, 47, 49, 52–53, 59, 61–62, 66–68, 74, 78, 80, 95–99, 101, 106, 116–119, 121, 123–125, 128–134, 137–138, 147–158, 160–170, 172–173, 177, 179, 181, 183, 185–187, 192, 195, 198, 205–206, 208, 210–218, 220–222, 224–225, 228, 230, 232, 247, 249–260, 262–263, 265–268, 271, 275–280, 282, 284–285-288, 290, 293–294, 296, 298–300, 305, 308, 312–313, 323–332, 335–337, 339–340, 352, 354, 357.

Franklin, John Hope. *Mirror to America.* Farrar, Straus Giroux, 2005, 167, 169, 172.

Roche, Brien, et al. *Law 101.* Sphinx Publishing, 2009.

Zackheim, Victoria (ed.). *The Face in the Mirror.* Prometheus Books, 2009, 39–45.

Articles

Abbey, Alan D. "The Eulogizer: Rabbi, wrestler, entrepreneur Rafael Halperin, Ralf Pinto, Algarve community founder." Jewish Telegraphic Agency, August 24, 2011. https://www.jta.org/2011/08/24/lifestyle/the-eulogizer-rabbi-wrestler-entrepreneur-rafael-halperin-ralf-pinto-algarve-community-founder.

"Alexander M. Bickel Dies." *New York Times*, November 8, 1974. https://www.nytimes.com/1974/11/08/archives/alexander-m-bickel-dies-constitutional-law-expert-a-legal.html.

"Biography of Joseph Goldstein." Yale Law School Open Scholarship Repository. https://openyls.law.yale.edu/bitstream/handle/20.500.13051 /16916/05_19YaleL_PolyRev1_2000_.pdf.

Broeklundian, 1959. https://academicworks.cuny.edu/bc_arch_1959/80/.

Calabresi, Guido. "Tribute to Joseph Goldstein." Yale Law School Open Scholarship Repository. https://openyls.law.yale.edu/bitstream/handle /20.500.13051/1312/Tribute_to_Joseph_Goldstein.pdf.

Dershowitz, Alan. "Increasing Community Control over Corporate Crime. A Problem in the Law of Sanctions." *The Yale Law Journal*, Dec., 1961, Vol. 71, No. 2 (Dec., 1961), pp. 280–306. https://openyls .law.yale.edu/bitstream/handle/20.500.13051/14742/27_71Yal eLJ280_1961_1962_.pdf.

Dershowitz, Alan. "Mad About Music." WQXR, January 1, 2006. https: //www.wqxr.org/story/47061-alan-m-dershowitz/transcript/.

Dershowitz, Alan. "Tribute to Joseph Goldstein." Yale Law School Open Scholarship Repository. https://openyls.law.yale.edu/bitstream/handle /20.500.13051/16921/10_19YaleL_PolyRev17_2000_.pdf.

"Eugene V. Rostow '37." Yale Law School News, November 27, 2002. https://web.archive.org/web/20060114220904/http://www.law.yale .edu/outside/html/Public_Affairs/315/yls_article.htm.

Ferencz, Benjamin B. "Telford Taylor." *Columbia Journal of Transnational Law: Inmemoriam*, November 1, 1998. https://web.archive.org/web /20041223124028/http://www.benferencz.org/telford.htm.

"In loco parentis: Harry Gideonse and the Making of Brooklyn College." CUNY Academic Commons. https://countdown2030.commons.gc .cuny.edu/the-1940s/in-loco-parentis-harry-gideonse-and-the-making -of-brooklyn-college/.

"Jewish Groups Mourn Death of Stevenson; Was Great Friend of Jews." JTA, July 15, 1965. https://www.jta.org/archive/jewish-groups-mourn -death-of-stevenson-was-great-friend-of-jews.

"Our History." Brooklyn.edu. https://www.brooklyn.cuny.edu/web/about /history/ourhistory.php.

Roach, Ronald. "The Soul of David Levering Lewis." *Diverse*, December 29, 2004. https://www.diverseeducation.com/demographics/african -american/article/15080527/the-soul-of-david-levering-lewis.

The Editors of Encyclopaedia Britannica. "Abba Eban." Britannica, March 4, 2024. https://www.britannica.com/biography/Abba-Eban.

The Editors of Encyclopaedia Britannica. "Adlai Stevenson." Britannica, April 9, 2024. https://www.britannica.com/biography/Adlai-E-Stevenson.

The Editors of Encyclopaedia Britannica. "Adolf Eichmann." Britannica, March 15, 2024. https://www.britannica.com/biography/Adolf-Eichmann.

The Editors of Encyclopaedia Britannica. "City University of New York." Britannica, March 23, 2024. https://www.britannica.com/topic/The-City-University-of-New-York.

The Editors of Encyclopaedia Britannica. "Clarence Darrow." Britannica, April 14, 2024. https://www.britannica.com/biography/Clarence-Darrow.

The Editors of Encyclopaedia Britannica. "Felix Frankfurter." Britannica, March 4, 2024. https://www.britannica.com/biography/Felix-Frankfurter.

The Editors of Encyclopaedia Britannica. "Hillel." Britannica, April 13, 2024. https://www.britannica.com/biography/Hillel.

The Editors of Encyclopaedia Britannica. "John Hope Franklin." Britannica, March 21, 2024. https://www.britannica.com/biography/John-Hope-Franklin.

The Editors of Encyclopaedia Britannica. "Louis Brandeis." Britannica, February 16, 2024. https://www.britannica.com/biography/Louis-Brandeis.

The Editors of Encyclopaedia Britannica. "Suez Crisis." Britannica, March 27, 2024. https://www.britannica.com/event/Suez-Crisis.

The Editors of Encyclopaedia Britannica. "Thurgood Marshall." Britannica, March 28, 2024. https://www.britannica.com/biography/Thurgood-Marshall.

The Editors of Encyclopaedia Britannica. "Wall Street." Britannica, March 14, 2024. https://www.britannica.com/topic/Wall-Street-New-York-City.

The Editors of Encyclopaedia Britannica. "Yale University." Britannica, April 7, 2024. https://www.britannica.com/topic/Yale-University.

The Yale Law Journal Company, Inc. "About the Yale Law Journal." Yalelawjournal.org. https://www.yalelawjournal.org/about-the-yale-law-journal.

"Visit." Brooklyn College. https://www.brooklyn.cuny.edu/web/about/campus/visit

Wikipedia. "Abraham S. Goldstein." Wikipedia, October 25, 2023. https://en.wikipedia.org/wiki/Abraham_S._Goldstein.

Wikipedia. "Eugene V. Rostow." Wikipedia, April 10, 2024. https://en.wikipedia.org/wiki/Eugene_V._Rostow

Wikipedia. "Guido Calabresi." Wikipedia, April 5, 2024. https://en.wikipedia.org/wiki/Guido_Calabresi.

Wikipedia. "Harry Gideonse." Wikipedia, June 11, 2023. https://en.wikipedia.org/wiki/Harry_Gideonse.

Wikipedia. "John Hope Franklin." Wikipedia, December 14, 2023. https://en.wikipedia.org/wiki/John_Hope_Franklin.

Wikipedia. "John Hospers." Wikipedia, April 12, 2024. https://en.wikipedia.org/wiki/John_Hospers.

Wikipedia. "Joseph Goldstein." Wikipedia, January 3, 2024. https://en.wikipedia.org/wiki/Joseph_Goldstein_(legal_scholar).

Wikipedia. "Kaye Scholer." Wikipedia, March 16, 2024. https://en.wikipedia.org/wiki/Kaye_Scholer.

Wikipedia. "Milton Handler." Wikipedia, July 29, 2023. https://en.wikipedia.org/wiki/Milton_Handler.

Wikipedia. "Telford Taylor." Wikipedia, April 2, 2024. https://en.wikipedia.org/wiki/Telford_Taylor.

Wikipedia. "Timeline of United States history." Wikipedia, February 11, 2024. https://en.wikipedia.org/wiki/Timeline_of_United_States_history_(1950–1969).

Videos

Dershowitz, Alan. "Legally Speaking: Alan Dershowitz." University of California, YouTube video, May 5, 2011. https://youtu.be/bzP8ykQgkZw.

Franklin, John Hope. "John Hope Franklin lecturing at UCLA 2/11/1965." UCLA Communication Archive, YouTube video, June 30, 2014. https://www.youtube.com/watch?v=8E8XNSIz_9I.

Hospers, John. "A Conversation with John Hospers." Online Library of Liberty, YouTube video, May 24, 2021. https://www.youtube.com/watch?v=cGq2XtPXSoM.

Brooklyn College/other

Dershowitz Archives—Series 2.1; Alan Dershowitz's oral history with Philip Napoli; Alan Dershowitz's 2004 anecdotes document

Big Feet

Interviews

Alan Dershowitz, Justice Stephen Breyer, Lee McTurnan, Nathan Dershowitz, Guido Calabresi

Books

Bartholomew, Paul. "THE SUPREME COURT OF THE UNITED STATES, 1963–1964." Vol. 17, No. 4, December, 1964 of *The Western Political Quarterly*—595–607.

Dershowitz, Alan:

Taking the Stand. Crown Publishers, 2013, Chapter 3.

Defending Israel. All Points Books, 2019, 6, 8–18, 20–21, 24, 26, 29–40, 42–50.

Chutzpah. Touchstone, 1992, acknowledgments, 3–53, 56–65, 69–70, 73–74, 79–97, 101, 125–126, 134–135, 137, 139–142, 144–146, 149–150, 170, 172–178, 184–186, 192–195, 197, 199, 201–205, 213–214, 217, 219, 221–222, 227, 233–234, 236–237, 241–244, 250–263, 267–276, 289, 296, 304–306, 310–317, 324, 327–328, 342–354, 362.

Shouting Fire. Little, Brown, 2002.

The Best Defense. Vintage Books, 1983, 235, 306–311, 271, 281, 306.

Letters to a Young Lawyer. Basic Books, 2001.

The Vanishing American Jew. Little, Brown, 1997, acknowledgments, 7, 181, 187, 194, 215, 254, 266, 268–271, 280–281, 294–295, 302, 308, 310, 334.

America on Trial. Warner Books, 2004, 262–263, 307–312, 321–322, 325, 346–349, 362–363, 366–367, 468.

Roche, Brien, et al. *Law 101.* Sphinx Publishing, 2009.

U.S. Constitution https://books.google.co.tz/books?id=gIl2AAAAMAAJ&q=Dorothea+Chauncey+Freedman&redir_esc=y

Articles

Aflcio.org. "Arthur Goldberg." AFL-CIO. https://aflcio.org/about/history/labor-history-people/arthur-goldberg.

American Bar Association. "How Courts Work." Americanbar.org. https://www.americanbar.org/groups/public_education/resources/law_related_education_network/how_courts_work/court_officers/.

Barnes, Bart. "David L. Bazelon Dies." *The Washington Post*, February 20, 1993. https://www.washingtonpost.com/archive/local/1993/02/21/david-l-bazelon-dies/ee8a2864-0b59-483c-9b50-635eb2d75db8/.

Capshaw, Ron. "How Robert Kennedy's Assassination Foreshadowed the Rise of Palestinian Terrorism." *Tablet*, June 6, 2018. https://www.tabletmag.com/sections/news/articles/how-robert-kennedys-assassination-foreshadowed-the-rise-of-palestinian-terrorism.

Carson, Clayborne. "American civil rights movement." Britannica, March 19, 2024. https://www.britannica.com/summary/Key-Facts-About-the-American-Civil-Rights-Movement.

District of Columbia Courts. "Court of Appeals." Dccourts.gov. https://www.dccourts.gov/court-of-appeals.

Fogle, Jeanne Mason. "Washington, D.C." Britannica, April 11, 2024. https://www.britannica.com/place/Washington-DC/City-layout.

Hood, Roger. "Capital punishment." Britannica, March 22, 2024. https://www.britannica.com/summary/capital-punishment.

Jewish Virtual Library. "Arthur Goldberg." JewishVirtualLibrary.org. https://www.jewishvirtuallibrary.org/arthur-goldberg.

Maltz, Judy. "Bobby Kennedy's Little-known Visit." Haaretz, June 8, 2018. https://www.haaretz.com/us-news/2018-06-08/ty-article/bobby-kennedys-israel-visit-that-led-to-his-assassination/0000017f-e6c1-da9b-a1ff-eeef03020000.

Manchester, William. "Robert F. Kennedy." Britannica, April 13, 2024. https://www.britannica.com/biography/Robert-F-Kennedy.

Oyez.org "Arthur J. Goldberg." Oyez. https://www.oyez.org/justices/arthur_j_goldberg.

Saxon, Wolfgang. "From millions to jail, then crowning glory." *The Age*, January 21, 2008. https://www.theage.com.au/world/from-millions-to-jail-then-crowning-glory-20080121-ge6moh.

Sjclawclerks.sociallaw.com. "Law clerk history." Sjclawclerks.sociallaw. com. http://sjclawclerks.socialaw.com/about-us/law-clerk-history/.

Shils, Edward B. "Arthur Goldberg: proof of the American dream." *Monthly Labor Review*, January 1997. https://www.bls.gov/opub/mlr /1997/01/art5full.pdf.

Smentowski, Brian P. "Supreme Court of the United States." Britannica, April 13, 2024. https://www.britannica.com/topic/Supreme-Court-of-the -United-States.

The Editors of Encyclopaedia Britannica. "Arthur J. Goldberg." Britannica, March 6, 2024. https://www.britannica.com/biography/Arthur-J -Goldberg.

The Editors of Encyclopaedia Britannica. "Byron R. White." Britannica, April 15, 2024. https://www.britannica.com/biography/Byron-R-White.

The Editors of Encyclopaedia Britannica. "Hugo Black." Britannica, February 23, 2024. https://www.britannica.com/biography/Hugo-L-Black.

The Editors of Encyclopaedia Britannica. "J. Edgar Hoover." Britannica, March 13, 2024. https://www.britannica.com/biography/J-Edgar-Hoover.

The Editors of Encyclopaedia Britannica. "John Marshall Harlan." Britannica, March 11, 2024. https://www.britannica.com/biography/John-Marshall -Harlan-United-States-jurist-1833–1911.

The Editors of Encyclopaedia Britannica. "Supreme Court of the United States." Britannica, April 13, 2024. https://www.britannica.com /topic/Supreme-Court-of-the-United-States.

The Editors of Encyclopaedia Britannica. "Warren E. Burger." Britannica, February 19, 2024. https://www.britannica.com/biography/Warren-E -Burger.

The Editors of Encyclopaedia Britannica. "William Brennan." Britannica, February 19, 2024. https://www.britannica.com/biography/William -Joseph-Brennan-Jr.

The Editors of Encyclopaedia Britannica. "William O. Douglas." Britannica, February 28, 2024. https://www.britannica.com/biography/William-O -Douglas.

Thomas, Sophie. "The Best Shakespeare Quotes about Life." *London Theatre*, May 25, 2022.

Urofsky, Melvin I. "New York Times Co. v. Sullivan." Britannica, March
2, 2024. https://www.britannica.com/event/New-York-Times-Co-v
-Sullivan/The-Supreme-Courts-ruling.
U.S. Department of Justice. "David L. Bazelon." Justice.gov. https://www
.justice.gov/enrd/david-l-bazelon.
Wikipedia. "Alan Dershowitz." Wikipedia, April 15, 2024. https://en
.wikipedia.org/wiki/Alan_Dershowitz.

Videos
Dershowitz, Alan. "Alan Dershowitz at the National Constitution Center,
March 27, 2014." National Constitution Center, March 27, 2014.
https://www.youtube.com/watch?v=rj6JPDHEUIA.
Goldberg, Arthur. "Arthur Goldberg discusses U.S. as a world power
1968." Historycomestolife, YouTube video. March 16, 2011. https:
//www.youtube.com/watch?v=dDa73hEuLsc.

Brooklyn College/other
Brooklyn College newspaper from 1955, 1956, 1957, 1958, 1959;
Dershowitz Archives—Series 2.1; Alan Dershowitz's oral history inter-
view with Philip Napoli; Alan Dershowitz's 2004 anecdotes document

Boy Professor
Interviews
Alan Dershowitz, Dr. Noam Chomsky, Harvey Silverglate, Norman
Ringel, Nathan Dershowitz, Elon Dershowitz, Marty Weinberg, Stuart
Eizenstat, Aharon Barak, Yitzhak Zamir, Michael Walzer

Books
Dershowitz, Alan:
The Best Defense. Vintage Books, 1983, 117, 206, 406–410, 384–396.
Taking the Stand. Crown Publishers, 2013, page 144–145 & Chapter 4.
Chutzpah. Touchstone, 1992, acknowledgments, 3–53, 56–65, 69–70,
73–74, 79–97, 101, 125–126, 134–135, 137, 139–142, 144–146,
149–150, 170, 172–178, 184–186, 192–195, 197, 199, 201–205,
213–214, 217, 219, 221–222, 227, 233–234, 236–237, 241–244,

250–263, 267–276, 289, 296, 304–306, 310–317, 324, 327–328, 342–354, 362.

Defending Israel. All Points Books, 2019, 6, 8–18, 20–21, 24, 26, 29–40, 42–50.

Dershowitz on Killing. Hot Books, 2023.

Epps, Archie. *Malcolm X: Speeches at Harvard.* Paragon House, 1991.

Friel, Howard. *Chomsky and Dershowitz.* Olive Branch Press, 2014, 52–55, 57–63, 65–66.

Murphy, Bruce Allen; Owens, Arthur. "Felix Frankfurter (1882–1965)." *Great American Judges: An Encyclopedia*, Vol. 1, Santa Barbara, 2003.

Roche, Brien, et al. *Law 101.* Sphinx Publishing, 2009.

Articles

AFL-CIO. "Arthur Goldberg." Aflcio.org. https://aflcio.org/about/history /labor-history-people/arthur-goldberg.

"Archibald Cox." *The New York Times*, May 31, 2004. https://www .nytimes.com/2004/05/31/us/archibald-cox-special-watergate-prosecutor -dies-at-92.html.

Baker, Lisle R. "The Advocates." Open Vault, GBH Archives. https: //openvault.wgbh.org/exhibits/advocates/related-content.

"Bernard G. Segal." University of Pennsylvania Almanac. https://almanac .upenn.edu/archive/v43/n36/deaths.html.

Brown, Theodore Dr. "Noam Chomsky." *Am J Public Health*, August 2018. https://www.ncbi.nlm.nih.gov/pmc/articles/PMC6050830/.

"Charles Nesson." Berkman Klein Center. https://cyber.harvard.edu/people /cnesson.

Clarida, Matthew Q. "Ted Kennedy '54-'56." *The Harvard Crimson*, May 27, 2013. https://www.thecrimson.com/article/2013/5/27/teddy_boy _senate_1962/.

Dershowitz, Alan. "Comments of Alan Dershowitz." *Journal of Legal Education* Vol. 20, No. 4 (1968), pp. 439–443. https://www.jstor.org /stable/42891898.

Dershowitz, Alan. "On 'Preventive Detention.'" *The New York Review*, March 13, 1969. https://www.nybooks.com/articles/1969/03/13/on- preventive-detention/.

Dershowitz, Alan. "Psychiatry and the Legal Process: A Knife That Cuts Both Ways." *JUDICATURE* 370, 1968.

Dershowitz, Alan. "The Psyche and the Law: The Twain Do Meet," *Harvard Law Record*, October 22, 1964.

Dershowitz, Alan. "They were virtual strangers." *The New York Times*, September 14, 1969. https://www.nytimes.com/1969/09/14/archives/they-were-virtual-strangers-yet-the-government-charged-them-with.html.

Ferber, Michael K. "Involvement in the Vietnam war." Michaelkferber.com. https://www.michaelkferber.com/politics-public-affairs/the-boston-five.

Fitchburg Sentinel, October 2, 1969. https://newspaperarchive.com/fitchburg-sentinel-oct-02-1969-p-13/.

Harvard Law School. "About." https://hls.harvard.edu/about/.

Harvard Law School. "Gallery of Event Spaces." https://hls.harvard.edu/office-of-event-scheduling-and-support/gallery-of-event-spaces/.

Harvard University. "Lowell Lecture Hall." https://websites.harvard.edu/memhall/home-2/lowell-lecture-hall-a/.

Jewish Virtual Library. "Arthur Goldberg." Jewishvirtuallibrary.org. https://www.jewishvirtuallibrary.org/arthur-goldberg.

"Khartoum Resolution." United Nations. https://www.un.org/unispal/document/auto-insert-193039/.

"Law Faculty." *The Harvard Crimson*, March 25, 1969. https://www.thecrimson.com/article/1969/3/25/law-faculty-loses-expert-on-us/.

Levy, Daniel S. "Behind the Anti-War Protests." *Time*, January 19, 2018. https://time.com/5106608/protest-1968/.

Malcolm X. "Zionist Logic." *The Egyptian Gazette*, September 17, 1964. http://www.malcolm-x.org/docs/gen_zion.htm.

Mamiya, Lawrence A. "Malcolm X." Britannica, March 28, 2024. https://www.britannica.com/biography/Malcolm-X.

Manchester, William. "Robert F. Kennedy." Britannica, April 13, 2024. https://www.britannica.com/biography/Robert-F-Kennedy.

McGilvray, James A. "Noam Chomsky." Britannica, March 3, 2024. https://www.britannica.com/biography/Noam-Chomsky/Rule-systems-in-Chomskyan-theories-of-language.

Merriam-Webster. "Civil commitment." Merriam-webster.com. https://www.merriam-webster.com/legal/civil%20commitment.

Narvaez, Alfonso A. "Paul Michael Bator." *The New York Times*, February 25, 1989. https://www.nytimes.com/1989/02/25/obituaries/paul-michael-bator-is-dead-at-59-lawyer-teacher-also-served-us.html.

Nashua Telegraph, February 19, 1968. Archived at Newspaper Archive. https://newspaperarchive.com/nashua-telegraph-feb-19–1968-p-20/.

Navasky, Victor S. "The Yales vs. The Harvards." *The New York Times*, September 11, 1966. https://www.nytimes.com/1966/09/11/archives/the-yales-vs-the-harvards-legal-division-yale-doesnt-teach-you-any.html.

Norman, Russell P. "Book Review of Psychoanalysis, Psychiatry, and the Law." *William & Mary Law Review*, Volume 9, Issue 4, Article 27. https://scholarship.law.wm.edu/cgi/viewcontent.cgi?article=3024&context=wmlr.

Office of the Solicitor General. "Solicitor General: Erwin N. Griswold." Justice.gov. https://www.justice.gov/osg/bio/erwin-n-griswold.

Oyez. "Arthur J. Goldberg." Oyez.org. https://www.oyez.org/justices/arthur_j_goldberg.

Pace, Eric. "Paul A. Freund." *The New York Times*, February 6, 1992. https://www.nytimes.com/1992/02/06/us/paul-a-freund-authority-on-constitution-dies-at-83.html.

"Paul Krassner Leads Fire Island Incursion." *Village Voice*, July 28, 2010. https://www.villagevoice.com/2010/07/28/paul-krassner-leads-fire-island-incursion/.

Putzel, Michael & Pyle, Richard. "Chappaquiddick." *The Ledger*, February 22, 1976. https://news.google.com/newspapers?id=s4gsAAAAIBAJ&pg=7143%2C5292039.

Raskin, Marcus, Waskow, Arthur, and Chomsky, Noam. "A Call to Resist Illegitimate Authority." Issues and Controversies in American History, reprinted at Encyclopedia.com. https://www.encyclopedia.com/social-sciences/news-wires-white-papers-and-books/raskin-marcus-waskow-arthur-and-chomsky-noam.

"Remembering Alan Stone." *Harvard Law Today*, February 4, 2022. https://hls.harvard.edu/today/in-memoriam-alan-stone-1929–2022/.

Science and Media Museum. "From the Moon to Your Living Room." Scienceandmediamuseum.org.uk, July 8, 2019. https://www.scienceand mediamuseum.org.uk/objects-and-stories/moon-to-living-room -apollo-11-broadcast.

Spector, Ronald H. "Vietnam War." Britannica, April 7, 2024. https: //www.britannica.com/summary/Key-Facts-of-the-Vietnam-War.

Spero, Josh. "No stranger to controversy, Dershowitz remains unapologetic." *The Times*, June 11, 2011. Archived at the Wayback Machine, March 14, 2006.

Storrin, Matt. "Folk Mass Honors RFK." *The Boston Globe*, June 7, 1969. Archived September 18, 2017, at the Wayback Machine.

Syracuse Post Standard, July 13, 1967. https://newspaperarchive.com /syracuse-post-standard-jul-13–1967-p-79/.

The Editors of Encyclopaedia Britannica. "American Civil Liberties Union." Britannica, April 14, 2024. https://www.britannica.com/topic /American-Civil-Liberties-Union.

The Editors of Encyclopaedia Britannica. "Arthur J. Goldberg." Britannica, March 6, 2024. https://www.britannica.com/biography /Arthur-J-Goldberg.

The Editors of Encyclopaedia Britannica. "Benjamin Spock." Britannica, April 9, 2024. https://www.britannica.com/biography/Benjamin-Spock.

The Editors of Encyclopaedia Britannica. "Cambridge." Britannica, April 14, 2024. https://www.britannica.com/place/Cambridge-Massachusetts.

The Editors of Encyclopaedia Britannica. "Chappaquiddick incident." Britannica. https://www.britannica.com/event/Chappaquiddick-incident.

The Editors of Encyclopaedia Britannica. "Chicago Seven." Britannica, March 28, 2024. https://www.britannica.com/event/Chicago-Seven-law -case.

The Editors of Encyclopaedia Britannica. "Edgartown." Britannica. March 19, 2024. https://www.britannica.com/place/Edgartown.

The Editors of Encyclopaedia Britannica. "Harvard University." Britannica, April 14, 2024. https://www.britannica.com/topic/Harvard-University.

The Editors of Encyclopaedia Britannica. "Richard Nixon." Britannica, April 3, 2024. https://www.britannica.com/summary/Richard-Nixon.

The Editors of Encyclopaedia Britannica. "Ted Kennedy." Britannica, March 31, 2024. https://www.britannica.com/biography/Ted-Kennedy -American-senator.

The Editors of Encyclopaedia Britannica. "William Kunstler." Britannica. https://www.britannica.com/biography/William-Kunstler.

The Editors of Encyclopaedia Britannica. "United Nations Resolution 242." Britannica. https://www.britannica.com/topic/United-Nations -Resolution-242.

The University of Sydney. "The Chappaquiddick Incident." School of Physics, November 2017. http://www.physics.usyd.edu.au/~cross /FORENSIC-PHYSICS/Chappaquiddick.htm.

Time. "Trauma: Everything Was Not Enough." June 14, 1968. https: //content.time.com/time/subscriber/article/0,33009,900131,00.html.

Times Machine, September 14, 1969. https://timesmachine.nytimes .com/timesmachine/1969/09/14/302053382.html?pageNumber=153.

Times Machine, September 14, 1969. https://timesmachine.nytimes. com/timesmachine/1969/09/14/302053382.html?pageNumber=174.

Wall, Michael. "Hussein and Nasser." *The Guardian*, May 31, 2019. https://www.theguardian.com/world/2019/may/31/hussein-and -nasser-sign-defence-agreement-archive-1967.

Wikipedia. "Aharon Barak." Wikipedia, January 31, 2024. https://en .wikipedia.org/wiki/Aharon_Barak.

Wikipedia. "Assassination of Robert F. Kennedy." Wikipedia, April 4, 2024. https://en.wikipedia.org/wiki/Assassination_of_Robert_F._Kennedy# /media/File:Rfk_assassination.jpg.

Wikipedia. "Chappaquiddick incident." Wikipedia, February 26, 2024. https://en.wikipedia.org/wiki/Chappaquiddick_incident.

Wikipedia. "Stuart E. Eizenstat." Wikipedia, December 16, 2023. https://en .wikipedia.org/wiki/Stuart_E._Eizenstat.

Wikipedia. "Telford Taylor." Wikipedia, April 2, 2024. https://en .wikipedia.org/wiki/Telford_Taylor.

Wikipedia. "Yitzhak Zamir." Wikipedia, January 3, 2024. https://en .wikipedia.org/wiki/Yitzhak_Zamir.

Zimmerberg, Betty. "Radical Lawyer." *The Harvard Crimson*, October 4, 1969. https://www.thecrimson.com/article/1969/10/4/radical-lawyer -advocates-new-social-role/.

Videos

"Celebrating Alan Dershowitz: Teacher." YouTube, October 30, 2013. https://www.youtube.com/watch?v=qUMVXLkygtE&t=3131s%5C.

Dershowitz, Alan. "Alan Dershowitz on Protestors (1970)." YouTube, August 31, 2017. https://www.youtube.com/watch?v=LnfgxenJgqM.

Dershowitz, Alan. "Ford Hall Forum—Taking the Stand." YouTube, November 25, 2013. https://www.youtube.com/watch?v=Ad7vPcEZ MBM&t=1797s.

Brooklyn College/other

Dershowitz Archives : Series 10.1—all boxes, Series 2.3—Box 1, Series 2.1—Box 1, Series 6.2—Box 1, Series 6.2—Box 1, Series 6.1—Boxes 1, 2, & 3, Series 13.1—Box 16, Series 3.2—Box 26, Series 9.1—Box 3, Series 4.1—Boxes 1 & 2, Series 8.1—Box 1, Series 6.2—Box 2, Series 3.1—Box 9, Series 3.1—Boxes 5, 6, 7, 8, & 9, Series 3.4—Box 2, Series 4.3—Box 9, Series 7.5—Box 3, Series 3.4—Box 8, Series 5.3—Box 1, Series 4.3—Box 3 & 5, Series 3.2—Box 4, Series 3.1—Box 19, Series 14.1—Oversize Box 2, Series 8.1—Box 1, Series 8.2—Box 1, Series 8.1—Box 1; Alan Dershowitz's oral history interview with Philip Napoli; Alan Dershowitz's 2004 anecdotes document

Next Year in Jerusalem!

Interviews

Alan Dershowitz, Judy Beck, Nathan Dershowitz, Elon Dershowitz, Harvey Silverglate, Jeanne Baker, Norman Sohn, Nadine Strossen, Michael Walzer, Mark Cohen, Joel Klein, Zecharia Dor-Shav, Nathan Lewin, Justice Stephen Breyer

Books

Barsky, Robert F. *Noam Chomsky: A Life of Dissent.* MIT Press, 1998, 13, 170–171, 180–182, 186.

Chomsky, Noam, & Barsamian, David. *Chronicles of Dissent.* Common Courage Press, 1992, 346–348.

Dershowitz, Alan:

> *The Best Defense.* Vintage Books, 1983, Chapter 1, 163–168, first half of Chapter 6, first half of Chapter 7, 353.
>
> *Taking the Stand.* Crown Publishers, 2013, 190–197, 82–83, 423–424, 434–436, 452–453, 97–101, 210–211, 145–147, 283–285, 426–428, 159–162, 203–204, 420–421, 302–303, 121–130, 389–391.
>
> *Chutzpah.* Touchstone, 1992, 313–316, 80–82, 263, 86, 62, 100, 60, 199–200, 252, 13, 14, 73–74, 235–236.
>
> *Defending Israel.* All Points Books, 2019, last page of Chapter 3, totality of Chapters 4, 5, & 6.
>
> *Letters to a Young Lawyer.* Basic Books, 2001, 78, 154.

Friel, Howard. *Chomsky and Dershowitz.* Olive Branch Press, 2014, 52–55, 57–63, 65–66.

Netanyahu, Benjamin. *Bibi: My Story.* Threshold Editions, 2022.

Taylor, Telford. *Courts of Terror.* Vintage, 1976, x, 5–11, 13–15, 18–41, 43, 45–47, 51–58, 60, 65–66, 69–70, 140, 151, 168–169.

Articles

"50 Years Ago, the U.S. Supreme Court Overturned All Existing Death Penalty Laws in Furman v. Georgia." Texas Coalition to Abolish the Death Penalty. Accessed April 15, 2024. https://tcadp.org/2022/06/26/50-years-ago-the-u-s-supreme-court-overturned-all-existing-death-penalty-laws-in-furman-v-georgia/.

"Aharon Barak." Wikipedia, January 31, 2024. https://en.wikipedia.org/wiki/Aharon_Barak.

Ball, Charles H. "Professor Recalls Netanyahu's Intense Studies in Three Fields." *MIT News* | Massachusetts Institute of Technology. Accessed April 15, 2024. https://news.mit.edu/1996/netanyahu-0605.

"Benjamin Netanyahu." Encyclopædia Britannica, April 15, 2024. https://www.britannica.com/biography/Benjamin-Netanyahu.

Botwright, Ken O. "Professor says Israel is 'racist.'" *The Boston Globe*, April 18, 1973. Archived at Newspapers.com.

Bruck, Connie. "Alan Dershowitz, Devil's Advocate." *The New Yorker*, July 29, 2019. https://www.newyorker.com/magazine/2019/08/05/alan-dershowitz-devils-advocate.

Chomsky, Noam, and Alan Dershowitz. Exchange with Alan Dershowitz. Accessed April 15, 2024. https://chomsky.info/19730401–2/.

"Dancing to the First Amendment." *The New York Times*, June 27, 1972. https://www.nytimes.com/1972/06/27/archives/dancing-to-the-first -amendment.html.

"Danville Bee Newspaper Archives, Nov 21, 1974, p. 5." NewspaperArchive .com, November 21, 1974. https://newspaperarchive.com/danville-bee -nov-21–1974-p-5/.

"Dershowitz Calls for Mideast Peace: 'Israel Should Give up Arab Land.'" *The Harvard Crimson*, March 20, 1974. https://www.thecrimson.com /article/1974/3/20/dershowitz-calls-for-mideast-peace-israel/.

Dershowitz, Alan. "Due Process of Law in the Trial of Soviet Jews." Brill, July 5, 1974. https://brill.com/display/book/edcoll/9789004422858 /BP000013.xml.

Dershowitz, Alan. "Law and Order." *The New York Times*, February 21, 1971. https://www.nytimes.com/1971/02/21/archives/crimes-of-degree -law-and-order.html.

Dershowitz, Alan. "Letters to the Editor." *The New York Times*, November 11, 1971. https://www.nytimes.com/1971/11/11/archives/powells -nomination.html.

Dershowitz, Alan. "Preventive Detention of Citizens during a National Emergency—A Comparison between Israel and the United States." Brill, November 7, 1971. https://brill.com/display/book/edcoll/978900 4422827/BP000023.xml.

Dershowitz, Alan. "The Confession by Artur London. Translated by Alastair Hamilton." *The New York Times*, February 7, 1971. https: //www.nytimes.com/1971/02/07/archives/the-confession-by-artur -london-translated-by-alastair-hamilton-442.html.

Dershowitz, Alan. "The Morality of Consent." *The New York Times*, September 21, 1975. https://www.nytimes.com/1975/09/21/archives /the-morality-of-consent-by-alexander-m-bickel-156-pp-new-haven -yale.html.

Donadio, Rachel. "The Story of 'Night.'" *The New York Times*, January 20, 2008. https://www.nytimes.com/2008/01/20/books/review/Donadio -t.html.

"Eighth Amendment." Encyclopædia Britannica, March 8, 2024. https:
//www.britannica.com/topic/Eighth-Amendment#ref1097119.

"Elie Wiesel." Encyclopædia Britannica, April 10, 2024. https://www
.britannica.com/biography/Elie-Wiesel.

Executives, Key. "Benjamin Netanyahu Connects Education with Peace
at Alma Mater Mit—Key Executives." August 30, 2022. https://csuite
spotlight.com/2021/07/29/benjamin-netanyahu-connects-education
-with-peace-at-alma-mater-mit/.

"Exodus." Encyclopædia Britannica. Accessed April 15, 2024. https:
//www.britannica.com/topic/Exodus-by-Uris.

"Former Prisoners of the 'Little Camp' in Buchenwald." Photograph.
United States Holocaust Memorial Museum. Accessed April 15, 2024.
https://encyclopedia.ushmm.org/content/en/photo/former-prisoners
-of-the-little-camp-in-buchenwald.

"Gerald R. Ford." The White House, December 23, 2022. https://www
.whitehouse.gov/about-the-white-house/presidents/gerald-r-ford/.

"Golda Meir's Trip Ends with Appeal." The New York Times, December
23, 1974. https://www.nytimes.com/1974/12/23/archives/golda-meirs
-trip-ends-with-appeal-she-raises-276million-for-israel.html.

Goldberg, Arthur, and Alan Dershowitz. "Constitutionality of the Death
Penalty in America." Death Penalty Information Center. Accessed
April 15, 2024. https://deathpenaltyinfo.org/facts-and-research/history
-of-the-death-penalty/constitutionality-of-the-death-penalty-in
-america.

"High Court Ruling Sought on Death Penalty Question." The New
York Times, May 12, 1971. https://www.nytimes.com/1971/05/12
/archives/high-court-ruling-sought-on-death-penalty-question.html.

"High Hopes: Chancellor of the New York City Public School System."
PBS, September 30, 2002. https://www.pbs.org/newshour/show/high
-hopes-chancellor-of-the-new-york-city-public-school-system.

"History of Harvard Hillel." Harvard Hillel. Accessed April 15, 2024.
https://hillel.harvard.edu/history.

Karalexis v. Byrne, 306 F. supp. 1363. Accessed April 15, 2024. https:
//casetext.com/case/karalexis-v-byrne.

"Letters to the Editor." *The New York Times*, November 24, 1975. https://www.nytimes.com/1975/11/24/archives/letters-to-the-editor.html.

"Lewis F. Powell Jr.." Wikipedia, April 10, 2024. https://en.wikipedia.org/wiki/Lewis_F._Powell_Jr.

"Noam Chomsky." Encyclopædia Britannica, March 3, 2024. https://www.britannica.com/biography/Noam-Chomsky.

Rosen, Jonathan. "Abraham's Drifting Children." *The New York Times*. Accessed April 15, 2024. https://archive.nytimes.com/www.nytimes.com/books/97/03/30/reviews/970330.30rosent.html.

Reeves, Richard. "4-Term Governor." *The New York Times*, November 4, 1970. https://www.nytimes.com/1970/11/04/archives/4term-governor-victory-helps-party-retain-control-of-the.html.

Sexton, Paul. "Gimme Some Truth: When John Lennon Faced US Deportation." uDiscover Music, July 18, 2023. https://www.udiscovermusic.com/stories/when-john-lennon-faced-us-deportation/.

"Stanford Daily Newspaper Archives, May 18, 1972, p. 3." Newspaper Archive.com, May 18, 1972. https://newspaperarchive.com/stanford-daily-may-18–1972-p-3/.

"Stanford Daily Newspaper Archives, May 31, 1972, p. 9." Newspaper Archive.com, May 31, 1972. https://newspaperarchive.com/stanford-daily-may-31–1972-p-9/.

"The Jerusalem Post—Jpost.Com Israel News." *The Jerusalem Post*. Accessed April 15, 2024. https://www.jpost.com/.

"Timeline of United States History (1970–1989)." Wikipedia, April 9, 2024. https://en.wikipedia.org/wiki/Timeline_of_the_history_of_the_United_States_(1970–1989).

"Vietnam War." Encyclopædia Britannica, April 7, 2024. https://www.britannica.com/event/Vietnam-War.

"Warren E. Burger." Encyclopædia Britannica, February 19, 2024. https://www.britannica.com/biography/Warren-E-Burger.

"Watergate and the White House: The 'third-rate burglary' that toppled a president." Accessed April 15, 2024. https://www.usnews.com/news/articles/2014/08/08/watergate-and-the-white-house-the-third-rate-burglary-that-toppled-a-president.

"Watergate Scandal." Encyclopædia Britannica, April 12, 2024. https://www.britannica.com/event/Watergate-Scandal.

"Yom Kippur War." Encyclopædia Britannica, March 13, 2024. https://www.britannica.com/event/Yom-Kippur-War.

Videos

"Alan Dershowitz on Saving the Life of Supreme Justice Athur Goldberg." YouTube, December 22, 2013. https://www.youtube.com/watch?v=5eozxK8YKxo%3B.

"American Archive of Public Broadcasting." American Archive of Public Broadcasting. Accessed April 15, 2024. https://americanarchive.org/catalog/cpb-aacip-15–95w6mspx.

"Everything That Happened Leading up to Nixon's Resignation." YouTube, November 29, 2020. https://www.youtube.com/watch?v=Ypi_nqe2P9I%3B.

"Public Affairs; Alan Dershowitz and Noam Chomsky: A Lasting Peace in the Middle East." American Archive of Public Broadcasting. Accessed April 15, 2024. https://americanarchive.org/catalog/cpb-aacip-15–149p8mf2.

"Public Affairs; Alan Dershowitz and Noam Chomsky: A Lasting Peace in the Middle East." American Archive of Public Broadcasting. Accessed April 15, 2024. https://americanarchive.org/catalog/cpb-aacip-15–8279d3vs.

"The Road to Peace & Israel's Image in America." C-Span. Accessed April 15, 2024. https://www.c-span.org/video/?7700–1%2Froad-peace-israels-image-america%3B.

"What Alan Dershowitz Said about Impeachment during Watergate." YouTube, January 31, 2020. https://www.youtube.com/watch?v=L2wagmgiP5I%3B.

"Why Noam Chomsky Doesn't Love America." YouTube, May 21, 2021. https://www.youtube.com/watch?v=3LwjaNYHEFM%3B.

Brooklyn College/other

Dershowitz Archives: Series 6.2—Boxes 2, 3, 4, 5, 6, & 7, Series 9.1—Box 3, Subgroup 8—U.S. v. Mike Gravel, 1971–72, Subgroup 8—"I am Curious Yellow" / Grove Press vs U.S.—Box 1 & 2, Subgroup

8—H. Bruce Franklin vs. Stanford University—Boxes 1, 2, & 3, U.S. vs. Sheldon Seigel—Boxes 1, 2, 3, & 4, Series 5.1a—Boxes 1, 2, 3, & 4, Series 3.2—Box 13, Series 3.2—Box 1, Series 7.4—Box 4, Series 3.4—Box 6, Series 2.3—Box 1, Series 7.3—Box 2, Miscellaneous cases—K—Box 1—Kennedy/Kopechne inquest; Alan Dershowitz's oral history with Philip Napoli; Alan Dershowitz's 2004 anecdotes document

For Me but Not for Thee

Interviews

Alan Dershowitz, Carolyn Cohen, Elon Dershowitz, Nathan Dershowitz, Natan Sharansky, Jeanne Baker, Stuart Eizenstat, Woody Allen, Susan Estrich, Dana Cernea, Nadine Strossen, Eli Noam, Harvey Silverglate, Nathan Lewin, anonymous relative of the Tison brothers, Judy Beck, Israel Ringel, Barry Shrage, Judge Aharon Barak

Books

Albany Law Review. Vol. 71, 2008.

Bailey, F. Lee. *For the Defense.* Signet, 1976, 278–280.

Clarke, James W. *Last Rampage.* Arizona, 1988, 47–53.

Dershowitz, Alan:

> *The Best Defense.* Vintage Books, 1983, picture inserts, Chapter 1, Chapter 2, Chapter 3, Chapter 4, Chapter 6, Chapter 7, Chapter 8, Chapter 9, 392–396, 190–192.

> *Taking the Stand.* Crown Publishers, 2013. –311–314, 302, 389–397, 236, 130–140, 289, 276–278, 496, 157–159, 420, 377, 428, 433–434, 213–218, 197–200, 191, picture inserts.

> *Defending Israel.* All Points Books, 2019, Chapter 7, 95–99, 84, 127–131, 145–147.

> *Reversal of Fortune.* Random House, 1986, dedication, acknowledgments, xiii-xv, xvii-xxvi, 3–17, 19–22, 24–25, 28–35, 37, 41–43, 47–48, 50–55, 59–61, 64–71, 73, 74–93, 99–100, picture inserts, 105, 109–123, 128–131, 136–145, 149, 154–160, 165–172, 176–179, 181, 183–189, 193–196, 198–208, 211–213, 215–217, 220, 222–225, 228–230, 232–238, 241–248, 250, 252–261, 264–265, 267, 271.

Chutzpah. Touchstone, 1992, 82, 236–237, 170–171 re Skokie, 233, 234, 235, 250–260, 86, 93–101, 184–186, 70–71.

Eizenstat, Stuart. *President Carter.* Thomas Dunne Books, 2018, 487, 600.

Estrich, Susan. *Real Rape.* Harvard University Press, 1987, preface, 1–3, 6–7.

Sharansky, Avital with Ilana Ben-Josef. *Next Year in Jerusalem.* New York: William Morrow and Company, 1979.

Sharansky, Natan. *Never Alone.* Hachette Book Groups, 2020, picture inserts, 114–119.

Articles

ABC News. "Ted Kennedy: The Day the Presidency Was Lost." August 28, 2009. https://abcnews.go.com/Politics/TedKennedy/story?id=8436 488%3B.

"About Us—John Simon Guggenheim Memorial Foundation" John Simon Guggenheim Memorial Foundation. Accessed April 15, 2024. https://www.gf.org/about-us/.

"Aharon Barak." Wikipedia, January 31, 2024. https://en.wikipedia.org /wiki/Aharon_Barak.

"Alan Dershowitz, from the Death Penalty to Roman Polanski." *The New York Times*, December 12, 2015. https://www.nytimes.com /interactive/2015/12/12/business/alan-dershowitz-timeline.html# /#time392_11342.

Associated Press. "Moscow Prison for Us Reporter Was Used in Stalin's Purges." AP News, March 31, 2023. https://apnews.com/article /moscow-lefortovo-prison-gershkovich-russia-wall-street-journal -2b160207d8c08f8ca0cc30b619daf6e9.

Bandow, Doug. "The Rise and Fall of Nicolae Ceausescu, 'the Romanian Fuehrer.'" Cato Institute, December 31, 2019. https://www.cato.org /commentary/rise-fall-nicolae-ceausescu-romanian-fuehrer.

"Barbara Walters." D23, December 31, 2022. https://d23.com/walt-disney -legend/barbara-walters/.

Betts, Jennifer. "US Divorce Rates over Time and What the Numbers Really Mean." LoveToKnow, June 5, 2023. https://www.lovetoknow .com/life/relationships/historical-divorce-rate-statistics.

Bruck, Connie. "Alan Dershowitz, Devil's Advocate." *The New Yorker*, July 29, 2019. https://www.newyorker.com/magazine/2019/08/05/alan -dershowitz-devils-advocate.

Buckley, William F. "Be Loyal to Your God—Don't See the Movie." *The Washington Post*, August 15, 1988. https://www.washingtonpost.com /archive/opinions/1988/08/16/be-loyal-to-your-god_dont-see-the -movie/6f5ce63e-314c-42cc-870e-107ec04e71ef/.

"Camp David Accords." Encyclopædia Britannica, April 1, 2024. https: //www.britannica.com/event/Camp-David-Accords.

"Clearing the Throat." *The Harvard Crimson*. September 15, 1980. https://www.thecrimson.com/article/1980/9/15/clearing-the-throat -pyour-honor-if/.

Clendinen, Dudley. "Jurors Find von Bulow Guilty of Trying Twice to Kill Wife." *The New York Times*, March 17, 1982. https://www.nytimes .com/1982/03/17/nyregion/jurors-find-von-bulow-guilty-of-trying -twice-to-kill-wife.html.

Clendinen, Dudley. "Prosecution and Defense Outline von Bulow Cases." *The New York Times*, February 3, 1982. https://www.nytimes .com/1982/02/03/us/prosecution-and-defense-outline-von-bulow -cases.html.

Cohen, Marns F. "Dershowitz to Argue von Bulow Appeal." *The Harvard Crimson*, November 20, 1982. https://www.thecrimson.com/article /1982/11/20/dershowitz-to-argue-von-bulow-appeal/.

Cotler, Irwin. "A remarkable man, a remarkable legacy." Maclean's, December 6, 2013. https://macleans.ca/news/world/a-remarkable-man-a-remarkable -legacy/.

"Danville Bee Newspaper Archives, Nov 21, 1974, p. 5." Newspaper Archive.com, November 21, 1974. https://newspaperarchive.com /danville-bee-nov-21–1974-p-5/.

Dershowitz, Alan. "Free Free Speech." *The New York Times*, February 9, 1979. https://www.nytimes.com/1979/02/09/archives/freefreespeech .html.

Dershowitz, Alan. "Let the Punishment (Published 1975)." *The New York Times*, December 28, 1975. https://www.nytimes.com/1975/12/28 /archives/let-the-punishment-fit-the-crime-indeterminate-prison -sentences-a.html%20-;.

Dershowitz, Alan. "The Source of Justice in the Mind of a Justice." *The New York Times*, February 22, 1981. https://www.nytimes.com/1981/02/22/books/the-source-of-justice-in-the-mind-of-a-justice.html.

Dershowitz, Alan. "The Special Victim Is Not New in the Law." *The New York Times*, March 27, 1977. https://www.nytimes.com/1977/03/27/archives/the-special-victim-is-not-new-in-the-law-but-the-elderly-of-new.html.

Dershowitz, Alan. "Unequal Justice." *The New York Times*, January 25, 1976. https://www.nytimes.com/1976/01/25/archives/unequal-justice-counselor-counsel-thyself.html.

Doorn, John van. "A Look Into the Future." *NEXT* magazine, April 1981.

"Firing Line (TV Program)." Wikipedia, March 12, 2024. https://en.wikipedia.org/wiki/Firing_Line_(TV_program).

"First Lebanon War." The Kahan Commission of Inquiry. Accessed April 15, 2024. https://www.jewishvirtuallibrary.org/the-kahan-commission-of-inquiry.

Freedman, Eliyahu. "Irwin Cotler, Who Advocated for Natan Sharansky and Nelson Mandela, Awarded Israel's Presidential Medal of Honor." *The Canadian Jewish News*, September 7, 2023. https://thecjn.ca/news/irwin-cotler-who-advocated-for-natan-sharansky-and-nelson-mandela-awarded-israels-presidential-medal-of-honor/.

Freedman, Monroe H., and Alan. "Israeli Torture, They Said." *The New York Times*, June 2, 1978. https://www.nytimes.com/1978/06/02/archives/israeli-torture-they-said.html.

Goldstein, Tom. "Notables Aid Convicted 'Deep Throat' Star." *The New York Times*, June 29, 1976. https://www.nytimes.com/1976/06/29/archives/notables-aid-convicted-deep-throat-star.html.

"Helsinki Accords." Encyclopædia Britannica. Accessed April 15, 2024. https://www.britannica.com:443/event/Helsinki-Accords.

"Inside the Sanctum Sanctorum; Douglas." *The New York Times*. Accessed April 15, 2024. https://timesmachine.nytimes.com/timesmachine/1980/11/02/112166239.html?pageNumber=110%3B.

"Irwin Cotler." encyclopedia.com. Accessed April 15, 2024. https://www.encyclopedia.com/religion/encyclopedias-almanacs-transcripts-and-maps/cotler-irwin.

"Jimmy Carter Summary." Encyclopædia Britannica. Accessed April 15, 2024. https://www.britannica.com/summary/Jimmy-Carter.

Kuznetsov, Eduard S. "FLIGHT FROM THE GULAG." *The New York Times*, April 27, 1980. https://www.nytimes.com/1980/04/27/archives/flight-from-the-gulag-april-25–1979-april-26–1979-kuznetsov-april.html.

Niven, David. "Why Do You Want to be President?" Medium, August 26, 2015. https://medium.com/@nivenpolitics/why-do-you-want-to-be-president-29ce11fbf164.

"Nicolae Ceaușescu." Encyclopædia Britannica, March 28, 2024. https://www.britannica.com/biography/Nicolae-Ceausescu.

"P.L.O. Is a Friend of the News Media." *The New York Times*, March 2, 1982. https://www.nytimes.com/1982/03/02/opinion/l-plo-is-a-friend-of-the-news-media-226971.html.

"Palestine Liberation Organization." Encyclopædia Britannica, April 10, 2024. https://www.britannica.com/topic/Palestine-Liberation-Organization.

"Register of the Firing Line (Television Program) Broadcast Records." Online Archive of California. Accessed April 15, 2024. https://oac.cdlib.org/findaid/ark:/13030/kt6m3nc88c/entire_text/.

Staff, CIE. "Zionism Is Racism UNGA Resolution 3379." CIE, July 3, 2018. https://israeled.org/resources/documents/zionism-racism-unga-resolution-3379/.

"Stuart E. Eizenstat." Wikipedia, December 16, 2023. https://en.wikipedia.org/wiki/Stuart_E._Eizenstat.

Susan Estrich. Accessed April 15, 2024. https://www.estrichgoldin.com/susan-estrich.

"Susan Estrich." Wikipedia, February 26, 2023. https://en.wikipedia.org/wiki/Susan_Estrich.

"The General Election Campaign." Encyclopædia Britannica. Accessed April 15, 2024. https://www.britannica.com/event/United-States-presidential-election-of-1976/The-general-election-campaign#ref285488.

"Time Magazine Cover: Anatoli Shcharansky—July 24, 1978." *Time*. https://content.time.com/time/covers/0,16641,19780724,00.html.

Tison v. Arizona, 481 U.S. 137 (1987). Accessed April 15, 2024. https://www.quimbee.com/cases/tison-v-arizona.

Tsai, Michelle. "Why Did William F. Buckley Jr. Talk like That?" Slate Magazine, February 29, 2008. https://slate.com/news-and-politics/2008/02/why-did-william-f-buckley-jr-talk-like-that.html.

"Umberto Terracini, 88, an Italian Communist." *The New York Times*, December 8, 1983. https://www.nytimes.com/1983/12/08/obituaries/umberto-terracini-88-an-italian-communist.html

"US & Canada | Latest News & Updates." BBC News. Accessed April 15, 2024. https://www.bbc.com/news/world/us_and_canada.

"Von Bulow Gets 30 Years in Murder Attempts." *The New York Times*, May 8, 1982. https://www.nytimes.com/1982/05/08/nyregion/von-bulow-gets-30-years-in-murder-attempts.html.

"Where Your Money Goes." Combined Jewish Philanthropies of Greater Boston. Accessed April 15, 2024. https://www.cjp.org/about-us/where-your-money-goes.

"William F. Buckley Jr." Wikipedia, April 12, 2024. https://en.wikipedia.org/wiki/William_F._Buckley_Jr.

"William F. Buckley, Jr." Encyclopædia Britannica, April 10, 2024. https://www.britannica.com/biography/William-F-Buckley-Jr.

"Woody Allen." Encyclopædia Britannica, April 9, 2024. https://www.britannica.com/biography/Woody-Allen.

"Yasser Arafat." Encyclopædia Britannica, March 13, 2024. https://www.britannica.com/biography/Yasser-Arafat.

Videos

"ABC World News Tonight July 10 1978 | Max Robinson's Debut." You Tube, April 11, 2019. https://www.youtube.com/watch?v=eHTg1Mlcnnw%3B.

"A Case of Justice: African Americans and the United States Judicial System." Open Vault, GBH Archive, June 19, 1979. https://openvault.wgbh.org/catalog/V_9505CAA825F0444382DD673438C672E8.

"American Archive of Public Broadcasting." American Archive of Public Broadcasting. Accessed April 15, 2024. https://americanarchive.org/catalog/cpb-aacip-507-m901z42q4j-.

"Celebrating Alan Dershowitz: Public Intellectual." YouTube, October
    30, 2013. https://www.youtube.com/watch?v=mtbXjn2Z_qw&t=1916s
    %3B.
"Firing Line with William F. Buckley Jr.: Deep Throat and the First
    Amendment." YouTube, January 30, 2017. https://www.youtube
    .com/watch?v=BtRVdFGCteM&t=570s%3B.
"First Amendment: Alan Dershowitz." Open Vault, GBH Archive, March
    3, 1977. https://openvault.wgbh.org/catalog/A_07572339C5234070
    85C7199F0E6569E4.
"In the News—Dershowitz on Judge Garland." YouTube, March 17,
    2016. https://www.youtube.com/watch?v=sWdWYoNVboU.
"Should Your State Carry Out Death Sentences?" Open Vault, GBH
    Archive, June 24, 1979. https://openvault.wgbh.org/catalog/V_E88
    C09C767DA48A3A64C9FB078446FCC.
"Skokie: Invaded, but Not Conquered Film Trailer." YouTube, January 8,
    2013. https://www.youtube.com/watch?v=r8X8Q0pzwyw%3B.
"The MacNeil/Lehrer Report; 7066; Insanity Defense for John Hinckley."
    American Archive of Public Broadcasting. Accessed April 15, 2024.
    https://americanarchive.org/catalog/cpb-aacip-507-th8bg2j874.
The Trials of Alan Dershowitz, John Curtin, 2023. https://www.docnyc
    .net/film/the-trials-of-alan-dershowitz/.

Brooklyn College/other

Dershowitz Archives: Series 6.2—Box 23, Series 6.2—Boxes 2, 5, 6, 7,8,
    9, 11, 15, & 18, Series 11.2, Series 1.1—Box 8, Series 4.3—Box 3,
    Series 5.1c—Boxes 12, 13, & 14, Subgroup 7—Box 19, Subgroup
    8—Box 1, H—Miscellaneous Cases—Box 2, U.S. vs. Deep Throat
    & Herbert Streicher (Harry Reems), 1970s—Boxes 1, 2, & 3, People
    of the State of New York vs. Bernard Bergman, 1970s—Box 1, Tison
    vs Arizona 1976–1990—Box 3, Series 9.1—Boxes 2 & 3, Series
    7.5—Box 2, Series 7.5—Box 2 & 3, Series 7.9—Box 8, Series 7.4—
    Box 3, Series 3.1—Box 19, Subgroup 7, Chutzpah—Box 10, Series
    5.5—Box 1, Series 4.3—Box 10, Sami Esmail, 1970s—Box 1; Alan
    Dershowitz's oral history with Philip Napoli; Alan Dershowitz's 2004
    anecdotes document; Alan Dershowitz's picture collection in Martha's

Vineyard residence; Alan Dershowitz's picture collection in New York City apartment

On the Threshold
Interviews
Alan Dershowitz, Carolyn Cohen, Elon Dershowitz, Nathan Dershowitz, Natan Sharansky, Jeanne Baker, Stuart Eizenstat, Woody Allen, Susan Estrich, Dana Cernea, Nadine Strossen, Eli Noam, Harvey Silverglate, Nathan Lewin, anonymous relative of the Tison brothers, Judy Beck, Israel Ringel, Barry Shrage, Judge Aharon Barak

Books
Albany Law Review. Vol. 71, 2008.
Bailey, F. Lee. *For the Defense*. Signet, 1976, 278–280.
Clarke, James W. *Last Rampage*. Arizona, 1988, 47–53.
Dershowitz, Alan:
　The Best Defense. Vintage Books, 1983, picture inserts, Chapter 1, Chapter 2, Chapter 3, Chapter 4, Chapter 6, Chapter 7, Chapter 8, Chapter 9, 392–396, 190–192.
　Taking the Stand. Crown Publishers, 2013. –311–314, 302, 389–397, 236, 130–140, 289, 276–278, 496, 157–159, 420, 377, 428, 433–434, 213–218, 197–200, 191, picture inserts.
　Defending Israel. All Points Books, 2019, Chapter 7, 95–99, 84, 127–131, 145–147.
　Reversal of Fortune. Random House, 1986, dedication, acknowledgments, xiii-xv, xvii-xxvi, 3–17, 19–22, 24–25, 28–35, 37, 41–43, 47–48, 50–55, 59–61, 64–71, 73, 74–93, 99–100, picture inserts, 105, 109–123, 128–131, 136–145, 149, 154–160, 165–172, 176–179, 181, 183–189, 193–196, 198–208, 211–213, 215–217, 220, 222–225, 228–230, 232–238, 241–248, 250, 252–261, 264–265, 267, 271.
　Chutzpah. Touchstone, 1992, 82, 236–237, 170–171 re Skokie, 233, 234, 235, 250–260, 86, 93–101, 184–186, 70–71.
Eizenstat, Stuart. *President Carter*. Thomas Dunne Books, 2018, 487, 600.
Estrich, Susan. *Real Rape*. Harvard University Press, 1987, preface, 1–3, 6–7.

Sharansky, Avital with Ilana Ben-Josef. *Next Year in Jerusalem*. New York: William Morrow and Company, 1979.

Sharansky, Natan. *Never Alone*. Hachette Book Groups, 2020, picture inserts, 114–119.

Articles

"About Us—John Simon Guggenheim Memorial Foundation." John Simon Guggenheim Memorial Foundation. Accessed April 15, 2024. https://www .gf.org/about-us/.

"Aharon Barak." Wikipedia, January 31, 2024. https://en.wikipedia.org /wiki/Aharon_Barak.

"Alan Dershowitz, from the Death Penalty to Roman Polanski." *The New York Times*, December 12, 2015. https://www.nytimes.com/interactive /2015/12/12/business/alan-dershowitz-timeline.html#/#time392 _11342.

Associated Press. "Moscow Prison for Us Reporter Was Used in Stalin's Purges." AP News, March 31, 2023. https://apnews.com/article/moscow -lefortovo-prison-gershkovich-russia-wall-street-journal-2b160207 d8c08f8ca0cc30b619daf6e9.

Bandow, Doug. "The Rise and Fall of Nicolae Ceausescu, 'the Romanian Fuehrer.'" Cato Institute, December 31, 2019. https://www.cato.org /commentary/rise-fall-nicolae-ceausescu-romanian-fuehrer.

"Barbara Walters." D23, December 31, 2022. https://d23.com/walt-disney -legend/barbara-walters/.

Betts, Jennifer. "US Divorce Rates over Time and What the Numbers Really Mean." LoveToKnow, June 5, 2023. https://www.lovetoknow .com/life/relationships/historical-divorce-rate-statistics.

Bruck, Connie. "Alan Dershowitz, Devil's Advocate." *The New Yorker*, July 29, 2019. https://www.newyorker.com/magazine/2019/08/05/alan -dershowitz-devils-advocate.

Buckley, William F. "Be Loyal to Your God—Don't See the Movie." *The Washington Post*, August 15, 1988. https://www.washingtonpost.com /archive/opinions/1988/08/16/be-loyal-to-your-god_dont-see-the-movie /6f5ce63e-314c-42cc-870e-107ec04e71ef/.

"Camp David Accords." Encyclopædia Britannica, April 1, 2024. https://www.britannica.com/event/Camp-David-Accords.

Clendinen, Dudley. "Jurors Find von Bulow Guilty of Trying Twice to Kill Wife." *The New York Times*, March 17, 1982. https://www.nytimes.com/1982/03/17/nyregion/jurors-find-von-bulow-guilty-of-trying-twice-to-kill-wife.html.

Clendinen, Dudley. "Prosecution and Defense Outline von Bulow Cases." *The New York Times*, February 3, 1982. https://www.nytimes.com/1982/02/03/us/prosecution-and-defense-outline-von-bulow-cases.html.

"Clearing the Throat." *The Harvard Crimson*. September 15, 1980. https://www.thecrimson.com/article/1980/9/15/clearing-the-throat-pyour-honor-if/.

Cohen, Marns F. "Dershowitz to Argue von Bulow Appeal." *The Harvard Crimson*, November 20, 1982. https://www.thecrimson.com/article/1982/11/20/dershowitz-to-argue-von-bulow-appeal/.

Cotler, Irwin. "A remarkable man, a remarkable legacy." Maclean's, December 6, 2013. https://macleans.ca/news/world/a-remarkable-man-a-remarkable-legacy/.

"Danville Bee Newspaper Archives, Nov 21, 1974, p. 5." Newspaper Archive.com, November 21, 1974. https://newspaperarchive.com/danville-bee-nov-21–1974-p-5/.

Dershowitz, Alan. "Free Free Speech." *The New York Times*, February 9, 1979. https://www.nytimes.com/1979/02/09/archives/freefreespeech.html.

Dershowitz, Alan. "Let the Punishment (Published 1975)." *The New York Times*, December 28, 1975. https://www.nytimes.com/1975/12/28/archives/let-the-punishment-fit-the-crime-indeterminate-prison-sentences-a.html%20-.

Dershowitz, Alan. "The Source of Justice in the Mind of a Justice." *The New York Times*, February 22, 1981. https://www.nytimes.com/1981/02/22/books/the-source-of-justice-in-the-mind-of-a-justice.html.

Dershowitz, Alan. "The Special Victim Is Not New in the Law." *The New York Times*, March 27, 1977. https://www.nytimes.com/1977/03/27/archives/the-special-victim-is-not-new-in-the-law-but-the-elderly-of-new.html.

Dershowitz, Alan. "Unequal Justice." *The New York Times*, January 25, 1976. https://www.nytimes.com/1976/01/25/archives/unequal-justice-counselor-counsel-thyself.html.

Doorn, John van. "A Look Into the Future." *NEXT* magazine, April 1981.

"Firing Line (TV Program)." Wikipedia, March 12, 2024. https://en.wikipedia.org/wiki/Firing_Line_(TV_program).

"First Lebanon War." The Kahan Commission of Inquiry. Accessed April 15, 2024. https://www.jewishvirtuallibrary.org/the-kahan-commission-of-inquiry.

Freedman, Eliyahu. "Irwin Cotler, Who Advocated for Natan Sharansky and Nelson Mandela, Awarded Israel's Presidential Medal of Honor." *The Canadian Jewish News*, September 7, 2023. https://thecjn.ca/news/irwin-cotler-who-advocated-for-natan-sharansky-and-nelson-mandela-awarded-israels-presidential-medal-of-honor/.

Freedman, Monroe H., and Alan. "Israeli Torture, They Said." *The New York Times*, June 2, 1978. https://www.nytimes.com/1978/06/02/archives/israeli-torture-they-said.html.

Goldstein, Tom. "Notables Aid Convicted 'Deep Throat' Star." *The New York Times*, June 29, 1976. https://www.nytimes.com/1976/06/29/archives/notables-aid-convicted-deep-throat-star.html.

"Helsinki Accords." Encyclopædia Britannica. Accessed April 15, 2024. https://www.britannica.com:443/event/Helsinki-Accords.

"Inside the Sanctum Sanctorum; Douglas." *The New York Times*. Accessed April 15, 2024. https://timesmachine.nytimes.com/timesmachine/1980/11/02/112166239.html?pageNumber=110%3B.

"Irwin Cotler." encyclopedia.com. Accessed April 15, 2024. https://www.encyclopedia.com/religion/encyclopedias-almanacs-transcripts-and-maps/cotler-irwin.

"Jimmy Carter Summary." Encyclopædia Britannica. Accessed April 15, 2024. https://www.britannica.com/summary/Jimmy-Carter.

Kuznetsov, Eduard S. "Flight from the Gulag." *The New York Times*, April 27, 1980. https://www.nytimes.com/1980/04/27/archives/flight-from-the-gulag-april-25-1979-april-26-1979-kuznetsov-april.html.

"Nicolae Ceaușescu." Encyclopædia Britannica, March 28, 2024. https://www.britannica.com/biography/Nicolae-Ceausescu.

Niven, David. "Why Do You Want to be President?" *Medium*, August 26, 2015. https://medium.com/@nivenpolitics/why-do-you-want-to-be-president-29ce11fbf164.

"P.L.O. Is a Friend of the News Media." *The New York Times*, March 2, 1982. https://www.nytimes.com/1982/03/02/opinion/l-plo-is-a-friend-of-the-news-media-226971.html.

"Palestine Liberation Organization." Encyclopædia Britannica, April 10, 2024. https://www.britannica.com/topic/Palestine-Liberation-Organization.

"Register of the Firing Line (Television Program) Broadcast Records." Online Archive of California. Accessed April 15, 2024. https://oac.cdlib.org/findaid/ark:/13030/kt6m3nc88c/entire_text/.

Staff, CIE. "Zionism Is Racism UNGA Resolution 3379." CIE, July 3, 2018. https://israeled.org/resources/documents/zionism-racism-unga-resolution-3379/.

"Stuart E. Eizenstat." Wikipedia, December 16, 2023. https://en.wikipedia.org/wiki/Stuart_E._Eizenstat.

Susan Estrich. Accessed April 15, 2024. https://www.estrichgoldin.com/susan-estrich.

"Susan Estrich." Wikipedia, February 26, 2023. https://en.wikipedia.org/wiki/Susan_Estrich.

"Ted Kennedy: The Day the Presidency Was Lost." ABC News, August 28, 2009. https://abcnews.go.com/Politics/TedKennedy/story?id=8436488%3B.

"The General Election Campaign." Encyclopædia Britannica. Accessed April 15, 2024. https://www.britannica.com/event/United-States-presidential-election-of-1976/The-general-election-campaign#ref285488.

"Time Magazine Cover: Anatoli Shcharansky—July 24, 1978." *Time*. https://content.time.com/time/covers/0,16641,19780724,00.html.

Tison v. Arizona, 481 U.S. 137 (1987). https://www.quimbee.com/cases/tison-v-arizona.

Tsai, Michelle. "Why Did William F. Buckley Jr. Talk like That?" Slate Magazine, February 29, 2008. https://slate.com/news-and-politics/2008/02/why-did-william-f-buckley-jr-talk-like-that.html.

"Umberto Terracini, 88, an Italian Communist." *The New York Times*, December 8, 1983. https://www.nytimes.com/1983/12/08/obituaries /umberto-terracini-88-an-italian-communist.html.

"Von Bulow Gets 30 Years in Murder Attempts." *The New York Times*, May 8, 1982. https://www.nytimes.com/1982/05/08/nyregion/von -bulow-gets-30-years-in-murder-attempts.html.

"Where Your Money Goes." Combined Jewish Philanthropies of Greater Boston. Accessed April 15, 2024. https://www.cjp.org/about-us/where -your-money-goes.

"William F. Buckley Jr.." Wikipedia, April 12, 2024. https://en.wikipedia .org/wiki/William_F._Buckley_Jr.

"William F. Buckley, Jr.." Encyclopædia Britannica, April 10, 2024. https://www.britannica.com/biography/William-F-Buckley-Jr.

"Woody Allen." Encyclopædia Britannica, April 9, 2024. https://www .britannica.com/biography/Woody-Allen.

"Yasser Arafat." Encyclopædia Britannica, March 13, 2024. https://www .britannica.com/biography/Yasser-Arafat.

Videos

"ABC World News Tonight July 10 1978 | Max Robinson's Debut." YouTube, April 11, 2019. https://www.youtube.com/watch?v=eHTg1 Mlcnnw%3B.

"American Archive of Public Broadcasting." American Archive of Public Broadcasting. Accessed April 15, 2024. https://americanarchive.org /catalog/cpb-aacip-507-m901z42q4j-.

"Celebrating Alan Dershowitz: Public Intellectual." YouTube, October 30, 2013. https://www.youtube.com/watch?v=mtbXjn2Z_qw&t=1916s %3B.

"Firing Line with William F. Buckley Jr.: Deep Throat and the First Amendment." YouTube, January 30, 2017. https://www.youtube .com/watch?v=BtRVdFGCteM&t=570s%3B.

GBH Openvault. Accessed April 15, 2024. https://openvault.wgbh.org /catalog/A_07572339C523407085C7199F0E6569E4 .

GBH Openvault. Accessed April 15, 2024. https://openvault.wgbh.org /catalog/V_9505CAA825F0444382DD673438C672E8.

GBH Openvault. Accessed April 15, 2024. https://openvault.wgbh.org/catalog/V_E88C09C767DA48A3A64C9FB078446FCC.

"In the News—Dershowitz on Judge Garland." YouTube, March 17, 2016. https://www.youtube.com/watch?v=sWdWYoNVboU.

"Skokie: Invaded, but Not Conquered Film Trailer." YouTube, January 8, 2013. https://www.youtube.com/watch?v=r8X8Q0pzwyw%3B.

"The MacNeil/Lehrer Report; 7066; Insanity Defense for John Hinckley." American Archive of Public Broadcasting. Accessed April 15, 2024. https://americanarchive.org/catalog/cpb-aacip-507-th8bg2j874.

The Trials of Alan Dershowitz, John Curtin, 2023. https://www.docnyc.net/film/the-trials-of-alan-dershowitz/

Brooklyn College/other

Dershowitz Archives: Series 6.2—Box 23, Series 6.2—Boxes 2, 5, 6, 7,8, 9, 11, 15, & 18, Series 11.2, Series 1.1—Box 8, Series 4.3—Box 3, Series 5.1c—Boxes 12, 13, & 14, Subgroup 7—Box 19, Subgroup 8—Box 1, H—Miscellaneous Cases—Box 2, U.S. vs. Deep Throat & Herbert Streicher (Harry Reems), 1970s—Boxes 1, 2, & 3, People of the State of New York vs. Bernard Bergman, 1970s—Box 1, Tison vs Arizona 1976–1990—Box 3, Series 9.1—Boxes 2 & 3, Series 7.5—Box 2, Series 7.5—Box 2 & 3, Series 7.9—Box 8, Series 7.4—Box 3, Series 3.1—Box 19, Subgroup 7, Chutzpah—Box 10, Series 5.5—Box 1, Series 4.3—Box 10, Sami Esmail, 1970s—Box 1; Alan Dershowitz's oral history with Philip Napoli; Alan Dershowitz's 2004 anecdotes document; Alan Dershowitz's picture collection in Martha's Vineyard residence; Alan Dershowitz's picture collection in New York City apartment

Outnumbered

Interviews

Alan Dershowitz, Carolyn Cohen, Elon Dershowitz, Nathan Dershowitz, Raymond Tison, Ricky Tison, Eliot Spitzer, Maura Kelley, Jamie Raskin, Jeffrey Toobin, Alex Kozinski, Zvi Dershowitz, Shirley Ringel, Mark Levin, Zecharia Dor-Shav, Stephen Trachtenberg, Hal Miller-Jacobs, Barry Zimmerman, Carl & Joan Meshenberg, Bernie Beck,

Harvey Silverglate, Woody Allen, Kenneth Sweder, Joel Klein, Jeanne Baker, Sandor Frankel, Susan Estrich, Dana Cernea, Judy Beck, Natan Sharansky, Judge Aharon Barak, Dr. Noam Chomsky

Books

Dershowitz, Alan:

> *The Best Defense.* Vintage Books, 1983, Acknowledgments, 117–118, 277–278, 318, 384–417, Introduction; back and front covers.

> *Defending Israel.* All Points Books, 2019, 109–126.

> *Chutzpah.* Touchstone, 1992, 94–97, 139–150, 256–260, 296, 316–317, 324, 172–173, 134–135, 264–266, 250, picture inserts, 191–196, 197, 201–205, 241–244, 262, 328, 343–349, 82–91, 79, 14–15, 28–34.

> *Taking the Stand.* Crown Publishers, 2013, 200, 207, 503, 378, 401, 228–247, 429–431, 409, 270, 423, 454, 170–171, 360, 277–278, 424–425, 382, 218–227.

> *Reversal of Fortune.* Random House, 1986, dedication, acknowledgments, xiii-xv, xvii-xxvi, 3–17, 19–22, 24–25, 28–35, 37, 41–43, 47–48, 50–55, 59–61, 64–71, 73, 74–93, 99–100, picture inserts, 105, 109–123, 128–131, 136–145, 149, 154–160, 165–172, 176–179, 181, 183–189, 193–196, 198–208, 211–213, 215–217, 220, 222–225, 228–230, 232–238, 241–248, 250, 252–261, 264–265, 267, 271.

> *Taking Liberties.* Contemporary Books, 1988, introduction, numbers: 10, 11, 19, 21, 22, 23, 30, 32, 39, 40, 45, 54, 59, 60, 65, 72, 75, 76, 78, 83, 86, 94, 99, 100, 104, 108, 116, 129, 132, 138, 141, 142, 143.

> *America on Trial.* Warner Books, 2004, 262–263, 307–312, 321–322, 325, 346–349, 362–363, 366–367, 468.

Elkind, Peter. *Rough Justice.* Portfolio, 2010, 20.

Gilbert, Martin. *Shcharansky: Hero of our Time.* Viking Adult, 1986.

Hayward, Steven F. *The Age of Reagan: The Conservative Counterrevolution.* Crown Forum, 2009, 433–435.

Masters, Brooke A. *Spoiling for a Fight.* An Owl Book, 2007, 11, 30–31.

Sharansky, Natan. *Fear No Evil.* PublicAffairs, 1998.

Sharansky, Natan. *Never Alone*. Hachette Book Groups, 2020, picture inserts, 114–119.

Zackheim, Victoria (ed.). *The Face in the Mirror*. Prometheus Books, 2009, 39–45.

Articles

Anderson, Leslie. "Defense lawyer Alan Dershowitz: Hate mail is badge of honor." UPI, April 7, 1985. https://www.upi.com/Archives/1985/04 /07/Defense-lawyer-Alan-Dershowitz-Hate-mail-is-badge-of-honor /1849481698000/.

"Anti-Defamation League." Encyclopædia Britannica, April 10, 2024. https://www.britannica.com/topic/Anti-Defamation-League.

"Antonin Scalia." Encyclopædia Britannica, April 5, 2024. https://www .britannica.com/biography/Antonin-Scalia.

"An Undeserved Honor." *The Harvard Crimson*, June 9, 1987. https: //www.thecrimson.com/article/1987/6/9/an-undeserved-honor -pbhbarvard-is-once/.

Appel, Richard J."The ABC's of Ted Koppel's 'Nightline.'" *The Harvard Crimson*, June 6, 1984. https://www.thecrimson.com/article/1984/6 /6/the-abcs-of-ted-koppels-nightline/.

"Attorney General: Edwin Meese, III." Office of the Attorney General, United States Department of Justice, October 25, 2022. https://www .justice.gov/ag/bio/meese-edwin-iii.

Bishop, Joseph W. "The Best Defense, by Alan M. Dershowitz." *Commentary Magazine*, October 1982. https://www.commentary.org/articles/joseph -bishop-2/the-best-defense-by-alan-m-dershowitz/.

"Bowers v. Hardwick, 478 U.S. 186 (1986)." Justia Law. Accessed April 15, 2024. https://supreme.justia.com/cases/federal/us/478/186/.

Bruck, Connie. "Alan Dershowitz, Devil's Advocate." *The New Yorker*, July 29, 2019. https://www.newyorker.com/magazine/2019/08/05/alan -dershowitz-devils-advocate.

Brumberg, Abraham. "A New Deal in Poland?" *The New York Review*, January 15, 1987. https://www.nybooks.com/articles/1987/01/15/a -new-deal-in-poland/.

"Claus von Bulow: Socialite Acquitted of Killing His Wife after a Trial That Gripped America." *The Independent*, May 31, 2019. https://www.independent.co.uk/news/obituaries/claus-von-bulow-death -sunny-insulin-reversal-of-fortune-alan-dershowitz-death-a8937336 .html.

Clendinem, Dudley. "Von Bulow's 2 Convictions." *The New York Times*, April 28, 1984.[*] https://www.nytimes.com/1984/04/28/us/von -bulow-s-2-convictions-voided-on-appeal.html.

Cohen, Marns F. "Dershowitz to Argue von Bulow Appeal." *The Harvard Crimson*, November 20, 1982. https://www.thecrimson.com/article /1982/11/20/dershowitz-to-argue-von-bulow-appeal/.

Craft, Nikki. "Alan Dershowitz, Joseph Mengele and Me: The Limits of Libertarian Ideology." 1987. http://www.nostatusquo.com/ACLU/Porn /Dershowitz.html.

Cunha, Robert F. Jr. "Von Bulow Trial Begins Without Dershowitz." *The Harvard Crimson*, April 9, 1985. https://www.thecrimson.com /article/1985/4/9/von-bulow-trial-begins-without-dershowitz/.

Davis, Lawrence J. "Dershowitz Modifies." *The Harvard Crimson*, May 3, 1984. https://www.thecrimson.com/article/1984/5/3/dershowitz -modifies-role-in-von-bulow/.

"Dershowitz, Alan M. 1938–" Encyclopedia.com. https://www.encyclopedia .com/arts/educational-magazines/dershowitz-alan-m-1938.

Dershowitz, Alan. "How the First Amendment Saved Jamie Raskin's Father." *Newsweek*, February 12, 2021. https://www.newsweek.com /how-first-amendment-saved-jamie-raskins-father-opinion-1568724.

Dershowitz, Alan. "Justice: While the Meese Commission Played Fast and Loose with Our Liberties, Reagan's AIDS Commission May Be Playing Politics with Our Lives." *Penthouse*, December 1987.

Dershowitz, Alan. "President's Willful Blindness." *Seattle Times*, November 3, 1987.

Dershowitz, Alan. "Reagan-Meese Hypocrisy." *Seattle Times*, July 30, 1987.

Dershowitz, Alan. "Unseemly and Worse Reaganites Now Appreciate the Fifth." *Seattle Times*, December 12, 1986.

"Dershowitz Writes Book On Von Bulow Defense." *The Harvard Crimson*, February 5, 1986. https://www.thecrimson.com/article/1986/2/5/dershowitz-writes-book-on-von-bulow/.

"Elena Kagan." Encyclopædia Britannica, March 15, 2024. https://www.britannica.com/biography/Elena-Kagan.

"Eliot Spitzer." Jewish Virtual Library, Accessed April 15, 2024. https://www.jewishvirtuallibrary.org/eliot-spitzer.

"Eliot Spitzer." Wikipedia, April 14, 2024. https://en.wikipedia.org/wiki/Eliot_Spitzer.

Ephron, Nora. "Pulling Victory out of the Black Bag." *The New York Times*, June 15, 1986. https://www.nytimes.com/1986/06/15/books/pulling-victory-out-of-the-black-bag.html.

Glass, Andrew. "Reagan lifts sanctions on Poland, Feb. 19, 1987." *Politico*, February 19, 2019. https://www.politico.com/story/2019/02/19/reagan-lifts-sanctions-on-poland-feb-19-1987-1173436.

Hakim, Danny. "Gilded Path to Political Stardom, with Detours." *The New York Times*, October 12, 2006. https://www.nytimes.com/2006/10/12/nyregion/12spitzer.html.

"Harvard Law Review." Internet Archive. Accessed April 15, 2024. https://archive.org/details/100HarvLRev99s.

Hentoff, Nat. "She Didn't Stand for the Pledge of Allegiance." *The Washington Post*, December 5, 1984. https://www.washingtonpost.com/archive/politics/1984/12/06/she-didnt-stand-for-the-pledge-of-allegiance/0ac6b8d0–53c8–4f29–8ee5–9cb4bf01e1e3/.

Hertzberg, Arthur. "Reagan and the Jews: Arthur Hertzberg." *The New York Review of Books*, September 15, 2020. https://www.nybooks.com/articles/1985/01/31/reagan-and-the-jews/.

"Jamie Raskin." Wikipedia, April 10, 2024. https://en.wikipedia.org/wiki/Jamie_Raskin.

"Jeffrey Toobin." Wikipedia, April 2, 2024. https://en.wikipedia.org/wiki/Jeffrey_Toobin.

"Jim Cramer." Encyclopædia Britannica, April 3, 2024. https://www.britannica.com/biography/Jim-Cramer.

"Kagan's a Not-so-Leftist Liberal." *Los Angeles Times*, June 27, 2010. https://www.latimes.com/archives/la-xpm-2010-jun-27-la-na-kagan-profile-20100627-story.html.

Krebs, Albin. "Roy Cohn, Aide to McCarthy and Fiery Lawyer, Dies at 59." *The New York Times*, August 3, 1986. https://archive.nytimes .com/www.nytimes.com/library/national/science/aids/080386sci-aids .html.

"Larry King." Encyclopædia Britannica, March 28, 2024. https://www .britannica.com/biography/Larry-King.

"Late night with David Letterman (a guest stars & air dates guide)." Accessed April 15, 2024. https://epguides.com/LateNightwithDavidLetterman/.

Levmore, Rachel. "Should the Government 'get' Involved?" *The Forward*, May 2, 2012. https://forward.com/opinion/155597/should-the-government -get-involved/.

MacQuarrie, Brian. "Alan Dershowitz Recalls Former Client Claus von Bülow." *The Boston Globe*, May 30, 2019. https://www.bostonglobe .com/metro/2019/05/30/alan-dershowitz-recalls-former-client-claus -von-bulow/xqT0bA0jvwb76sJUvvjxhP/story.html.

Margolick, David. "Taking a Stand against Standing for The Pledge of Allegiance." *The New York Times*, November 30, 1984. https://www .nytimes.com/1984/11/30/us/taking-a-stand-against-standing-for -the-pledge-of-allegiance.html.

Michigan Law Review, Vol. 82, 8, 1984. https://repository.law.umich.edu /cgi/viewcontent.cgi?article=3478&context=mlr.

"Natan Sharansky Is Released and Arrives in Israel." Aish.com, May 2, 2023. https://aish.com/natan-sharansky-is-released-and-arrives-in-israel/.

"Nelson Mandela Summary." Encyclopædia Britannica. Accessed April 15, 2024. https://www.britannica.com/summary/Nelson-Mandela.

Nemy, Enid. "Claus von Bülow, Society Figure in High-Profile Case, Dies at 92." *The New York Times*, May 30, 2019. https://www.nytimes .com/2019/05/30/obituaries/claus-von-bulow-dead.html.

"Newspapers Fact Sheet." Pew Research Center's Journalism Project, November 10, 2023. https://www.pewresearch.org/journalism/fact-sheet /newspapers/.

Rosenfeld, Megan. "Von Bulow, the Second Time Around." *The Washington Post*, April 14, 1985. https://www.washingtonpost.com /archive/lifestyle/1985/04/15/von-bulow-the-second-time-around /cd544635–4089-4fef-96f9–79e8bb901093/.

"Roy Cohn." Wikipedia, April 10, 2024. https://en.wikipedia.org/wiki/Roy_Cohn.

"Solidarity." Encyclopædia Britannica, March 22, 2024. https://www.britannica.com/topic/Solidarity.

"Spies and Scapegoats." *The New York Times*, August 14, 1983. https://www.nytimes.com/1983/08/14/books/spies-and-scapegoats.html.

"Staff." DC Medical Care LLC. Accessed April 15, 2024. https://www.dcmedicalcare.com/staff.

Swan, Christopher. "Redgrave's Latest Role Is in Court." *Christian Science Monitor*, November 6, 1984. https://www.csmonitor.com/1984/1106/110610.html.

"The Best Defense." *Kirkus Reviews*, May 17, 1982. https://www.kirkusreviews.com/book-reviews/a/alan-m-dershowitz-4/the-best-defense-3/.

"'The Best Defense.'" *The New York Times*, July 4, 1982. https://www.nytimes.com/1982/07/04/books/l-the-best-defense-251187.html.

"The Lawyer of Last Resort." *The New York Times*, June 13, 1982. https://www.nytimes.com/1982/06/13/books/the-lawyer-of-last-resort.html.

Taylor, Stuart. "Justices Seem to Widen Death Penalty." *The New York Times*, April 22, 1987. https://www.nytimes.com/1987/04/22/us/supreme-court-roundup-justices-seem-to-widen-death-penalty.html.

United States of America v. H. Daniel Whitman. Justia Law, 1985. https://law.justia.com/cases/federal/appellate-courts/F2/771/1348/379955/.

Valentine, Paul W. "Claus von Bulow, cleared of attempted murder of his wife, dies at 92." *Stuff*, May 30, 2019. https://www.stuff.co.nz/world/americas/113146399/claus-von-bulow-cleared-of-attempted-murder-of-his-millionaire-wife-dies-at-92.

Widdicombe, Ben. "How Claus von Bulow Became the Original True Crime Star." *Town & Country*, May 31, 2019. https://www.townandcountrymag.com/society/money-and-power/a27675062/claus-von-bulow-dead/.

Videos

"1985 Throwback: 'Roy Cohn vs. Alan Dershowitz.'" YouTube, August 21, 2020. https://www.youtube.com/watch?v=e3x7uDkP0cY%3B.

"Alan Dershowitz on the Claus von Bulow Case (1986)." YouTube, October 27, 2008. https://www.youtube.com/watch?v=_GA1vZSvDA0%3B.

"American Archive of Public Broadcasting." American Archive of Public Broadcasting. Accessed April 15, 2024. https://americanarchive.org/catalog/cpb-aacip-507–8p5v698x8c.

Bülow, Claus von. NBC 10 WJAR. Interviewed by Tim Taricani, Facebook video. https://www.facebook.com/watch/?v=638656483315260

"Celebrating Alan Dershowitz: Public Intellectual." YouTube, October 30, 2013. https://www.youtube.com/watch?v=mtbXjn2Z_qw&t=2382s%3B.

"Fear No Evil with Natan Sharansky." YouTube, March 14, 2018. https://www.youtube.com/watch?v=lgfHP7Xag6Y&t=876s%3B.

Brooklyn College/Other

Dershowitz Archives: Tison vs Arizona 1976–1990—Box 3 & Box 21, 5.1c Anatoly Shcharansky, 1977–1986—Box 12, Box 14, Series 7.5 Editorials, 1969–2003—Box 2, Series 1.1—Box 9, Series 1.2—Box 1, Series 14.1: Oversize clippings / articles / calendars—Box 4, Series 6.2—Boxes 8, 9, 10, 11, 12, 13, 14, & 15, Series 9.1—Box 2, Box 3, Series 10.2—Box 2, Series 4.1—Box 2, Series 7.1—The Best Defense: Boxes 23, 24, & 25, Series 7.1—Reversal of Fortune: Boxes 1 & 8, Series 11.1—Box 1, Series 4.3—Box 3, Series 10.2—Boxes 1, 5, 6, 7, & 28, Series 6.2—Box 23, Series 5.5—Box 1, Series 11. 4—Box 1, Series 14.1—Oversize Box 7, Oversize Box 9; Alan Dershowitz's oral history with Philip Napoli; Alan Dershowitz's 2004 anecdotes document; Pictures of Alan's Martha's Vineyard home

Help Wanted
Interviews

Alan Dershowitz, Carolyn Cohen, Elon Dershowitz, Nathan Dershowitz, Harvey Silverglate, Sandor Frankel, Richard Sandler, Stephen Joel Trachtenberg, Ted Cruz, Mike Pompeo, Justice Stephen Breyer, Mike Tyson, Raymond Tison, Ricky Tison, Woody Allen, Jim Bakker, Dr. Noam Chomsky

Books

Allen, Woody. *Apropos of Nothing*. Arcade Publishing, 2020, 237–283.

Bakker, Jim. *I Was Wrong*. Nelson, 1996, 17–19, 186–187, 199–201, 218, 220, 233–234, 239–244, 256–259, 261–264.

Dershowitz, Alan:

    Taking the Stand. Crown Publishers, 2013, 200, 92–93, 364–365, 83, 357–358, 278, 241, 362–363, 292–293, 428–429, 401–404, 325–341, 377–382, 250, picture inserts.

    Chutzpah. Touchstone, 1992, 350–354; 3–11, 18–19, Acknowledgments, Dedication, 342, 227, 79, 284–312, 365, 327, 260–263, 348, 137–139, front and back covers, 150–162, 192–193, 173–178, 199–201, 267–276, picture inserts, 125–126.

    Defending Israel. All Points Books, 2019, 132–133, 143, 181, 84.

    Contrary to Popular Opinion. Pharos Books, 1992, 156–158, 333.

    Letters to a Young Lawyer. Basic Books, 2001, 188.

    The Abuse Excuse. Back Bay Books, 1994, 87.

Farrow, Mia. *What Falls Away*. Bantam Books, 1998, 249–303.

Frankel, Sandor. *The Accidental Philanthropist*. Skyhorse Publishing, 2021, 84–113.

Tyson, Mike. *Undisputed Truth*. Plume, 2014, 8–9, 255, 268–272.

Articles

"800 Students Gather for 'thinking' Class." *The Harvard Crimson*, February 12, 1994. https://www.thecrimson.com/article/1994/2/12/800-students-gather-for-thinking-class/.

"Alan Dershowitz, from the Death Penalty to Roman Polanski." *The New York Times*, December 12, 2015. https://www.nytimes.com/interactive/2015/12/12/business/alan-dershowitz-timeline.html#/#time392_11347.

"Alan Dershowitz: Objection to a false narrative." Opinion, *The Washington Post*, August 6, 2019. https://www.washingtonpost.com/opinions/alan-dershowitz-objection-to-a-false-narrative/2019/08/06/b7a8bf44-b799-11e9-8e83-4e6687e99814_story.html.

"All of Mia Farrow's 14 Adopted and Biological Children." *Daily Mail Online*, February 22, 2021. https://www.dailymail.co.uk/news/fb-9285643/All-Mia-Farrows-14-adopted-biological-children.html.

Anderson, Leslie. "Defense lawyer Alan Dershowitz: Hate mail is badge of honor." UPI, April 7, 1985 https://www.upi.com/Archives /1985/04/07/Defense-lawyer-Alan-Dershowitz-Hate-mail-is-badge -of-honor/1849481698000/.

"Appeals Court Upholds Leona Helmsley's Conviction." UPI, July 30, 1991. https://www.upi.com/Archives/1991/07/30/Appeals-court-upholds -Leona-Helmsleys-conviction/5001680846400/.

Applebome, Peter. "Judge Cuts Bakker's Prison Term, Making Parole Possible in 4 Years." *The New York Times*, August 24, 1991. https: //www.nytimes.com/1991/08/24/us/judge-cuts-bakker-s-prison-term -making-parole-possible-in-4-years.html.

"Bakker Committed for Psychiatric Tests." *The New York Times*, September 1, 1989. https://www.nytimes.com/1989/09/01/us/bakker -committed-for-psychiatric-tests.html.

"Barack Obama." Encyclopædia Britannica, April 13, 2024. https://www .britannica.com/biography/Barack-Obama.

Baughman, Judith S., et al. "Noam Chomsky." *American Decades*. Detroit: Gale, 2006.

"Bill Clinton." Encyclopædia Britannica, April 10, 2024. https://www .britannica.com/biography/Bill-Clinton.

Cain, Áine. "The Life of Secretary of State Mike Pompeo, the West Point Valedictorian and Former CIA Director Who's in Hot Water Amid an Inspector General Scandal." *Business Insider*, May 20, 2020. https://www.businessinsider.com/who-is-mike-pompeo-2017–11.

"Chutzpah." Simon & Schuster. Accessed April 15, 2024. https://www .simonandschuster.com/books/Chutzpah/Alan-M-Dershowitz /9780671760892.

"Clinton Apologizes for Remarks about Cuomo : Politics: Democratic Candidate, in a Private Phone Conversation, Implied That the New York Governor Behaves like a Mafioso." *Los Angeles Times*, January 29, 1992. https://www.latimes.com/archives/la-xpm-1992–01-29-mn-927 -story.html.

Cohen, Roger. "Jewish Group Attacks Author of 'Chutzpah.'" *The New York Times*, July 17, 1991. https://www.nytimes.com/1991/07/17 /books/jewish-group-attacks-author-of-chutzpah.html.

"Getting to the Heart of the American Family." *Life*, June 1, 1992.

Fischoff, Maya E. "Dershowitz, Ogletree Clash at Law School." *The Harvard Crimson*, May 8, 1992. https://www.thecrimson.com/article /1992/5/8/dershowitz-ogletree-clash-at-law-school/.

Harris, Art. "Jim Bakker, Driven by Money or Miracles?" *The Washington Post*, August 28, 1989. https://www.washingtonpost.com /archive/lifestyle/1989/08/29/jim-bakker-driven-by-money-or-miracles /525a2b1b-95c7–447a-980a-e81b2357d36a/.

"Jamin Dershowitz." WNBA.com. Accessed April 15, 2024. https://www .wnba.com/archive/wnba/about_us/dershowitz_bio.html.

"Jim Bakker Enters Halfway House after Serving 4 1/2 Years in Prison." *Los Angeles Times*, July 2, 1994. https://www.latimes.com/archives /la-xpm-1994–07-02-mn-11000-story.html.

"Jim Bakker." Encyclopædia Britannica. Accessed April 15, 2024. https: //www.britannica.com/biography/Jim-Bakker.

"Jim Bakker Freed from Jail to Stay in a Halfway House." *The New York Times*, July 2, 1994. https://www.nytimes.com/1994/07/02/us/jim -bakker-freed-from-jail-to-stay-in-a-halfway-house.html.

"Jim Bakker Gets PPP Loans during Legal Fight on Fraud Claims." AP News, April 30, 2021. https://apnews.com/article/virus-outbreak -ap-top-news-michael-brown-health-mo-state-wire-2c690094065ece 9ba147feb4b18812d2.

"Jonathan Pollard." Encyclopædia Britannica, March 3, 2024. https: //www.britannica.com/biography/Jonathan-Pollard.

Kampeas, Ron. "Late Governor Mario Cuomo: A Sicilian Altar Boy Turned New York Shabbos Goy." *Haaretz*, January 4, 2015. https: //www.haaretz.com/jewish/2015–01-04/ty-article/cuomo-married -liberalism-and-sensitivity-to-the-orthodox/0000017f-db12-db5a -a57f-db7a35cf0000.

Kirsch, Jonathan. "Book Review: Dershowitz Charms with His 'Chutzpah'." *Los Angeles Times*, May 29, 1991. https://www.latimes .com/archives/la-xpm-1991–05-29-vw-2307-story.html.

Margolick, David. "At the Bar; Dershowitz Wows 'em Again! (Is There No Escaping This Guy?)" *The New York Times*, February 15, 1991. https://www.nytimes.com/1991/02/15/news/at-the-bar-dershowitz -wows-em-again-is-there-no-escaping-this-guy.html.

Marks, Peter. "Dershowitz Says Farrow Involved Him." *The New York Times*, April 16, 1993. https://www.nytimes.com/1993/04/16/nyregion /dershowitz-says-farrow-involved-him.html.

Marks, Peter. "Dershowitz Testimony Turns into 3-Hour Shouting Match." *The New York Times*, April 17, 1993. https://www.nytimes.com /1993/04/17/nyregion/dershowitz-testimony-turns-into-3-hour -shouting-match.html.

"Mia Farrow." Encyclopædia Britannica, April 14, 2024. https://www .britannica.com/biography/Mia-Farrow.

"Mike Tyson." Encyclopædia Britannica, April 14, 2024. https://www .britannica.com/biography/Mike-Tyson.

"Moses Farrow: 'I'd Be Very Happy to Take My Father's Surname.'" *The Guardian*, December 11, 2020. https://www.theguardian.com/film/2020 /dec/11/moses-farrow-id-be-very-happy-to-take-my-fathers-surname.

"Mstislav Rostropovich." Encyclopædia Britannica, April 4, 2024. https: //www.britannica.com/biography/Mstislav-Rostropovich.

Nemy, Enid. "Leona Helmsley, Hotel Queen, Dies at 87." *The New York Times*, August 20, 2007. https://www.nytimes.com/2007/08/20 /nyregion/20cnd-helmsley.html.

"O.J. Simpson Trial." Encyclopædia Britannica, April 11, 2024. https: //www.britannica.com/event/O-J-Simpson-trial.

"Oslo Accords." Encyclopædia Britannica, March 27, 2024. https://www. britannica.com/topic/Oslo-Accords.

"Pamyat." Encyclopedia.com, Accessed April 15, 2024. https://www.ency clopedia.com/history/encyclopedias-almanacs-transcripts-and-maps/pamyat.

Recio, Maria. "Ted Cruz's family story: Poignant but incomplete." McClatchy DC, February 23, 2016. https://www.mcclatchydc.com /news/politics-government/election/article24782596.html.

"Robert Smigel as Alan Dershowitz, et al." *Saturday Night Live*, Getty Images, September 26, 1992. https://www.gettyimages.com/detail /news-photo/episode-1-pictured-robert-smigel-as-alan-dershowitz -jan-news-photo/140765761.

Smerconish, Michael. "The Pulse: Dershowitz and His Life at Harvard Law." *The Philadelphia Inquirer*, April 6, 2014. https://www.inquirer .com/philly/news/20140406_The_Pulse__Dershowitz_and_his_life _at_Harvard_Law.html.

Staff, J. "Allow Clinton, a Good Friend of Israel, to Finish Term." *Jewish News of Northern California*, September 25, 1998. https://jweekly.com/1998/09/25/allow-clinton-a-good-friend-of-israel-to-finish-term/.

Tannenbaum, Rob. "Mike Tyson Opens up about Sobriety, Therapy." *Rolling Stone*, June 25, 2018. https://www.rollingstone.com/culture/culture-news/mike-tyson-on-ditching-club-life-and-getting-sober-56592/.

"Ted Cruz." Encyclopædia Britannica, April 11, 2024. https://www.britannica.com/biography/Ted-Cruz.

"Trying to Save Leona." *New York Magazine*, March 1, 1990.

"United States Presidential Election of 1992." Encyclopædia Britannica. Accessed April 15, 2024. https://www.britannica.com/event/United-States-presidential-election-of-1992.

"Whitey Bulger." Encyclopædia Britannica, March 27, 2024. https://www.britannica.com/biography/Whitey-Bulger.

Williams, Marjorie, and Ruth Marcus. "Courting Fame, Fanning Flames." *The Washington Post*, February 9, 1991. https://www.washingtonpost.com/archive/lifestyle/1991/02/10/courting-fame-fanning-flames/0eae368c-9019-4736-baea-ed1705c72a8d/.

Videos

"ABC News 20/20: Barbara Walters Interviews Michael Milken: 1993: Broadcast TV Edit: VHS Format." YouTube, November 26, 2022. https://youtu.be/1fEo8hLHcxg?si=fiOTcTNl0Rba17I5.

"Alan Dershowitz on Teaching Ted Cruz at Harvard Law School." YouTube, April 13, 2016. https://youtu.be/sc9rubga1lY?si=KBPSo6zJHjciF55V.

"American Archive of Public Broadcasting." American Archive of Public Broadcasting. Accessed April 15, 2024. https://americanarchive.org/catalog/cpb-aacip_15–901zc7rs7f.

Charlie Rose. Accessed April 15, 2024. https://charlierose.com/videos/14850; https://charlierose.com/videos/18189.

"Jim and Tammy Present PTL the Second Decade." YouTube, January 19, 2019. https://www.youtube.com/watch?v=XuARY5fK0oQ&t=1402s.

"The Road to Peace & Israel's Image in America." C-Span. Accessed April 15, 2024. https://www.c-span.org/video/?7700-1%2Froad-peace-israels -image-america%E2%80%94aipac+1989%3B.

The Trials of Alan Dershowitz, John Curtin, 2023. https://www.docnyc .net/the-trials-of-alan-dershowitz/.

"Woody Allen Cold Opening—Saturday Night Live." YouTube, October 5, 2013. https://youtu.be/iDAgPyZSbis?si=xah-EIHV5KfRPBCT.

Brooklyn College/Other

Dershowitz Archives: Series 9.1—Box 3, New York vs. Harry and Leona Helmsley: Series 1: Box 2, Series V. Correspondence—Box 18, Series VII. Press and Media—Box 24; U.S. v. James O. Bakker, 1980s-1990s: Boxes 2 & 4; U.S. vs Michael Milken, 1980–1984—Boxes 5, 11, 23, 26, & 35, State of Indiana vs Michael G. Tyson: Series 1—Box 5, Box 8; Series 2: Box 17, Box 26; Series 3: Box 31; Series 7: Boxes 41, 42, 45, & 46; Woody Allen v. Maria Villiers Farrow—Box 1, State of California vs. Christian Brando, 1990–1995—Boxes 1 & 2, Series 1.2—Box 3, Series 6.2—Boxes 16, 18, & 19, Series 6.2—Box 23, Series 5.4: Holocaust—Box 1, Series 7.1—Box 9, Series 1.1—Box 13, Tison vs Arizona 1976–1990—Boxes 3 & 21, Series 10.1—Boxes 1, 2, & 3; "AMD Guide"

Trails of Deceit

Interviews

Alan Dershowitz, Carolyn Cohen, Elon Dershowitz, Nathan Dershowitz, Gen. Elyezer Shkedi, Robert Shapiro, O. J. Simpson, Geraldo Rivera, Robert F. Kennedy Jr., Itamar Ringel, Itamar Rabinovich, Mark Levin, Judge Aharon Barak, Ted Cruz, Justice Stephen Breyer, Shirley Ringel, Maura Kelley, Norman Ringel, Barry Zimmerman, Hal Miller-Jacobs, Carl & Joan Meshenberg, Zecharia Dor-Shav, Norman Sohn, Alan Zwiebel

Books

Dershowitz, Alan:

> *Taking the Stand.* Crown Publishers, 2013, 284, 237–247, 365–376, 432, 361–362, 303–305, 272, 458–459.

> *Defending Israel.* All Points Books, 2019, 132–163.

> *Sexual McCarthyism.* Basic Books, 1998, acknowledgments, 3, 4, 9–18, 21, 23–27, 30–36, 39, 67–68, 70, 77, 91, 94, 103, 115, 124, 137, 145, 149, 150–152, 181, 186–191, 199, 207, 209, 212, 217, 218–220, 232, 234, 236–238, 265.

> *Supreme Injustice.* Oxford University Press, 2001, 4–7, 9–12, 20–25, 31–33, 37–38, 43–44, 46, 48, 56, 63, 64, 69–70, 80–82, 90, 108–109, 119–120, 124, 126, 131–132, 137, 141, 146, 153, 168, 169, 171–172, 175, 177–179, 181, 188, 200, 202–203, 206.

> *Reasonable Doubts.* Simon & Schuster, 1996, dedication, introduction, 19, 20–32, 38, 42–55, 57–58, 60–62, 64–66, 69, 73–78, 80–86, 99, 101, 103–107, 113, 119, 123–125, 130, 141, 146, 151, 153, 155, 157, 159, 160–162, 164–166, 172–175, 181, 188–190, 196, 198–199.

> *Guilt by Accusation.* Hot Books, 2019, 26–31.

> *The Price of Principle.* Hot Books, 2022, 74–76.

> *The Case for Israel.* Wiley, 2003, introduction, back cover, dedication, acknowledgments, Conclusion, 121.

> *Shouting Fire.* Little, Brown, 2002, 335, 192–193.

Groening, Matt. *The Simpsons: A Complete Guide to Our Favorite Family.* First Edition, HarperPerennial, page 173.

Shapiro, Robert. *The Search for Justice.* Grand Central Pub, 1996, 54–55, 80–81, 111–112, 249, 391.

Articles

"A Chronology: Key Moments in the Clinton-Lewinsky Saga." CNN. Accessed April 15, 2024. https://edition.cnn.com/ALLPOLITICS/1998/resources/lewinsky/timeline/.

"Alan Dershowitz: Al Gore, His Legal Team and I Tried to Find Uncounted Presidential Votes, Lobbied Officials and Fought in the Courts in 2000. the Only Difference Now? The Candidate's Name Is

Donald Trump . . . That's Why This Prosecution Is an Outrage." *Daily Mail Online*, August 16, 2023. https://www.dailymail.co.uk/news /article-12413181/ALAN-DERSHOWITZ-Al-Gore-2000-Donald -Trump-indictment.html.

"Albert Dershman, Who Can Hold Three Billiard Balls in His Mouth." Yarn. Accessed April 15, 2024. https://getyarn.io/yarn-clip/391ea9 3f-5440-40ee-8b76-b21659132fef.

Anderson, Leslie. "Defense lawyer Alan Dershowitz: Hate mail is badge of honor." UPI, April 7, 1985. https://www.upi.com/Archives/1985 /04/07/Defense-lawyer-Alan-Dershowitz-Hate-mail-is-badge-of -honor/1849481698000/.

Arenson, Karen W. "Commencements; College Honors Man It Tried to Discredit." *The New York Times*, June 2, 2001. https://www.nytimes .com/2001/06/02/nyregion/commencements-college-honors-man-it -tried-to-discredit.html.

Baker, KC. "Nicole Brown Simpson and Ron Goldman Were Murdered 25 Years Ago Today: 'The Pain Is Always There.'" *People*, June 12, 2019. https://people.com/crime/nicole-brown-simpson-ron-goldman -murders-25-years-ago/.

Barron, James. "Charlie Rose Never Runs out of Things to Say." *The New York Times*, June 13, 1993. https://www.nytimes.com/1993/06/13/arts /television-charlie-rose-never-runs-out-of-things-to-say.html.

"Basic Law: Human Dignity and Liberty—17 March 1992 (Historical Text)." palquest, March 17, 1992. https://www.palquest.org/en/historictext /33424/basic-law-human-dignity-and-liberty.

"Benjamin Netanyahu." Encyclopædia Britannica, April 15, 2024. https: //www.britannica.com/biography/Benjamin-Netanyahu.

"Bill Clinton." Encyclopædia Britannica, April 10, 2024. https://www .britannica.com/biography/Bill-Clinton.

Blumenkrantz, Zohar, Rina Rozenberg Kandel, and Shelly Appelberg. "El Al CEO Eliezer Shkedy to Step Down after 4 Years." Haaretz, December 1, 2013. https://www.haaretz.com/2013-12-01/ty-article/.premium /el-al-ceo-stepping-down/0000017f-e0e6-d7b2-a77f-e3e7966a0000.

Bronner, Ethan. "The New New Historians." *The New York Times*, November 9, 2003. https://www.nytimes.com/2003/11/09/books/the -new-new-historians.html.

Caldwell, Ellen C. "O.J. Simpson: Media Spectacle Then and Now." *JSTOR Daily*, April 25, 2016. https://daily.jstor.org/o-j-simpson -media-and-spectacle-then-and-now/.

"Carly Simon, Center, Alan Dershowitz, Right, and an Unidentified Man." Getty Images. Accessed April 15, 2024. https://www.gettyimages .com/detail/news-photo/carly-simon-center-alan-dershowitz-right -and-an-news-photo/141034876.

"Deconstructing Camp David." *Al Jazeera*, September 28, 2003. https: //www.aljazeera.com/news/2003/9/28/deconstructing-camp-david.

"Direct Access: Alan M. Dershowitz." *The Washington Post*, January 15, 1999. https://www.washingtonpost.com/wp-srv/politics/talk/zforum /dershowitz011599.htm.

"Elena Kagan." Encyclopædia Britannica, March 15, 2024. https://www .britannica.com/biography/Elena-Kagan.

Eliezer Shkedy. Accessed April 15, 2024. https://www.jewishvirtuallibrary .org/eliezer-shkedy.

Eilperin, Juliet, and Ruth Marcus. "Both Sides Harden Impeachment Views." *The Washington Post*, December 1, 1998. https://www.washing tonpost.com/archive/politics/1998/12/02/both-sides-harden -impeachment-views/5d13cb8d-b394-470b-a61c-bf7a871c18d5/.

Galloway, Stephen. "A Conversation with Marcia Clark: Rape, Scientology Flirtation and When She Law Saw O.J." *The Hollywood Reporter*, March 30, 2016. https://www.hollywoodreporter.com/movies/movie -features/marcia-clark-her-rape-scientology-878889/.

"Geraldo Rivera." Encyclopædia Britannica, April 3, 2024. https://www .britannica.com/biography/Geraldo-Rivera.

Finkelstein, Norman. "The Glove Does Fit: A Reply to Alan Dershowitz." The Electronic Intifada, September 30, 2003. https://electronicintifada .net/content/glove-does-fit-reply-alan-dershowitz/4814.

"Hi Reddit—I am Christopher Darden, Prosecutor on O.J. Simpson's Murder Trial. Ask Me Anything!" Reddit thread, July 22, 2017. https://www.reddit.com/r/IAmA/comments/6oybbr/hi_reddit_i_am _christopher_darden_prosecutor_on/.

Impeachment of president William Jefferson Clinton—the eviden-tiary record pursuant to S. Res. 16—index to Senate document

106–3, vols. I-XXIV—volume XXI—hearing of the full committee—"consequences of perjury and related crimes" (December 1, 1998) ser. no. 67. Accessed April 15, 2024. https://www.govinfo.gov/content/pkg/GPO-CDOC-106sdoc3/html/GPO-CDOC-106sdoc3–21.htm;

"Intifada." Encyclopædia Britannica, April 11, 2024. https://www.britannica.com/topic/intifada.

Itzkoff, Dave. "Alan Dershowitz in Two Eras of SNL Impeachment Parodies, 22 Years Apart, as Played by Jimmy Fallon (in 1998) and Jon Lovitz (Tonight)." Twitter, January 25, 2020. https://twitter.com/ditzkoff/status/1221290259666948096.

Jackson, Abby. "O.J. Simpson's Lawyer Alan Dershowitz: 'This Was Not the Dream Team—This Was the Nightmare Team.'" Yahoo! Finance, February 8, 2016. https://uk.finance.yahoo.com/news/o-j-simpsons-lawyer-alan-204510057.html.

"Jeffrey Epstein." Encyclopædia Britannica, April 9, 2024. https://www.britannica.com/biography/Jeffrey-Epstein.

"Johnnie Cochran." Encyclopædia Britannica, April 12, 2024. https://www.britannica.com/biography/Johnnie-L-Cochran-Jr.

"Ken Starr." Encyclopædia Britannica. Accessed April 15, 2024. https://www.britannica.com/biography/Kenneth-W-Starr.

Kiner, Deb. "From Dance Recital and Dinner to Dead—the Murder of Nicole Brown Simpson and Ron Goldman in 1994." PennLive, April 11, 2024. https://www.pennlive.com/crime/2021/06/from-dance-recital-and-dinner-to-dead-the-murder-of-nicole-brown-simpson-and-ron-goldman-in-1994.html.

Kingsley, Patrick. "He's 86 and Long Retired. Why Are Israelis Protesting Outside His Home?" The New York Times, May 5, 2023. https://www.nytimes.com/2023/05/05/world/middleeast/aharon-barak-israel-judicial-overhaul.html.

"Larry David." Encyclopædia Britannica, April 11, 2024. https://www.britannica.com/biography/Larry-David.

"Lawdragon 500 Limelight: Robert Shapiro." Lawdragon, December 21, 2023. https://www.lawdragon.com/lawyer-limelights/2023–01–31-lawdragon-500-limelight-robert-.

"Majority Opinion." Encyclopædia Britannica. Accessed April 15, 2024. https://www.britannica.com/event/Bush-v-Gore/Majority-opinion.

"Mark Fuhrman." Encyclopædia Britannica. Accessed April 15, 2024. https://www.britannica.com/biography/Mark-Fuhrman.

"Mark Levin." Wikipedia, April 14, 2024. https://en.wikipedia.org/wiki/Mark_Levin.

"Natalie Portman." Encyclopædia Britannica, April 15, 2024. https://www.britannica.com/biography/Natalie-Portman.

"Nicole Simpson's Grisly Death Described to Jury." *Chicago Tribune*, August 19, 2021. https://www.chicagotribune.com/news/ct-xpm-1995–06-08–9506080167-story.html.

"O.J. Simpson Trial." Encyclopædia Britannica, April 11, 2024. https://www.britannica.com/event/O-J-Simpson-trial.

"O.J. Simpson trial: Night of the murders timeline." CNN/Wayback Machine, December 11, 2007. https://web.archive.org/web/20130306203826/http://articles.cnn.com/2007–12-11/us/court.archive.simpson14_1_pablo-fenjves-ronald-goldman-allan-park?_s=PM:US.

"Q&A on the Override Clause." The Israel Democracy Institute, May 17, 2018. https://en.idi.org.il/articles/23521.

"Portman's Peers." *The Globe and Mail*, December 3, 2004. https://www.theglobeandmail.com/arts/portmans-peers/article18278890/.

Reich, J.E. "Inside Nicole Brown Simpson and Ron Goldman's Relationship." Nicki Swift, May 27, 2022. https://www.nickiswift.com/478981/inside-nicole-brown-simpson-and-ron-goldmans-relationship/.

Roberts, Roxanne, and Kimberly Palmer. "Morocco's King of Hearts." *The Washington Post*, June 20, 2000. https://www.washingtonpost.com/archive/lifestyle/2000/06/21/moroccos-king-of-hearts/8e9a8515-b0d4–4e84-a0d7–39e09e1eacaf/.

"Robert F. Kennedy, Jr.." Encyclopædia Britannica, April 13, 2024. https://www.britannica.com/biography/Robert-F-Kennedy-Jr.

Rose, Stephen. "Mike Wallace, Left, Ted Danson with Wife Mary Steenburgen, Alan Dershowitz." Getty Images, July 25, 1999. https://www.gettyimages.co.uk/detail/news-photo/mike-wallace-left-ted-danson-with-wife-mary-steenburgen-news-photo/585797923.

Scharnick, Jaquelyn M. "People in the News: Jeffrey E. Epstein." *The Harvard Crimson*, June 5, 2003. https://www.thecrimson.com/article /2003/6/5/people-in-the-news-jeffrey-e/.

Scharnick, Jaquelyn M. "Mogul Donor Gives Harvard More Than Money." *The Harvard Crimson*, May 1, 2003. https://www.thecrimson.com /article/2003/5/1/mogul-donor-gives-harvard-more-than/.

Schoenberg, Abigail F. "Professors Reflect on Natalie Portman." *The Harvard Crimson*, March 1, 2011. https://www.thecrimson.com/article /2011/3/1/harvard-natalie-portman-dershowitz/.

"Senators' Final Statements by Date." *The Washington Post*, n.d. Accessed April 15, 2024. https://www.washingtonpost.com/wp-srv/politics/special /clinton/stories/bystatetext021399.htm.

Spargo, Chris. "Mark Fuhrman's Racist Tapes: The Full Transcript of Key OJ Simpson Detective Saying n-Word 41 Times and Detailing Racially-Motivated Violence Involving Members of LAPD." *Daily Mail Online*, March 30, 2016. https://www.dailymail.co.uk/news /article-3514002/Mark-Fuhrman-s-racist-tapes-transcript-key-witness -OJ-Simpson-case-saying-N-word-41-TIMES-detailing-incidents -racially-motivated-violence-involving-members-LAPD.html.

"The Trial of Orenthal James Simpson: An Account." Famous Trials. Accessed April 15, 2024. https://famous-trials.com/simpson/1862-home.

"Ted Cruz." Encyclopædia Britannica, April 11, 2024. https://www .britannica.com/biography/Ted-Cruz.

Tufano, Nora A. "FM Cribs: Alan M. Dershowitz." *The Harvard Crimson*, October 29, 2010. https://www.thecrimson.com/article/2010/10/29 /dershowitz-one-walls-cohen/.

"Twenty Years Out, Racial Gap Narrows on Simpson Verdict." ABC News, September 25, 2015. https://abcnews.go.com/Politics/twenty -years-racial-gap-narrows-simpson-verdict/story?id=33926204.

Villarreal, David. "Dershowitz Editorial Draws Fire." *The Harvard Crimson*, March 18, 2002. https://www.thecrimson.com/article/2002/3/18 /dershowitz-editorial-draws-fire-an-article/.

Ward, Vicky. "The Talented Mr. Epstein." *Vanity Fair*, March 1, 2003. https://www.vanityfair.com/news/2003/03/jeffrey-epstein-200303.

"Why Did So Many People Hate Bill Clinton? An Exchange Among Conservatives." History News Network. Accessed April 15, 2024. https://historynewsnetwork.org/article/12761.

"Yeshiva University Milestones." Accessed April 15, 2024. https://www.tiki-toki.com/timeline/entry/23605/Yeshiva-University-Milestones.

Videos

"(RAW) 1995: O.J. Simpson Verdict Is Not Guilty." YouTube, June 9, 2014. https://www.youtube.com/watch?v=rurKd569xRw%3B.

"Alan Dershowitz and Roger Ailes." YouTube, June 9, 2019. https://www.youtube.com/watch?si=.

"Alan Dershowitz." Charlie Rose. Accessed April 15, 2024. https://charlierose.com/videos/9616.

"ASC Panel on the OJ Simpson Trial." YouTube, February 11, 2013. https://www.youtube.com/watch?v=BW45TxN3FEE&t=3235s%3B.

"Celebrating Alan Dershowitz: Public Intellectual." YouTube, October 30, 2013. https://www.youtube.com/watch?v=mtbXjn2Z_qw%3B.

"Christopher Darden vs Alan Dershowitz Live—the OJ Simpson Trial." YouTube, July 12, 2016. https://www.youtube.com/watch?v=ozqQohSCdfE%3B.

"CNNs Crossfire K Furman vs Alan Dershowitz (1997)." YouTube, January 14, 2018. https://www.youtube.com/watch?v=E52oSaTRYq0.

"Consequences of Perjury and Related Crimes." C-Span. December 1, 1988. https://www.c-span.org/video/?116024-1/consequences-perjury-related-crimes.

"Jeffrey Epstein's Lawyer Alan Dershowitz vs Douglas Murray | Full Debate." YouTube, January 4, 2024. https://www.youtube.com/watch?v=DME_3KSWNUM&t=613s.

"OJ Simpson Trial—June 16th, 1995—Part 1." YouTube, September 23, 2016. https://www.youtube.com/watch?v=7Pg92Ao1VNk%3B.

"Prof. Alan Dershowitz at Shaare Zedek Luncheon." YouTube, May 2, 2018. https://youtu.be/OdyXHZBs47g.

The Trials of Alan Dershowitz. John Curtin, 2003.

"The Fuhrman Tapes with Transcript—O.J. Simpson Murder Trial." YouTube, March 30, 2016. https://www.youtube.com/watch?v=C6pymcUV8v4%3B.

"What Alan Dershowitz and Ken Starr Used to Say about Impeachment."
  YouTube, January 28, 2020. https://www.youtube.com/watch?v=oxBJ
  gGro3ik%3B.
"William F. Buckley, Jr.; Alan Dershowitz." Charlie Rose. Accessed April
  15, 2024. https://charlierose.com/videos/26500.

Brooklyn College/Other
Dershowitz Archives: Series 9.1—Box 4, Series 1.2—Videos—TV Clips—
  Box 20, State of California vs. O.J. Simpson—Boxes 1, 2, 3, 5, 6, &
  14, Series 6.2—Special Correspondence—Boxes 19, 20, 21, & 22,
  Series 7.1—Supreme Injustice—Box 3, U.S. vs Susan McDougal—
  Box 1, George W. Bush vs. Albert Gore—Boxes 1, 2, 3, & 4, Series
  7.1—Case for Israel—Box 1, Series 7.4—Box 1, Series 6.2—Boxes 23
  & 23A, Series 1.2—Box 2; Alan Dershowitz's oral history with Philip
  Napoli; Alan Dershowitz's 2004 anecdotes document; Pictures from
  Alan Dershowitz's apartment in New York City

David *and* Goliath
Interviews
Alan Dershowitz, Carolyn Cohen, Elon Dershowitz, Nathan Dershowitz,
  anonymous family member of Alan's, Robert F. Kennedy Jr., Geraldo
  Rivera, Prof. I. Glenn Cohen, Glenn Greenwald, Ehud Olmert,
  Dr. Noam Chomsky, Stuart Eizenstat, Jeffrey Toobin, Eliot Spitzer,
  Zecharia Dor-Shav, Yitz Greenberg Mike Huckabee, Joel Pollak,
  Steven Pinker, Sarah Neely, Geoffrey Robertson

Books
Chomsky, Noam, & Barsamian, David. *Chronicles of Dissent*. Common
  Courage Press, 1992, 346–348.
Dershowitz, Alan:
  Taking the Stand. Crown Publishers, 2013, 458–459, 410–411, 429, 289,
    442, 320–321, 245–246, 446–450, 171, 457, 148–152, 291, 303.
  Defending Israel. All Points Books, 2019, Chapter 11, Chapter 12,
    Chapter 13, 131, 127, 241–246, 126, 250–251, 230–231, 227–
    229, 229–230.

Guilt by Accusation. Hot Books, 2019, 28–31.
The Case Against Israel's Enemies. Wiley, 2008.
The Best Defense. Vintage Books, 1983, 235.
The Price of Principle. Hot Books, 2022, 74–76, 43–52.
The Case for Peace. Wiley, 2005.
Preemption. Norton, 2006, 176–177.

Articles

Admin. "Geneva—Alan Dershowitz Hauled Away from Protest at Ahmadinejad Hotel." VINnews, April 20, 2009. https://vinnews.com /2009/04/20/geneva-alan-dershowitz-hauled-away-from-protest-at -ahmadinejad-hotel/.

"Alan Dershowitz Talks Obama and Israel." *Vineyard Gazette*, August 3, 2009. https://vineyardgazette.com/news/2009/08/03/alan-dershowitz -talks-obama-and-israel.

Alan M. Dershowitz. "Netanyahu, Show the U.S. That Israel Does Know Its Own Best Interests." *Haaretz*, January 23, 2013. https://www .haaretz.com/opinion/2013–01-23/ty-article/.premium/alan-dershowitz -a-ripe-time-for-peace-talks/0000017f-f405-d47e-a37f-fd3d5b910000.

"Ariel Sharon Summary." Encyclopædia Britannica. Accessed April 15, 2024. https://www.britannica.com/summary/Ariel-Sharon.

"At Intelligence Squared Us Debate Audience Says: 'Freedom of the Press Does Extend to State Secrets.'" NBCNews.com, June 9, 2011. https: //www.nbcnews.com/id/wbna43343727.

"At Intelligence Squared Us Debate Audience Says: 'Freedom of the Press Does Extend to State Secrets.'" News Powered by Cision. June 9, 2011. https://news.cision.com/intelligence-squared/r/at-intelligence-squared -us-debate-audience-says-freedom-of-the-press-does-extend-to-state -secrets-,c9133352.

"At the Birthplace of U.S. Liberty, Eroticized Hatred of Israel." *Jewish News of Northern California*, April 9, 2004. https://jweekly.com/2004/04/09 /at-the-birthplace-of-u-s-liberty-eroticized-hatred-of-israel/.

"Barack Obama." Encyclopædia Britannica, April 13, 2024. https://www .britannica.com/biography/Barack-Obama.

Barkan, Ross. "The Tragedy of Eliot Spitzer." March 11, 2023. https://rosselliotbarkan.com/p/the-tragedy-of-eliot-spitzer.

"Benjamin Netanyahu." Encyclopædia Britannica, April 15, 2024. https://www.britannica.com/biography/Benjamin-Netanyahu.

Brown, Jeannette. "Dershowitz Visits." Newuniversity.org, December 3, 2007. https://newuniversity.org/2007/12/03/dershowitz_visits_on_anniv50/.

"Chomsky Is Citation Champ." MIT News, April 15, 1992. https://news.mit.edu/1992/citation-0415.

Cohen, Patricia. "Dershowitz vs. Finkelstein: When a Scholarly Clash Turns Vitriolic." The New York Times, April 17, 2007. https://www.nytimes.com/2007/04/16/arts/16iht-feud.1.5305993.html.

Cummings, William. "Six Big Leaks from Julian Assange's WikiLeaks over the Years." USA Today, April 14, 2019. https://www.usatoday.com/story/news/politics/2019/04/11/julian-assange-six-wikileaks-most-memorable-revelations/3434371002/.

David, Dennis. "SAZF shouldn't honour Dershowitz." PoliticsWeb, March 27, 2011. https://www.politicsweb.co.za/about/sazf-shouldnt-honour-dershowitz.

Dershowitz, Alan. "Finkelstein's Bigotry." Wall Street Journal, May 4, 2007. https://www.wsj.com/articles/SB117824380227591804.

Dershowitz, Alan. "Arafat Died an Uncontrite Terrorist." The Forward, November 19, 2004. https://forward.com/opinion/4549/arafat-died-an-uncontrite-terrorist/.

Dershowitz, Alan. "Norway to Jews: You're Not Welcome Here." Wall Street Journal, March 29, 2011. https://www.wsj.com/articles/SB10001424052748704474804576222561887244764.

Dershowitz, Alan. "The Entrapment of Eliot." Wall Street Journal, March 13, 2008. https://www.wsj.com/articles/SB120536943121332151.

Dershowitz, Alan. "Why I Support Israel and Obama." HuffPost, May 25, 2011. https://www.huffpost.com/entry/why-i-support-israel-and_b_135660.

Dershowitz, Elon. "In LA. Just Got Back from Israel. Amazing Trip with Dad. He's Elvis over There." Twitter, May 29, 2010. https://twitter.com/elondershowitz/status/14946728625.

Deutch, Gabby. "Harvard Chabad, a Citywide Jewish Empire, Gets a New Endowment." eJewishPhilanthropy, November 18, 2022. https://ejewishphilanthropy.com/harvard-chabad-a-citywide-jewish-empire-gets-a-new-endowment/.

Donaghue, Erin. "NYPD Says It Wasn't Required to Monitor Jeffrey Epstein's Sex Offender Registration." CBS News, July 11, 2019. https://www.cbsnews.com/news/jeffrey-epstein-nypd-says-it-wasnt-required-to-monitor-sex-offender-registration/.

"Ehud Olmert." Encyclopædia Britannica, April 12, 2024. https://www.britannica.com/biography/Ehud-Olmert.

"Elena Kagan." Encyclopædia Britannica, March 15, 2024. https://www.britannica.com/biography/Elena-Kagan.

Finkelstein, Norman. "Should Alan Dershowitz Target Himself for Assassination?" CounterPunch.org, August 12, 2006. https://www.counterpunch.org/2006/08/12/should-alan-dershowitz-target-himself-for-assassination/.

"Four Years since the Arrest and Imprisonment of WikiLeaks Publisher Julian Assange." World Socialist Web Site. April 11, 2023. https://www.wsws.org/en/articles/2023/04/11/zhqs-a11.html.

"Glenn Greenwald." Encyclopædia Britannica, March 2, 2024. https://www.britannica.com/biography/Glenn-Greenwald.

Goldsmith, Samuel. "Jeffrey Epstein Pleads Guilty to Prostitution Charges." New York Post, June 30, 2008. https://nypost.com/2008/06/30/jeffrey-epstein-pleads-guilty-to-prostitution-charges/.

Finkelstein, Norman G. The Holocaust Industry: Reflections on the Exploitation of Jewish Suffering. Verso, 2015.

"Intifada." Encyclopædia Britannica, April 11, 2024. https://www.britannica.com/topic/intifada.

"Jeffrey Epstein." Encyclopædia Britannica, April 9, 2024. https://www.britannica.com/biography/Jeffrey-Epstein.

"Jeffrey Epstein: Palm Beach Police Say Lawyer Tried to Discredit Teenage Girl." The Palm Beach Post, July 11, 2019. https://www.palmbeachpost.com/story/news/2006/07/29/jeffrey-epstein-palm-beach-police-say-lawyer-tried-to-discredit-teenage-girl/4712840007/.

"Jeffrey Epstein's Donations to Young Pupils Prompts US Virgin Islands Review." *The Guardian*, January 13, 2015. https://www.theguardian .com/us-news/2015/jan/13/jeffrey-epstein-donations-us-virgin-islands -review.

"Julian Assange." Encyclopædia Britannica, April 11, 2024. https://www .britannica.com/biography/Julian-Assange.

Krieger, Hilary Leila. "Ross, Dershowitz: Obama Has Israel's Back on Iran." *The Jerusalem Post*, September 21, 2012. https://www.jpost .com/The-US-Presidential-race/Ross-Dershowitz-Obama-has-Israels -back-on-Iran.

"Larry David." Encyclopædia Britannica, April 11, 2024. https://www .britannica.com/biography/Larry-David.

Loewenstein, Antony. "Meeting Alan Dershowitz in Sydney." Antony Loewenstein, October 3, 2010. https://antonyloewenstein.com /meeting-alan-dershowitz-in-sydney/.

Marra, Andrew. "Jeffrey Epstein craved big homes, elite friends—and, investigators say, underage girls." *Palm Beach Post News*/Wayback Machine, August 14, 2006. https://web.archive.org/web/20110616194257 /http://www.palmbeachpost.com/localnews/content/local_news /epaper/2006/08/14/m1a_EPSTEIN_0814.html.

"Mahmoud Ahmadinejad." Encyclopædia Britannica, February 21, 2024. https://www.britannica.com/biography/Mahmoud-Ahmadinejad.

McGreal, Chris. "When Desmond Tutu Stood up for the Rights of Palestinians, He Could Not Be Ignored." *The Guardian*, December 30, 2021. https://www.theguardian.com/commentisfree/2021/dec/30/desmond -tutu-palestinians-israel.

McKay, Caroline M, and Zoe A. Y. Weinberg. "Dershowitz Joins Legal Team for Wikileaks." *The Harvard Crimson*, February 15, 2011. https://www .thecrimson.com/article/2011/2/15/dershowitz-case-wikileaks-new/.

Meier, Barry. "Alan Dershowitz on the Defense (His Own)." *The New York Times*, December 12, 2015. https://www.nytimes.com/2015/12/13 /business/alan-dershowitz-on-the-defense-his-own.html.

Mohler, Albert, and Albert Mohler. "Can We Be Good without God?" AlbertMohler.com, November 8, 2004. https://albertmohler.com /2004/11/08/can-we-be-good-without-god-2.

Molinari, Maurizio. "Alan Dershowitz: Why I Am Defending Julian Assange." La Stampa, February 18, 2011. https://www.lastampa.it/esteri /la-stampa-in-english/2011/02/18/news/alan-dershowitz-why-i -am-defending-julian-assange-1.36979806/.

Neuman, Johanna. "Kerry's entree to Jewish vote." Los Angeles Times, October 29, 2004. https://www.latimes.com/archives/la-xpm-2004 -oct-29-et-jewish29-story.html.

"Robert F. Kennedy, Jr.." Encyclopædia Britannica, April 13, 2024. https: //www.britannica.com/biography/Robert-F-Kennedy-Jr.

Shalev, Chemi. "Abbas Adopts 'Dershowitz Formula' for Resuming Talks With Israel." Haaretz, September 25, 2012. https://www.haaretz .com/2012–09-25/ty-article/abbas-to-recognize-israels-jewish-link /0000017f-f0b8-d223-a97f-fdfd2ac70000.

Shamir, Shlomo, and Natasha Mozgovaya. "Durban III Conference Opens in New York amid Allegations of Anti-Israel Bias." Haaretz. com, September 22, 2011. https://www.haaretz.com/2011–09-22/ty -article/durban-iii-conference-opens-in-new-york-amid-allegations -of-anti-israel-bias/0000017f-dc89-df9c-a17f-fe99dbad0000.

"Shortly before Noon, Cambridge Fire Officials Responded to a Call For . . ." Getty Images, January 21, 2009. https://www.gettyimages .com/detail/news-photo/shortly-before-noon-cambridge-fire-officials -responded-to-a-news-photo/1290406442.

Smink, Sam. "Jeffrey Epstein Spent Hours at Home during Work Release, 'Responsible for His Own Transportation.'" WPTV News, July 18, 2019. https://www.wptv.com/news/local-news/investigations/convicted -sex-offender-jeffrey-epstein-spent-hours-at-home-during-work-release -was-responsible-for-his-own-transportation-from-pbso-jail.

Sokol, Sam. "Dershowitz Presents Plan to Restart Peace Talks." The Jerusalem Post, April 29, 2013. https://www.jpost.com/diplomacy -and-politics/dershowitz-presents-plan-to-restart-peace-talks-311465.

"Star Lawyer Alan Dershowitz: 'Assange Is a New Kind of Journalist.'" DER SPIEGEL, February 22, 2011. https://www.spiegel.de/international /world/star-lawyer-alan-dershowitz-assange-is-a-new-kind-of-journalist -a-746942.html.

"Two-State Solution." Encyclopædia Britannica, March 27, 2024. https://www.britannica.com/topic/two-state-solution.

Wharton, Molly E. "Fifty Years of Alan Dershowitz." *The Harvard Crimson*, April 24, 2014. https://www.thecrimson.com/article/2014/4/24/fifty-years-retired-alan-dershowitz/.

Wiener, Jon. "Chutzpah and free speech." *Los Angeles Times*, July 11, 2005. https://www.latimes.com/archives/la-xpm-2005-jul-11-oe-wiener11-story.html.

Wu, June Q. "Harvard Law Prof. Receives Suspicious Powder." *The Harvard Crimson*, January 21, 2009. https://www.thecrimson.com/article/2009/1/21/harvard-law-prof-receives-suspicious-powder/.

Videos

"Alan Dershowitz and Jeffrey Toobin on Free Speech." YouTube, February 12, 2008. https://www.youtube.com/watch?v=fT7B183Ym0g%3B.

"Alan Dershowitz Responds to Being Named in Jeffrey Epstein Court Docs." YouTube, January 4, 2024. https://www.youtube.com/watch?v=5IUESiGbXq8.

"Alan Dershowitz, Jeffrey Epstein's Former Lawyer, Claims to Have Proof His Accuser Is Lying." YouTube, July 10, 2019. https://www.youtube.com/watch?v=eaz9dpk9Yyk&t=101s.

"Celebrating Alan Dershowitz: Litigator." YouTube, October 30, 2013. https://www.youtube.com/watch?v=WB-TD0tEQts.

"Celebrating Alan Dershowitz: Public Intellectual." YouTube, October 30, 2013. https://www.youtube.com/watch?v=mtbXjn2Z_qw&t=4453s.

"Celebrating Alan Dershowitz: Scholarship and Writing." YouTube, October 30, 2013. https://www.youtube.com/watch?v=d_CqB4wjm5w.

"Celebrating Alan Dershowitz: Teacher." YouTube, October 30, 2013. https://www.youtube.com/watch?v=qUMVXLkygtE%3B.

"Has God's Law Been Changed? Mike Huckabee and Alan Dershowitz Discuss." YouTube, July 8, 2022. https://www.youtube.com/watch?v=ZLlVwUkMtr0.

"Hot Take Grills Attorney Alan Dershowitz on Jeffrey Epstein." YouTube, May 19, 2020. https://www.youtube.com/watch?v=L2wrZXDFGVI.

"Jeffrey Epstein List: Over 150 People to Be Identified in Court Documents." YouTube, January 3, 2024. https://www.youtube.com/watch?v=lEJJfzfgYcs.

"Jeffrey Epstein's Lawyer Alan Dershowitz vs Douglas Murray | Full Debate." YouTube, January 4, 2024. https://www.youtube.com/watch?v=DME _3KSWNUM&t=613s%3B.

"Noam Chomsky Debates Alan Dershowitz + Q&A (2005)." YouTube, September 9, 2017. https://www.youtube.com/watch?v=4dvMdSuLK CE&t=25s.

"Norman Finkelstein vs Alan Dershowitz—a Lively Debate on Democracy Now." YouTube, January 12, 2020. https://www.youtube.com/watch ?v=GzqTWpPI5Qw.

Other

Pictures in Alan Dershowitz's New York apartment; Pictures in Alan Dershowitz's Martha's Vineyard home

To the "Dark Side"

Interviews

Alan Dershowitz, Carolyn Cohen, Elon Dershowitz, Nathan Dershowitz, Tony Lyons, Jamie Raskin, Jared Kushner, Jay Sekulow, O. J. Simpson, Megyn Kelly, Susan Estrich, Mike Pompeo, Yitz Greenberg, Mark Levin, Harvey Silverglate, Jeffrey Toobin, Donald Trump, Zecharia Dor-Shav, Susan Estrich, Kenneth Sweder, anonymous friend of Alan's, Sarah Neely, Hal Miller-Jacobs, Barry Zimmerman, Bernie Beck, Carl & Joan Meshenberg, Zvi Boyarsky, Geraldo Rivera, Robert F. Kennedy Jr., Mike Huckabee, Nathan Lewin, Geoffrey Robertson, Justice Stephen Breyer, Joel Klein, Maura Kelley, Robert Shapiro, Harvey Silverglate, Eliot Spitzer, Alex Kozinski, Steven Pinker, Joel Pollak, Stuart Eizenstat, Judge Aharon Barak

Books

Department of Justice. *The Mueller Report*. Skyhorse Publishing, 2019, 1–12.

Dershowitz, Alan:

Defending Israel. All Points Books, 2019, Chapter 13, Chapter 14, 259–265.

Guilt by Accusation. Hot Books, 2019, 5–8, 10–11, 19–22, 24–25, 27–28, 30–32, 36–40, 42–43, 45, 48–49, 53, 55, 57–58, 61, 67–72, 92, 96–97, 99, 100, 102–105, 107–109, 111–112, 119–132, 146, 149, 152.

The Case Against the Iran Deal. Rosetta Press, 2015, 68, 170, 171, 195.

The Case Against the Democratic House Impeaching Trump. Hot Books, 2019, 1–2, 7, 9, 13, 24–25, 29, 30, 45–47, 54, 57, 71, 73, 76–79, 86–87, 96, 103, 108, 111–113, 118–120, 132, 134, 136, 148–153, 172, 174, 187, 189, 202–203, 208–212, 275, 283–284, 285–286.

Terror Tunnels. Rosetta Books, 2014, 72.

The Case Against BDS. Bombardier Books, 2018, 30.

Defending the Constitution. Hot Books, 2020, 1, 3–9, 11–13, 25–27, 31–33, 37–38, 51–55, 62–63, 68–70, 73–77, 87–89, 94–99, 101–104, 106, 108–112, 119–121, 123–124, 128–133, 136–138, 140–141, 143, 146–147, 149–155, 162, 170–171, 207.

The Price of Principle. Hot Books, 2022, 74–76, 43–52.

Electile Dysfunction. Rosetta Books, 2016, 50–51, 70, 72–73, 74, 79, 84, 87, 90, 95, 97, 100, 102, 105–106, 108, 113.

The Case for Liberalism in an Age of Extremism. Hot Books, 2020, 4–7, 28–31, 41, 110–111, 114–117.

Trumped Up. Bombardier Books, 2017, 10–12, 18, 51–52, 70, 89, 127, 130, 137, 144, 168–169, 172, 174–175, 178–179, 180–181, 186–187.

Articles

"About the Aleph Institute." The Aleph Institute, n.d. https://aleph-institute.org/about/.

"Abraham Accords." Encyclopædia Britannica, n.d. https://www.britannica.com/topic/Abraham-Accords.

"Across the World, Shock and Uncertainty at Trump's Victory." *The New York Times*, November 9, 2016. https://www.nytimes.com/2016/11/09/world/europe/global-reaction-us-presidential-election-donald-trump.html.

"Alan (I Kept My Underwear on) Dershowitz Slams Barr for 'dead Wrong' Comments on "Trump Indictment." Democratic Underground Forums, August 5, 2023. www.democraticunderground.com/100218154669.

"Alan Dershowitz Defamation Lawsuit Reveals Another Jeffrey Epstein Accuser." CBS News, August 13, 2019. https://www.cbsnews.com /news/jeffrey-epstein-new-accuser-maria-farmer-revealed-in-alan -dershowitz-lawsuit/.

"Alan Dershowitz Mock Trial on Child Trafficking in the Bible Canceled after Epstein Suicide." CNBC, August 15, 2019. https://www.cnbc .com/2019/08/14/dershowitz-child-trafficking-mock-trial-canceled -after-epstein-suicide.html.

"Alan Dershowitz Slams Harvard's Decision to Drop Weinstein Lawyer as Dean: 'New Mccarthyism.'" Fox News, May 12, 2019. https://www .foxnews.com/us/alan-dershowitz-harvard-harvey-weinstein-lawyer -dean-new-mccarthyism.

"Alan Dershowitz Sued in Prince Andrew Sex Abuse Case." BBC News, January 7, 2015. https://www.bbc.com/news/world-us-canada-3070 8795.

"Alan Dershowitz wanted David Boies off Epstein-related suit. A top law-yer has replaced him." McClatchy News, November 3, 2019. https: //www.mcclatchydc.com/news/investigations/article236923193.html.

"Alan M. Dershowitz: A nightmare of false accusation that could happen to you." *Wall Street Journal*, January 14, 2015. https://www.wsj.com /articles/alan-m-dershowitz-a-nightmare-of-false-accusation-that-could -happen-to-you-1421280860.

Allman, William G. "The Lincoln Bedroom: Refurbishing a Famous White House Room." White House History, n.d. https://www.white househistory.org/the-lincoln-bedroom-refurbishing-a-famous-white -house-room.

"An Open Letter to the Senate." *The New York Times*. https://int.nyt .com/data/documenthelper/6765-v2–0-senate-open-letter crimes/77b77 a0e52cd5125550d/optimized/full.pdf.

Badcock, Merris. "Jeffrey Epstein, Sex Offenders Qualified for Work Release under PBSO's 2007 Policy." www.wflx.com, August 6, 2019. https://www.wflx.com/2019/08/06/jeffrey-epstein-sex-offenders -qualified-work-release-under-pbsos-policy/.

Beckett, Lois. "Harvey Weinstein Sentenced to 16 Additional Years for LA Rape Conviction." *The Guardian*, February 24, 2023. www.theguardian.com/world/2023/feb/23/harvey-weinstein-los-angeles-rape-conviction-sentencing.

Bendix, Trish. "Late Night Dissects Alan Dershowitz's Unimpeachable Logic." *The New York Times*, January 31, 2020. https://www.nytimes.com/2020/01/31/arts/television/seth-meyers-jimmy-kimmel-late-night-trump.html.

"Benjamin Netanyahu—‏והינתנ ‏וימינב‏." Facebook, February 27, 2019. https://www.facebook.com/Netanyahu/posts/10156187963162076.

Berg, Madeline. "Oscar Hero to Zero: How Harvey Weinstein's Power Enabled Him—and Led to His Decline." *Forbes*, October 14, 2017. https://www.forbes.com/sites/maddieberg/2017/10/13/oscar-hero-to-zero-how-harvey-weinsteins-power-enabled-him-and-led-to-his-decline/?sh=6cd4b49e3062.

Bidgood, Jess, and Julie Bosman. "On Martha's Vineyard, a Frosty Summer for Alan Dershowitz." *The New York Times*, July 4, 2018. https://www.nytimes.com/2018/07/03/us/marthas-vineyard-trump.html.

Bloom, Horace. *Donald Trump and Adolf Hitler: Making a Serious Comparison*. CreateSpace, 2016.

Bondarenko, Veronika. "Advisers 'tried to cheer up' an Angry Trump with Positive Comments on Travel Ban from Alan Dershowitz." *Business Insider*, March 16, 2017. https://www.businessinsider.com/president-trump-alan-dershowitz-travel-ban-muslims-2017-3.

Bowden, John. "Trump Cites Dershowitz in Claim That Mueller Should Not Have Been Appointed." *The Hill*, March 21, 2018. https://thehill.com/homenews/administration/379462-trump-cites-dershowitz-argument-that-special-counsel-never-should/.

Briquelet, Kate. "Epstein Victim: Dershowitz Says He's Exonerated. He Isn't." The Daily Beast, November 15, 2022. https://www.thedailybeast.com/epstein-victim-virginia-giuffre-says-alan-dershowitz-is-not-exonerated-no-matter-what-he-says.

Briquelet, Kate, Justin Rohrlich, and Katie Baker. "Epstein Victim Says She Was Forced into Threesome with Alan Dershowitz." The Daily Beast, December 13, 2022. https://www.thedailybeast.com/epstein-victim

-was-grilled-about-alan-dershowitzs-bleeding-penis-said-she-was
-forced-into-threesome.

Brown, Anna. "More than Twice as Many Americans Support than Oppose the #MeToo Movement." Pew Research Center's Social & Demographic Trends Project, September 29, 2022. www.pewresearch .org/social-trends/2022/09/29/more-than-twice-as-many-americans -support-than-oppose-the-metoo-movement/.

Brown, Connor W. K. "Harvard Law Prof. Emeritus Alan Dershowitz Joins Weinstein Defense Team in Class Action Suit." *The Harvard Crimson*, February 18, 2019. https://www.thecrimson.com/article/2019 /2/18/dershowitz-weinstein/.

Brown, Connor W. K., and Molly C. McCafferty. "Jeffrey Epstein Accuser Sues Harvard Law Professor Alan Dershowitz for Defamation." *The Harvard Crimson*, April 17, 2019. https://www.thecrimson.com/article /2019/4/17/dershowitz-defamation-suit/.

Bruck, Connie. "Alan Dershowitz, Devil's Advocate." *The New Yorker*, July 29, 2019. https://www.newyorker.com/magazine/2019/08/05/alan -dershowitz-devils-advocate.

Burke, Cathy. "Dershowitz to Newsmax TV: Klobuchar, Castro 'perfect' Ticket." Newsmax, June 27, 2019. https://www.newsmax.com/news max-tv/alan-dershowitz-amy-klobuchar-julian-castro-democrats /2019/06/26/id/922221/.

Campbell, Andy. "Hate Has Flourished in 2 Years since 'Unite the Right' Rally in Charlottesville." HuffPost, August 12, 2019. https://www .huffpost.com/entry/charlottesville-anniversary-hate-flourishes-unite -the-right.

Chiarella, Tom. "21 Hours with Alan Dershowitz." *Esquire*, January 29, 2020. www.esquire.com/news-politics/a30695201/alan-dershowitz -donald-trump-impeachment-interview/.

Chotiner, Isaac. "Alan Dershowitz-Fresh from Dinner with Trump-Says the President's Civil Liberties Are Being Violated." Slate Magazine, April 11, 2018. https://slate.com/news-and-politics/2018/04/alan -dershowitzfresh-from-dinner-with-trumpsays-the-presidents-civil -liberties-are-being-violated.html.

Concha, Joe. "Dershowitz Says He Could 'Enthusiastically' Vote for Biden over Trump." The Hill, June 13, 2019. https://thehill.com/homenews /media/448480-dershowitz-says-he-could-enthusiastically-vote-for -biden-over-trump/.

Concha, Joe. "Dershowitz to Maxine Waters: 'Being Black Does Not Give You a License to Call Me a Racist.'" The Hill, August 8, 2017. https: //thehill.com/homenews/media/345714-dershowitz-to-maxine-waters -being-black-does-not-give-you-a-license-to-call-me/.

Corum, Samuel. "Senate Impeachment Trial Of President Trump Continues." Getty Images, January 27, 2020. https://www.gettyimages .com/detail/news-photo/members-of-president-donald-trumps-defense -team-including-news-photo/1196884952.

Cowan, Richard. "Breaking with Republicans, Romney Votes 'Guilty' in Trump Impeachment Trial." Reuters, February 5, 2020. https://www .reuters.com/article/idUSKBN20005L/.

Crowley, Michael, and David M. Halbfinger. "Trump Releases Mideast Peace Plan That Strongly Favors Israel." The New York Times, January 28, 2020. www.nytimes.com/2020/01/28/world/middleeast/peace-plan .html.

"Dershowitz Friend Creates Fund to Fight Sex Abuse Defamation Case." Mediaite, May 17, 2015. https://www.mediaite.com/online/dershowitz -friends-create-fund-to-fight-sex-abuse-defamation-case/amp/.

Dershowitz, Alan, The Case Against Impeaching Trump. Hot Books, 2018.

Dershowitz, Alan. "The Epstein Documents Reveal How I Was Framed— but I'm Still Being Canceled." New York Post, January 12, 2024. https://nypost.com/2024/01/11/opinion/the-epstein-documents -reveal-how-i-was-framed-but-im-still-being-canceled/.

"Donald Trump." Encyclopædia Britannica, April 13, 2024. https://www .britannica.com/biography/Donald-Trump.

Dorman, Sam. "Harvard Law Professors Dershowitz, Tribe Square off over Trump Impeachment Defense." Fox News, January 30, 2020. https://www.foxnews.com/media/harvard-law-dershowitz-tribe -impeachment.

Dr. Miguna. "Alan Dershowitz Is a Certified Perennial Pedophile, but He Won't Be Arrested, Charged, Prosecuted and Punished Because He Is a Zionist. Zionism Is the Worst Plague since Slavery!"

Twitter, January 4, 2024. https://twitter.com/MigunaMiguna/status
/1742754595795796341.

"Elizabeth Warren." Harvard Law School, hls.harvard.edu/faculty
/elizabeth-warren/.

Eugene Gu, MD. "Alan Dershowitz Needs Our Thoughts and
Prayers . . ." Twitter, July 2, 2018. https://twitter.com/eugenegu
/status/1013909193936461824

"Famed Lawyer Says Trump 'clearly' Endorsed Palestinian State." Voice of
America, March 30, 2017. https://www.voanews.com/a/famed-lawyer-
says-trump-clearly-endorsed-palestinian-state/3788564.html.;

Flaherty, Colleen. "Alan Dershowitz Finds Himself Thrust into Academe's
Margins." Inside Higher Ed, February 2, 2020. https://www
.insidehighered.com/news/2020/02/03/alan-dershowitz
-finds-himself-thrust-academes-margins.

"Foreign Affairs since 1989: Continuing Tension Abroad." Encyclopædia
Britannica. Accessed April 15, 2024. https://www.britannica.com
/place/Iran/Foreign-affairs-since-1989-continuing-tension-abroad
#ref1267930.

Frankfurter, Rabbi Yitzchok. "Q&A with Alan Dershowitz." Ami Magazine,
December 26, 2017. https://www.amimagazine.org/2017/12/27/qa
-alan-dershowitz/.

Gardner, Eriq. "Alan Dershowitz Hired as Harvey Weinstein Consultant."
The Hollywood Reporter, April 17, 2023. https://www.hollywood
reporter.com/business/business-news/alan-dershowitz-has-been-hired
-by-harvey-weinsteins-lawyer-as-consultant-1108452/.

Gerstein, Josh. "Unsealed Documents Detail Alleged Epstein Victim's
Recruitment at Mar-a-Lago." Politico, August 9, 2019. https://www
.politico.com/story/2019/08/09/epstein-mar-a-lago-trump-1456221.

Gold, Matea. "The campaign to impeach President Trump has
begun." *The Washington Post*, January 20, 2017. https://www
.washingtonpost.com/news/post-politics/wp/2017/01/20/the
-campaign-to-impeach-president-trump-has-begun/.

Hale, Nathan. "Dershowitz Didn't Do Work on Conviction Appeal, Suit
Says." Law360, February 9, 2015. https://www.law360.com/articles
/619860/dershowitz-didn-t-do-work-on-conviction-appeal-suit-says.

Harris, Vice President Kamala. "Yesterday, Alan Dershowitz Made an Extraordinarily Dangerous Argument..." Twitter, January 30, 2020. https://twitter.com/VP/status/1222986716576911360.

"Harvey Weinstein." Encyclopædia Britannica, April 11, 2024. https://www.britannica.com/biography/Harvey-Weinstein.

Helmore, Edward. "Tony Lyons, the US Publisher Who Picks up Books 'cancelled' by Other Presses." *The Guardian*, January 27, 2022. www.theguardian.com/books/2022/jan/27/tony-lyons-skyhorse-publisher-cancelled-books.

Holtzman, Elizabeth. *The Case for Impeaching Trump*. Rosetta Books, 2018.

Huitson, Joseph. "'Un-American': Former Trump Lawyer Takes Aim at Caroline Kennedy." *Sky News*, April 4, 2023. www.skynews.com.au/world-news/united-states/she-fails-that-standard-united-states-ambassador-to-australia-caroline-kennedy-criticised-by-lawyer-alan-dershowitz/news-story/

Independent, Southlake. "'I Left My Underwear on'—Alan Dershowitz?" Twitter, January 12, 2024. https://twitter.com/SouthlakeIndep1/status/1745903791445000404.

"James Comey." Encyclopædia Britannica, n.d. https://www.britannica.com/biography/James-Comey.

"James Patterson on delving into a financier's scandal in 'filthy rich.'" Wall Street Journal. https://www.wsj.com/articles/james-patterson-on-delving-into-a-financiers-scandal-in-filthy-rich-1475924580.

"Jeffrey Epstein." Encyclopædia Britannica, April 9, 2024. https://www.britannica.com/biography/Jeffrey-Epstein.

"Jeffrey Toobin Accuses Alan Dershowitz of "Carrying Water' for President Trump." Twitter Video. March 21, 2018.

"Judge to Dershowitz: You Wrote the Book on Chutzpah, and It Shows." The Forward, October 17, 2019. https://forward.com/fast-forward/433224/alan-dershowitz-giuffre-jeffrey-epstein-chutzpah/.

Kaczynski, Andrew, and Em Steck. "Alan Dershowitz Called Trump Corrupt in 2016 and Said He Could Be Corrupt as President." CNN, January 28, 2020. https://www.cnn.com/2020/01/28/politics/dershowitz-2016-trump-corruption-kfile/index.html.

Karni, Annie. "Alan Dershowitz Adds Trump to the List of His High-Profile Clients." *The New York Times*, January 17, 2020. https://www.nytimes.com/2020/01/17/us/politics/alan-dershowitz-trump.html.

Karni, Annie, and Eliana Johnson. "Trump turns to Dershowitz as Mueller probe escalates." Politico. April 11, 2018 https://www.politico.com/story/2018/04/11/trump-alan-dershowitz-lawyer-516437.

Katherine Tangalakis-Lippert, Jacob Shamsian. "Alan Dershowitz Called for the Release of Epstein Court Documents. In Them, Virginia Giuffre Alleges They Had Sex at Least 6 Times." *Business Insider*. January 10, 2024. https://www.businessinsider.com/epstein-accuser-detailed-sex-with-alan-dershowitz-in-unsealed-document-2024-1.

Kay, Jeremy. "Harvey Weinstein Granted Access to Emails in Bid to Dismiss Criminal Case." Screen Daily, August 2, 2018. www.screendaily.com/news/harvey-weinstein-granted-access-to-emails-in-bid-to-dismiss-criminal-case/5131424.article.

Kegu, Jessica. "What Makes Trump's Tweets Racist? A Historian Explains." CBS News, July 17, 2019. https://www.cbsnews.com/news/trumps-tweets-racist-historian-explains-why/.

Kelley, Patrick, and Todd Ruger. "View from the Gallery: Senators Swap Notes and Jockey for Questions at Trump Trial." Roll Call, January 30, 2020. https://rollcall.com/2020/01/29/view-from-the-gallery-senators-swap-notes-and-jockey-for-questions-at-trump-trial/.

Kelley, Seth. "Megyn Kelly 'Good Morning America' Interview: Roger Ailes 'Tried to Kiss Me Three Times'" *Variety*, November 15, 2016. https://variety.com/2016/biz/news/megyn-kelly-good-morning-america-interview-roger-ailes-kiss-donald-trump-1201918433/.

Kornbluh, Jacob. "Dershowitz: 'Trump Knows How to Show Outrage.'" Jewish Insider, November 23, 2016. https://jewishinsider.com/2016/11/dershowitz-trump-knows-how-to-show-outrage/.

Lat, David. "Settlement Reached in Litigation between Alan Dershowitz, Paul Cassell, and Bradley Edwards." Above the Law, April 12, 2016. https://abovethelaw.com/2016/04/settlement-reached-in-litigation-between-alan-dershowitz-paul-cassell-and-bradley-edwards/.

Lederman, Josh. "AP Fact Check: Does US Believe Western Wall Is in Israel?" AP News, December 1, 2023. https://apnews.com/united-states-government-a89b8acbaa1749c4af50e85383e1ae20.

Levinthal, Dave. "Dershowitz Persuaded Rangel to Attend Netanyahu Speech." Center for Public Integrity, January 28, 2022. https://publicintegrity.org/politics/dershowitz-persuaded-rangel-to-attend-netanyahu-speech/.

Lillis, Mike. "Pelosi Says Trump Lawyers Have 'Disgraced' Themselves, Suggests Disbarment." The Hill, January 30, 2020. https://thehill.com/homenews/house/480709-pelosi-says-trump-lawyers-have-disgraced-themselves-suggests-disbarment/.

Lincoln, Ross A. "Alan Dershowitz Mocked over Missing Martha's Vineyard Invites." The Wrap, July 3, 2018. https://www.thewrap.com/alan-dershowitz-mocked-hard-after-complaining-he-lost-friends-for-defending-trump/.

McCafferty, Molly C., and Aidan F. Ryan. "Dershowitz Files Motion to Dismiss Defamation Case from Epstein Accuser." *The Harvard Crimson*, July 2, 2019. https://www.thecrimson.com/article/2019/7/2/dershowitz-dismiss-suit/.

McCafferty, Molly, and Aidan F. Ryan. "Epstein Allegedly Directed Second Woman to Have Sex with Harvard Prof. Dershowitz, Court Documents State." *The Harvard Crimson*, December 22, 2018. https://www.thecrimson.com/article/2018/12/22/epstein-dershowitz-lawsuit-allegations/.

"Megyn Kelly." Encyclopædia Britannica, April 11, 2024. https://www.britannica.com/biography/Megyn-Kelly.

Meier, Barry. "Alan Dershowitz on the Defense (His Own)." *The New York Times*, December 12, 2015. https://www.nytimes.com/2015/12/13/business/alan-dershowitz-on-the-defense-his-own.html.

"Mike Huckabee." Facebook. https://www.facebook.com/mikehuckabee/posts/10154873325067869/.

Nadeau, Barbie Latza. "Alan Dershowitz's Wife Blames #MeToo for Accusations against Her Husband." The Daily Beast, July 20, 2019.

Nassar, Tamara. "Israel Propagandist Alan Dershowitz Protested in Qatar." The Electronic Intifada, August 27, 2018. https://electronicintifada.net/blogs/tamara-nassar/israel-propagandist-alan-dershowitz-protested-qatar.

426   LEGAL GLADIATOR

426   LEGAL GLADIATOR

National Archives and Records Administration. https://trumpwhitehouse.archives.gov/briefings-statements/remarks-president-trump-prime-minister-conte-italian-republic-bilateral-meeting-hertfordshire-united-kingdom/.

National Archives and Records Administration. https://trumpwhitehouse.archives.gov/briefings-statements/remarks-president-trump-rosh-hashanah-national-press-call-jewish-faith-leaders-rabbis/.

"'Nonsense . . . Preposterous . . . Absurd': Critics Lecture Dershowitz about Trial Remarks." NBCNews.com, January 30, 2020. https://www.nbcnews.com/politics/trump-impeachment-inquiry/nonsense-preposterous-absurd-critics-lecture-prof-dershowitz-about-trial-remarks-n1126521.

"Perversion of Justice: Jeffrey Epstein." *Miami Herald*. https://www.miamiherald.com/topics/jeffrey-epstein.

Peters, Jeremy W. "Alan Dershowitz Is Enjoying This." *The New York Times*, July 7, 2018. https://www.nytimes.com/2018/07/07/us/politics/alan-dershowitz-trump.html.

"President Donald J. Trump Is Ending United States Participation in an Unacceptable Iran Deal." National Archives and Records Administration, May 8, 2018. https://trumpwhitehouse.archives.gov/briefings-statements/president-donald-j-trump-ending-united-states-participation-unacceptable-iran-deal/.

"Prince Andrew Named in US Lawsuit over Underage Sex Claims." *The Guardian*, January 3, 2015. https://www.theguardian.com/uk-news/2015/jan/02/prince-andrew-named-us-lawsuit-underage-sex-allegations.

"Proclamation on Recognizing the Golan Heights as Part of the State of Israel." National Archives and Records Administration, March 25, 2019. https://trumpwhitehouse.archives.gov/presidential-actions/proclamation-recognizing-golan-heights-part-state-israel/.

"Professor Dershowitz on Trump's Bluff." The Rush Limbaugh Show, June 23, 2017. https://www.rushlimbaugh.com/daily/2017/06/23/professor-dershowitz-on-trumps-bluff/amp/.

Przybyla, Heidi, and Adam Edelman. "Nancy Pelosi Announces Formal Impeachment Inquiry of Trump." NBCNews.com, September 24, 2019.

https://www.nbcnews.com/politics/trump-impeachment-inquiry
/pelosi-announce-formal-impeachment-inquiry-trump-n1058251.

Rahhal, Emily. "Alan Dershowitz Faces Protestors during Lecture." *The Colgate Maroon-News*, November 8, 2018. https://thecolgatemaroon news.com/1903/news/alan-dershowitz-faces-protestors-during-lecture/.

"Read Trump's Phone Conversation with Volodymyr Zelensky." *CNN*, September 25, 2019. www.cnn.com/2019/09/25/politics/donald -trump-ukraine-transcript-call/index.html.

"Remarks by President Trump at Hanukkah Reception and Signing of an Executive Order Combating Anti-Semitism." National Archives and Records Administration, December 11, 2019. https://trumpwhite house.archives.gov/briefings-statements/remarks-president-trump -hanukkah-reception-signing-executive-order-combating-anti-semitism/.

Ryan, Aidan F. "HLS Prof. Dershowitz Becomes Loud Trump Defender." *The Harvard Crimson*, January 26, 2018. https://www.thecrimson .com/article/2018/1/26/dershowitz-on-trump/.

"Roll Call 695, Bill Number: H. Res. 755, 116th Congress, 1st Session." Office of the Clerk, U.S. House of Representatives, December 18, 2019. https://clerk.house.gov/Votes/2019695.

"Roll Call 696, Bill Number: H. Res. 755, 116th Congress, 1st Session." Office of the Clerk, U.S. House of Representatives, December 18, 2019. https://clerk.house.gov/Votes/2019696.

"Russia Investigation of Donald Trump." Encyclopædia Britannica, n.d. https://www.britannica.com/biography/Donald-Trump/Russia -investigation#ref1261359.

Shamsian, Jacob. "Alan Dershowitz Says a New Memoir from His Accuser Proves His Innocence, but She's Not Dropping Her Lawsuit against Him." Business Insider. August 14, 2019. https://www.businessin sider.com/alan-dershowitz-epstein-documents-virginia-giuffre-memoir -prove-innocence-2019-8.

Sherman, Mark. "Dershowitz Says His Impeachment Argument Was Misinterpreted." PBS, January 30, 2020. https://www.pbs.org/newshour /nation/dershowitz-says-his-impeachment-argument-was-misinterpreted.

Staff, IE. "Law Professor Alan Dershowitz's Daughter Says Sexual Assault Charges against Him Are 'Ridiculous.'" Inside Edition, January 22,

2015. https://www.insideedition.com/9590-law-professor-alan-dershowitzs
-daughter-says-sexual-assault-charges-against-him-are-ridiculous.

Stern, Marlow. "Bill Maher Brutally Mocks Alan Dershowitz over Creepy
Jeffrey Epstein Ties." The Daily Beast, February 2, 2020. https://www
.thedailybeast.com/bill-maher-mocks-trump-lawyer-alan-dershowitz
-over-creepy-jeffrey-epstein-ties.

Sullivan, Eileen. "6 Takeaways from Senators' Questions to Impeachment
Lawyers." The New York Times, January 30, 2020. https://www
.nytimes.com/2020/01/29/us/politics/impeachment-trial-trump.html.

Swan, Jonathan. "Alan Dershowitz says he's still advising Jeffrey Epstein."
Axios, December 2, 2018. https://www.axios.com/2018/12/02/alan
-dershowitz-jeffrey-epstein-legal-advice.

Thomas, David. "Prominent US litigator David Boies to step down as law
firm leader." Reuters, November 17, 2023. https://www.reuters.com
/world/us/prominent-us-litigator-david-boies-step-down-law-firm
-leader-2023–11-17/.

Thomsen, Jacqueline. "Dershowitz to Trump: End Policy Separating
Immigrant Families at Border." The Hill, June 18, 2018. https:
//thehill.com/blogs/blog-briefing-room/news/392749-dershowitz-to
-trump-end-policy-separating-immigrant-families-at/.

Thors, Lucas. "Dershowitz Presents New Book amid Protests." The
Martha's Vineyard Times, September 6, 2019. https://www.mvtimes
.com/2019/09/05/dershowitz-presents-new-book-amid-protests/.

Tribe, Laurence. "My Retired Former Colleague…" Twitter, December 7,
2017. https://twitter.com/tribelaw/status/938792171733258240.

"Trump Holds Chat with Alan Dershowitz during Mar-a-Lago Christmas
Eve Dinner." Times of Israel, December 25, 2019. https://www
.timesofisrael.com/trump-holds-chat-with-alan-dershowitz-during-mar
-a-lago-christmas-eve-dinner/.

Trump, Donald J. "They Never Even Saw the Transcript of the Call. A
Total Witch Hunt!" X, September 24, 2019. https://twitter.com
/realDonaldTrump/status/1176605750657003520

"Two-State Solution." Encyclopædia Britannica, March 27, 2024. https:
//www.britannica.com/topic/two-state-solution.

"US Lawyer Dershowitz Sues in Prince Andrew Sex Claim Case." BBC News, January 7, 2015. https://www.bbc.com/news/uk-30692699.

Ward, Vicky. "The inside Story of How a Kosher Meat Kingpin Won Clemency under Trump." CNN, August 9, 2019. https://www.cnn.com/2019/08/09/politics/kushner-rubashkin-trump-clemency/index.html.

Mandery, Evan. "What happened to Alan Dershowitz?" Politico, May 11, 2018. https://www.politico.com/magazine/story/2018/05/11/alan-dershowitz-donald-trump-what-happened-218359/.

"Why Jeffrey Epstein Death Fuels so Many Conspiracy Theories." MSNBC, July 2, 2023. https://www.msnbc.com/opinion/msnbc-opinion/jeffrey-epstein-death-fuels-many-conspiracy-theories-rcna92112.

Williams, Jennifer. "Obama Just Took a Parting Shot at Israel—and Trump—at the UN." Vox, December 23, 2016. https://www.vox.com/world/2016/12/23/14071550/united-nations-vote-israeli-settlements-obama-trump.

Wilson, Mark. "Sen. Kamala Harris Greets Legal Counsel for President Donald Trump . . ." Getty Images, January 29, 2020. https://www.gettyimages.com/detail/news-photo/sen-kamala-harris-greets-legal-counsel-for-president-donald-news-photo/1202789782.

Zuylen-Wood, Simon van. "The World v. Alan Dershowitz." *Boston Magazine*, March 7, 2017. https://www.bostonmagazine.com/news/2016/12/11/alan-dershowitz/2/.

Videos

ABC News Live. "Rep. Adam Schiff Responds to Alan Dershowitz." Facebook, January 30, 2020. m.facebook.com/ABCNewsLive/videos/rep-adam-schiff-responds-to-alan-dershowitzs-astonishing-argument-yesterday-on-q/184839526220892/?locale2=sw_KE.

"According to Alan Dershowitz, Anything Trump Does Is Legal If It's Done in Pursuit of His Reelect." *YouTube*. January 29, 2020. https://www.youtube.com/watch?v=cXXPRImhn_E.

"Alan Dershowitz Defends President Trump on Senate Floor." *YouTube*. January 27, 2020. https://www.youtube.com/watch?v=9cGk4BRHckA.

"Alan Dershowitz on Developments in the Mueller Probe." *YouTube*. April 3, 2018. https://www.youtube.com/watch?si=DKV56ptkhh19cHL3.

"Alan Dershowitz, Attorney Denies Sexual Allegations Following Defamation Hearing." *YouTube*. September 25, 2019. https://www.youtube.com/watch?v=b10QDfOZ8ho.

BBC Newsnight. "Jeffrey Epstein's Former Lawyer, Alan Dershowitz, on His Client—BBC Newsnight." *YouTube*. August 20, 2019. https://www.youtube.com/watch?v=QRVO9k2IiSc.

CBS Sunday Morning. "Alan Dershowitz: 'President Trump Encourages Incivility.'" *YouTube*. July 22, 2018. https://www.youtube.com/watch?v=I_utStqZBwA.

CNN. "Dershowitz on Impeachment Reversal: I Am Much More Correct Right Now." *YouTube*. January 21, 2020. https://www.youtube.com/watch?v=Nb1C98SYKk4&t=432s.

CNN. "Toobin to Alan Dershowitz: What Side Are You On?" *YouTube*. January 17, 2020. https://www.youtube.com/watch?v=xmf2PodFgi4&t=416s.

CNN. "Watch Dershowitz's Former Student Challenge His Argument." *YouTube*. January 30, 2020. https://www.youtube.com/watch?v=B6ssCGcFpW8.

Fox News Insider. "Dershowitz: Martha's Vineyard Liberals Who Shunned Me Are Actually Helping Trump." *YouTube*. July 6, 2018. https://www.youtube.com/watch?v=G1Qy8V7rJRo.

Law & Crime Network. "SHOUT OUT: The Miami Herald's Investigation of Jeffrey Epstein." *YouTube*. January 25, 2019. https://www.youtube.com/watch?v=WP8Dcfp_dAs.

Miami Herald. "How Teen Runaway Virginia Roberts Became One of Jeffrey Epstein's Victims." *YouTube*. https://www.youtube.com/watch?v=qLAzubOpOtg.

"Mitt Romney SHOCKED Alan Dershowitz with His Decision | Huckabee." *YouTube*. February 8, 2020. https://www.youtube.com/watch?v=DFunrEUkPyA.

MSNBC. "Sen. Chuck Schumer Calls Alan Dershowitz's Impeachment Logic 'a Load of Nonsense'" *YouTube*. January 30, 2020. https://www.youtube.com/watch?v=Hbjr9wso8F0.

MSNBC. "Alan Dershowitz on Allegations: 'Totally False' | Msnbc." YouTube. January 9, 2015. https://www.youtube.com/watch?v=GaZhc DWoQ7s.

PBS NewsHour. "WATCH: Dershowitz Says Charges against Trump Are 'Outside' of Impeachment Offenses." *YouTube*, January 27, 2020. https://www.youtube.com/watch?v=uqmhfyH09jM&t=1s.

PBS NewsHour. "WATCH: Dershowitz Says Charges against Trump Are 'Outside' of Impeachment Offenses." *YouTube*, January 27, 2020. https://www.youtube.com/watch?v=uqmhfyH09jM.

PBS NewsHour. "Watch Israeli Prime Minister Benjamin Netanyahu's Full Speech to Congress." *YouTube*, March 3, 2015 https://www .youtube.com/watch?v=-pOs99OZN1g.

Stand With Us. "Prof. Alan Dershowitz Speaks out against the Iran Deal and Strongly Criticizes Both US President Barack Obama and Iran's Hassan Rouhani" Facebook. September 30, 2015. https://www.facebook .com/StandWithUs/videos/prof-alan-dershowitz-speaks-out-against -the-iran-deal-and-strongly-criticizes-bo/10153236897937689/.

The Dershow With Alan Dershowitz. "Are Trumps Recent Statements Antisemitic?" *YouTube*. December 14, 2022. https://www.youtube .com/watch?v=oYqbp0Xc-BI.

The Majority Report w/ Sam Seder. "Total Creep Dershowitz Brags about 'Perfect Sex Life' to Laura Ingraham." *YouTube*. July 20, 2019. https: //www.youtube.com/watch?v=fFYHDmZwgco.

The Trials of Alan Dershowitz. John Curtin, 2023.

The View. "Alan Dershowitz on Jeffrey Epstein Case." X. May 2, 2019. https://twitter.com/TheView/status/1124004154505084928.

The View. "Dershowitz Says His Job Is to Defend the Constitution, 'Not Any Particular President." *YouTube*. January 29, 2020. https://www .youtube.com/watch?v=fEX9ZcfB5jQ.

The View. "Video Alan Dershowitz on Why People Assume He Supports Trump." ABC News. July 10, 2018. https://abcnews.go.com/theview /video/alan-dershowitz-people-assume-supports-trump-56488507.

TODAY. "Alan Dershowitz Strongly Denies Sex Slave Scandal." *YouTube*. January 22, 2015. https://www.youtube.com/watch?v=ObmC6TO6xqo.

"Trump Lawyer Alan Dershowitz Shocks at the Impeachment Trial | the Daily Show." *YouTube*. January 29, 2020. https://www.youtube.com/watch?v=0qEaZCSxDyQ.

"Trump Praises Pompeo for Berating NPR Reporter." *YouTube*. January 28, 2020. https://www.youtube.com/watch?v=v8KkFECkgAw.

"Video Reveals Alan Dershowitz Patting Mike Pompeo on the Back after Pres. Trump Praised the Secretary of State for His Verbal Altercation with an NPR . . . | by Anderson Cooper " www.facebook.com. January 28, 2020. https://www.facebook.com/AC360/videos/video-reveals-alan-dershowitz-patting-mike-pompeo-on-the-back-after-pres-trump-p/2681060981990105/.

Voice of America. "Jerusalem U.S. Embassy Opening Ceremony." *YouTube*, May 14, 2018, www.youtube.com/watch?v=fdH7aYkS5V8.

WPLG Local 10. "Alan Dershowitz: Alleged Sex Slave Victim 'Still a Prostitute.'" *YouTube*. April 17, 2019. https://www.youtube.com/watch?v=_GlK8dr6MP0.

Taking the Stand
Interviews

Alan Dershowitz, Carolyn Cohen, Elon Dershowitz, Nathan Dershowitz, Tony Lyons, Jamie Raskin, Jared Kushner, Jay Sekulow, O. J. Simpson, Megyn Kelly, Susan Estrich, Mike Pompeo, Yitz Greenberg, Mark Levin, Harvey Silverglate, Jeffrey Toobin, Donald Trump, Zecharia Dor-Shav, Susan Estrich, Kenneth Sweder, anonymous friend of Alan's, Sarah Neely, Hal Miller-Jacobs, Barry Zimmerman, Bernie Beck, Carl & Joan Meshenberg, Zvi Boyarsky, Geraldo Rivera, Robert F. Kennedy Jr., Mike Huckabee, Nathan Lewin, Geoffrey Robertson, Justice Stephen Breyer, Joel Klein, Maura Kelley, Robert Shapiro, Harvey Silverglate, Eliot Spitzer, Alex Kozinski, Steven Pinker, Joel Pollak, Stuart Eizenstat, Judge Aharon Barak

Books

Department of Justice. *The Mueller Report*. Skyhorse Publishing, 2019, 1–12.

Dershowitz, Alan:

Defending Israel. All Points Books, 2019, Chapter 13, Chapter 14, 259–265.

Guilt by Accusation. Hot Books, 2019, 5–8, 10–11, 19–22, 24–25, 27–28, 30–32, 36–40, 42–43, 45, 48–49, 53, 55, 57–58, 61, 67–72, 92, 96–97, 99, 100, 102–105, 107–109, 111–112, 119–132, 146, 149, 152.

The Case Against the Iran Deal. Rosetta Press, 2015, 68, 170, 171, 195.

The Case Against the Democratic House Impeaching Trump. Hot Books, 2019, 1–2, 7, 9, 13, 24–25, 29, 30, 45–47, 54, 57, 71, 73, 76–79, 86–87, 96, 103, 108, 111–113, 118–120, 132, 134, 136, 148–153, 172, 174, 187, 189, 202–203, 208–212, 275, 283–284, 285–286.

Terror Tunnels. Rosetta Books, 2014, 72.

The Case Against BDS. Bombardier Books, 2018, 30.

Defending the Constitution. Hot Books, 2020, 1, 3- 9, 11–13, 25–27, 31–33, 37–38, 51–55, 62–63, 68–70, 73–77, 87–89, 94–99, 101–104, 106, 108–112, 119–121, 123–124, 128–133, 136–138, 140–141, 143, 146–147, 149–155, 162, 170–171, 207.

The Price of Principle. Hot Books, 2022, 74–76, 43–52.

Electile Dysfunction. Rosetta Books, 2016, 50–51, 70, 72–73, 74, 79, 84, 87, 90, 95, 97, 100, 102, 105–106, 108, 113.

The Case for Liberalism in an Age of Extremism. Hot Books, 2020, 4–7, 28–31, 41, 110–111, 114–117.

Trumped Up. Bombardier Books, 2017, 10–12, 18, 51–52, 70, 89, 127, 130, 137, 144, 168–169, 172, 174–175, 178–179, 180–181, 186–187.

Articles

See Articles for "To the 'Dark Side'"

Videos

ABC News Live. "Rep. Adam Schiff Responds to Alan Dershowitz." *Facebook*, 30 Jan. 2020, m.facebook.com/ABCNewsLive/videos/rep-adam-schiff-responds-to-alan-dershowitzs-astonishing-argument-yesterday-on-q/184839526220892/?locale2=sw_KE.

"According to Alan Dershowitz, Anything Trump Does Is Legal If It's Done in Pursuit of His Reelect. . . ." *YouTube*. January 29, 2020. https://www.youtube.com/watch?v=cXXPRImhn_E.

"Alan Dershowitz Defends President Trump on Senate Floor." *YouTube*. January 27, 2020. https://www.youtube.com/watch?v=9cGk4BRHckA.

"Alan Dershowitz on Developments in the Mueller Probe.". *YouTube*. April 3, 2018. https://www.youtube.com/watch?si=DKV56ptkhh19cHL3&v=xKzs4HK2azc&feature=youtu.be

"Alan Dershowitz, Attorney Denies Sexual Allegations Following Defamation Hearing." *YouTube*. September 25, 2019. https://www.youtube.com/watch?v=b10QDfOZ8ho&pp=ygUgYWxhbiBkZXJzaG93aXR6IHZpcmdpbmlhIGdpdWZmcmU%3D.

BBC Newsnight. "Jeffrey Epstein's Former Lawyer, Alan Dershowitz, on His Client—BBC Newsnight." *YouTube*. August 20, 2019. https://www.youtube.com/watch?v=QRVO9k2IiSc.

CBS Sunday Morning. "Alan Dershowitz: 'President Trump Encourages Incivility.'" *YouTube*. July 22, 2018. https://www.youtube.com/watch?v=I_utStqZBwA.

CNN. "Dershowitz on Impeachment Reversal: I Am Much More Correct Right Now." *YouTube*. January 21, 2020. https://www.youtube.com/watch?v=Nb1C98SYKk4&t=432s.

CNN. "Toobin to Alan Dershowitz: What Side Are You On?" *YouTube*. January 17, 2020. https://www.youtube.com/watch?v=xmf2PodFgi4&t=416s.

CNN. "Watch Dershowitz's Former Student Challenge His Argument." *YouTube*. January 30, 2020. https://www.youtube.com/watch?v=B6ssCGcFpW8.

Fox News Insider. "Dershowitz: Martha's Vineyard Liberals Who Shunned Me Are Actually Helping Trump." *YouTube*. July 6, 2018. https://www.youtube.com/watch?v=G1Qy8V7rJRo.

"Jeffrey Toobin Accuses Alan Dershowitz of "Carrying Water' for President Trump." Twitter Video. March 21, 2018.

Law & Crime Network. "SHOUT OUT: The Miami Herald's Investigation of Jeffrey Epstein." *YouTube*. January 25, 2019. https://www.youtube.com/watch?v=WP8Dcfp_dAs.

Miami Herald. "How Teen Runaway Virginia Roberts Became One of Jeffrey Epstein's Victims." *YouTube*. https://www.youtube.com/watch?v=qLAzubOpOtg.

"Mitt Romney SHOCKED Alan Dershowitz with His Decision | Huckabee." *YouTube*. February 8, 2020. https://www.youtube.com/watch?si=ao1Uq8I17FPFe0x&v=DFunrEUkPyA&feature=youtu.be.

MSNBC. "Sen. Chuck Schumer Calls Alan Dershowitz's Impeachment Logic 'a Load of Nonsense'" *YouTube*. January 30, 2020. https://www.youtube.com/watch?v=Hbjr9wso8F0.

MSNBC. "Alan Dershowitz on Allegations: 'Totally False' | Msnbc." YouTube. January 9, 2015. https://www.youtube.com/watch?v=GaZhcDWoQ7s.

PBS NewsHour. "WATCH: Dershowitz Says Charges against Trump Are 'Outside' of Impeachment Offenses." *YouTube*. January 27, 2020. https://www.youtube.com/watch?v=uqmhfyH09jM&t=1s.

PBS NewsHour. "WATCH: Dershowitz Says Charges against Trump Are 'Outside' of Impeachment Offenses." *YouTube*. https://www.youtube.com/watch?v=uqmhfyH09jM.

PBS NewsHour. 2015. "Watch Israeli Prime Minister Benjamin Netanyahu's Full Speech to Congress." *YouTube*. https://www.youtube.com/watch?v=-pOs99OZN1g.

Stand With Us. "Prof. Alan Dershowitz Speaks out against the Iran Deal and Strongly Criticizes Both US President Barack Obama and Iran's Hassan Rouhani" Facebook. September 30, 2015. https://www.facebook.com/StandWithUs/videos/prof-alan-dershowitz-speaks-out-against-the-iran-deal-and-strongly-criticizes-bo/10153236897937689/.

The Dershow With Alan Dershowitz. "Are Trumps Recent Statements Antisemitic?" *YouTube*. December 14, 2022. https://www.youtube.com/watch?v=oYqbp0Xc-BI.

The Majority Report w/ Sam Seder. "Total Creep Dershowitz Brags about 'Perfect Sex Life' to Laura Ingraham." *YouTube*. July 20, 2019. https://www.youtube.com/watch?v=fFYHDmZwgco.

The Trials of Alan Dershowitz. John Curtin, 2023.

The View. "Alan Dershowitz on Jeffrey Epstein Case." X. May 2, 2019. https://twitter.com/TheView/status/1124004154505084928.

The View. "Dershowitz Says His Job Is to Defend the Constitution, 'Not Any Particular President'" *YouTube*. January 29, 2020. https://www.youtube.com/watch?v=fEX9ZcfB5jQ.

The View. "Video Alan Dershowitz on Why People Assume He Supports Trump." ABC News. July 10, 2018. https://abcnews.go.com/theview/video/alan-dershowitz-people-assume-supports-trump-56488507.

TODAY. "Alan Dershowitz Strongly Denies Sex Slave Scandal" *YouTube*. January 22, 2015. https://www.youtube.com/watch?v=ObmC6TO6xqo.

"Trump Lawyer Alan Dershowitz Shocks at the Impeachment Trial | the Daily Show." *YouTube*. January 29, 2020. https://www.youtube.com/watch?v=0qEaZCSxDyQ.

"Trump Praises Pompeo for Berating NPR Reporter." *YouTube*. January 28, 2020. https://www.youtube.com/watch?v=v8KkFECkgAw.

Video Reveals Alan Dershowitz Patting Mike Pompeo on the Back after Pres. Trump Praised the Secretary of State for His Verbal Altercation with an NPR . . . | by Anderson Cooper " www.facebook.com. January 28, 2020. https://www.facebook.com/AC360/videos/video-reveals-alan-dershowitz-patting-mike-pompeo-on-the-back-after-pres-trump-p/2681060981990105/.

Voice of America. "Jerusalem U.S. Embassy Opening Ceremony." *YouTube*, 14 May 2018, www.youtube.com/watch?v=fdH7aYkS5V8.

WPLG Local 10. "Alan Dershowitz: Alleged Sex Slave Victim 'Still a Prostitute.'" *YouTube*. April 17, 2019. https://www.youtube.com/watch?v=_GlK8dr6MP0.

Epilogue

Interviews

Alan Dershowitz, Carolyn Cohen, Elon Dershowitz, Nathan Dershowitz, Geraldo Rivera, Tony Lyons, Donald Trump, Megyn Kelly, Harvey Silverglate, Joel Pollak, Jeffrey Toobin, Jim Bakker, Steven Pinker, Glenn Greenwald, Justice Steven Breyer, Goeffrey Robertson, Eliot Spitzer, Mike Pompeo, Jamie Raskin, Mike Huckabee, Sarah Neely, anonymous friend of Alan's, Robert Shapiro, Robert F. Kennedy Jr., Ted Cruz, Susan Estrich, Nadine Strossen

Books

Dershowitz, Alan:
   Get Trump. Hot Books, 2023.
   War Against the Jews. Hot Books, 2023.
   The Case for Vaccine Mandates. Hot Books, 2021.

Articles

"Alan Dershowitz and Elon Musk on Free Speech and Anti-Semitism." Alan Dershowitz Newsletter. October 6, 2023. https://dersh.substack .com/p/alan-dershowitz-and-elon-musk-on.

Atkins, Dorothy. "CNN Beats Alan Dershowitz's $300M Defamation Suit." www.law360.com. April 4, 2023. https://www.law360.com/amp /articles/1593738.

Coleman, Oli. "Larry David 'Screamed' at Alan Dershowitz at Grocery Store over Trump Ties." Page Six. August 18, 2021. https://pagesix .com/2021/08/18/larry-david-screamed-at-alan-dershowitz-at-grocery -store-over-trump-ties/.

Dershowitz, Alan. "Three Compromises to Fix Israeli Judicial Reform— Opinion." *Jerusalem Post*. February 15, 2023. https://www.jpost.com /opinion/article-731609

"Dinner with Bibi Netanyahu—up Close, Personal, And, Surprisingly, Funny." *The New York Sun*. September 24, 2023. https://www.nysun .com/article/dinner-with-bibi-netanyahu-up-close-personal-and-surprisingly -funny.

"Donald Trump Becomes the First President Charged with Criminal Activity." NPR. April 6, 2023. https://www.npr.org/2023/04/05/1168 256845/donald-trump-becomes-the-first-president-charged-with -criminal-activity.

Dye, Liz. "Alan Dershowitz Will Defend Free Speech by Suing the Library." Above the Law. July 25, 2022. https://abovethelaw.com/2022/07/alan -dershowitz-will-defend-free-speech-by-suing-the-library/.

Giuffre, Virginia, David Boies, and Alan Dershowitz. n.d. "AGREED STATEMENT from ALL PARTIES." https://static.foxnews.com /foxnews.com/content/uploads/2022/11/Agreed-Statement.pdf.

Jacoby, Jenny. "Who Is Alan Dershowitz and Why Is He Coming to Campus?" *The Miami Hurricane*. February 4, 2024. https://th emiamihurricane.com/2024/02/04/who-is-alan-dershowitz-and-why -is-he-coming-to-campus/.

Klasfeld, Adam. "Alan Dershowitz's Accuser Virginia Giuffre Reveals When Trial Might Begin—and She Intends to Testify." Law & Crime. July 18, 2022. https://lawandcrime.com/high-profile/alan-dershowitzs -accuser-virginia-giuffre-reveals-when-trial-might-begin-and-she -intends-to-testify/.

Quinn, Melissa, and Graham Kates. "Trump's 4 Indictments in Detail: A Quick-Look Guide to Charges, Trial Dates and Key Players for Each Case" www.cbsnews.com. August 29, 2023. https://www.cbsnews.com/news /trump-indictments-details-guide-charges-trial-dates-people-case/.

Thorpe, Lindsey. "Harvard Student Organizations Blame 'Israeli Regime' for Unfolding Violence." Boston 25 News. October 10, 2023. https: //www.boston25news.com/news/local/harvard-student-organizations -blame-israeli-regime-unfolding-violence/V5TFTW4GW REERB7BLD7BDKPNDY/.

Videos

"Alan Dershowitz Says There Was No Incitement in Trump's Speech before Violence at the Capitol." *YouTube*. January 11, 2021. https: //www.youtube.com/watch?v=I9I23rr3ejc.

"Alan Dershowitz Speaks at 'We Stand with Israel' Rally Sept 21 2023." *YouTube*. AFSI. September 26, 2023. https://www.youtube.com /watch?v=MZKVAbSmP4U.

"Alan Dershowitz's Secret to Staying Sharp While Getting Older: Having a Big Enemies List." n.d. *YouTube*. @MegynKelly. https://www.youtube .com/shorts/-t2d0FvTncw.

"Counting of Electoral College Votes, Part 1 | C-SPAN.org." 2021. www.c -Span.org. January 6, 2021. https://www.c-span.org/video/?507663–3 /counting-electoral-college-votes-part-1.

"Dershowitz Calls for 'Total, Unconditional Surrender' of Hamas." *YouTube*. December 17, 2023. https://youtu.be/B25JJQuZwOQ.

"HEATED DEBATE: Cornel West, Alan Dershowitz Spar over Israel-Hamas War." *YouTube*. October 12, 2023. https://youtu.be/svOc4Ki68_U.

"Israel-Hamas War: 'IDF Are the Bigger Terrorist Group!' Piers Morgan Debates Panel over Palestine." *YouTube*. November 30, 2023. https://www.youtube.com/watch?v=k-sIbtnz1eI.

"Legal Expert Warns This Is 'Most Serious Violation of the Rule of Law.'" *YouTube*. March 21, 2023. https://www.youtube.com/watch?v=SRVpjkNCO6s.

"Maryland Rep. Jamie Raskin Named Lead Impeachment Manager for Trial against President Donald Trump." *Baltimore Sun*. January 13, 2021. https://www.baltimoresun.com/2021/01/13/maryland-rep-jamie-raskin-named-lead-impeachment-manager-for-trial-against-president-donald-trump/.

Montanaro, Domenico. "Senate Acquits Trump in Impeachment Trial–Again." NPR, February 13, 2021. www.npr.org/sections/trump-impeachment-trial-live-updates/

"Norman Finkelstein vs Alan Dershowitz on Israel-Palestine War with Piers Morgan | the Full Debate.". *YouTube*. December 13, 2023. https://www.youtube.com/watch?v=uHqs15gOv4k.

"Pelosi Statement on Two Years since January 6th Insurrection | Representative Nancy Pelosi." *Pelosi.house.gov*, 6 Jan. 2023, pelosi.house.gov/news/press-releases/pelosi-statement-on-two-years-since-january-6th-insurrection.

"Sen. Romney: This Was 'an Insurrection Incited by the President'." CNN January 7, 2021. https://www.cnn.com/videos/politics/2021/01/07/mitt-romney-riot-violence-reaction-capitol-certification-sot-vpx.cnn.

"Trump Faces the 'Most Dangerous Indictment in Political History': Harvard Professor." *YouTube*. June 6, 2023. https://youtu.be/wjG4PoteCWw.

"Virginia Roberts Giuffre Responds to Alan Dershowitz's Challenge Re: Her Sexual Abuse Allegation." *YouTube*. July 5, 2020. https://www.youtube.com/watch?v=G7Kgp4YZtMU.

"WATCH LIVE: Donald Trump Host First 2024 Presidential Campaign Rally in Waco." *YouTube*. March 25, 2023. https://www.youtube.com/watch?v=HPpQ8wWYmsA.

"WATCH: Israeli Prime Minister Benjamin Netanyahu Addresses the 2023 United Nations General Assembly." *YouTube*. PBS NewsHour. September 22, 2023. https://www.youtube.com/watch?v=kNH85jgzJ0Y.

"What Donald Trump Told Alan Dershowitz Ahead of His Impending Arrest and Arraignment." *YouTube*. April 4, 2023. https://www.youtube.com/watch?v=vy_s4XlNOeo.

Trials of Alan Dershowitz—produced by John Curtin, 2023. https://www.youtube.com/watch?v=IfnJi7yLKgE.

Appendix: Human Alan

Interviews

Alan Dershowitz, Carolyn Cohen, Elon Dershowitz, Sarah Neely, Zecharia Dor-Shav

Eyewitness information was also supplied from events I attended and visits I had with Alan Dershowitz in Miami, Israel, New York City, and Martha's Vineyard.

INDEX